Journey to the Polar Sea

Library of Congress Cataloging-in-Publication Data
TK

ISBN 1-57488-314-3   (alk.paper)

Printed in Spain on acid-free paper that meets the American National Standards Institute Z39-48 Standard.

Brassey's, Inc.
22841 Quicksilver Drive
Dulles, Virginia 20166

First Edition

10 9 8 7 6 5 4 3 2 1

Printed and bound in Spain by Bookprint, SL, Barcelona

Narrative of a

Journey to the Shores of the Polar Sea

in the Years 1819-20-21-22

John Franklin

new introduction by
James P. Delgado

1908 introduction by
Captain Scott

Brassey's, Inc.
Washington, D.C.

CONTENTS

INTRODUCTION TO THIS EDITION

James P. Delgado

It is ironic that in death John Franklin's contributions to Arctic exploration outweighed those he made while alive. Franklin's disappearance in the summer of 1845, together with 128 other officers and crew members of His Majesty's Ships *Erebus* and *Terror*, spurred a search of the Canadian Arctic archipelago that involved dozens of ships and thousands of men. In all, 32 separate expeditions searched for Franklin over a ten year period that ended in 1859. Even then, the scarce clues – a note sealed in a stone cairn, a trail of bodies and abandoned boats and equipment – left more questions unanswered than solved. And of Franklin himself, no trace was ever found, only a few pieces of silver plate and a medal purchased from the local Inuit peoples of the Arctic who possessed them. Indeed, very few of the dead were ever found, and fewer yet had their names attached to the bones and scraps of uniform that were collected from the frozen north.

The tragedy of the death of Franklin and his men, and the mystery that still swirls around the ill-fated expedition has kept Franklin's name alive even now, more than 150 years after his death. Arguably the most famous Arctic explorer, John Franklin remains very much in the public consciousness because of his failure to escape the grip of the ice and the gruesome results that followed. It is also ironic, too, that Franklin first gained fame, during his lifetime, for another ill-starred expedition. The near failure of Franklin's first overland Arctic expedition made between 1819 and 1822, with its tales of starvation, suffering, cannibalism and murder, propelled him into the ranks of contemporary celebrity. Famous upon his return, and particularly following the publication of the first edition of this volume, as the "man who ate his boots," the Arctic career of John Franklin is defined more by misfortune than triumphant achievement.

Franklin's fate was foreshadowed by the Arctic expedition recounted in the pages that follow. His three-year sojourn in the wilderness succeeded in mapping part of the Arctic coast, but the expedition ended in disaster, Franklin pushed his men too far, exhausting overloaded voyageurs. Sparse supplies ran out, and starvation and scurvy set in. More than half the expedition died as the survivors huddled down in winter quarters with lichen scraped off rocks, bones, scraps of hides and their own boots as the only source of food. One voyageur seemingly went mad and was executed by one of Franklin's officers on suspicion of murder and cannibalism. When finally rescued by the local Indians, Franklin and his remaining men were days away from death.

What compelled this man, supported by his government, to venture into an extreme environment at the top of the world? British pride, nationalism, science, and personal ambition combined with the right timing to thrust Franklin into the last acts of a three hundred year quest to find a Northwest Passage.

The Search for the Northwest Passage

The career of John Franklin spans the climactic years of Britain's search for a Northwest Passage. The dream of a water passage across the top of the world was a four-century obsession of various European powers. But the desire for the long-sought prize burned brightest in Britain. The island kingdom rose to prominence through command of the seas. In the sixteenth century, English sea dogs first challenged the global hegemony of Portugal and Spain. It was at this time, too, that the concept of a Northwest Passage first arose. The Iberian powers controlled the sea routes to the riches of the Orient, either by way of Cape Horn at the end of the Americas or the Cape of Good Hope at the tip of Africa. To find and hold an English route to the Far East was to challenge the Iberians for global mastery.

English-sponsored voyages as early as 1497 sought a sea route to "Cathay." John Cabot, sailing from Bristol just five years after Columbus' first voyage, discovered a "New Found Lande" instead of a passage to the Orient, but his voyage inspired other English ventures across the Atlantic. His son Sebastian between 1508 and 1509 may have reached Hudson Strait and the entrance to Hudson's Bay. But he sailed no further north, and the English quest for a Northwest Passage languished for decades.

England renewed the quest during the reign of Elizabeth I. In 1576, soldier and adventurer Sir Humphrey Gilbert published *A Discourse for a Discoverie for a New Pasage to Cathaia*. Convinced that a Northwest Passage existed, Gilbert argued that "it were the onely way for our princes, to possesse the wealthe of all the Easte parts (as they terme them) of the world, which is infinite" and "the Queenes Majesties dominions are neerer the Northwest passage then any other great princes that mighte passe that way." Gilbert's words came at a time when one of Elizabeth's sea dogs, the adventurer, sometime pirate and master mariner Martin Frobisher, was seeking backing for a voyage north to find the passage.

Frobisher's three voyages, between 1576 and 1578, reached the shores of Baffin Island and encountered the native Inuit of the region, but the chance discovery of a "black ore" that English assayers mistakenly believed would yield gold and silver diverted attention from a passage to a mining venture. The "ore" was actually hornblende, but Frobisher and his backers, including the Queen, were swept up with gold fever. When, at the conclusion of a third and expensive expedition, the "ore" was finally discovered to be worthless rock, Frobisher's voyages to the north ended.

The frozen seas and wind-swept lands Frobisher described inspired a return by England to those shores within a few years. In 1585 and again in 1586 and 1587, John Davis, sponsored by a group of London and Devon merchants sailed north, past Frobisher's "straites" to reconnoitre the region for a passage. Davis probed the entrances to both Baffin Bay (now known as Davis Strait) and Hudson's Bay. Returning home from his third voyage in September 1587, he wrote to his sponsors that "with Gods great mercy" he had "sailed threescore leagues further then my determination at my departure. I have bene in 73 leagues, finding the sea all open, and forty leagues between land and land. The passage is most probable, the execution easie . . ."

Picking up where Davis left off, other mariners sought the passage in the early seventeenth century. The 1610-1611 voyage of Henry Hudson entered a "Furious Overfall" described by John Davis, and followed it to a "large sea." A better navigator than a leader of men, Hudson was marooned by his mutinous crew and left to die in an open boat with his son and several "poor, sick lame men." The mutineers finally managed to reach home, where news of a potential passage spared their lives. Hudson's discovery of Hudson Strait and Hudson Bay spurred what eventually proved to be a fruitless 162-year search of the bay's shores for an entrance to the Northwest Passage.

One of the mutineers, Robert Bylot, joined by navigator William Baffin, ventured out of Hudson's Bay in 1616 to sail north through Davis Strait. In their small ship, *Discovery*, the expedition followed the Greenland coast into another vast bay. In one amazing summer, they mapped the ice-choked shores of the bay, which was named for Baffin. It was the entrance to the Canadian Arctic archipelago – the Northwest Passage. One "sound," which they named for patron Sir James Lancaster, was the doorway, but ice closed it off. It was not until 1819, following in their wake, that a British ship would enter the passage by way of Lancaster Sound.

The numerous searches of Hudson's Bay finally ended in the middle of the eighteenth century. Failure to find a passage from the bay, or anywhere else on the eastern shores of America, inspired British explorers to search the western shore on the Pacific coast in the last decades of the century. They did so in the name of science and British prestige, though, not for commercial gain. In the intervening centuries since 1576, Britain had defeated its Portuguese, Spanish and Dutch rivals for control of the sea. In the second half of the eighteenth century, British voyages of scientific exploration commanded by James Cook mapped the Pacific, collected information about the heavens, lands, flora, fauna and the native peoples. Cook's voyages exemplified Britain's global reach and interests on the high seas.

In 1778, the Admiralty sent Cook north, along the coast of North America, to seek a entrance from the Pacific to the Northwest Passage. In November, Cook's ships *Resolution* and *Discovery* followed the coast of Alaska and the Aleutian Islands, rediscovering a strait first charted by Vitus Bering nearly forty years previous. Bering's Russian-sponsored voyages had charted the northern seas and the coast of Alaska for the Tsar. Now Cook retraced Bering's route, mapping the narrow strait before pushing north into freezing seas. Ice halted *Resolution* and *Discovery* at the edge of the Chukchi Sea; Cook named his northernmost landfall "Icy Cape" before retreating. Cook had indeed charted the Pacific entrance to the passage, but it would be decades before the true significance of what he charted was realized.

British interest in the passage, and the far northern regions where it obviously lay, inspired voyages other than Cook's. In June 1773, the ships *Racehorse* and *Carcass* sailed between Greenland and Svalbard, pushing north towards the North Pole. Commanded by Captain Constantine Phipps, the expedition was a test of the theory of an "open polar sea," separated from the rest of the world's oceans by a fringe of ice. Once the icy barrier was passed, a navigable sea lay atop the world. The ice at 80 degrees, 43 minutes North, stopped Phipps' ships. Phipps's observations were added to the Admiralty's as yet scanty knowledge of the polar regions. But in the minds of some, one fact was clear. If a sea route lay across the top of the world, it would have to lie near the continent on the northern shores of America.

George Vancouver, one of Cook's more promising young officers, was next to attempt to locate the passage. During a four-year voyage to the Pacific, Vancouver probed the north west coast for a passage. He verified the claim of an American sea captain, Charles Barkley, that a vast opening existed on the coast near the 49th parallel. But Vancouver disproved Barkley's suggestion that the strait was in fact the entrance to a Northwest Passage, perhaps a near mythical strait vaguely described in the sixteenth century as the "straits of Juan de Fuca." De Fuca, a Greek in the service of Spain, claimed to have discovered a large strait on a secret voyage. His account, published during the early years of England's quest for the passage, had often been cited as proof of a passage through the continent.

Vancouver, pushing up the "supposed strait of Juan de Fuca" at the same time as a Spanish expedition, joined them in meticulously charting the coast. Numerous inlets penetrated the interior coastline, but they ultimately came to a close in narrow, high fiords. Vancouver, writing aboard his ship *Discovery* in 1794, reported that his expedition had "truly determined the non-existence of any water communication between this and the opposite side of America within the bounds of our investigation, beyond all doubts and disputance . . ."

But even as Phipps and Cook had shown that an icy barrier closed the north, and Vancouver had proved that no passage lay through the more temperate continental mass, two other British explorers had pushed overland to stand on the shores of an icy but apparently navigable sea at the northern edge of North America. On July 18, 1771, fur trader Samuel Hearne, after a long march overland, stood on the shores of the Arctic Ocean. With a native Chippewayan guide, Matonabbee, Hearne followed the Coppermine River north to its mouth. Searching for copper mines and open waters that might be the "polar sea," Hearne found both. "The sea is full of islands and shoals, as far as I could see," he wrote. "I erected a mark, and took possession of the coast."

Hearne's glimpse of the Arctic Ocean was followed by that of another overland explorer, the fur trader Alexander Mackenzie. In 1789 Mackenzie set out by birchbark canoe to find a great river which, according to the local Indians, flowed into the sea. Thinking it might be the Pacific Ocean, Mackenzie and a Copper Indian guide entered the river and followed it north on a two-week journey to the Arctic Ocean. Disappointed at not reaching the Pacific, Mackenzie had nonetheless charted a river that now bears his name and a small segment of Arctic coast. On a second trip, Mackenzie worked overland to the west, reaching the shores of the Pacific in what is now British Columbia in July 1793. He narrowly missed meeting up with George Vancouver's expedition, also on the coast at that time. But while the two did not meet, their separate accounts showed that a passage, if it existed, had to lie in the icy regions north of the continental landmass.

But the time was not ripe to pursue the passage in the Arctic. As the eighteenth century ended, Britain was engulfed in a global war with France and Spain, and thoughts of exploration and science faded into the background. The new century, with its continuation of the war, and a new conflict with the United States saw the Royal Navy and the British government preoccupied with matters other than seeking new lands or ocean passages.

The climactic years of the search for the Northwest Passage began in 1818, after the Napoleonic Wars. The renewed quest for the passage was largely at the urging of John Barrow, Second Secretary of the Admiralty and an advocate for exploration. Barrow collected accounts of early explorers, including the now nearly mythical Bylot/Baffin voyage, as well as "traders in the service of the Hudson's Bay and North-West Companies" and "scattered remarks of whale fishers and casual travellers such as Hearne and Mackenzie." To Barrow, the evidence, particularly the currents flowing out of Davis Strait, Hudson's Strait, and along the coast of Spitzbergen, proved that "the water supplied through the Strait of Behring . . . into the Polar Sea, was discharged, by some opening, or other, yet to be discovered, into the Atlantic." This would have to be the long-sought Northwest Passage.

Centuries of probing had however suggested that the probable route was blocked by ice. But a five-century long "Little Ice Age" that gripped the world was ending. Whalers working in the seas off Greenland and in Baffin Bay began reporting that the ice was retreating. In 1818, the reports of experienced whaling captain William Scoresby, Jr. excited Barrow's interest. Scoresby wrote "I observed on my last voyage about two thousand square leagues (eighteen thousand square miles) of the surface of the Greenland seas . . . perfectly devoid of ice . . ." The door to the Northwest Passage was probably open, and Barrow turned the attention of the Admiralty and the Royal Navy to it.

Over the next three decades, several expeditions sailed for the Arctic, laden with eager explorers and scientific instruments. Out of their endeavours, as well as those of fur traders in the employ of the Hudson's Bay Company, a gradual map of the Canadian Arctic archipelago emerged. A number of possible routes existed in the narrow channels, shoals and ice-choked straits. Finding the correct route, thwarting the ice that closed in each winter, and surviving months of imprisonment in an unforgiving landscape epitomized the promise and the tragedy inherent with each expedition.

The first of these new British expeditions to seek the passage commenced in 1818 under the command of John Ross. Ross's instructions were both simple and direct: "find a passage, by sea, between the Atlantic and Pacific . . . by way of Davis' Strait . . ." Ross sailed in HMS *Isabella*, while his second in command, W. Edward Parry, followed in HMS *Alexander*. At the same time, Barrow sent two other ships to see if the ice barrier that stopped Phipps in 1773 was still there. David Buchan, commanding HMS *Dorothea*, and John Franklin, commanding HMS *Trent*, sailed toward Spitzbergen only to be stopped by the ice.

Ross unfortunately was not stopped by ice, but turned a blind eye toward the probable route, Lancaster Sound, which was now free of its icy barrier. *Isabella* and *Alexander* headed into the 45-mile wide sound, but just as his officers saw a strait, Ross claimed that he "distinctly saw the land round the bottom of the bay, forming a chain of mountains." Ross was wrong, and his stubborn belief "that there was no passage in this direction" ended the expedition on a sour note. Barrow was infuriated and Ross's career and reputation were damaged. Ross was ridiculed, particularly by Barrow, who said that Ross's claims of mountains were "a pitiable excuse for running away home."

The Admiralty immediately dispatched another expedition to Lancaster Sound. Commanded by W. Edward Parry, in HMS *Hecla*, with HMS *Griper*, a small gun brig under the command of Lieut. Matthew Liddon, the expedition pushed past Ross's imaginary mountains and entered the Arctic in 1819. "We now began to flatter ourselves," Parry wrote, "that we had fairly entered the Polar Sea." *Hecla* and *Griper* sailed 600 miles west through waters not hitherto navigated by another ship. When ice finally stopped the expedition in September, Parry realized that his position was well north of where Hearne had glimpsed the Arctic Ocean in 1771.

Parry's crews survived a year-long sojourn, moored in a frozen sea at a sheltered anchorage off Melville Island that Parry named "Winter Harbour." When the ice freed *Hecla* and *Griper* in August 1820, Parry retraced his tracks and sailed home to a hero's welcome. Parry returned to the Arctic three other times. In 1821, Parry sailed into the northern reaches of Hudson's Bay with *Hecla* and HMS *Fury*, with Lieut. George F. Lyon commanding *Hecla*. The purpose of this voyage was to see if a half-forgotten strait sighted by a mid-eighteenth century expedition led to the Northwest Passage. Freezing in for a long winter, Parry, Lyon and their men made contact with the local Inuit, exchanged gifts and learned much from their native hosts.

Inuit-drawn charts of the area told Parry that he was anchored off a 50-mile wide peninsula that separated Hudson's Bay from the Arctic Sea. Beyond it, was "one wide-extended sea." At the tip of the peninsula was a strait, which Parry reached only to find it closed by ice. Frustrated by not being able to sail through, Parry spent a second winter with the Inuit before returning home in 1823. Parry's third voyage, again in *Hecla* and *Fury,* sailed in May 1824, this time to push south from Lancaster Sound and follow the coast toward the land and sea west of "Hecla and Fury Strait."

The voyage did not progress far before the ships were frozen in for the winter. When the ice freed the ships, Parry progressed another short distance before the ice caught *Hecla* and *Fury* and shoved the hapless *Fury* ashore on a narrow beach surrounded by high cliffs. With exceptional effort, Parry, his second in command, Henry Hoppner, and their men worked to save *Fury*. The ship was a total loss, though, and with an overloaded *Hecla*, Parry retreated from the Arctic, arriving home in November 1825. He would not return until 1827, on his fourth and final voyage, this time yet again attempting to sail north to the pole.

Parry's successes outweighed his failures, however, and Barrow and the Admiralty continued to push north, mounting other expeditions to complement Parry's. Two overland expeditions, each led by John Franklin, pushed out of Canada to the shores of the Arctic Ocean. Franklin's first expedition, between 1819-1821, proved a disaster, replete with starvation, murder, and cannibalism. But in 1823, as the Admiralty assessed the records of the various expeditions, they realized that the evidence pointed to more than one possible passage that could be found. To ensure success, four separate expeditions were sent north, to push from all directions – Lancaster Sound, Hudson Bay, the Mackenzie River, and Bering Strait. This was the genesis of Parry's third, ill-fated expedition, as well as Franklin's second overland trek along the course of the Mackenzie and thence west, together with two other attempts by sea.

Frederick William Beechey, a veteran of Parry's voyages, and now in command of HMS *Blossom*, was ordered to try for a passage from the Pacific. The Admiralty instructed Beechey to enter the Arctic through the Bering Strait, and to then push east to rendezvous with Franklin. George Lyon, commanding *Griper*, was to return to Parry's winter quarters north of Hudson's Bay and strike out from there, overland, to the west, where Parry would hopefully be. Beechey and Franklin successfully concluded their tasks without meeting each other – both turning back unaware that they were only 160 miles apart. But Parry's expedition came to grief with the loss of *Fury* and *Hecla*'s retreat. George Lyon fared no better in *Griper*. The brig was mauled by winter storms and nearly wrecked. Finally, with his ship and crew strained beyond their tolerances, Lyon also retreated.

With the failure of their all-out effort, Barrow and the Admiralty faltered in their quest for the passage. Into the breach stepped John Ross. The disgraced Arctic veteran, with help from supporters, his own funds, and finally with begrudging assistance from the Admiralty mounted a private expedition to seek the Northwest Passage. Sailing in a small paddlewheel steamer, *Victory*, in June 1829 Ross was joined by his nephew, James Clark Ross, himself a veteran of Parry's expeditions, as second-in-command.

Victory succeeded in pushing farther south than Parry had reached with *Fury* and *Hecla*, following an inlet that Ross believed was the passage. It was instead a dead end, terminating in a bay Ross named the Gulf of Boothia. *Victory* froze in for the winter, while a frustrated Ross ordered that the steam machinery, which had proved itself useless, be dismantled and tossed on the beach. Disappointment notwithstanding, the two Rosses and their men made contact with the local Netsilik Inuit and surveyed the surrounding lands. They discovered their position relative to Hecla and Fury Strait, mapped the eastern shores of the Boothia Peninsula, and reconnoitred the northern shores of another land mass which they believed was a peninsula, which they named "King William's Land." On a sledging trip, James Ross, working with instruments to map magnetic variation, fixed the location of the magnetic North Pole, a major scientific achievement.

But the expedition was trapped. Unable to work *Victory* north after two long winters, John Ross ordered the tiny steamer abandoned in May 1832. Scurvy was setting in, and his men were slowly dying. A desperate dash by foot over the ice reached Fury Beach, where supplies that Parry had cached from his wrecked ship ensured Ross's survival. A shelter, built from abandoned wood and canvas housed the men of *Victory* during the winter of 1832-1833. In July 1833, they pushed out over the water in small boats, reaching Lancaster Sound in mid-August. There, a whaling ship was sighted. "No time . . . was lost: the boats were launched, and signals made . . ." Ross wrote in his account of his rescue. After chasing the whaling ship all morning, they were finally sighted. The ship stopped and lowered a boat and approached that of Ross and his men. "The mate in command addressed us, by presuming that we had met with some misfortune and lost our ship. This being answered in the affirmative, I requested to know the name of the vessel . . . it was 'the *Isabella* of Hull, once commanded by Captain Ross,' on which I stated I was the identical man in question . . ." Ross was delighted to report that the mate "assured me that I had been dead two years."

Ross's disappearance had spurred an overland search for him by George Back, a veteran of Franklin's two overland expeditions. Back received word of Ross's rescue while trekking in the north, but took the opportunity to continue north, reaching the Arctic coast by following a large river, then known as the "Great Fish," but now known as the Back River. Back's brief survey of the coast in August 1834 showed that "King William's Land" could be an island instead of a peninsula. Back drew a strait separating the mainland from King William's Land, but his plots were vague and could not connect his positions with those on Franklin's or Ross's charts.

The glimpses of the region that the two Rosses and Back brought back from the Arctic did spur another try at the Passage. Public acclaim for the heroic Rosses led to a knighthood for John Ross, a promotion for James Ross, and financial reward. It also helped inspire the Admiralty to send Back into Hudson's Bay, this time in command of HMS *Terror*. Back's instructions were nearly identical to Lyon's in 1823; anchor near Parry's winter quarters, hike overland and chart the shoreline until he reached the mouth of the Great Fish River – his stopping point in 1834. But the voyage, which started with high hopes in June 1836, ended badly. Caught by the ice in Hudson's Bay and frozen into the middle of heaving ice pack, *Terror* drifted for ten awful months at the mercy of the sea and the ice. When the ship was finally freed in July 1837, Back hastily retreated, his crew constantly manning the pumps to keep the badly damaged *Terror* from sinking.

The 1830s ended with the Admiralty seemingly out of contention for the Northwest Passage. The Hudson's Bay Company sent its own expedition, under the command of two of its traders, Peter Dease and Thomas Simpson in 1837. Retracing Franklin's footsteps from his second overland expedition, Dease and Simpson closed the 160-mile gap left between Franklin and Beechey's expeditions. They then turned east, and mapped the coast toward Back's River, crossing the sea that lay north of the coast to reach the shores of Victoria Island. Their surveys filled in, with less cost, effort or fanfare, what the naval expeditions had not. But the coast and the waters north of Back's river – particularly the region around King William's Land, as well as what lay between the southern coast of Victoria Island and Parry's "Winter Harbour" of 1819-1820 – was unknown.

The Admiralty however was not interested. James Ross, in command of the repaired *Terror* and her sister ship, HMS *Erebus*, instead journeyed toward another pole, south to Antarctica on a three year voyage of exploration and science between 1839 and 1843. Stopping at Tasmania, the ships officers were entertained by the Lieut. Governor, John Franklin, who found his own interest in polar expeditions rekindled. So too, on Ross's return, was that of the Admiralty, which soon made plans to send *Terror* and *Erebus* to the Arctic for yet another crack at the Northwest Passage.

Barrow led the charge, pointing out in 1844 that Lancaster Sound was the entrance to the Northwest Passage. If another nation was now to sail, after so many British voyages, through the passage, "England by her neglect of it after having opened the East and West doors should be laughed at by all the world for having hesitated to cross the threshold." The Admiralty agreed and offered command of the expedition to James Ross. The recently married Ross declined, but recommended that the command go to John Franklin, himself recently returned from Tasmania. The 59-year-old Franklin was perhaps too old, but Edward Parry seconded the recommendation, writing to the First Lord of the Admiralty that Franklin "is a fitter man than any I know, and if you don't let him go, the man will die of disappointment."

The Admiralty gave the command of the expedition to Franklin in February 1845. His orders were to follow in the wake of Parry's 1819-1820 expedition and from where Parry was stopped by ice to then go south or north, but trending westward, "towards Bering Strait in as straight a line as is permitted by ice or any unknown land." With Franklin ultimately went 129 officers and men, among them Captain Francis Rawdon Moira Crozier, commanding *Terror*, and Commander James Fitzjames commanding *Erebus*. The Admiralty fitted both ships with steam engines and propellers, supplies for three years, and a library of 2,900 books. As the London *Times* opined in May 1845, "The Lords Commissioners of the Admiralty have, in every respect, provided most liberally for the comforts of the officers and men of an expedition which may, with the facilities of the screw propeller, and other advantages of modern science, be attended with great results." Nothing, it seemed, thanks to advance planning, experience and the benefits of modern technology, could go wrong.

Erebus and *Terror* sailed on May 19, 1845 from the Thames, and after reaching Greenland, moved out across Baffin Bay. On July 28, the whalers *Enterprise* and *Prince of Wales* spotted them. After a brief visit, the four ships departed company. *Erebus* and *Terror* and their crews sailed into Lancaster Sound and vanished into the Arctic. No word came from the north for years, and finally it became obvious that disaster had struck.

In all, 32 separate expeditions were mounted, both by governments and private individuals, to find Franklin and his men. The search for Franklin, at first to rescue the men of *Erebus* and *Terror*, and then finally to learn of their fate, lasted from

1847 to 1859, involving dozens of ships and thousands of men. The search also dominated the popular consciousness, not only in Britain, but also throughout much of the rest of the world. The Arctic, first introduced to the public as a fatal landscape courtesy of Franklin's first, ill-fated expedition, had that reputation firmly set as a result of Franklin's final voyage. The search for Franklin also firmly established the reputation of his faithful wife, Lady Jane. Jane Franklin's numerous appeals, her private financing of expeditions to learn her husband's fate, and her unrelenting drive to assure that Franklin's place as the discoverer of the Northwest Passage earned Jane her own fame. "Lady Franklin's Lament," a folk song in which she beseeches searchers to tell her "that my Franklin yet lives," is a lasting reminder of this remarkable woman.

The Franklin search also resolved the question of where the Northwest Passage lay. It was indeed in the Canadian Arctic archipelago, but it was not one single passage. Rather, the intricate maze of islands and shoals provided a number of potential passages, whenever the ice shifted to open the door. This was particularly shown by the 1849-1855 voyages of the ships *Enterprise* and *Investigator*. Richard Collinson, in command of *Enterprise*, pushed east into Arctic, passing Point Barrow, finally reaching the southeast corner of Victoria Island, where Dease and Simpson had first planted the British flag in 1839. Commander Robert McClure pushed *Investigator* east and then north into Prince of Wales Strait, off the west coast of Victoria Island. Wintering there, McClure sledged over the ice to the northern end of the strait. There, McClure realized, he was standing at a point spotted but not reached by Parry in 1820. As ship's interpreter, Johann Miertsching wrote in his diary, "so the problem of the Northwest Passage, disputed for 300 years, was solved."

McClure was unable to wrest his own ship free of the ice, however. In August 1851, McClure worked *Investigator* west and then north around Banks Island, only to freeze in again at an anchorage McClure named Mercy Bay. Finally, three years into his voyage, running out of supplies and realizing that if he was ever to meet Franklin, it would be in another life, McClure decided to abandon his ship and trek over land and ice with his men. He was saved at the last when a party from another searching expedition, led by Edward Belcher, reached the stranded *Investigator*. Lieut. Bedford Pim of HMS *Resolute* led McClure and his men east to rescue in June 1853. When McClure reached England, he and Collinson were both rewarded for the discovery of "a" Northwest Passage, as both had closed the last links on paper. But the routes were closed with ice, unnavigable and of no value save as a laurel for headstrong if not resolute explorers.

All the more amazing for those who clung to the belief that the Navy's efforts alone had wrested the secret of the passage from the Arctic were the incredible sledging journeys of Hudson's Bay Company explorer Dr. John Rae. Under the company's orders to complete the mapping of the Arctic coast, Rae mapped the Melville Peninsula and the southern end of the Boothia P eninsula on foot between 1846 and 1847, filling in all the gaps left by the Admiralty expeditions. In 1848, Rae, again on company orders, returned to the region to search for Franklin. He was unsuccessful, although he returned in 1851 and traversed the southern and eastern shores of Victoria Island. Then, in a fourth expedition, between 1853 and 1854, Rae trekked up the Boothia Peninsula, crossed over the ice to King William's Land, which he proved was an island, not a peninsula, and learned of Franklin's fate from the local Inuit.

Erebus and *Terror*, trapped in the ice, had been abandoned. The crews had marched away from the ships, and died, some resorting to cannibalism at the end.

Rae's findings were confirmed in 1858-1859, when a private expedition, led by Leopold McClintock, and financed by Lady Franklin, reached King William Island. McClintock and Lieut. William R. Hobson discovered skeletons, abandoned boats and equipment, and a brief note that reported that Franklin was dead, as were several other officers and men, and that the ships had been abandoned in a quest to reach Back's River. These few words from beyond the grave were the only record of what befell Franklin and his men. Since then, only the accounts of the Inuit, and the physical record of bodies and scattered relics from the lost ships have been available to provide a clearer sense of what happened.

When McClintock returned from the Arctic with definite news of Franklin's death and confirmation of Rae's reports, British interest in the Northwest Passage dropped away. The quest for the passage died with the news of Franklin's own death. Britain, at war in the Crimea and again embroiled in matters other than exploration, did not return to the Arctic until the Nares expedition of the 1870s. The actual conquest of the passage by ship, when it finally came, was made between 1903-1905 by a small Norwegian fishing sloop converted into a vessel of exploration. Under the command of Roald Amundsen, the tiny *Gjoa* threaded past King William Island, wintering with the Netsilik Inuit at a harbour Amundsen named "Gjoa Haven." In his treks across the island, Amundsen discovered more traces of Franklin's lost expedition. He also re-established the position of the magnetic North Pole, first plotted by James Ross in 1831.

The Northwest Passage, despite Amundsen's feat, remained a difficult goal to attain. Whalers, traders and trappers followed in the wake of the explorers and settled in among the native Inuit, and whaling ships and trading schooners, as well as the occasional government vessel navigated the waters of the passage. It was until 1940-1942, though, that another ship went all the way through. The small Royal Canadian Mounted Police schooner *St. Roch*, under the command of Norwegian-born Henry A. Larsen, made it through, west to east, during an extended wartime passage. In 1944, Larsen returned to the western Arctic and then south to his homeport of Vancouver, British Columbia, essentially retracing Parry's 1819-1820 voyage before threading through Prince of Wales Strait, past the spot where the ice had stopped McClure and *Investigator* in 1851.

The conquest of the Northwest Passage was followed by other transits after 1944; even so, deliberate voyages all the way through remain relatively rare and the subject of comment even at the dawn of the 21st century. Most travellers reach the Arctic by air, not ship, and tourists now venture where early explorers struggled and occasionally died. For them, as well as the inhabitants of the north, there is one figure whose name is remembered. It is John Franklin, whose fate attracted the attention of the world, and whose career and the mysteries of his final, fatal voyage continue to be scrutinized more than a century and a half after his death.

John Franklin and His Expeditions

Franklin is best known either as a name laden with the symbolism of an expedition gone badly, or as an image – a symbol in its own right. The man himself is often lost in the power of the name – "Franklin," or in the engraved portraits that depict him as an idealized British naval officer. He sits in them uniformed, decorated, eyes resolutely fixed on some distant object or goal, perhaps the elusive Northwest Passage itself. The only photograph of John Franklin shows him, shadowed and dimly, on the eve of departure aboard *Erebus*. Franklin was 59, suffering from a cold, and the image shows it. For the modern viewer, looking at the silvery daguerreotype, the blurred features, the shadows around the eyes and the pasty rendering of the flesh hint at death waiting in the frozen north. It is a powerful image in its own right, a very different view than the heroic engravings or the brightly coloured porcelain figures of him. There, in moulded magnificence he stands upright in full dress uniform, often joined by a similar figure of Jane, Lady Franklin. They were perfectly suited to garish, overdone Victorian parlours and drawing rooms. These porcelain statuettes, like those done earlier for Nelson, reflect nothing of the real man, only the western cult of death that occasionally encapsulates and apotheosises larger-than-life public figures who die heroically or before their time.

Who was the real John Franklin? He was a short, stout, balding man who became, even in his own lifetime, larger than life. He inspired tremendous loyalty from his junior officers and men, from his colleagues, and from his wife. Seaman John Hepburn stayed by Franklin's side throughout the perils of the disastrous first overland expedition and returned, along with John Richardson, to search the Arctic in his old age for their former commander and friend. John Ross, also in his own old age, ventured north to rescue his colleague, and Lady Jane Franklin spent large sums of money and years of effort to equip expeditions seeking her lost husband.

Why this loyalty? Because the man himself was incredibly loyal. Franklin actively sought to find Hepburn a good post after the overland expedition, and did not take him on the second expedition because to do so would upset Hepburn's domestic tranquillity. He was a man who remained in touch with John Ross even through the winter of Barrow's discontent, who actively corresponded with his sisters and remained close to his family throughout his life. He was a man who carefully packed and carried a handmade flag made for him by his ailing first wife, the poet Eleanor Porden. It is a measure of his humanity that he carried the flag on his second expedition to the shores of the polar sea, news of Eleanor's death still fresh in his mind. Standing on the shore, alone as his men pitched camp, Franklin unfurled the flag to the wind. He wrote in his journal, "I will not attempt to describe my emotions as it expanded to the breeze . . ."

John Franklin was the youngest son of a grocer, one of five boys in a family with twelve children. Born above his father's shop on April 16, 1786 in Spilsby, several miles from the sea in eastern Lincolnshire, Franklin grew up in a small market town. Historian Richard C. Davis, assessing the careers of Franklin's brothers as well as John's, notes that none followed their father's "modest trade." The circumstances of Franklin's birth and upbringing inspired him to "value social standing and economic success." Unlike his businessman, trader or barrister brothers, however, John chose the sea.

It was not necessarily an unwise choice of career. With his father's assistance, Franklin shipped out of nearby Hull at age 14 aboard a trader running between that port and Lisbon, part of a regular trade that sustained English markets with brigs and schooner sailing with the regularity of a modern semi-trailer route along the motorway. The voyage down the Channel to Portugal must have whetted the boy's appetite for the sea. Franklin then shipped aboard HMS *Polyphemus* as a first-rate volunteer, the likely choice for a boy seeking to become an officer in the Royal Navy without the money to immediately become a midshipman. Sent to the Baltic, Franklin saw combat when his ship was engaged in the Battle of Copenhagen. *Polyphemus,* part of Nelson's fleet, helped to defeat Napoleon's Danish allies, then sailed home in the summer of 1801.

Franklin's choice of the Royal Navy paid off as the boy was promoted to midshipman and joined the company of HMS *Investigator*, under the command of Captain Matthew Flinders, Franklin's uncle. Flinders' orders were to proceed into the Indian Ocean, and even in that time of war, continue the Navy's charting of Australia. It was an auspicious voyage for Franklin, who under his uncle's tutelage learned navigation, surveying and scientific observation, all vital skills for him later to assume the world stage as an explorer in his own right. He also learned command, as he was given a boat with a crew to survey on his own as *Investigator* circumnavigated the great southern continent and mapped its shores. He also learned about the harsh realities of both exploration and command when he and his boat crew were wrecked on a small sandbar off the Australian coast and stranded for 51 days.

When Franklin returned home in 1804, he spent a short leave with his family. He then joined the crew of the 74-gun ship HMS *Bellerophon*, which blockaded Brest. The ship then sailed to Cadiz, and joined the rest of the British fleet assembled under Horatio Nelson in 1805. *Bellerophon* fought at the Battle of Trafalgar. Franklin stood on the deck through the action, serving as Signals Lieutenant. The thunderous hammering of the cannon partially deafened him for life.

After Trafalgar, Franklin remained with *Bellerophon*, joining HMS *Bedford* in 1807 as Master's Mate. Franklin remained with the ship through the peacetime routine of patrols, but it was employment, while many other officers languished on the beach at half pay after the post-war reduction of the Navy. Franklin gained promotion, to acting Lieutenant, and in 1813, returned to combat when *Bedford* participated in the War of American Independence. Franklin's actions included the attack on New Orleans; he was wounded and decorated. He was also promoted to full Lieutenant, and when *Bedford* went home, remained in the American theatre as Lieutenant of HMS *Forth*.

When *Forth* returned home after the Treaty of Ghent and the end of the war, Franklin ended up on the beach in the Fall of 1815, on half pay and his future uncertain. He applied to the Admiralty for a position with any voyage of exploration. The chance came at last in 1818, when Barrow's plans for a renewed crack at the Northwest Passage and the North Pole gave Franklin command of HMS *Trent*. Despite the failure of his ship and Buchan's *Dorothea* to reach the pole, Franklin distinguished himself. In 1819, Barrow favoured him with command of his own expedition, the overland trek to the shores of the Polar Sea that is the focus of the volume that follows.

Franklin's orders were to proceed along Hearne's route to the polar sea, following the Coppermine River to its mouth and then following the coastline "to amend the very defective geography of the northern part of America." With Franklin went three fellow officers of the Royal Navy, surgeon John Richardson and midshipmen George Back and Robert Hood. Seaman John Hepburn was the fourth naval member of the party. They relied on the support of the fur traders of the rival North West and Hudson's Bay companies, who were to provide voyageurs to haul supplies, equipment, and hunt.

Sailing in the Hudson's Bay Company supply ship *Prince of Wales* to Hudson's Bay, Franklin and his men landed at York Factory, the Hudson's Bay Company's major depot and post on the bay, on August 30, 1819. They left York Factory on September 9, working north by way of the forts and posts of the H.B.C. and the North West Company. After wintering at the H.B.C.'s post at Cumberland House, 690 miles from York Factory, Franklin pushed on in January 1820. In the Spring,

Franklin, Richardson, Hood, Back and Hepburn, with their party of voyageurs and native guides and hunters worked farther north and built a winter camp they named Fort Enterprise.

After wintering at the fort, with few supplies, Franklin's expedition headed for the Coppermine River in June 1821, dragging heavy 180 lb packs and two birchbark canoes. Reaching the river's mouth on July 17, they took their fragile craft out into the Arctic Ocean and paddled east, following the coast. It was a difficult trip, as Franklin charted a shore he described as "sterile and inhospitable . . . One trap-cliff succeeds another with tiresome uniformity . . ." Fighting the ice and fatigue, they mapped 550 miles of the coast before turning back and heading south in a desperate race for Fort Enterprise. Winter was coming on, food was running out, and the entire party was exhausted.

The race to the Fort was also a race with death. Many of the party failed to make it. The canoes were broken and discarded, food ran out, and the men eked out a miserable existence by scraping the lichen off the rocks and boiling it. Franklin split his men into three groups – one, led by George Back, moved on to find help and food from the Indians who lived near Fort Enterprise. Hood, unable to digest the lichen and starving, was too weak to continue. Franklin left Richardson and Hepburn, along with some of the voyageurs, to nurse Hood and then rejoin the main party. Franklin then pushed on, following Back's trail.

When Franklin reached Fort Enterprise, he found it abandoned. There was no food, only a note from Back. The midshipman had arrived at the empty fort two days earlier and pushed on to find the Indians, then heading south for the winter. Franklin waited at Fort Enterprise with his men, boiling old hides, burnt bones and indeed their boots to keep alive. When Richardson and Hepburn arrived at the fort in October, without Hood, they brought back a tale of madness, murder and cannibalism. One voyageur, either insane or in extreme desperation, had apparently been killing and eating his fellow voyageurs. Left alone with Hood by the unsuspecting Richardson and Hepburn, he shot the hapless midshipman in the head. Fearing they were next, the two remaining Britons ambushed and executed the voyageur.

Great tragedy awaited them at Fort Enterprise, where starvation and scurvy continued to claim lives. Richardson was shocked to find Franklin and the other survivors mired in "filth and wretchedness . . ." with "the ghastly countenances, dilated eye-balls, and sepulchral voices . . ." Rescue came too late for most, for when Back arrived in November with food and help, nearly all the voyageurs had died. With food, Franklin's remaining crew slowly regained their strength over the winter. Reaching York Factory on July 14, 1822, Franklin ended his journals after a three-year, 5,500 mile journey into the heart of despair and wretchedness.

But when he returned home, Franklin discovered he was a hero. Franklin's travails in the Canadian wilderness on that arduous adventure gained him lasting fame back home. Known thereafter as the "man who ate his boots," Franklin's story was snapped up by an eager audience – the volume went through four editions in eighteen months, was translated into French and German, was published in the United States, and then appeared in an abridged version with the account of Franklin's second overland expedition. It was an incredible book for its time. At the dawn of a new period of polar exploration, Franklin's *Narrative*, in the words of historian Maurice Hodgson, presented "a new Arctic: starvation, murder and cannibalism, the extremities of human suffering."

Franklin's story was republished after his disappearance into the Arctic, and remained in print throughout much of the nineteenth century. When republished in

1908 (in the edition here reproduced) Franklin's fame was such that Robert Falcon Scott, then Britain's most famous polar explorer, penned a brief introduction. But Franklin was, as Richard Davis notes, a "modest man." The fame that commenced in 1822 embarrassed the icon himself even as he appreciated the benefits of success in 1822 as he recovered from his ordeal. He settled in, made money from his book, and married the poet Eleanor Porden.

One of the benefits was a second expedition, again across the land to the Arctic Ocean's shores. To ensure that there would be no repeat of the last expedition's problems, particularly starvation and relying on others to supply the expedition, the Admiralty planned for a year, consulted with the Hudson's Bay Company, laid out the route carefully and cached food along the way. Four specially built boats were provided, and a larger complement of officers and crew assembled. When Franklin departed in 1825, leaving his ailing wife and infant daughter behind, his expedition sailed with every possible contingency having been considered.

Franklin's party began their trek north just as news of the death of Eleanor Franklin reached John. On arriving at the Mackenzie River in August 1825, Franklin's party started down it to the sea, and by mid-month reached the shores of the Arctic Ocean. Standing on a high hill, with Eleanor's flag blowing in the breeze, an emotion-choked Franklin watched the "sea . . . in all its majesty, entirely free from ice and without any visible obstruction to navigation . . ."

Rather than push on, Franklin ordered a retreat to winter quarters, a fort that his crew had named, over his objections, Fort Franklin. There the 51 man party waited through the winter of 1825-1826. With the spring, they broke out their gear, splitting into two parties. In the summer, the two groups, one under Franklin, the other under his second in command and good friend John Richardson, a veteran of the first expedition, moved east and west of the mouth of the Mackenzie. Franklin's plan was to meet up with Beechey and the *Blossom* to the west, while Richardson pushed for the Coppermine's mouth.

Franklin's crew made their way to within 160 miles of Beechey's position before weather and ice turned them back. It had been a hard trip, including a near-disastrous encounter with plundering Inuit. Only Franklin's cool-headed and calm determination to stand his ground, but not shoot, had saved the day. Richardson, with his crew, had succeeded in his mission, and when the two explorers met again at Fort Franklin in September 1826, they compiled notes and charts that showed an amazing mapping of 1,500 miles of the Arctic coast. Their successful return in September 1827 resulted in another published narrative, more accolades for Franklin, rewards for all the officers concerned, and a burning desire in Franklin's heart to keep at the task.

In a letter to Admiralty, he urged them to continue the quest in the far north. "Each succeeding attempt has added a step towards the completion . . . and it is sincerely to be hoped that Great Britain will not relax her efforts until the question of a north west passage has been satisfactorily set at rest." Unfortunately for Franklin, he was not to participate in the ongoing push for the passage.

Franklin's life and career took a different direction upon his return to England. He remarried, to Jane Griffith, a family friend, in 1828. Jane was a perfect companion, an intellectual match, if not more intelligent than John and with as keen a desire to explore and learn. Knighted by his king, Captain Sir John Franklin was also given command of the 26-gun HMS *Rainbow*. After a three-year tour of duty in the Mediterranean, and joined by Jane during a winter ashore in Corfu in 1831-1832, Franklin returned to England at the end of 1833. Officers without commands were placed on half-pay and kept in limbo until new orders arrived. Franklin, who hated being idle, pushed for a diplomatic post.

In 1836, he was appointed Lieut. Governor of Van Diemen's Land (now Tasmania) and arrived at that Australian colony in January 1837 with Jane. Both took an active interest in the colony. But after running afoul of his superiors for terminating a colonial secretary with better political connections than his own, Franklin found himself relieved of his post and sent home in 1843. For the next two years, Franklin and his friends fought to clear his reputation and career as a colonial administrator. Then the Admiralty and fate intervened, and command of the Arctic expedition with *Erebus* and *Terror* came his way. After a spate of farewells and letters, he left just as Jane planned her own round-the-world travels to occupy her time until John returned home again. Other than his last letters, posted as *Erebus* and *Terror* cleared Baffin Bay, the last word Jane ever had was a brief note from Captains Crozier and Fitzjames in the aftermath of the abandonment of the ships, "Sir John Franklin died on the 11th June, 1847 ..." Jane's quest for Franklin, and when it was clear he was gone, her push to secure his reputation for posterity is as much a testament to her love as well as her to her determination. She was a remarkable woman. Franklin's epitaph, penned by his nephew, Alfred, Lord Tennyson, is carved in marble above a bust of the explorer in Westminster Abbey:

> Not here: the white North has thy Bones; and thou,
> Heroic Sailor-Soul,
> Art passing on thine happier voyage now
> Toward no earthly pole.

Bibliographical Note

The story of Franklin and his expeditions has been the subject of considerable inquiry and publication. Franklin himself published the accounts of his two Arctic land expeditions; in the aftermath of his disappearance, these were republished and combined into a 'memoir' of sorts. Other accounts include biographies, such as Sherard Osborn's *The Career, Last Voyage and Fate of Sir John* Franklin, A.H. Beesly's *Sir John Franklin, A Narrative of His Life*, John Ross's *Rear Admiral Sir John Franklin*, H.D. Trail's *Life of Sir John Franklin* and A.H. Markham's *Life of Sir John Franklin*, all similarly named products of the nineteenth century, and the more recent and freshly titled *Franklin, Happy voyager* by G.F. Lamb and Paul Nanton's *Arctic Breakthrough: Franklin's Expeditions, 1819-1847*.

Franklin's first overland expedition and its participants is the subject of several books. In addition to Franklin's own *Narrative*, here republished for the first time in the twenty-first century, an essential companion is Richard C. Davis, ed., *Sir John Franklin's Journals and Correspondence: The First Arctic Land Expedition, 1819-1822*, (Toronto and Ottawa: The Champlain Society and the Royal Canadian Geographical Society, 1990s) which transcribes, edits and annotates Franklin's surviving journals as well as a selection of important correspondence. Davis's perceptive introduction does an outstanding job of assessing the expedition, its participants, and what went wrong. Also essential are the collected works edited by C.S. Houston, *To the Arctic by Canoe, 1819-1821: The Journals and Paintings of Robert Hood, Midshipman With Franklin* (Kingston and Montreal: McGill-Queen's University Press, 1974), *Arctic Ordeal: The Journal of John Richardson*

(Kingston and Montreal: McGill-Queen's University Press, 1984), *Arctic Artist: The Journal and Paintings of George Back, Midshipman With Franklin* (Kingston and Montreal: McGill-Queen's University Press, 1994).

Another important addition to the literature of the first overland expedition is archaeologist Timothy C. Losey's *An Interdisciplinary Investigation of Fort Enterprise, Northwest Territories, 1970* Occasional Publication No. 9 (Tomahawk, Alberta: University of Alberta/The Boreal Institute of Northern Studies, 1973) which reports on the excavation of Franklin's winter quarters, the scene of much of the suffering during the first overland expedition.

Biographies of the participants are found in summary form in the various edited journals and accounts, as well as Richard C. Davis, *Lobsticks and Stone Cairns: Human Landmarks in the Arctic* (Calgary: University of Calgary Press, 1996), detailed accounts published as "Arctic Profiles" in *Arctic*, the scholarly journal of the Arctic Institute of North America. Paul Nanton and Davis, both in *Arctic Breakthrough* and Sir *John Franklin's Journals* also include biographies. A full biography of Richardson is found in Robert E. Johnson's *Sir John Richardson: Arctic Explorer, Natural Historian, Naval Surgeon* (London: Taylor and Francis, 1976).

Finally, the mystery of Franklin's last expedition, and the death of Franklin, his officers and crews has been the subject of a number of books. The classic work, recently republished, is Richard J. Cyriax, *Sir John Franklin's Last Arctic Expedition* (London: Methuen & Co., 1939) with the reprint edition (1997) by the Arctic Press, Plaistow & Sutton Coldfield. Recent scholarship emphasises the forensic evidence from the bodies and bones of Franklin's men in Owen Beattie and John Geiger, *Frozen in Time* (Saskatoon: Western Producer Prairie Books, 1987). Also highly recommended is David Woodman's assessment of the Inuit accounts of Franklin's demise, in two books, *Unravelling the Franklin Mystery* (Kingston and Montreal: McGill-Queen's University Press, 1991) and *Strangers Among Us* (Kingston and Montreal: McGill-Queen's University Press, 1995).

The story of the quest for the Northwest Passage has inspired authors for over a century, and a small library of hundreds of volumes exists on the subject. The two most recent books are Ann Savours, *The Search for the Northwest Passage* (London and New York: Chatham Publishing, 1999) and James P. Delgado, *Across the Top of the World: The Quest for the Northwest Passage* (Vancouver, Toronto, New York and London: Douglas & McIntyre/Facts on File/British Museum Press, 1999), which complement each other. Savour's *Search for the Northwest Passage* is a detailed-filled historical account. *Across the Top of the World* is an historical, archaeological and maritime tour of the three-century quest. Science as well as geographical discovery played a significant role in the quest, as detailed by Trevor Levere in *Science and the Canadian Arctic: A Century of Exploration, 1818-1918* (Cambridge: Cambridge University Press, 1993).

INTRODUCTION
TO 1908 EDITION

Captain R. F. Scott

In days of hurried action I have been astonished at the depth of interest which a re-perusal of this wonderful old narrative has held for me. Wonderful it is in its simplicity and its revelation of the simplicity of character and faith of the man who wrote it. It is old only by comparison – scarcely ninety years have elapsed since the adventures it described were enacted – yet such a period has never held a fuller measure of change or more speedily passed current events into the limbo of the past.

Nothing could more vividly impress this change than the narrative itself. We are told that Mr. Back missed his ship at Yarmouth but succeeded in rejoining her at Stromness, having travelled 'nine successive days almost without rest.' What a vision of post-chaises, sweating horses and heavy roads is suggested! And if the contrast with present-day conditions in our own Islands is great, how much greater is it in that vast Dominion through which Franklin directed his pioneer footsteps. As he followed the lonely trails to Fort Cumberland, or sailed along the solitary shores of Lake Winnipeg, how little could he guess that in less than a century a hundred thousand inhabitants would dwell by the shore of the great lake or that its primeval regions would one day provide largely the bread of his countrymen.

There civilization has followed fast indeed, and ever it presses forward on the tracks of the pioneer. But even today if we follow Franklin we must come again to the wild – to the great Barren Lands and to the ice-bound limit of a Continent – regions where for ninety years season has succeeded season without change – where few have passed since his day and Nature alone holds sway. For those who would know what *is* as well as for those who would know what *has been*, this narrative still holds its original interest; all must appreciate that it records the work of a great traveller and a gallant man whose fame deserves to live.

BIBLIOGRAPHY
TO 1908 EDITION

Sir John Franklin's Voyages into the Polar Seas:-

F. W. Beechey, Voyage of Discovery toward the North Pole in H.M. Ships *Dorothea* and *Trent* (with summary of earlier attempts to reach the Pacific by the North), 1818; Narrative of a Journey to the Shores of the Polar Sea, in the Years 1819–22, by John Franklin, 1823, 1824; Narrative of a Second Expedition to the Shores of the Polar Sea in the Years 1825–27, by John Franklin, 1828.

Publications concerning the Search for Sir John Franklin:-

Report of the Committee appointed by the Lords Commissioners of the Admiralty to inquire into and report on the Recent Arctic Expeditions in search of Sir John Franklin, 1851; Papers relative to the Recent Arctic Expeditions in search of Sir John Franklin and the Crews of H.M.S. *Erebus* and *Terror*, 1854; Further Papers relative to the Search, 1855; R. King, The Franklin Expedition from First to Last, 1855; R. Huish, Recent Expeditions to the Polar Regions, including all the Voyages in search of Sir J. Franklin, 1855; E. K. Kane, Arctic Explorations, the Second Grinnell Expedition in search of Sir John Franklin, 1856; MacClintock, The Voyage of the *Fox* in the Arctic Seas. A narrative of the discovery of the fate of Sir John Franklin, 1859, 1861, 1869, 1908; Sir J. Leslie, Discovery and Adventure in the Polar Seas, with a Narrative of the Recent Expeditions in search of Sir John Franklin, 1860; J. A. Browne, The North-West Passage, and the Fate of Sir John Franklin, 1860; Sir Allen M. Young, The Search for Sir John Franklin, etc., 1875. Schwatka's Search, Sledging in the Arctic in search of Franklin Records, 1881; The Search for Franklin; American Expedition under Lieutenant Schwatka, 1878–80, 1882. J. H. Skewes, The True Secret of the Discovery of the Fate of Sir John Franklin, 1889.

Life: S. Osborn, Career, Last Voyage and Fate of Sir John Franklin (*Once a Week*, 1859), 1860. A Brave Man and his Belongings, by a Niece of the first Mrs. Franklin, 1874. A. H. Beesley, Sir John Franklin; the Narrative of his Life (The New Plutarch), 1881: A. H. Markham (The World's Great Explorers), 1891; G. B. Smith, Sir John Franklin and the Romance of the North-West Passage, 1895; H. D. Traill, 1896; H. Harbour, Arctic Explorers, 1904; E. C. Buley, Into the Polar Seas: The Story of Sir J. Franklin, etc., 1909.

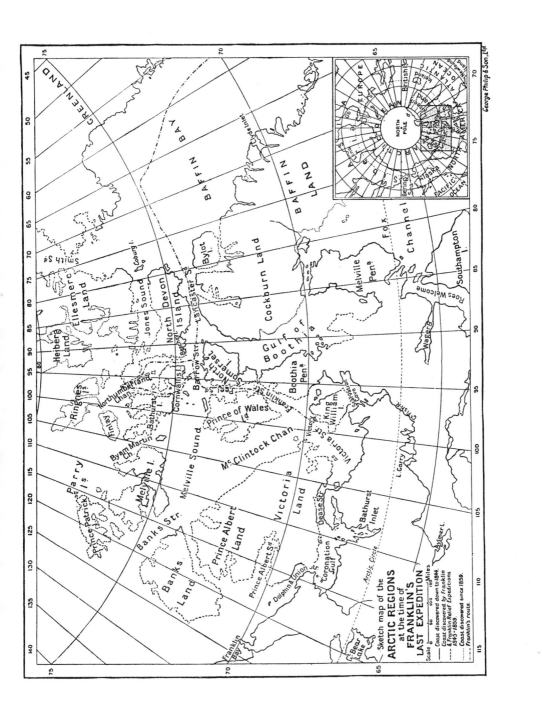

Sketch map of the
ARCTIC REGIONS
at the time of
FRANKLIN'S
LAST EXPEDITION

Scale 0   50   100   150 Miles

———— Coast discovered down to 1844.
- - - - Coast discovered by Franklin & Franklin Relief Expeditions 1848-1859.
········· Coast discovered since 1859.
—·—·— Franklin's route.

George Philip & Son, Ltd

NARRATIVE OF A JOURNEY TO THE SHORES OF THE POLAR SEA IN THE YEARS 1819-20-21-22

INTRODUCTION

His Majesty's Government having determined upon sending an Expedition from the Shores of Hudson's Bay by land, to explore the Northern Coast of America, from the Mouth of the Copper-Mine River to the eastward, I had the honour to be appointed to this service by Earl Bathurst, on the recommendation of the Lords Commissioners of the Admiralty; who, at the same time, nominated Doctor John Richardson, a Surgeon in the Royal Navy, Mr. George Back, and Mr. Robert Hood, two Admiralty Midshipmen, to be joined with me in the enterprise. My instructions, in substance, informed me that the main object of the Expedition was that of determining the latitudes and longitudes of the Northern Coast of North America, and the trending of that Coast from the Mouth of the Copper-Mine River to the eastern extremity of that Continent; that it was left for me to determine according to circumstances, whether it might be most advisable to proceed, at once, directly to the northward till I arrived at the sea-coast, and thence westerly towards the Copper-Mine River; or advance, in the first instance, by the usual route to the mouth of the Copper-Mine River, and from thence easterly till I should arrive at the eastern extremity of that Continent; that, in the adoption of either of these plans, I was to be guided by the advice and information which I should receive from the wintering servants of the Hudson's Bay Company, who would be instructed by their employers to co-operate cordially in the prosecution of the objects of the Expedition, and who would provide me with the necessary escort of Indians to act as guides, interpreters, game-killers, etc.; and also with such articles of clothing, ammunition, snow-shoes, presents, etc., as should be deemed expedient for me to take. That as another principal object of the Expedition was to amend the very defective geography of the northern part of North America, I was to be very careful to ascertain correctly the latitude and longitude of every remarkable spot upon our route, and of all the bays, harbours, rivers, headlands, etc., that might occur along the Northern Shore of North America. That in proceeding along the coast, I should erect conspicuous marks at places where ships might enter, or to which a boat could be sent;

and to deposit information as to the nature of the coast for the use of Lieutenant Parry. That in the journal of their route, I should register the temperature of the air at least three times in every twenty-four hours; together with the state of the wind and weather, and any other meteorological phenomena. That I should not neglect any opportunity of observing and noting down the dip and variation of the magnetic needle, and the intensity of the magnetic force; and should take particular notice whether any, and what kind or degree of, influence the Aurora Borealis might appear to exert on the magnetic needle; and to notice whether that phenomenon were attended with any noise; and to make any other observations that might be likely to tend to the further development of its cause, and the laws by which it is governed.

Mr. Back and Mr. hood were to assist me in all the observations above-mentioned, and to make drawings of the land, of the natives, and of the various objectives of Natural History; and, particularly, of such as Dr. Richardson, who, to his professional duties, was to add that of naturalist, might consider to be most curious and interesting.

I was instructed, on my arrival at, or near, the Mouth of the Copper-Mine River, to make every inquiry as to the situation of the spot whence native copper had been brought down by the Indians to the Hudson's Bay establishment, and to visit and explore the place in question; in order that Dr. Richardson might be enabled to make such observations as might be useful in a commercial point of view, or interesting to the science of mineralogy.

From Joseph Berens, Esq., the Governor of the Hudson's Bay Company, and the gentlemen of the Committee, I received all kinds of assistance and information, communicated in the most friendly manner previous to my leaving England; and I had the gratification of perusing the orders to their agents and servants in North America, containing the fullest directions to promote, by every means, the progress of the Expedition. I most cheerfully avail myself of this opportunity of expressing my gratitude to these gentlemen for their personal kindness to myself and the other officers, as well as for the benefits rendered by them to the Expedition; and the same sentiment is due towards the Gentlemen of the North-West Company, both in England and America, more particularly to Simon M'Gilliyray, Esq., of London, from whom I received much useful information, an cordial letters of recommendation to the partners and agents of that Company, resident on our line of route.

A short time before I left London I had the pleasure and advantage of an interview with the late Sir Alexander Mackenzie, who was one of the two persons who had visited the coast we were to explore. He afforded me, in the most open and kind manner, much valuable information and advice.

The provisions, instruments, and other articles, of which I had furnished a list, by direction of the Lords Commissioners of the Admiralty, were embarked on board the Hudson's Bay Company's ship *Prince of Wales*, appointed by the Committee to convey the Expedition to York Factory, their principal establishment in Hudson's Bay.

It will be seen, in the course of the Narrative how much reason I had to be satisfied with, and how great my obligations are to, all the gentlemen who were associated with me in the Expedition, whose kindness, good conduct, and cordial co-operation, have made an impression which can never be effaced from my mind. The unfortunate death of Mr. hood is the only drawback which I feel from the otherwise unalloyed pleasure of reflecting on that cordial unanimity which at all times prevailed among us in the days of sunshine, and in those of 'sickness and sorrow.'

To Dr. Richardson, in particular, the exclusive merit is due of whatever collections and observations have been made in the department of Natural History; and I am indebted to him in no small degree for his friendly advice and assistance in the preparation of the present narrative.

1. Given in the Appendix to the Quarto Edition.

The charts and drawings were made by Lieutenant Back, and the late Lieutenant hood. Both these gentlemen cheerfully and ably assisted me in making the observations and in the daily conduct of the Expedition. The observations made by Mr. hood, on the various phenomena presented by the Aurora Borealis,[1] will, it is presumed, present to the reader some new facts connected with this meteor. Mr. Back was mostly prevented from turning his attention to objects of science by the many severe duties which were required of him, and which obliged him to travel almost constantly every winter that we passed in America; to his personal exertions, indeed, our final safety is mainly to be attributed. And here I must be permitted to pay the tribute, due to the fidelity, exertion and uniform good conduct in the most trying situations, of John Hepburn, an English seaman, and our only attendant, to whom in the latter part of our journey we owe, under Divine Providence, the preservation of the lives of some of the party.

I ought, perhaps, to crave the reader's indulgence towards the defective style of this work, which I trust will not be refused when it is considered that mine has been a life of constant employment in my profession from a very early age. I have been prompted to venture upon the task solely by an imperious sense of duty, when called upon to undertake it.

In the ensuing Narrative the notices of the moral condition of the Indians as influenced by the conduct of the traders towards them, refer entirely to the state in which it existed during our progress through the country; but lest I should have been mistaken respecting the views of the Hudson's Bay Company on these points, I gladly embrace the opportunity which a Second Edition affords me of stating that the junction of the two Companies has enabled the Directors to put in practice the improvements which I have reason to believe they have long contemplated. They have provided for religious instruction by the appointment of two Clergymen of the established church, under whose direction school-masters and mistresses are to be placed at such stations as afford the means of support for the establishment of schools. The offspring of the voyagers and labourers are to be educated chiefly at the expense of the Company; and such of the Indian children as their parents may wish to send to these schools, are to be instructed, clothed, and maintained at the expense of the Church Missionary Society, which has already allotted a considerable sum for these purposes, and has also sent out teachers who are to act under the superintendence of the Rev. Mr. West, the principal chaplain of the Company.

We had the pleasure of meeting this gentleman at York Factory, and witnessed with peculiar delight that great benefit which already marked his zealous and judicious conduct. Many of the traders, and of the servants of the Company, had been induced to marry the women with whom they had cohabited; a material step towards the improvement of the females in that country.

Mr. West, under the sanction of the Directors, has also promoted a subscription for the distribution of the Bible in every part of the country where the Company's Fur Trade has extended, and which has met with very general support from the resident chief factors, traders, and clerks. The Directors of the Company are continuing to reduce the distribution of spirits gradually among the Indians, as well as towards their own servants, with a view to the entire disuse of them as soon as this most desirable object can be accomplished. They have likewise issued orders for the cultivation of the ground at each of the posts, by which means the residents will be far less exposed to famine whenever through the scarcity of animals, the sickness of the Indians, or any other cause, their supply of meat may fail.

It is hoped that intentions, so dear to every humane and pious mind, will, through the blessing of God, meet with the utmost success.

CHAPTER I

May, 1819

On Sunday, the 23rd of May, the whole of our party embarked at Gravesend on board the ship *Prince of Wales*, belonging to the Hudson's Bay Company, just as she was in the act of getting under weigh, with her consorts, the *Eddystone* and *Wear*. The wind being unfavourable, on the ebb tide being finished, the vessels were again anchored; but they weighed in the night and beat down as far as the Warp, where they were detained two days by a strong easterly wind.

Having learned from some of the passengers, who were the trading Officers of the Company, that the arrival of the ships at either of the establishments in Hudson's Bay, gives full occupation to all the boatmen in their service, who are required to convey the necessary stores to the different posts in the interior; that it was very probable a sufficient number of men might not be procured from this indispensable duty; and, considering that any delay at York Factory would materially retard our future operations, I wrote to the Under Secretary of State, requesting his permission to provide a few well-qualified steersmen and bowmen, at Stromness, to assist our proceedings in the former part of our journey into the interior.

May 30

The easterly wind, which had retarded the ship's progress so much, that we had only reached Hollesley Bay after a week's beating about, changed to W.S.W. soon after that anchorage had been gained. The vessels instantly weighed, and by carrying all sail, arrived in Yarmouth Roads at seven P.M.; the pilots were landed, and our course was continued through the anchorage. At midnight, the wind became light and variable, and gradually drew round to the N.W.; and, as the sky indicated unsettled weather, and the wind blew from an unfavourable quarter for ships upon that coast, the commander bore up again for Yarmouth, and anchored at eight A.M.

This return afforded us, at least, the opportunity of comparing the longitude of Yarmouth church, as shown by our chronometers, with its position as laid down by the Ordnance Trigonometrical Survey; and it was satisfactory to find, from the small difference in their results, that the chronometers had not experienced any alteration in their rates, in consequence of their being changed from an horizontal position in a room, to that of being carried in the pocket.

An untoward circumstance, while at this anchorage, cast a damp on our party at this early period of the voyage. Emboldened by the decided appearance of the N.W. sky, several of our officers and passengers ventured on shore for a few hours; but we had not been long in the town before the wind changed suddenly to S.E., which caused instant motion in the large fleet collected at this anchorage. The commander of our ship intimated his intention of proceeding to sea by firing guns; and the passengers hastened to embark. Mr. Back, however, had unfortunately gone upon some business to a house two or three miles distant from Yarmouth, along the line of the coast; from whence he expected to be able to observe the first symptoms of moving, which the vessels might make. By some accident, however, he did not make his appearance before the captain was obliged to make sail, that he might get the ships through the intricate passage of the Cockle Gat before it was dark. Fortunately, through the kindness of Lieutenant Hewit, of the *Protector*, I was enabled to convey a note to our missing companion, desiring him to proceed immediately by the coach to the Pentland Firth, and from thence across the passage to Stromness, which appeared to be the only way of proceeding by which he could rejoin the party.

June 3

The wind continuing favourable after leaving Yarmouth, about nine this morning we passed the rugged and bold projecting rock, termed Johnny Groat's house, and soon afterwards Duncansby Head, and then entered the Pentland Firth. A pilot came from the main shore of Scotland, and steered the ship in safety between the different islands, to the outer anchorage at Stromness, though the atmosphere was too dense for distinguishing any of the objects on the land. Almost immediately after the ship had anchored, the wind changed to N.W., the rain ceased, and a sight was then first obtained of the neighbouring islands, and of the town of Stromness, the latter of which, from this point of view, and at this distance, presented a pleasing appearance.

Mr. Geddes, the agent of the Hudson's Bay Company at this place, undertook to communicate my wish for volunteer boatmen to the different parishes, by a notice on the church door, which he said was the surest and most direct channel for the conveyance of information to the lower classes in these islands, as they invariably attend divine service there every Sunday. He informed me that the kind of men we were in want of would be difficult to procure, on account of the very increased demand for boatmen for the herring fishery, which had recently been established on the shores of these islands; that last year sixty boats and four hundred men only were employed in this service, whereas now there were three hundred boats and twelve hundred men engaged; and that owing to this unexpected addition to the fishery, he had been unable to provide the number of persons required for the service of the Hudson's Bay Company. This was unpleasant information, as it increased the apprehension of our being detained at York Factory the whole winter if boatmen were not taken from hence. I could not, therefore, hesitate in requesting Mr. Geddes to engage eight or ten men well adapted for our service, on such terms as he could procure them, though the Secretary of State's permission had not yet reached me.

Next to a supply of boatmen, our attention was directed towards the procuring of a house conveniently situated for trying the instruments and examining the rates of the chronometers. Mr. Geddes kindly offered one of his, which, though in an unfinished state, was readily accepted, being well situated for our purpose, as it was placed on an eminence, had a southern aspect, and was at a sufficient distance from the town to secure us from frequent interruption. Another advantage was its proximity to the Manse, the residence of the Rev. Mr. Clouston, the worthy and highly respected minister of Stromness; whose kind hospitality and the polite attention of his family the party experienced almost daily during their stay.

For three days the weather was unsettled, and few observations could be made except for the dip of the needle, which was ascertained to be 74° 37′ 48″, on which occasion a difference of eight degrees and a half was perceived between the observations, when the face of the instrument was changed from the east to the west, the amount being the greatest when it was placed with the face to the west. But, on the 8th, a westerly wind caused a cloudless sky, which enabled us to place the transit instrument in the meridian and to ascertain the variation of the compass to be 27° 50′ west. The sky becoming cloudy in the afternoon prevented our obtaining the corresponding observations to those gained in the morning; and the next day an impervious fog obscured the sky until noon. On the evening of this day, we had the gratification of welcoming our absent companion, Mr. Back. His return to our society was hailed with sincere pleasure by every one, and removed a weight of anxiety from my mind. It appears that he had come down to the beach at Caistor just as the ships were passing by, and had applied to some boatmen to convey him on board, which might have been soon accomplished but they, discovering the emergency of his case, demanded an exorbitant reward which he was not at the instant prepared to satisfy; and, in consequence, they positively refused to assist him. Though he had travelled nine successive days, almost without rest, he could not be prevailed upon to withdraw from the agreeable scene of a ball-room, in which he joined us, until a late hour.

On the 10th, the rain having ceased, the observations for ascertaining the dip of the needle were repeated; and the results compared with the former ones, gave a mean of 74° 33′ 20″. Nearly the same differences were remarked in reversing the face of the instrument as before. An attempt was also made to ascertain the magnetic force, but the wind blew too strong for procuring the observation to any degree of accuracy.

The fineness of the following day induced us to set up the different instruments for examination, and to try how nearly the observations made by each of them would agree; but a squall passed over just before noon, accompanied by heavy rain, and the hoped-for favourable opportunity was entirely lost. In the intervals between the observations, and at every opportunity, my companions were occupied in those pursuits to which their attention had been more particularly directed in my instructions. Whilst Dr. Richardson was collecting and examining the various specimens of marine plants, of which these islands furnish an abundant and diversified supply, Mr. Back and Mr. Hood took views and sketches of the surrounding scenery, which is extremely picturesque in many parts, and wants only the addition of trees to make it beautiful. The hills present the bold character of rugged sterility, whilst the valleys at this season are clothed with luxuriant verdure.

It was not till the 14th that, by appointment, the boatmen were to assemble at the house of Mr. Geddes, to engage to accompany the Expedition. Several persons collected, but, to my great mortification, I found they were all so strongly possessed with the fearful apprehension either that great danger would attend the service, or that we should carry them further than they would agree to go, that not a single man would engage with us; some of them, however, said they would consider the subject, and give me an answer on the following day. This indecisive conduct was extremely annoying to me, especially as the next evening was fixed for the departure of the ships.

At the appointed time on the following morning four men only presented themselves, and these, after much hesitation, engaged to accompany the Expedition to Fort Chipewyan if they should be required so far. The bowmen and steersmen were to receive forty pounds wages annually, and the middle men thirty-five pounds. They stipulated to be sent back to the Orkney Islands free of expense, and to receive their pay until the time of their arrival. Only these few men could be procured, although our requisition had been sent to almost every island, even as far as the northernmost point of Ronaldsha. I was much amused with the extreme caution these men used before they would sign the agreement; they minutely scanned all our intentions, weighed every circumstance, looked narrowly into the plan of our route, and still more circumspectly to the prospect of return. Such caution on the part of the northern mariners forms a singular contrast with the ready and thoughtless manner in which an English seaman enters upon any enterprise, however hazardous, without inquiring, or desiring to know where he is going, or what he is going about.

The brig *Harmony*, belonging to the Moravian Missionary Society, and bound to their settlement at Nain, on the coast of Labrador, was lying at anchor. With the view of collecting some Esquimaux words and sentences, or gaining any information respecting the manners and habits of that people, Doctor Richardson and myself paid her a visit. We found the passengers, who were going out as Missionaries, extremely disposed to communicate; but as they only spoke the German and Esquimaux languages, of which we were ignorant, our conversation was necessarily much confined: by the aid, however, of an Esquimaux and German Dictionary, some few words were collected, which we considered might be useful. There were on board a very interesting girl and a young man, who were natives of Disco, in Old Greenland; both of them had fair complexions, rather handsome features, and a lively manner; the former was going to be married to a resident Missionary, and the latter to officiate in that character. The commander of the vessel gave me a translation of the Gospel of St. John in the Esquimaux language, printed by the Moravian Society in London.

June 16

The wind being unfavourable for sailing I went on shore with Dr. Richardson, and took several lunar observations at the place of our former residence. The result obtained was latitude 58° 56' 56", N.; longitude 3° 17' 55" W.; variation 27° 50' W.; dip of the magnetic needle, 74° 33' 20". In the afternoon the wind changed in a squall some points towards the north, and the *Prince of Wales* made the preparatory signal for sea. At three P.M. the ships weighed, an hour too early for the tide; as soon as this served we entered into the passage between Hoy and Pomona, and had to beat through against a very heavy swell, which the meeting of a weather tide and a strong breeze had occasioned.

Some dangerous rocks lie near the Pomona shore, and on this side also the tide appeared to run with the greatest strength. On clearing the outward projecting points of Hoy and Pomona we entered at once into the Atlantic, and commenced our voyage to Hudson's Bay – having the *Eddystone, Wear* and *Harmony*, Missionary brig, in company.

The comparisons of the chronometers this day indicated that Arnold's Nos. 2148 and 2147 had slightly changed their rates since they had been brought on board; fortunately the rate of the former seems to have increased nearly in the same ratio as the other has lost, and the mean longitude will not be materially affected.

Being now fairly launched into the Atlantic, I issued a general memorandum for the guidance of the officers during the prosecution of the service on which we were engaged, and communicated to them the several points of information that were expected from us by my instructions. I also furnished them with copies of the signals which had been agreed upon between Lieutenant Parry and myself, to be used in the event of our reaching the northern coast of America and falling in with each other.

At the end of the month of June our progress was found to have been extremely slow, owing to a determined N.W. wind and much sea. We had numerous birds hovering round the ship; principally fulmars (*procellaria glacialis*) and shear-waters (*procellaria puffinus*), and not unfrequently saw shoals of grampusses sporting about, which the Greenland seamen term finners from their large dorsal fin. Some porpoises occasionally appeared, and whenever they did the crew were sanguine in their expectation of having a speedy change in the wind, which had been so vexatiously contrary, but they were disappointed in every instance.

Thursday, July 1

The month of July set in more favourably; and aided by fresh breezers, we advanced rapidly to the westward, attended daily by numerous fulmars and shearwaters. The Missionary brig had parted company on the 22nd of June. We passed directly over that part of the ocean where the 'Sunken Land of Buss' is laid down in the old, and continued in the Admiralty charts. Mr. Bell, the commander of the *Eddystone*, informed me that the pilot who brought his ship down the Thames told him that he had gained surroundings in twelve feet somewhere hereabout; and I am rather inclined to attribute the very unusual and cross sea we had in this neighbourhood to the existence of a bank, than to the effect of a gale of wind which we had just before experienced; and I cannot but regret that the commander of the ship did not try for soundings at frequent intervals.

By the 25th July we had opened the entrance of Davis Straits, and in the afternoon spoke the *Andrew Marvell*, bound to England with a cargo of fourteen fish. The master informed us that the ice had been heavier this season in Davis Straits than he had ever recollected, and that it lay particularly close to the westward, being connected with the shore to the northward of Resolution Island, and extending from thence within a short distance of the Greenland coast; that whales had been abundant, but the ice so extremely cross, that few could be killed. His ship, as well as several others, had suffered material injury, and two vessels had been entirely crushed between vast masses of ice in latitude 74° 40′ N., but the crews were saved. We inquired anxiously, but in vain, for intelligence respecting Lieutenant Parry and the ships under his command; but as he mentioned that the wind had been blowing strong from the northward for some time, which would, probably, have cleared Baffin's Bay of ice, we were disposed to hope favourably of his progress.

The clouds assumed so much the appearance of icebergs this evening, as to deceive most of the passengers and crew; but their imaginations had been excited by the intelligence we had received form the *Andrew Marvell*, that she had only parted from a cluster of them two days previous to our meeting.

On the 27th, being in latitude 57° 44′ 21″ N., longitude 47° 31′ 14″ W., and the weather calm, we tried our soundings, but did not reach the bottom. The register thermometer was attached to the line just about the lead, and is supposed to have descended six hundred and fifty fathoms. A well-corked bottle was also fastened to the line, two hundred fathoms above the lead, and went down four hundred and fifty fathoms. The change in temperature, shown by the register thermometer during the descent, was from 52° to 40.5; and it stood at the latter point when taken out of the tin case. The temperature of the water brought up in the bottle was 41°, being half a degree higher at four hundred and fifty than at six hundred and fifty fathoms, and four degrees colder than the water at the surface, which was then at 45°, whilst that of the air was 46°. This experiment in showing the water to be colder at a great depth than at the surface, and in proportion to the increase of the descent, coincides with the observations of Captain Ross and Lieutenant Parry, on their late voyage to these seas, but is contrary to the results obtained by Captain Buchan and myself on our recent voyage to the north, between Spitzbergen and Greenland, in which sea we invariably found the water brought from any great depth to be warmer than that at the surface.

On the 28th we tacked to avoid an extensive stream of sailing ice. The temperature of the water fell to 39.5° when we were near it, but was at 41° when at the distance of half a mile. The thermometer in the air remained steadily at 40°. Thus the proximity of this ice was not so decidedly indicated by the decrease of the temperature of either the air or water, as I have before witnessed, which was probably owing to the recent arrival of the stream at this point and its passing at too quick a rate for the effectual diffusion of its chilling influence beyond a short distance. Still the decrease in both cases was sufficient to have given timely warning for a ship's performing any evolution that would have prevented the coming in contact with it had the thickness of the weather precluded a distant view of the danger.

The approach to ice would be more evidently pointed out in the Atlantic, or wherever the surface is not so continually chilled by the passing and the melting of ice as in this sea; and I should strongly recommend a strict hourly attention to the thermometrical state of the water at the surface, in all parts where ships are exposed to the dangerous concussion of sailing icebergs, as a principal means of security.

The following day our ship came near another stream of ice and the approach to it was indicated by a decrease of the temperature of the water at the surface form 44° to 42°. A small pine-tree was picked up much shattered by the ice. In the afternoon of the 30th a very dense fog came on; and, about six P.M., when sailing before a fresh breeze, we were suddenly involved in a heavy stream of ice. Considerable difficulty was experienced in steering through the narrow channels between the different masses in this foggy weather, and the ship received several severe blows.

The water, as usual in the centre of the stream, was quite smooth, but we heard the waves beating violently against the outer edge of the ice. There was some earthy matter on several of the pieces, and the whole body bore the appearance of recent separation from the land. In the space of two hours we again got in the open sea, but had left our two consorts far behind; they followed our track by the guns we discharged. The temperature of the surface water was 35° when amongst the ice, 38° when just clear of it, and 41.5° at two miles distant.

On the 4th of August, when in latitude 59° 58′ N., longitude 59° 53′ W., we first fell in with large icebergs; and in the evening were encompassed by several of considerable magnitude, which obliged us to tack the ship in order to prevent our getting entangled amongst them. The estimated distance from the nearest part of the Labrador coast was then eighty-eight miles; here we tried for soundings without gaining the bottom. The ship passed through some strong ripplings, which evidently indicated a current, but its direction was not ascertained. We found, however, by the recent observations, that the ship had been set daily to the southward since we had opened David Straits. The variation of the compass was observed to be 52° 41′ W.

At nine P.M. brilliant coruscations of the Aurora Borealis appeared, of a pale ochre colour, with a slight tinge of red, in an arched form, crossing the zenith from N.W. to S.E., but afterwards they assumed various shapes and had a rapid motion.

On the 5th of August a party of the officers endeavoured to get on one of the larger icebergs, but ineffectually, owing to the steepness and smoothness of its sides, and the swell produced by its undulating motion. This was one of the largest we saw, and Mr. hood ascertained its height to be one hundred and forty-nine feet; but these masses of ice are frequently magnified to an immense size through the illusive medium of a hazy atmosphere, and on this account their dimensions have often been exaggerated by voyagers.

In the morning of the 7th the island of Resolution was indistinctly seen through the haze, but was soon afterwards entirely hidden by a very dense fog. The favourable breeze subsided into a perfect calm and left the ship surrounded by loose ice. At this time the *Eddystone* was perceived to be driving with rapidity towards some of the larger masses; the stern-boats of this ship and of the *Wear* were despatched to assist in towing her clear of them. At ten a momentary clearness presented the land distinctly at the distance of two miles; the ship was quite unmanageable, and under the sole governance of the currents, which ran in strong eddies between the masses of ice. Our consorts were also seen, the *Wear* being within hail, and the *Eddystone* at a short distance from us. Two attempts were ineffectually made to gain soundings, and the extreme density of the fog precluded us from any other means of ascertaining the direction in which we were driving until half-past twelve, when we had the alarming view of a barren rugged shore within a few yards towering over the mast-heads. Almost instantly afterwards the ship struck violently on a point of rocks projecting from the island; and the ship's side was brought so near to the shore that poles were prepared to push her off. This blow displaced the rudder and raised it several inches, but it fortunately had been previously confined by tackles. A gentle swell freed the ship from this perilous situation, but the current hurried us along in contact with the rocky shore, and the prospect was most alarming. On the outward bow was perceived a rugged and precipitous cliff whose summit was hid in the fog, and the vessel's head was pointed towards the bottom of a small bay into which we were rapidly driving. There now seemed to be no probability of escaping shipwreck, being without wind, and having the rudder in its present useless state; the only assistance was that of a boat employed in towing, which had been placed in the water between the ship and the shore at the imminent risk of its being crushed. The ship again struck in passing over a ledge of rocks, and happily the blow replaced the rudder, which enabled us to take advantage of a light breeze, and to direct the ship's head without the projecting cliff. But the breeze was only momentary, and the ship was a third time driven on shore on the rocky termination of the cliff. Here we remained stationary for some seconds and with little prospect of being removed from this perilous situation; but we were once more extricated by the swell from this ledge also, and carried still farther along the shore. The coast became now more rugged, and our view of it was terminated by another high projecting point on the starboard bow. Happily, before we had reached it, a light breeze enabled us to turn the ship's head to seaward, and we had the gratification to find, when the sails were trimmed, that shore drew off the shore. We had made but little progress, however, when she was violently forced by the current against a large iceberg lying aground.

Our prospect was now more alarming than at any preceding period; and it would be difficult for me to portray the anxiety and dismay depicted on the countenances of the female passengers and children, who were rushing on deck in spite of the endeavours of the officers to keep them below, out of the danger which was apprehended if the masts should be carried away. After the first concussion the ship was driven along the steep and rugged side of this iceberg with such amazing rapidity that the destruction of the masts seemed inevitable, and every one expected we should again be forced on the rocks in the most disabled state; but we providentially escaped this perilous result, which must have been decisive.

The dense fog now cleared away for a short time, and we discovered the *Eddystone* close to some rocks, having three boats employed in towing; but the *Wear* was not visible.

Our ship received water very fast; the pumps were instantly manned and kept in continual use, and signals of distress were made to the *Eddystone*, whose commander promptly came on board, and then ordered to our assistance his carpenter and all the men he could spare, together with the carpenter and boat's crew of the *Wear*, who had gone on board the *Eddystone* in the morning, and were prevented from returning to their own vessel by the fog. As the wind was increasing and the sky appeared very unsettled, it was determined the *Eddystone* should take the ship in two, that the undivided attention of the passengers and crew might be directed to pumping, and clearing the holds to examine whether there was a possibility of stopping the leak. We soon had reason to suppose the principal injury had been received from a blow near the stern-post, and, after cutting away part of the ceiling, the carpenters endeavoured to stop the rushing in of the water by forcing oakum between the timbers; but this had not the desired effect, and the leak, in spite of all our efforts at the pumps, increased so much that parties of the officers and passengers were stationed to bail out the water in buckets at different parts of the hold. A heavy gale came on, blowing from the land, as the night advanced; the sails were split, the ship was encompassed by heavy ice, and, in forcing through a closely-connected stream the tow-rope broke and obliged us to take a portion of the seamen from the pumps and appoint them to the management of the ship.

Fatigue, indeed, had caused us to relax in our exertions at the pumps during a part of the night of the 8th, and on the following morning upwards of five feet of water was found in the well. Renewed exertions were now put forth by every person, and before eight A.M. the water was so much reduced as to enable the carpenters to get at other defective places; but the remedies they could apply were insufficient to repress the water from rushing in, and our labours could but just keep the ship in the same state throughout the day, until six P.M.; when the strength of every one began to fail, the expedient of thrusting in felt, as well as oakum, was resorted to, and a plank nailed over all. After this operation a perceptible diminution in the water was made, and being encouraged by the change, we put forth our utmost exertion in bailing and pumping; and before night, to our infinite joy, the leak was so overpowered that the pumps were only required to be used at intervals of ten minutes. A sail, covered with every substance that could be carried into the leaks by the pressure of the water, was drawn under the quarter of the ship, and secured by ropes on each side.

As a matter of precaution in the event of having to abandon the ship, which was for some time doubtful, the elderly women and children were removed to the *Eddystone* when the wind was moderate this afternoon, but the young women remained to assist at the pumps, and their services were highly valuable, both for their personal labour, and for the encouragement their example and perseverance gave to the men.

At daylight, on the 9th, every eye was anxiously cast around the horizon in search of the *Wear*, but in vain; and the recollection of our own recent peril caused us to entertain considerable apprehensions for her safety. This anxiety quickened our efforts to exchange our shattered sails for new ones, that the ship might be got, as speedily as possible, near to the land, which was but just in sight, and a careful search be made for her along the coast. We were rejoiced to find that our leak did not increase by carrying sail, and we ventured in the evening to remove the sail which had been placed under the part where the injury had been received, as it greatly impeded our advance.

We passed many icebergs on the 10th, and in the evening we tacked from a level field of ice, which extended northward as far as the eye could reach. Our leak remained in the same state; the pumps discharged in three minutes the quantity of water which had been received in fifteen.

The ship could not be got near to the land before the afternoon of the 11th. At four P.M. we hove to, opposite to, and about five miles distant from, the spot on which we had first struck on Saturday. Every glass was directed along the shore (as they had been throughout the day) to discover any trace of our absent consort; but as none was seen, our solicitude respecting her was much increased, and we feared the crew might be wrecked on this inhospitable shore. Guns were frequently fired to apprize any who might be near of our approach; but as no one appeared, and no signal was returned, and the loose ice was setting down towards the ship, we bore up to proceed to the next appointed rendezvous. At eight P.M. we were abreast of the S.W. end of the island called Cape Resolution, which is a low point, but indicated at a distance by a lofty round-backed hill that rises above it. We entered Hudson's Straits soon afterwards.

The coast of Resolution Island should be approached with caution, as the tides appear to be strong and uncertain in their course. Some dangerous rocks lie above and below the water's edge, at the distance of five or six miles from East Bluff, bearing S. 32° E.

August 12

Having had a fresh gale through the night, we reached Saddleback Island by noon – the place of rendezvous; and looked anxiously, but in vain, for the *Wear*. Several guns were fired, supposing she might be hid from our view by the land; but as she did not appear, Captain Davidson, having remained two hours, deemed further delay inexpedient, and bore up to keep the advantage of the fair wind. The outline of this island is rugged; the hummock on its northern extremity appeared to me to resemble a decaved martello tower more than a saddle.

Azimuths were obtained this evening that gave the variation 58° 45′ W., which is greater than is laid down in the charts, or than the officers of Hudson's Bay ships have been accustomed to allow. We arrived abreast of the Upper Savage Island early in the morning, and as the breeze was moderate, the ship was steered as near to the shore as the wind would permit, to give the Esquimaux inhabitants an opportunity of coming off to barter, which they soon embraced.

Their shouts at a distance intimated their approach some time before we descried the canoes paddling towards us; the headmost of them reached us at eleven; these were quickly followed by others, and before noon about forty canoes, each holding one man, were assembled around the two ships. In the afternoon, when we approached nearer to the shore, five or six larger ones, containing the women and children, came up.

The Esquimaux immediately evinced their desire to barter, and displayed no small cunning in making their bargains, taking care not to exhibit too many articles at first. Their principal commodities were oil, sea-horse teeth, whalebone, seal-skin dresses, caps and boots, deerskins and horns, and models of their canoes; and they received in exchange small saws, knives, nails, tin-kettles, and needles. It was pleasing to behold the exultation, and to hear the shouts of the whole party, when an acquisition was made by any one; and not a little ludicrous to behold the eagerness with which the fortunate person licked each article with his tongue, on receiving it, as a finish to the bargain, and an act of appropriation. They in no instance omitted this strange practice, however small the article; the needles even passed individually through the ceremony. The women brought imitations of men, women, animals, and birds, carved with labour and ingenuity out of seahorse teeth. The dresses and the figures of the animals, were not badly executed, but there was no attempt at the delineation of the countenances; and most of the figures were without eyes, ears, and fingers, the execution of which would, perhaps, have required more delicate instruments than they possess. The men set most value on saws; *kuttee-swa-bak*, the name by which they distinguish them, was a constant cry. Knives were held next in estimation. An old sword was bartered from the *Eddystone*, and I shall long remember the universal burst of joy on the happy man's receiving it. It was delightful to witness the general interest excited by individual acquisitions. There was no desire shown by any one to over-reach his neighbour, or to press towards any part of the ship where a bargain was making, until the person in possession of the place had completed his exchange and removed; and if any article happened to be demanded from the outer canoes, the men nearest assisted willingly in passing the thing across. Supposing the party to belong to one tribe, the total number of the tribe must exceed two hundred persons, as there were, probably, one hundred and fifty around the ships, and few of these were elderly persons, or male children.

Their faces were broad and flat, the eyes small. The men were in general stout. Some of the younger women and the children had rather pleasing countenances, but the difference between these and the more aged of that sex, bore strong testimony to the effects which a few years produce in this ungenial climate. Most of the party had sore eyes, all of them appeared of a plethoric habit of body; several were observed bleeding at the nose during their stay near the ship. The men's dresses consisted of a jacket of seal-skin, the trowsers of bear-skin, and several had caps of the white fox-skin. The female dresses were made of the same materials, but differently shaped, having a hood in which the infants were carried. We thought their manner very lively and agreeable. They were fond of mimicking our speech and gestures; but nothing afforded them greater amusement than when we attempted to retaliate by pronouncing any of their words.

The canoes were of seal-skin, and similar in every respect to those used by the Esquimaux in Greenland; they were generally new and very complete in their appointments. Those appreciated to the women are of ruder construction, and only calculated for fine weather; they are, however, useful vessels, being capable of containing twenty persons with their luggage. An elderly man officiates as steersman, and the women paddle, but they have also a mast which carries a sail, made of dressed whale-gut.

When the women had disposed of all their articles of trade they resorted to entreaty; and the putting in practice many enticing gestures was managed with so much address as to procure them presents of a variety of beads, needles, and other articles in great demand among females.

It is probable these Esquimaux go from this shore to some part of Labrador to pass the winter, as parties of them have been frequently seen by the homeward-bound Hudson's Bay ships in the act of crossing the Strait.

They appear to speak the same language as the tribe of Esquimaux who reside near to the Moravian settlements in Labrador: for we perceived they used several of the words which had been given to us by the Missionaries at Stromness.

Towards evening the Captain, being desirous to get rid of his visitors, took an effectual method by tacking from the shore; our friends then departed apparently in high glee at the harvest they had reaped. They paddled away very swiftly, and would, doubtless, soon reach the shore, though it was distant ten or twelve miles.

Not having encountered any of the ice which usually arrests the progress of ships in their outward passage through the Straits, and being consequently deprived of the usual means of replenishing our stock of water, which had become short, the Captain resolved on going to the coast of Labrador for a supply. Dr. Richardson and I gladly embraced this opportunity to land and examine this part of the coast. I was also desirous to observe the variation on shore, as the azimuths, which had been taken on board both ships since our entrance into the Straits, had shown a greater amount than we had been led to expect; but unluckily the sun became obscured. The beach consisted of large rolled stones of gneiss and sienite, amongst which many pieces of ice had grounded, and it was with difficulty that we effected a landing in a small cove under a steep cliff. These stones were worn perfectly smooth; neither in the interstices, nor at the bottom of the water, which was very clear, were there any vestiges of seaweed.

The cliff was from forty to fifty feet high and quite perpendicular, and had at its base a small slip of soil formed of the debris of a bed of clay-slate. From this narrow spot Dr. Richardson collected specimens of thirty different species of plants; and we were about to scramble up a shelving part of the rock, and go into the interior, when we perceived the signal of recall, which the master had caused to be made, in consequence of a sudden change in the appearance of the weather.

On the evening of the 19th we passed Digge's Islands, the termination of Hudson's Strait. Here the *Eddystone* parted company, being bound to Moose Factory at the bottom of the Bay. A strong north wind came on, which prevented our getting round the north end of Mansfield; and, as it continued to blow with equal strength for the next five days, we were most vexatiously detained in beating along the Labrador coast, and near the dangerous chain of islands, the Sleepers, which are said to extend from the latitude of 60° 10′ to 57° 00′ N. The press of sail which of necessity we carried, caused the leak to increase, and the pumps were kept in constant use.

A favouring wind at length enabled us, on the 25th, to shape our course across Hudson's Bay. Nothing worthy of remark occurred during this passage, except the rapid decrease in the variation of the magnetic needle. The few remarks respecting the appearance of the land, which we were able to make in our quick passage through these Straits, were transmitted to the Admiralty; but as they will not be interesting to the general reader, and may not be sufficiently accurate for the guidance of the Navigator, they are omitted in this narrative.

On the 28th we discovered the land to the southward of Cape Tatnam, which is so extremely low that the tops of the trees were first discerned; the soundings at the time were seventeen fathoms, which gradually decreased to five as the shore was approached. Cape Tatnam is not otherwise remarkable than as being the point from which the coast inclines rather more to the westward towards York Factory.

The opening of the morning of the 30th presented to our view the anchorage at York Flats, and the gratifying sight of a vessel at anchor, which we recognised, after an anxious examination, to be the *Wear*. A strong breeze blowing from the direction of the Flats, caused the water to be more shallow than usual on the sandy bar, which lies on the seaward side of the anchorage, and we could not get over it before two P.M., when the tide was nearly at its height.

Immediately after our arrival, Mr. Williams, the Governor of the Hudson's Bay Company's posts, came on board, accompanied by the Commander of the *Wear*. The pleasure we felt in welcoming the latter gentleman can easily be imagined, when it is considered what reason we had to apprehend that he and his crew had been numbered with the dead. We learned that one of the larger masses of ice had providentially drifted between the vessel's side and the rocks just at the time he expected to strike, to which he secured it until a breeze sprang up and enabled him to pursue his voyage.

The Governor acquainted me that he had received information from the Committee of the Hudson's Bay Company of the equipment of the Expedition, and that the officers would come out in their first ship. In the evening Dr. Richardson, Mr. Hood, and I, accompanied him to York Factory, which we reached after dark; it is distant from the Flats seven miles. Early next morning the honour of a salute was conferred on the members of the Expedition.

Having communicated to the Governor the objects of the Expedition, and that I had been directed to consult with him and the senior servants of the Company as to the best mode of proceeding towards the execution of the service, I was gratified by his assurance that his instructions from the Committee directed that every possible assistance should be given to forward our progress, and that he should feel peculiar pleasure in performing this part of his duty. He introduced me at once to Messrs. Charles, Swaine, and Snodie, masters of districts who, from long residence in the country, were perfectly acquainted with the different modes of travelling, and the obstructions which might be anticipated. At the desire of these gentlemen, I drew up a series of questions respecting the points on which we required information; to which, two days afterwards, they had the kindness to return very explicit and satisfactory answers; and on receiving them I requested the Governor to favour me with his sentiments on the same subject in writing, which he delivered to me on the following day.

Having learned that Messrs. Shaw, M'Tavish, and several other partners of the N.-W. Company, were under detention at this place, we took the earliest opportunity of visiting them; when having presented the general circular, and other introductory letters, with which I had been furnished by their agent Mr. Simon M'Gillivray, we received from them the most friendly and full assurance of the cordial endeavours of the wintering partners of their company to promote the interests of the Expedition. The knowledge we had now gained of the state of the violent commercial opposition existing in the country, rendered this assurance highly gratifying; and these gentlemen added to the obligation by freely communicating that information respecting the interior of the country, which their intelligence and long residence so fully qualified them to give.

I deemed it expedient to issue a memorandum to the officers of the Expedition, strictly prohibiting any interference whatever in the existing quarrels, or any that might arise, between the two Companies; and on presenting it to the principals of both the parties, they expressed their satisfaction at the step I had taken.

The opinions of all the gentlemen were so decidedly in favour of the route by Cumberland House, and through the chain of posts to the Great Slave Lake, that I determined on pursuing it, and immediately communicated my intention to the Governor, with a request that he would furnish me with the means of conveyance for the party as speedily as possible.

It was suggested in my instructions that we might probably procure a schooner at this place, to proceed north as far as Wager Bay; but the vessel alluded to was lying at Moose Factory, completely out of repair; independently of which, the route directly to the northward was rendered impracticable by the impossibility of procuring hunters and guides on the coast.

I found that as the Esquimaux inhabitants had left Churchill a month previous to our arrival, no interpreter from that quarter could be procured before their return in the following spring. The Governor, however, undertook to forward to us, next season, the only one amongst them who understood English, if he could be induced to go.

The Governor selected one of the largest of the Company's boats for our use on the journey, and directed the carpenters to commence refitting it immediately; but he was only able to furnish us with a steersman; and we were obliged to make up the rest of the crew with the boatmen brought from Stromness, and our two attendants.

York Factory, the principal depôt of the Hudson's Bay Company, stands on the west bank of Hayes River, about five miles above its mouth, on the marshy peninsula which separates the Hayes and Nelson Rivers. The surrounding country is flat and swampy, and covered with willows, poplars, larch, spruce, and birch-trees; but the requisition for fuel has expended all the wood in the vicinity of the fort, and the residents have now to send for it to a considerable distance. The soil is alluvial clay, and contains imbedded rolled stones. Though the bank of the river is elevated about twenty feet, it is frequently overflown by the spring floods, and large portions are annually carried away by the disruption of the ice, which grounding in the stream, have formed several muddy islands. These interruptions, together with the various collection of stones that are hid at high water, render the navigation of the river difficult; but vessels of two hundred tons burthen may be brought through the proper channels as high as the Factory.

The principal buildings are placed in the form of a square, having an octagonal court in the centre; they are two storeys in height, and have flat roofs covered with lead. The officers dwell in one portion of this square, and in the other parts the articles of merchandise are kept: the workshops, storehouses for the furs, and the servants' houses are ranged on the outside of the square, and the whole is surrounded by a stockade twenty feet high. A platform is laid from the house to the pier on the bank for the convenience of transporting the stores and furs, which is the only promenade the residents have on this marshy spot during the summer season. The few Indians who now frequent this establishment belong to the *Swampy Crees*. There were several of them encamped on the outside of the stockade. Their tents were rudely constructed by tying twenty or thirty poles together at the top, and spreading them out at the base so as to form a cone; these were covered with dressed moose-skins. The fire is placed in the centre, and a hole is left for the escape of the smoke. The inmates had a squalid look, and were suffering under the combined afflictions of whooping-cough and measles; but even these miseries did not keep them from an excessive indulgence in spirits, which they unhappily can procure from the traders with too much facility; and they nightly serenaded us with their monotonous drunken songs. Their sickness at this time was particularly felt by the traders, this being the season of the year when the exertion of every hunter is required to procure their winter's stock of geese, which resort in immense flocks to the extensive flats in this neighbourhood. These birds, during the summer, retire far to the north, and breed in security; but when the approach of winter compels them to seek a more southern climate, they generally alight on the marshes of this bay, and flatten there for three weeks or a month, before they take their final departure from the country. They also make a short halt at the same spots in their progress northwards in the spring. Their arrival is welcomed with joy, and the *goose hunt* is one of the most plentiful seasons of the year. The ducks frequent the swamps all the summer.

The weather was extremely unfavourable for celestial observations during our stay, and it was only by watching the momentary appearances of the sun that we were enabled to obtain fresh rates for the chronometers, and allow for their errors from Greenwich time. The dip of the needle was observed to be 79° 29′ 07″, and the difference produced by reversing the face of the instrument was 11° 3′ 40″. A succession of fresh breezes prevented our ascertaining the intensity of the magnetic force. The position of York Factory, by our observations, is in latitude 57° 00′ 03″ N., longitude 92° 26′ W. The variation of the compass 6° 00′ 21″ E.

CHAPTER II

Passage up Hayes, Steel and Hill Rivers – Cross Swampy Lake –
Jack River – Knee Lake and Magnetic Islet – Trout River – Holy
Lake – Weepinapannis River – Windy Lake – White Fall Lake and
River – Echemamis and Sea Rivers – Play Green Lakes – Lake
Winipeg – River Saskatchawan – Cross, Cedar and Pine Island
Lakes – Cumberland House

September, 1819

On the 9th of September, our boat being completed, arrangements were made for our departure as soon as the tide should serve. But, when the stores were brought down to the beach, it was found that the boat would not contain them all. The whole, therefore, of the bacon, and part of the flour, rice, tobacco, and ammunition, were returned into the store. The bacon was too bulky an article to be forwarded under any circumstances; but the Governor undertook to forward the rest next season. In making the selection of articles to carry with us, I was guided by the judgment of Governor Williams, who assured me that tobacco, ammunition, and spirits could be procured in the interior, otherwise I should have been very unwilling to have left these essential articles behind. We embarked at noon, and were honoured with a salute of eight guns and three cheers from the Governor and all the inmates of the fort, who had assembled to witness our departure. We gratefully returned their cheers, and then made sail, much delighted at having now commenced our voyage into the interior of America. The wind and tide failing us at the distance of six miles above the Factory, and the current being too rapid for using oars to advantage, the crew had to commence tracking, or dragging the boat by a line, to which they were harnessed. This operation is extremely laborious in these rivers. Our men were obliged to walk along the steep declivity of a high bank, rendered at this season soft and slippery by frequent rains, and their progress was often further impeded by fallen trees, which, having slipped from the verge of the thick wood above, hung on the face of the bank in a great variety of directions. Notwithstanding these obstacles, we advanced at the rate of two miles an hour, one-half of the crew relieving the other at intervals of an hour and a half. The banks of the river, and its islands, composed of alluvial soil, are well covered with pines, larches, poplars, and willows. The breadth of the stream, some distance above the Factory, is about half a mile, and its depth, during this day's voyage, varied from three to nine feet.

At sunset we landed, and pitched the tent for the night, having made a progress of twelve miles. A large fire was quickly kindled, supper speedily prepared, and as readily despatched, when we retired with our buffalo robes on, and enjoyed a night of sound repose.

It may here be stated, that the survey of the river was made by taking the bearings of every point with a pocket compass, estimating the distances, and making a connected eye-sketch of the whole. This part of the survey was allotted to Messrs. Back and Hood conjointly: Mr. Hood also protracted the route every evening on a ruled map after the courses and distances had been corrected by observations for latitude and longitude, taken by myself as often as the weather would allow. The extraordinary talent of this young officer in this line of service proved of the greatest advantage to the Expedition, and he continued to perform that duty until his lamented death, with a degree of zeal and accuracy that characterised all his pursuits.

The next morning our camp was in motion at five A.M., and we soon afterwards embarked with the flattering accompaniment of a fair wind: it proved, however, too light to enable us to stem the stream, and we were obliged to resume the fatiguing operation of tracking; sometimes under cliffs so steep that the men could scarcely find a footing, and not infrequently over spots rendered so miry by the small streams that trickled from above, as to be almost impassable. In the course of the day we passed the scene of a very melancholy accident. Some years ago, two families of Indians, induced by the flatness of a small beach, which lay betwixt the cliff and the river, chose it as the site of their encampment. They retired quietly to rest, not aware that the precipice, detached from the bank, and urged by an accumulation of water in the crevice behind, was tottering to its base. It fell during the night, and the whole part was buried under its ruins.

The length of our voyage today was, in a direct line, sixteen miles and a quarter, on a S.S.W. course. We encamped soon after sunset, and the tent was scarcely pitched when a heavy rain began, which continued all night.

Sixteen miles on the 11th, and five on the following morning, brought us to the commencement of Hayes River, which is formed by the confluence of the Shamatawa and Steel Rivers. Our observations place this spot in latitude 56° 22' 32" N., longitude 93° 1' 37" W. It is forty-eight miles and a half from York Factory including the windings of the river. Steel River, through which our course lay, is about three hundred yards wide at its mouth; its banks have more elevation than those of Hayes River, but they shelve more gradually down to the stream, and afford a tolerably good towing path, which compensates, in some degree, for the rapids and frequent shoals that impede its navigation. We succeeded in getting about ten miles above the mouth of the river, before the close of day compelled us to disembark.

We made an effort, on the morning of the 13th, to stem the current under sail, but as the course of the river was very serpentine, we found that greater progress could be made by tracking. Steel River presents much beautiful scenery; it winds through a narrow, but well wooded valley, which at every turn disclosed to us an agreeable variety of prospect, rendered more picturesque by the effect of the season on the foliage, now ready to drop from the trees. The light yellow of the fading poplars formed a fine contrast to the dark evergreen of the spruce, whilst the willows of an intermediate hue, served to shade the two principal masses of colour into each other. The scene was occasionally enlivened by the bright purple tints of the dogwood, blended with the browner shades of the dwarf birch, and frequently intermixed with the gay yellow flowers of the shrubby cinquefoil. With all these charms, the scene appeared desolate from the want of human species. The stillness was so great, that even the twittering of the *whiskey-johneesh*, or cinereous crow, caused us to start. Our voyage today was sixteen miles on a S.W. course.

September 14

We had much rain during the night, and also in the morning, which detained us in our encampment later than usual. We set out as soon as the weather cleared up; and in a short time arrived at the head of Steel River, where it is formed by the junction of Fox and Hill Rivers. These two rivers are nearly of equal width, but the latter is the most rapid. Mr. M'Donald, on his way to Red River, in a small canoe, manned by two Indians, overtook us at this place. It may be mentioned as a proof of the dexterity of the Indians, and the skill with which they steal upon their game, that they had on the preceding day, with no other arms than a hatchet, killed two deer, a hawk, a curlew, and a sturgeon. Three of the Company's boats joined us in the course of the morning and we pursued our course up Hill River in company. The water in this river was so low, and the rapids so bad, that we were obliged several times, in the course of the day, to jump into the water, and assist in lifting the boat over the large stones which impeded the navigation. The length of our voyage today was only six miles and three-quarters.

The four boats commenced operations together at five o'clock the following morning; but our boat being overladen, we soon found that we were unable to keep pace with the others; and, therefore, proposed to the gentlemen in charge of the Company's boats, that they should relieve us of part of our cargo. This they declined doing, under the plea of not having received orders to that effect, notwithstanding that the circular, with which I was furnished by Governor Williams, strictly enjoined all the Company's servants to afford us every assistance. In consequence of this refusal we dropped behind, and our steersman, who was inexperienced, being thus deprived of the advantage of observing the route followed by the guide, who was in the foremost boat, frequently took a wrong channel. The tow-line broke twice, and the boat was only prevented from going broadside down the stream, and breaking to pieces against the stones, by the officers and men leaping into the water, and holding her head to the current until the line could be carried again to the shore. It is but justice to say, that in these trying situations, we received much assistance from Mr. Thomas Swaine, who with great kindness waited for us with the boat under his charge at such places as he apprehended would be most difficult to pass. We encamped at sunset, completely jaded with toil. Our distance made good this day was twelve miles and a quarter.

The labours of the 16th commenced at half-past five, and for some time the difficulty of getting the boats over the rapids was equal to what we experienced the day before. Having passed a small brook, however, termed *Half-way Creek*, the river became deeper, and although rapid, it was smooth enough to be named by our Orkney boatmen *Still-water*. We were further relieved by the Company's clerks consenting to take a few boxes of our stores into their boats. Still we made only eleven miles in the course of the day.

The banks of Hill River are higher, and have a more broken outline, than those of Steel or Hayes Rivers. The cliffs of alluvial clay rose in some places to the height of eighty or ninety feet above the stream, and were surmounted by hills about two hundred feet high, but the thickness of the wood prevented us from seeing far beyond the mere banks of the river.

September 17

About half-past five in the morning we commenced tracking, and soon came to a ridge of rock which extended across the stream. From this place the boat was dragged up several narrow rocky channels, until we came to the Rock Portage, where the stream, pent in by a range of small islands, forms several cascades. In ascending the river, the boats with their cargoes are carried over one of the islands, but in the descent they are shot down the most shelving of the cascades. Having performed the operations of carrying, launching, and restowing the cargo, we plied the oars for a short distance, and landed at a depôt called Rock House. Here we were informed that the rapids in the upper parts of Hill River were much worse and more numerous than those we had passed, particularly in the present season, owing to the unusual lowness of the water. This intelligence was very mortifying, especially as the gentlemen in charge of the Company's boats declared that they were unable to carry any part of our stores beyond this place; and the traders, guides, and most experienced of the boatmen, were of opinion, that unless our boat was still further lightened, the winter would put a stop to our progress before we could reach Cumberland House, or any eligible post. Sixteen pieces were therefore necessarily left with Mr. Bunn, the gentlemen in charge of the post, to be forwarded by the Athabasca canoes next season, this being their place of rendezvous.

After this we recommenced our voyage, and having pulled nearly a mile, arrived at Borrowick's Fall, where the boat was dragged up with a line, after part of the cargo had been carried over a small portage. From this place to the Mud Portage, a distance of a mile and three-quarters, the boats were pushed on with poles against a very rapid stream. Here we encamped, having come seven miles during the day on a S.W. course. We had several snow showers in the course of the day, and the thermometer at bed-time stood at 30°.

On the morning of the 18th, the country was clothed in the livery of winter, a heavy fall of snow having taken place during the night. We embarked at the usual hour, and in the course of the day, crossed the Point of Rocks and Brassa Portages, and dragged the boats through several minor rapids. In this tedious way we only made good about nine miles.

On Sunday the 19th we hauled the boats up several short rapids, or, as the boatmen term them, expressively enough, *spouts*, and carried them over the Portages of Lower Burntwood and Morgan's Rocks; on the latter of which we encamped, having proceeded, during the whole day, only one mile and three-quarters.

The upper part of Hill River swells out considerably, and at Morgan's Rocks, where it is three-quarters of a mile wide, we were gratified with a more extensive prospect of the country than any we had enjoyed since leaving York Factory. The banks of the river here, consisting of low flat rocks with intermediate swamps, permitted us to obtain views of the interior, the surface of which is broken into a multitude of cone-shaped hills. The highest of these hills, which gives a name to the river, has an elevation not exceeding six hundred feet. From its summit, thirty-six lakes are said to be visible. The beauty of the scenery, dressed in the tints of autumn, called forth our admiration, and was the subject of Mr. Hood's accurate pencil. On the 20th we passed Upper Burntwood and Rocky Ledge Portages, besides several strong *spouts*; and in the evening arrived at Smooth Rock Portage, where we encamped, having come three miles and a half. It is not easy for any but an eye-witness to form an adequate idea of the exertions of the Orkney boatmen in the navigation of this river. The necessity they are under of frequently jumping into the water to lift the boats over the rocks, compels them to remain the whole day in wet clothes, at a season when the temperature is far below the freezing-point. The immense loads, too, which they carry over the portages, is not more a matter of surprise than the alacrity with which they perform these laborious duties.

At six on the morning of the 21st, we left our encampment, and soon after arrived at the Mossy Portage, where the cargoes were carried through a deep bog for a quarter of a mile. The river swells out, above this portage, to the breadth of several miles, and as the islands are numerous there are a great variety of channels. Night overtook us before we arrived at the *Second Portage*, so named from its being the second in the passage down the river. Our whole distance this day was one mile and a quarter.

On the 22nd our route led us amongst many wooded islands, which, lying in long vistas, produced scenes of much beauty. In the course of the day we crossed the Upper Portage, surmounted the Devil's Landing Place, and urged the boat with poles through Groundwater Creek. At the upper end of this creek, our bowman having given the boat too great a sheer, to avoid the rock, it was caught on the broadside by the current, and, in defiance of our utmost exertions, hurried down the rapid. Fortunately, however, it grounded against a rock high enough to prevent the current from oversetting it, and the crews of the other boats having come to our assistance, we succeeded, after several trials, in throwing a rope to them, with which they dragged our almost sinking vessel stern foremost up the stream, and rescued us from our perilous situation. We encamped in the dusk of the evening amidst a heavy thunder-storm, having advanced two miles and three-quarters.

About ten in the morning of the 23rd we arrived at the *Dramstone*, which is hailed with pleasure by the boats' crews, as marking the termination of the laborious ascent of Hill River. We complied with the custom from whence it derives its name, and soon after landing upon Sail Island prepared breakfast. In the meantime our boatmen cut down and rigged a new mast, the old one having been thrown overboard at the mouth of Steel River, where it ceased to be useful. We left Sail Island with a fair wind, and soon afterwards arrived at a depôt situated on Swampy Lake, where we received a supply of mouldy *pemmican*.[1] Mr. Calder and his attendant were the only tenants of this cheerless abode, and their only food was the wretched stuff with which they supplied us, the lake not yielding fish at this season. After a short delay at this post, we sailed through the remainder of Swampy Lake, and slept at the Lower Portage in Jack River; the distance sailed today being sixteen miles and a half.

Jack River is only eight miles long; but being full of bad rapids, it detained us considerably. At seven in the morning of the 24th, we crossed the Long Portage, where the woods, having caught fire in the summer, were still smoking. This is a common accident, owing to the neglect of the Indians and voyagers in not putting out their fires, and in a dry season the woods may be seen blazing to the extent of many miles. We afterwards crossed the Second, or Swampy Portage, and in the evening encamped on the Upper Portage, where we were overtaken by an Indian bringing an answer from Governor Williams to a letter I had written to him on the 15th, in which he renewed his injunctions to the gentlemen of the boats accompanying us, to afford us every assistance in their power. The Aurora Borealis appeared this evening in form of a bright arch, extending across the zenith in a N.W. and S.E. direction. The extent of our voyage today was two miles.

About noon, on the 25th, we entered Knee Lake, which has a very irregular form, and near its middle takes a sudden turn, from whence it derives its names. It is thickly studded with islands, and its shores are low and well wooded. The surrounding country, as far as we could see, is flat, being destitute even of the moderate elevations which occur near the upper part of Hill River. The weather

1 Buffalo meat, dried and pounded, and mixed with melted fat.

was remarkably fine, and the setting sun threw the richest tints over the scene that I remember ever to have witnessed.

About half a mile from the bend or *knee* of the lake, there is a small rocky islet, composed of magnetic iron ore, which affects the magnetic needle at a considerable distance. Having received previous information respecting this circumstance, we watched our compasses carefully, and perceived that they were affected at the distance of three hundred yards, both on the approach to and departure from the rock: on decreasing the distance, they became gradually more and more unsteady, and on landing they were rendered quite useless; and it was evident that the general magnetic influence was totally overpowered by the local attraction of the ore. When Kater's compass was held near to the ground on the N.W. side of the island, the needle dipped so much that the card could not be made to traverse by any adjustment of the hand; but on moving the same compass about thirty yards to the west part of the islet, the needle became horizontal, traversed freely, and pointed to the magnetic north. The dipping needle being landed on the S.W. point of the islet, was adjusted as nearly as possible on the magnetic meridian by the sun's bearings, and found to vibrate freely, when the face of the instrument was directed to the east or west. The mean dip it gave was 80° 37′ 50″. When the instrument was removed from the N.W. to the S.E. point, about twenty yards distant, and placed on the meridian, the needle ceased to traverse, but remained steady at an angle of 60°. On changing the face of the instrument, so as to give a S.E. and N.W. direction to the needle, it hung vertically. The position of the slaty strata of the magnetic ore is also vertical. Their direction is extremely irregular, being much contorted.

Knee Lake towards its upper end becomes narrower, and its rocky shores are broken into colonial and rounded eminences, destitute of soil, and of course devoid of trees. We slept at the western extremity of the lake, having come during the day nineteen miles and a half on a S.W. course.

We began the ascent of Trout River early in the morning of the 27th, and in the course of the day passed three portages and several rapids. At the first of these portages the river falls between two rocks about sixteen feet, and it is necessary to launch the boat over a precipitous rocky bank. This cascade is named the *Trout-Fall*, and the beauty of the scenery afforded a subject for Mr. Hood's pencil. The rocks which form the bed of this river are slaty, and present sharp fragments, by which the feet of the boatmen are much lacerated, obtains the expressive name of *Knife Portage*. The length of our voyage today was three miles.

On the 28th we passed through the remainder of Trout River; and, at noon, arrived at Oxford House on Holey Lake. This was formerly a post of some consequence to the Hudson's Bay Company, but at present it exhibits unequivocal signs of decay. The Indians have of late years been gradually deserting the low or swampy country and ascending the Saskatchawan, where animals are more abundant. A few Crees were at this time encamped in front of the fort. They were suffering under whooping-cough and measles, and looked miserably dejected. We endeavoured in vain to prevail on one of them to accompany us for the purpose of killing ducks, which were numerous but too shy for our sportsmen. We had the satisfaction, however, of exchanging the mouldy pemmican obtained at Swampy Lake for a better kind, and received, moreover, a small but very acceptable supply of fish. Holey Lake, viewed from an eminence behind Oxford House, exhibits a pleasing prospect; and its numerous islands, varying much in shape and elevation, contribute to break that uniformity of scenery which proves so palling to a traveller in this country. Trout of a great size, frequently exceeding forty pounds' weight, abound in this lake. We left Oxford House in the afternoon and encamped on an island about eight miles distant, having come during the day nine miles and a quarter.

At noon, on the 29th, after passing through the remainder of Holey Lake, we entered the Weepinapannis, a narrow grassy river, which runs parallel to the lake for a considerable distance, and forms its south bank into a narrow peninsula. In the morning we arrived at the Swampy Portage, where two of the boats were broken against the rocks. The length of the day's voyage was nineteen miles and a half.

In consequence of the accident yesterday evening we were detained a considerable time this morning until the boats were repaired, when we set out, and after ascending a strong rapid, arrived at the portage by John Moore's Island. Here the river rushes with irresistible force through the channels formed by two rocky islands; and we learned that last year a poor man, in hauling a boat up one of these channels, was, by the breaking of the line, precipitated into the stream and hurried down the cascade with such rapidity that all efforts to save him were ineffectual. His body was afterwards found and interred near the spot.

The Weepinapannis is composed of several branches which separate and unite again and again, intersecting the country in a great variety of directions. We pursued the principal channel, and having passed the Crooked Spout, with several inferior rapids, and crossed a small piece of water named Windy Lake, we entered a smooth deep stream about three hundred yards wide, which has got the absurd appellation of the Rabbit Ground. The marshy banks of this river are skirted by low barren rocks, behind which there are some groups of stunted trees. As we advanced, the country, becoming flatter, gradually opened to our view, and we at length arrived at a shallow, reedy lake, the direct course through which leads to the Hill Portage. This route has, however, of late years been disused, and we therefore turned towards the north, and crossing a small arm of the lake arrived at Hill Gates by sunset; having come this day eleven miles.

October 1

Hill Gates is the name imposed on a romantic defile, whose rocky walls, rising perpendicularly to the height of sixty or eighty feet, hem in the stream for three-quarters of a mile, in many places so narrowly that there is a want of room to ply the oars. In passing through this chasm we were naturally led to contemplate the mighty but, probably, slow and gradual effects of the water in wearing down such vast masses of rock; but in the midst of our speculations the attention was excited anew to a grand and picturesque rapid which, surrounded by the most wild and majestic scenery, terminated the defile. The brown fishing-eagle had built its nest on one of the projecting cliffs. In the course of the day we surmounted this and another dangerous portage called the Upper and Lower Hill Gate Portages, crossed a small sheet of water, termed the White Fall Lake, and entering the river of the same name, arrived at the White Fall about an hour after sunset, having come fourteen miles on a S.W. course.

The whole of the 2nd of October was spent in carrying the cargoes over a portage of thirteen hundred yards in length, and in launching the empty boats over three several ridges of rock which obstruct the channel and produce as many cascades. I shall long remember the rude and characteristic wildness of the scenery which surrounded these falls; rocks piled on rocks hung in rude and shapeless masses over the agitated torrents which swept their bases, whilst the bright and variegated tints of the mosses and lichens that covered the face of the cliffs, contrasting with the dark green of the pines which crowned their summits, added both beauty and grandeur to the scene. Our two companions, Back and Hood, made accurate sketches of these falls. At this place we observed a conspicuous *lopstick*, a kind of land-mark, which I have not hitherto noticed, notwithstanding its great use in pointing out the frequented routes. It is a pine-tree divested of its lower branches and having only a small tuft at the top remaining. This operation is usually performed at the instance of some individual emulous of fame. He treats his companions with rum, and they in return strip the tree of its branches and ever after designate it by his name.

In the afternoon, whilst on my way to superintend the operations of the men, a stratum of loose moss gave way under my feet, and I had the misfortune to slip from the summit of a rock into the river betwixt two of the falls. My attempts to regain the bank were, for a time, ineffectual, owing to the rocks within my reach having been worn smooth by the action of the water; but after I had been carried a considerable distance down the stream, I caught hold of a willow by which I held until two gentleman of the Hudson's Bay Company came in a boat to my assistance. The only bad consequence of this accident was an injury sustained by a very valuable chronometer (No. 1733), belonging to Daniel Moore, Esq., of Lincoln's Inn. One of the gentlemen to whom I delivered it immediately on landing, in his agitation let it fall, whereby the minute-hand was broken, but the works were not in the smallest degree injured, and the loss of the hand was afterwards supplied.

During the night the frost was severe; and at sunrise on the 3rd the thermometer stood at 25°. After leaving our encampment at the White Fall we passed through several lakes connected with each other by narrow, deep, grassy streams, and at noon arrived at the Painted Stone. Numbers of musk-rats frequent these streams; and we observed, in the course of the morning, many of their mud-houses rising in a conical form to the height of two or three feet above the grass of the swamps in which they were built.

The Painted Stone is a low rock, ten or twelve yards across, remarkable for the marshy streams which arise on each side of it, taking different courses. On the one side the water-course which we had navigated from York Factory commences. This spot may therefore be considered as one of the smaller sources of Hayes River. On the other side of the stone the Echemamis rises, and taking a westerly direction falls into Nelson River. It is said that there was formerly a stone placed near the centre of this portage on which figures were annually traced and offerings deposited by the Indians; but the stone has been removed many years, and the spot has ceased to be held in veneration. Here we were overtaken by Governor Williams, who left York Factory on the 20th of last month in an Indian canoe. He expressed much regret at our having been obliged to leave part of our stores at the Rock depôt, and would have brought them up with him had he been able to procure and man a boat, or a canoe of sufficient size.

Having launched the boats over the rock, we commenced the descent of the Echemamis. This small stream has its course through a morass, and in dry seasons its channel contains, instead of water, merely a foot or two of thin mud. On these occasions it is customary to build dams that it may be rendered navigable by the accumulation of its waters. As the beavers perform this operation very effectually, endeavours have been made to encourage them to breed in this place, but it has not hitherto been possible to restrain the Indians from killing that useful animal whenever they discover its retreats. On the present occasion there was no want of water, the principal impediment we experienced being from the narrowness of the channel, which permitted the willows of each bank to meet over our heads and obstruct the men at the oars. After proceeding down the stream for some time, we came to a recently-constructed beaver-dam through which an opening was made sufficient to admit the boat to pass. We were assured that the breach would be closed by the industrious creature in a single night. We encamped about eight miles from the source of the river, having come during the day seventeen miles and a half.

On the 4th we embarked amidst a heavy rain and pursued our route down the Echemamis. In many parts of the morass, by which the river is nourished and through which it flows, is intersected by ridges of rock which cross the channel, and require the boat to be lifted over them. In the afternoon we passed through a shallow piece of water overgrown with bulrushes, and hence named Hairy Lake; and in the evening encamped on the banks of Blackwater Creek, by which this lake empties itself into Sea River; having come during the day twenty miles and three-quarters.

On the morning of the 5th we entered Sea River, one of the many branches of Nelson River. It is about four hundred yards wide, and its waters are of a muddy white colour. After ascending the stream for an hour or two, and passing through Carpenter's Lake, which is merely an expansion of the river to about a mile in breadth, we came to the Sea River Portage, where the boat was launched across a smooth rock to avoid a fall of four or five feet. Re-embarking at the upper end of the portage, we ran before a fresh gale through the remainder of Sea River, the lower part of Play Green Lake, and entering Little Jack River, landed and pitched our tents. Here there is a small log-hut, the residence of a fisherman, who supplies Norway House with trout and sturgeon. He gave us a few of these fish, which afforded an acceptable supper. Our voyage this day was thirty-four miles.

October 6

Little Jack River is the name given to a channel that winds among several large islands which separate Upper and Lower Play Green Lakes. At the lower end of this channel Big Jack River, a stream of considerable magnitude, falls into the lake. Play Green is a translation of the appellation given to that lake by two bands of Indians, who met and held a festival on an island situated near its centre. After leaving our encampment we sailed through Upper Play Green Lake and arrived at Norway Point in the forenoon.

The waters of Lake Winipeg and of the rivers that run into it, the Saskatchawan in particular, are rendered turbid by the suspension of a large quantity of white clay. Play Green Lake and Nelson River, being the discharges of the Winipeg, are equally opaque, a circumstance that renders the sunken rocks, so frequent in these waters, very dangerous to boats in a fresh breeze. Owing to this one of the boats that accompanied us, sailing at the rate of seven miles an hour, struck upon one of these rocks. Its mast was carried away by the shock, but fortunately no other damage sustained. The Indians ascribe the muddiness of these lakes to an adventure of one of their deities, a mischievous fellow, a sort of Robin Puck, whom they hold in very little esteem. This deity, who is named Weesakootchaht, possesses considerable power, but makes a capricious use of it, and delights in tormenting the poor Indians. He is not, however, invincible, and was soiled in one of his attempts by the artifice of an old woman, who succeeded in taking him captive. She called in all the women of the tribe to aid in his punishment, and he escaped from their hands in a condition so filthy that it required all the waters of the Great Lake to wash him clean; and ever since that period it has been entitled to the appellation of Winnipeg, or Muddy water.

Norway Point forms the extremity of a narrow peninsula which separates Play

Green and Winipeg Lakes. Buildings were first erected here by a party of Norwegians, who were driven away from the colony at Red River by the commotions which took place some time ago. It is now a trading post belonging to the Hudson's Bay Company. On landing at Norway House we met with Lord Selkirk's colonists, who had started from York Factory the day before us. – These poor people were exceedingly pleased at meeting with us again in this wild country; having accompanied them across the Atlantic they viewed us in the light of old acquaintances. This post was under the charge of Mr. James Sutherlands, to whom I am indebted for replacing a minute-hand on the chronometer, which was broken at the White Fall, and I had afterwards the satisfaction of finding that it went with extraordinary regularity.

The morning of the 7th October was beautifully clear, and the observations we obtained place Norway House in latitude 53° 41′ 38″ N., and longitude 98° 1′ 24″ W.; the variation of the magnetic needle 14° 12′ 41″ E., and its dip 83° 40′ 10″. Though our route from York Factory has rather inclined to the S.W., the dip, it will be perceived, has gradually increased. The difference produced by reversing the face of the instrument was 7° 39′. There was too much wind to admit of our observing, with any degree of accuracy, the quantity of the magnetic force.

We left Norway House soon after noon, and the wind being favourable, sailed along the northern shore of Lake Winipeg the whole of the ensuing night; and on the morning of the 8th landed on a narrow ridge of sand, which, running out twenty miles to the westwards, separates Limestone Bay from the body of the Lake. When the wind blows hard from the southward it is customary to carry boats across this isthmus and to pull up under its lee. From Norwegian Point to Limestone Bay the shore consists of high clay cliffs, against which the waves beat with violence during strong southerly winds. When the wind blows from the land and the waters of the lake are low, a narrow sandy beach is uncovered and affords a landing-place for boats. The shores of Limestone Bay are covered with small fragments of calcareous stones. During the night the Aurora Borealis was quick in its motions, and various and vivid in its colours. After breakfasting we re-embarked, and continued our voyage until three P.M., when a strong westerly wind arising, we were obliged to shelter ourselves on a small island, which lies near the extremity of the above-mentioned peninsula. This island is formed of a collection of small rolled pieces of limestone, and was remembered by some of our boatmen to have been formerly covered with water. For the last ten or twelve years the waters of the lake have been low, but our information did not enable us to judge whether the decrease was merely casual, or going on continually, or periodical. The distance of this island from Norway House is thirty-eight miles and a half.

The westerly winds detained us all the morning of the 9th, but at two P.M. the wind chopped round to the eastward; we immediately embarked, and the breeze afterwards freshening, we reached the mouth of the Saskatchawan at midnight, having run thirty-two miles.

Sunday, October 10

The whole of this day was occupied in getting the boats from the mouth of the river to the foot of the grand rapid, a distance of two miles. There are several rapids in this short distance, during which the river varies its breadth from five hundred yards to half a mile. Its channel is stony. At the grand rapid the Saskatchawan forms a sudden bend from south to east, and works its way through a narrow channel deeply worn into the limestone strata. The stream, rushing with impetuous force over a rock and uneven bottom, presents a sheet of foam, and seems to bear with impatience the straitened confinement of its lofty banks. A flock of pelicans and two or three brown fishing eagles were fishing in its agitated waters, seemingly with great success. There is a good sturgeon fishery at the foot of the rapid. Several golden plovers, Canadian grosbeaks, crossbills, woodpeckers and pintailed grouse were shot today; and Mr. Back killed a small striped marmot. This beautiful little animal was busily employed in carrying in its distended pouches the seeds of the American vetch to its winter hoards.

The portage is eighteen hundred yards long, and its western extremity was found to be in 53° 08′ 25″ North latitude, and 99° 28′ 02″ West longitude. The route from Canada to the Athabasca joins that from York Factory at the mouth of the Saskatchawan, and we saw traces of a recent encampment of the Canadian voyagers. Our companions in the Hudson's Bay boats, dreading an attack from their rivals in trade, were on the alert at this place. They examined minutely the spot of encampment to form a judgment of the number of canoes that had preceded them; and they advanced, armed, and with great caution, through the woods. Their fears, however, on this occasion were fortunately groundless.

By noon on the 12th, the boats and their cargoes having been conveyed across the portage, we embarked and pursued our course. The Saskatchawan becomes wider above the Grand Rapid, and the scenery improves. The banks are high, composed of white clay and limestone, and their summits are richly clothed with a variety of firs, poplars, birches and willows. The current runs with great rapidity, and the channel is in many places intricate and dangerous from broken ridge of rock jutting into the stream. We pitched our tents at the entrance of Cross Lake, having advanced only fives miles and a half.

Cross Lake is extensive, running towards the N.E., it is said, for forty miles. We crossed it at a narrow part, and pulling through several winding channels, formed by a group of islands, entered Cedar Lake, which, next to Lake Winipeg, is the largest sheet of fresh water we had hitherto seen. Ducks and geese resort hither in immense flocks in the spring and autumn. These birds are now beginning to go off, owing to its muddy shores having become quite hard through the nightly frosts. At this place the Aurora Borealis was extremely brilliant in the night, its coruscations darting at times over the whole sky, and assuming various prismatic tints, of which the violet and yellow were predominant.

After pulling, on the 14th, seven miles and a quarter on the lake, a violent wind drove us for shelter to a small island, or rather a ridge of rolled stones, thrown up by the frequent storms which agitate this lake. The weather did not moderate the whole day, and we were obliged to pass the night on this exposed spot. The delay, however, enabled us to obtain some lunar observations. The wind having subsided, we left our resting-place the following morning, crossed the remainder of the lake, and in the afternoon arrived at Muddy Lake, which is very appropriately named, as it consists merely of a few channels winding amongst extensive mud banks, which are overflowed during the spring floods. We landed at an Indian tent, which contained two numerous families amounting to thirty souls. These poor creatures were badly clothed, and reduced to a miserable condition by the whooping-cough and measles. At the time of our arrival they were busy in preparing a sweating-house for the sick. This is a remedy which they consider, with the addition of singing and drumming, to be the grand specific for all diseases. Our companions having obtained some geese in exchange for rum and tobacco, we proceeded a few more miles and encamped on Devil's Drum Island, having come during the day twenty miles and a half. A second party of Indians were encamped on an adjoining island, a situation chosen for the purpose of killing geese and ducks.

On the 16th we proceeded eighteen miles up the Saskatchawan. Its banks are low, covered with willows, and lined with drift timber. The surrounding country is swampy and intersected by the numerous arms of the river. After passing for twenty or thirty yards through the willow thicket on the banks of the stream we entered an extensive marsh, varied only by a distant line of willows, which marks the course of a creek or branch of the river. The branch we navigated today is almost five hundred yards wide. The exhalations from the marshy soil produced a low fog, although the sky above was perfectly clear. In the course of the day we passed an Indian encampment of three tents, whose inmates appeared to be in a still more miserable condition than those we saw yesterday. They had just finished the ceremony of conjuration over some of their sick companions; and a dog, which had been recently killed as a sacrifice to some deity, was hanging to a tree where it would be left (I was told) when they moved their encampment.

We continued our voyage up the river to the 20th with little variation of scenery or incident, travelling in that time about thirty miles. The near approach of winter was marked by severe frosts, which continued all day unless when the sun chanced to be unusually bright, and the geese and ducks were observed to take a southerly course in large flocks. On the morning of the 20th we came to a party of Indians encamped behind the bank of the river on the borders of a small marshy lake for the purpose of killing water-fowl. Here we were gratified with the view of a very large tent. Its length was about forty feet, its breadth eighteen, and its covering was moose deer leather, with apertures for the escape of the smoke from the fires which are placed at each end; a ledge of wood was placed on the ground on both sides the whole length of the tent, within which were the sleeping-places, arranged probably according to families; and the drums and other instruments of enchantment were piled up in the centre. Amongst the Indians there were a great many half-breeds, who led an Indian life. Governor Williams gave a dram and a piece of tobacco to each of the males of the party.

On the morning of the 21st a heavy fall of snow took place, which lasted until two in the afternoon. In the evening we left the Saskatchawan and entered the Little River, one of the two streams by which Pine Island Lake discharges its waters. We advanced today fourteen miles and a quarter. On the 22nd the weather was extremely cold and stormy, and we had to contend against a strong head wind. The spray froze as it fell, and the oars were so loaded with ice as to be almost unmanageable. The length of our voyage this day was eleven miles.

The following morning was very cold; we embarked at daylight and pulled across a part of Pine Island Lake, about three miles and a half to Cumberland House. The margin of the lake was so incrusted with ice that we had to break through a considerable space of it to approach the landing-place. When we considered that this was the effect of only a few days' frost at the commencement of winter, we were convinced of the impracticality of advancing further by water this season, and therefore resolved on accepting Governor Williams's kind invitation to remain with him at this post. We immediately visited Mr. Connolly, the resident partner of the North-West Company, and presented to him Mr. M'Gillivray's circular letter. He assured us that he should be most desirous to forward our progress by every means in his power, and we subsequently had ample proofs of his sincerity and kindness. The unexpected addition of our party to the winter residents at this post rendered an increase of apartments necessary; and our men were immediately appointed to complete and arrange an unfinished building as speedily as possible.

November 8

Some mild weather succeeded to the severe frosts we had at our arrival; and the lake had not been entirely frozen before the 6th; but this morning the ice was sufficiently firm to admit of sledges crossing it. The dogs were harnessed at a very early hour, and the winter operations commenced by sending for a supply of fish from Swampy River, where men had been stationed to collect it just before the frost set in. Both men and dogs appeared to enjoy the change; they started in full glee and drove rapidly along. An Indian, who had come to the house on the preceding evening to request some provision for his family, whom he represented to be in a state of starvation, accompanied them. His party had been suffering greatly under the epidemic diseases of whooping-cough and measles; and the hunters were still in too debilitated a state to go out and provide them with meat. A supply was given to him, and the men were directed to bring his father, an old and faithful hunter, to the house, that he might have the comforts of nourishment and warmth. He was brought accordingly, but these attentions were unavailing as he died a few days afterwards. Two days before his death I was surprised to observe him sitting for nearly three hours, in a piercingly sharp day, in the saw-pit, employed in gathering the dust and throwing it by handfuls over his body, which was naked to the waist. As the man was in possession of his mental faculties, I conceived he was performing some devotional act preparatory to his departure, which he felt to be approaching, and induced by the novelty of the incident, I went twice to observe him more closely; but when he perceived that he was noticed, he immediately ceased his operation, hung down his head, and by his demeanour intimated that he considered my appearance an intrusion. The residents at the fort could give me no information on the subject, and I could not learn that the Indians in general observe any particular ceremony on the approach of death.

November 15

The sky had been overcast during the last week; the sun shone forth once only, and then not sufficiently for the purpose of obtaining observations. Faint coruscations of the Aurora Borealis appeared on evening, but their presence did not in the least affect the electrometer or the compass. The ice daily became thicker in the lake, and the frost had now nearly overpowered the rapid current of the Saskatchawan River; indeed, parties of men who were sent from both the forts to search for the Indians and procure whatever skins and provisions they might have collected, crossed that stream this day on the ice. The white partridges made their first appearance near the house, which birds are considered as the infallible harbingers of severe weather.

Monday, November 22

The Saskatchawan and every other river were now completely covered with ice, except a small stream not far from the fort through which the current ran very powerfully. In the course of the week we removed into the house our men had prepared since our arrival. We found it at first extremely cold notwithstanding that a good fire was kept in each apartment, and we frequently experienced the extremes of heat and cold on opposite sides of the body.

November 24

We obtained observations for the dip of the needle and intensity of the magnetic force in a spare room. The dip was 83° 9′ 45″, and the difference produced by reserving the face of the instrument 13° 3′ 6″. When the needle was faced to the west it hung nearly perpendicular. The Aurora Borealis had been faintly visible for a short time the preceding evening. Some Indians arrived in search of provision, having been totally incapacitated from hunting by sickness; the poor creatures looked miserably ill, and they represented their distress to have been extreme. Few recitals are more affecting than those of their sufferings during unfavourable seasons and in bad situations for hunting and fishing. Many assurances have been given me that men and women are not yet living who have been reduced to feed upon the bodies of their own family to prevent actual starvation; and a shocking case was cited to us of a woman who had been principal agent in the destruction of several persons, and amongst the number her husband and nearest relatives, in order to support life.

November 28

The atmosphere had been clear every day during the last week, about the end of which snow fell, when the thermometer rose from 20° below to 16° above zero. The Aurora Borealis was twice visible, but faint on both occasions. Its appearance did not affect the electrometer, nor could we perceive the compass to be disturbed.

The men brought supplies of moose meat from the hunter's tent, which is pitched near the Basquiai Hill, forty or fifty miles from the house, and whence the greatest part of the meat is procured. The residents have to send nearly the same distance for their fish, and on this service horse-sledges are used. Nets are daily set in Pine Island Lake which occasionally procure some fine sturgeon, tittameg and trout, but not more than sufficient to supply the officers' table.

December 1

The day was so remarkably fine that we procured another set of observations for the dip of the needle in the open air; the instrument being placed firmly on as rock, the results gave 83° 14′ 22″. The change produced by reversing the face of the instrument was 12° 50′ 55″.

There had been a determined thaw during the last three days. The ice on the Saskatchawan River and some parts of the lake broke up, and the travelling across either became dangerous. On this account the absence of Wilks, one of our men, caused no small anxiety. He had incautiously undertaken the conduct of a sledge and dogs, in company with a person, going to Swampy River for fish. On their return, being unaccustomed to driving, he became fatigued, and seated himself on his sledge, where his companion left him, presuming that he would soon rise and hasten to follow his track. He however returned safe in the morning, and reported that, foreseeing night would set in before he could get across the lake, he prudently retired into the woods before dark, where he remained until daylight; when the men who had been despatched to look for him met him returning to the house, shivering with cold, he having been unprovided with the materials for lighting a fire; which an experienced voyager never neglects to carry.

We had mild weather until the 20th of December. On the 13th there had been a decided thaw that caused the Saskatchawan, which had again frozen, to re-open, and the passage across it was interrupted for two days. We now received more agreeable accounts from the Indians, who were recovering strength and beginning to hunt a little; but it was generally feared that their spirits had been so much depressed by the loss of their children and relatives that the season would be far advanced before they could be roused to any exertion in searching for animals beyond what might be necessary for their own support. It is much to be regretted that these poor men, during their long intercourse with Europeans, have not been taught how pernicious is the grief which produces total inactivity, and that they have not been furnished with any of the consolations which the Christian religion never fails to afford. This, however, could hardly have been expected from persons who have permitted their own offspring, the half-casts, to remain in lamentable ignorance on a subject of such vital importance. It is probable, however, that an improvement will soon take place among the latter class, as Governor Williams proposes to make the children attend a Sunday school, and has already begun to have divine service performed at his post.

The conversations which I had with the gentlemen in charge of these posts convinced me of the necessity of proceeding during the winter into the Athabasca department, the residents of which are best acquainted with the nature and resources of the country to the north of the Great Slave Lake; and whence only guides, hunters and interpreters can be procured. I had previously written to the partners of the North-West Company in that quarter, requesting their assistance in forwarding the Expedition, and stating that we should require. But, on reflecting upon the accidents that might delay these letters on the road, I determined on proceeding to the Athabasca as soon as I possibly could, and communicated my intention to Governor Williams and Mr. Connolly, with a request that I might be furnished, by the middle of January, with the means of conveyance for three persons, intending that Mr. Back and Hepburn should accompany me, whilst Dr. Richardson and Mr. Hood remained till the spring at Cumberland House.

After the 20th of December the weather became cold, the thermometer constantly below zero. Christmas Day was particularly stormy; but the gale did not prevent the full enjoyment of the festivities which are annually given at Cumberland House on this day. All the men who had been despatched to different parts in search of provision or furs returned to the fort on the occasion and were regaled with a substantial dinner and a dance in the evening.

January 1, 1820

The new year was ushered in by repeated discharges of musketry; a ceremony which has been observed by the men of both the trading Companies for many years. Our party dines with Mr. Connolly, and were treated with a beaver, which we found extremely delicate. In the evening his voyagers were entertained with a dance, in which the Canadians exhibited some grace and much agility; and they contrived to infuse some portion of their activity and spirits into the steps of their female companions. The half-breed women are passionately fond of this amusement, but a stranger would imagine the contrary on witnessing their apparent want of animation. On such occasions they affect a sobriety of demeanour which I understand to be very opposite to their general character.

January 10

This day I wrote to Governor Williams and Mr. Connolly, requesting them to prepare two canoes, with crews and appointments, for the conveyance of Dr.

Richardson and Mr. Hood, with our stores, to Chipewyan as soon as the navigation should open, and had the satisfaction of receiving from both these gentlemen renewed assurances of their desire to promote the objects of the Expedition. I conceived it to be necessary, previous to my departure, to make some arrangement respecting the men who were engaged at Stromness. Only one of them was disposed to extend his engagement and proceed beyond the Athabasca Lake; and, as there was much uncertainty whether the remaining three could get from the Athabasca to York Factory sufficiently early to secure them a passage in the next Hudson's Bay ship, I resolved not to take them forward, unless Dr. Richardson and Mr. Hood should fail in procuring other men from these establishments next spring, but to despatch them down to York to bring up our stores to this place: after which they might return to the coast in time to secure their passage in the first ship.

I delivered to Dr. Richardson and Mr. Hood a memorandum containing the arrangements which had been made with the two Companies, respecting their being forwarded in the spring, and some other points of instruction for their guidance in my absence; together with directions to forward the map of our route which had been finished, since our arrival, by Mr. Hood, the drawing and the collections of natural history by the first opportunity to York Factory for conveyance to England.[1]

The houses of the two Companies at this post are situated close to each other at the upper extremity of a narrow island, which separates Pine Island Lake from the Saskatchawan River, and are about two miles and three-quarters from the latter in a northern direction. They are log-houses, built without much regard to comfort, surrounded by lofty stockades and flanked with wooden bastions. The difficulty of conveying glass into the interior has precluded its use in the windows, where its place is poorly supplied by parchment, imperfectly made by the native women from the skin of the reindeer. Should this post, however, continue to be the residence of Governor Williams, it will be much improved in a few years, as he is devoting his attention to that point. The land around Cumberland House is low, but the soil, from having a considerable intermixture of limestone, is good, and capable of producing abundance of corn and vegetables of every description. Many kinds of pot-herbs have already been brought to some perfection, and the potatoes bid fair to equal those of England. The spontaneous productions of nature would afford ample nourishment for all the European animals. Horses feed extremely well even during the winter, and so would oxen if provided with hay, which might be easily done.[2] Pigs also improve, but require to be kept warm in the winter. Hence it appears that the residents might easily render themselves far less dependant on the Indians for support, and be relieved from the great anxiety which they too often suffer when the hunters are unsuccessful. The neighbourhood of the houses has been much cleared of wood from the great demand for fuel; there is, therefore, little to admire in the surrounding scenery, especially in its winter garb; few animated objects occur to enliven the scene; an occasional fox, marten, rabbit or wolf and a few birds contribute the only variety. The birds which remained were ravens, magpies, partridges, crossbills and woodpeckers. In this universal stillness the residents at a post feel little disposed to wander abroad except when called forth by their occupations; and as ours were of a kind best performed in a warm room we imperceptibly acquired a sedentary habit. In going out, however, we never suffered the slightest inconvenience from the change of temperature, though the thermometer in the open air stood occasionally thirty degrees below zero.

The tribe of Indians who reside in the vicinity and frequent these establishments is that of the Crees, or Knisteneaux. They were formerly a powerful and

---

1 As Samuel Wilks, who had accompanied the Expedition from England, proved to be quite unequal to the fatigue of the journey, I directed him to be discharged in the spring, and sent to England by the next ship.

2 'The wild buffalo scrapes away the snow with its feet to get at the herbage beneath, and the horse, which was introduced by the Spanish invaders of Mexico, and may be said to have become naturalised, does the same; but it is worthy of remark, that the ox more lately brought from Europe, has not yet acquired an art so necessary for procuring its food.' – (Extract from Dr. Richardson's Journal.)

numerous nation which ranged over a very extensive country, and were very successful in their predatory excursions against their neighbours, particularly the northern Indians and some tribes on the Saskatchawan and Beaver Rivers; but they have long ceased to be held in any fear, and are now, perhaps, the most harmless and inoffensive of the whole Indian race. This change is entirely attributed to their intercourse with Europeans; and the vast reduction in their numbers occasioned, I fear, principally by the injudicious introduction of ardent spirits. They are so passionately fond of this poison that they will make any sacrifice to obtain it. They are good hunters and in general active. Having laid the bow and arrow altogether aside and the use of snares, except for rabbits and partridges, they depend entirely on the Europeans for the means of gaining subsistence, as they require guns and a constant supply of powder and shot; so that these Indians are probably more completely under the power of the trader than any of the other tribes. As I only saw a few straggling parties of them during short intervals, and under favourable circumstances of sickness and famine, I am unable to give, from personal observation, any detail of their manners and customs; and must refer the reader to Dr. Richardson's account of them in the following chapter. That gentleman, during his longer residence at the post, had many opportunities of seeing them and acquiring their language.

January 17

This morning of the sporting part of our society had rather a novel diversion: intelligence having been brought that a wolf had borne away a steel trap, in which he had been caught, a party went in search of the marauder and took two English bulldogs and a terrier which had been brought into the country this season. On the first sight of the animal the dogs became alarmed and stood barking at a distance, and probably would not have ventured to advance had they not seen the wolf fall by a shot from one of the gentlemen; they then, however, went up and behaved courageously, and were enraged by the bites they received. The wolf soon died of its wounds, and the body was brought to the house, where a drawing of it was taken by Mr. Hood and the skin preserved by Dr. Richardson. Its general features bore a strong resemblance to many of the dogs about the fort, but it was larger and had a more ferocious aspect. Mr. Back and I were too much occupied in preparing for our departure on the following day to join this excursion.

The position of Cumberland House, by our observations, is, latitude 53° 56′ 40″ N.; longitude 102° 16′ 41″ W. by the chronometers; variations 17° 17′ 29″ E.; dip of the needle, 83° 12′ 50″. The whole of the travelling distance between York Factory and Cumberland House is about six hundred and ninety miles.

CHAPTER III

Dr. Richardson's residence at Cumberland House – His account
of the Cree Indians.

January 19, 1820

From the departure of Messrs. Franklin and Back, on the 19th of January, for Chipewyan, until the opening of the navigation in the spring, the occurrences with the Expedition were so much in the ordinary routine of a winter's residence at Fort Cumberland, that they may be, perhaps, appropriately blended with the following general but brief account of that district and its inhabitants.

Cumberland House was originally built by Hearne, a year or two after his return from the Copper-Mine River, and has ever since been considered by the Hudson's Bay Company as a post of considerable importance. Previous to that time, the natives carried their furs down to the shore of Hudson's Bay, or disposed of them nearer home to the French Canadian traders, who visited this part of the country as early as the year 1697.

The Cumberland House district, extending about one hundred and fifty miles from east to west along the banks of the Saskatchawan, and about as far from north to south, comprehends, on a rough calculation, upwards of twenty thousand square miles, and is frequented at present by about one hundred and twenty Indian hunters. Of these a few have several wives, but the majority only one; and, as some are unmarried, we shall not err greatly in considering the number of married women as only slightly exceeding that of the hunters. The women marry very young, have a custom of suckling their children for several years, and are besides exposed constantly to fatigue and often to famine; hence they are not prolific, bearing upon an average not more than four children, of whom two may attain the age of puberty. Upon these data, the amount of each family may be stated at five, and the whole Indian population in the district at five hundred.

This is but a small population for such an extent of country, yet their mode of life occasionally subjects them to great privations. The winter of our residence at Cumberland House proved extremely severe to the Indians. The whooping-cough made its appearance amongst them in the autumn, and was followed by the measles, which in the course of the winter spread through the tribe. Many died, and most of the survivors were so enfeebled as to be unable to pursue the necessary avocations of hunting and fishing. Even those who experienced only a slight attack, or escaped the sickness altogether, dispirited by the scenes of misery which environed them, were rendered incapable of affording relief to their distressed relations, and spent their time in conjuring and drumming to avert the pestilence. Those who were able to came to the fort and received relief, but many who had retired with their families to distant corners, to pursue their winter hunts, experienced all the horrors of famine. One evening, early in the month of January, a poor Indian entered the North-West Company's House, carrying his only child in his arms, and followed by his starving wife. They had been hunting apart from the other bands, had been unsuccessful, and whilst in want were seized with the epidemical disease. An Indian is accustomed to starve, and it is not easy to elicit from him an account of his sufferings. This poor man's story was very brief; as soon as the fever abated, he set out with his wife for Cumberland House, having been previously reduced to feed on the bits of skin and offal, which remained about their encampment. Even this miserable fare was exhausted, and they walked several days without eating, yet exerting themselves far beyond their strength that they might save the life of the infant. It died almost within sight of the house. Mr. Connolly, who was then in charge of the post, received them with the utmost humanity, and instantly placed food before them; but no language can describe the manner in which the miserable father dashed the morsel from his lips and deplored the loss of his child. Misery may harden a disposition naturally bad, but it never fails to soften the heart of a good man.

The *origin* of the Crees, to which nation the Cumberland House Indians belong, is, like that of the other aborigines of American, involved in obscurity; but the researches now making into the nature and affinities of the languages spoken by the different Indian tribes, may eventually throw some light on the subject. Indeed, the American philologists seem to have succeeded already in classing the known dialects into three languages: – 1st. The Floridean, spoken by the Creeks, Chickesaws, Choctaws, Cherokees, Pascagoulas, and some other tribes, who inhabit the southern parts of the United States. 2nd. The Iroquois, spoken by the Mengwe, or Six Nations, the Wyandots, the Nadowessies, and Asseeneepoytuck. 3rd. The Lenni-lenapè, spoken by a great family more widely spread than the other two, and from which, together with a vast number of other tribes, are sprung our Crees. Mr. Heckewelder, a missionary, who resided long amongst these people, and from whose paper, (published in the *Transactions of the American Philosophical Society*,) the above classification is taken, states that the Lenapè have a tradition amongst them, of their ancestors having come from the westward, and taken possession of the whole country from the Missouri to the Atlantic, after driving away or destroying the original inhabitants of the land, whom they termed Alligewi. In this migration and contest, which endured for a series of years, the Mengwe, or Iroquois, kept pace with them, moving in a parallel but more northerly line, and finally settling on the banks of the St. Lawrence, and the great lakes from whence it flows. The Lenapè, being more numerous, peopled not only the greater part of the country at present occupied by the United States, but also sent detachments to the northward as far as the banks of the River Mississippi and the shores of Hudson's Bay. The principal of their northern tribes are now known under the names of Saulteurs or Chippewyas, and Crees; the former inhabiting the country betwixt Lakes Winipeg and Superior, the latter frequenting the shores of Hudson's Bay, from Moose to Churchill, and the country from thence as far to the westward as the plains which lie betwixt the forks of the Saskatchawan.

The Crees, formerly known by the French Canadian traders under the appellation of Knisteneaux, generally designated themselves as Eithinyoowuc (*men*), or, when they wish to discriminate themselves from the other Indian nations, as Nathehwy-withinyoowuc (*Southern-men*).[1]

The original character of the Crees must have been much modified by their long intercourse with Europeans; hence it is to be understood, that we confine ourselves in the following sketch to their present condition, and more particularly to the Crees of Cumberland House. The moral character of a hunter is acted upon

1 Much confusion has arisen from the great variety of names, applied without discrimination to the various tribes of Salteurs and Crees. Heckewelder considers the Crees of Moose Factory to be a branch of that tribe of the Lenapè, which is named Minsi, or Wolf Tribe. He has been led to form this opinion from the similarity of the name given to these people by Monsieur Jeremie, namely, Monsonies; but the truth is, that their real name is Mongsoa-eythinyoowuc, or Moose-deer Indians; hence the name of the factory and river on which it is built. The name Knisteneaux, Kristeneaux, or Killisteneaux, was anciently applied to a tribe of Crees, now termed Maskegons, who inhabit the river Winipeg. This small tribe still retains the peculiarities of customs and dress, for which it was remarkable many years ago, as mentioned by Mr. Henry, in the interesting account of his journeys in these countries. They are said to be great rascals. The great body of the Crees were at that time named Opimmitish Ininiwuc, or Men of the Woods. It would, however, be an endless task to attempt to determine the precise people designated by the early French writers. Every small band, naming itself from its hunting grounds, was described as a different nation. The Chippeways who frequented the Lake of the Woods were named from a particular act of pillage – Pilliers, or Robbers: and the name Saulteurs, applied to a principal band that frequented the Sault St. Marie, has been by degrees extended to the whole tribe. It is frequently pronounced and written Sotoos.

by the nature of the land he inhabits, the abundance or scarcity of food, and we may add, in the present case, his means of access to spirituous liquors. In a country so various in these respects as that inhabited by the Crees, the causes alluded to must operate strongly in producing a considerable difference of character amongst the various hordes. It may be proper to bear in mind also, that we are about to draw the character of a people whose only rule of conduct is public opinion, and to try them by a morality founded on divine revelation, the only standard that can be referred to by those who have been educated in a land to which the blessings of the Gospels have extended.

Bearing these considerations in mind then, we may state the Crees to be a vain, fickle, improvident, and indolent race, and not very strict in their adherence to truth, being great boasters; but, on the other hand, they strictly regard the rights of property,[1] are susceptible of the kinder affections, capable of friendship, very hospitable, tolerably kind to their women, and withal inclined to peace.

Much of the faulty part of their character, no doubt, originates in their mode of life; accustomed as a hunter to depend greatly on chance for his subsistence, the Cree takes little thought of tomorrow; and the most offensive part of his behaviour – the habit of boasting – has been probably assumed as a necessary part of his armour, which operates upon the fears of his enemies. They are countenanced, however, in this failing, by the practice of the ancient Greeks, and perhaps by that of every other nation in its ruder state. Every Cree fears the medical or conjuring powers of his neighbour; but at the same time exalts his own attainments to the skies. 'I am God-like,' is a common expression amongst them, and they prove their divinity-ship by eating live coals, and by various tricks of a similar nature. A medicine bag is an indispensable part of a hunter's equipment. It is generally furnished with a little bit of indigo, blue vitriol, vermilion, or some other showy article; and is, when in the hands of a noted conjurer, such an object of terror to the rest of the tribe, that its possessor is enabled to fatten at his ease upon the labours of his deluded countrymen.

A fellow of this description came to Cumberland House in the winter of 1819. Notwithstanding the then miserable state of the Indians, the rapacity of this wretch had been preying upon their necessities, and a poor hunter was actually at the moment pining away under the influence of his threats. The mighty conjurer, immediately on his arrival at the House, began to trumpet forth his powers, boasting, among other things, that although his hands and feet were tied as securely as possible, yet when placed in a conjuring-house, he would speedily disengage himself by the aid of two or three familiar spirits, who were attendant on his call. He was instantly taken at his word, and that his exertions might not be without an aim, a *capot* or great coat was promised as the reward of his success. A conjuring-house having been erected in the usual form, that is, by sticking four willows in the ground and tying their tops to a hoop at the height of six or eight feet, he was fettered completely by winding several fathoms of rope round his body and extremities, and placed in its narrow apartment, not exceeding two feet in diameter. A moose-skin being thrown over the frame, secluded him from our view. He forthwith began to chant a kind of hymn in a very monotonous tone. The rest of the Indians, who seemed in doubt respecting the powers of a devil when put in competition with those of a white man, ranged themselves around and watched the result with anxiety. Nothing remarkable occurred for a long time. The conjurer continued his song at intervals, and it was occasionally taken up by those without. In this manner an hour and a half elapsed; but at length our attention, which had begun to flag, was roused by the violent shaking of the conjuring-house. It was instantly whispered round the circle, that at least one devil had crept under the

1 This is, perhaps, true of the Cumberland House Crees alone: many of the other tribes of Crees are stated by the traders to be thieves.

moose-skin. But it proved to be only the 'God-like man' trembling with cold. He had entered the lists, stripped to the skin, and the thermometer stood very low that evening. His attempts were continued, however, with considerable resolution for half an hour longer, when he reluctantly gave in. He had found no difficulty in slipping through the noose when it was formed by his countrymen; but, in the present instance, the knot was tied by Governor Williams, who is an expert sailor. After this unsuccessful exhibition his credit sunk amazingly, and he took the earliest opportunity of sneaking away from the fort.

About two years ago a conjurer paid more dearly for his temerity. In a quarrel with an Indian he threw out some obscure threats of vengeance which passed unnoticed at the time, but were afterwards remembered. They met in the spring at Carlton House, after passing the winter in different parts of the country, during which the Indian's child died. The conjurer had the folly to boast that he had caused its death, and the enraged father shot him dead on the spot. It may be remarked, however, that both these Indians were inhabitants of the plains, and had been taught, by their intercourse with the turbulent Stone Indians, to set but comparatively little value on the life of a man.

It might be thought that the Crees have benefited by their long intercourse with civilised nations. That this is not so much the case as it ought to be, is not entirely their own fault. They are capable of being, and I believe willing to be, taught; but no pains have hitherto been taken to inform their minds,[1] and their white acquaintances seem in general to find it easier to descend to the Indian customs, and modes of thinking, particularly with respect to women, than to attempt to raise the Indians to theirs. Indeed such a lamentable want of morality has been displayed by the white traders in their contests for the interests of their respective companies, that it would require a long series of good conduct to efface from the minds of the native population the ideas they have formed of the white character. Notwithstanding the frequent violations of the rights of property they have witnessed, and but too often experienced, in their own persons, these savages, as they are termed, remain strictly honest. During their visits to a post, they are suffered to enter every apartment in the house, without the least restraint, and although articles of value to them are scattered about, nothing is ever missed. They scrupulously avoid moving anything from its place, although they are often prompted by curiosity to examine it. In some cases, indeed, they carry this principle to a degree of self-denial which would hardly be expected. It often happens that meat, which has been paid for, (if the poisonous draught it procures them can be considered as payment,) is left at their lodges until a convenient opportunity occurs of carrying it away. They will rather pass several days without eating than touch the meat thus intrusted to their charge, even when there exists a prospect of replacing it.

The hospitality of the Crees is unbounded. They afford a certain asylum to the half-breed children when deserted by their unnatural white fathers; and the infirm, and indeed every individual in an encampment, share the provisions of a successful hunter as long as they last. Fond too as a Cree is of spirituous liquors, he is not happy unless all his neighbours partake with him. It is not easy, however, to say what share ostentation may have in the apparent munificence in the latter article; for when an Indian, by a good hunt, is enabled to treat the others with a keg of rum, he becomes the chief of a night, assumes no little stateliness of manner, and is treated with deference by those who regale at his expense. Prompted also by the desire of gaining a *name*, they lavish away the articles they purchase at the trading posts, and are well satisfied if repaid in praise.

1 Since these remarks were written with the union of the rival Companies has enabled the gentlemen, who have now the management of the fur trade, to take some decided steps for the religious instruction and improvements of the natives and half-breed Indians, which have been more particularly referred to in the introduction.

Gaming is not uncommon amongst the Crees of all the different districts, but it is pursued to greater lengths by those bands who frequent the plains, and who, from the ease with which they obtain food, have abundant leisure. The game most in use amongst them, termed *puckesann*, is played with the stones of a species of *prunus* which, from the circumstance, they term *puckesann-meena*. The difficulty lies in guessing the number of stones which are tossed out of a small wooden dish, and the hunters will spend whole nights at the destructive sport, staking their most valuable articles, powder and shot.

It has been remarked by some writers that the aboriginal inhabitants of America are deficient in passion for the fair sex. This is by no means the case with the Crees; on the contrary, their practice of seducing each other's wives, proves the most fertile source of their quarrels. When the guilty pair are detected, the woman generally receives a severe beating, but the husband is, for the most part, afraid to reproach the male culprit until they get drunk together at the fort; then the remembrance of the offence is revived, a struggle ensues, and the affair is terminated by the loss of a few handfuls of hair. Some husbands, however, feel more deeply the injury done to their honour, and seek revenge even in their sober moments. In such cases it is not uncommon for the offended party to walk with great gravity up to the other, and deliberately seizing his gun, or some other article of value, to break it before his face. The adulterer looks on in silence, afraid to make any attempt to save his property. In this respect, indeed, the Indian character seems to differ from the European, that an Indian, instead of letting his anger increase with that of his antagonist, assumes the utmost coolness, lest he should push him to extremities.

Although adultery is sometimes punished amongst the Crees in the manner above described, yet it is no crime, provided the husband receives a valuable consideration for his wife's prostitution. Neither is chastity considered as a virtue in a female before marriage, that is, before she becomes the exclusive property of one hunter.

The Cree women are not in general treated harshly by their husbands, and possess considerable influence over them. They often eat, and even get drunk, in consort with the men; a considerable portion of the labour, however, falls to the lot of the wife. She makes the hut, cooks, dresses the skins, and for the most part, carries the heaviest load: but, when she is unable to perform her task, the husband does not consider it beneath his dignity to assist her. In illustration of this remark, I may quote the case of an Indian who visited the fort in winter. This poor man's wife had lost her feet by the frost, and he was compelled, not only to hunt, and do all the menial offices himself, but in winter to drag his wife with their stock of furniture from one encampment to another. In the performance of this duty, as he could not keep pace with the rest of the tribe in their movements, he more than once nearly perished of hunger.

These Indians, however, capable as they are of behaving thus kindly, affect in their discourse to despise the softer sex, and on solemn occasions, will not suffer them to eat before them, or even come into their presence. In this they are countenanced by the white residents, most of whom have Indian or half-breed wives, but seem afraid of treating them with the tenderness or attention due to every female, lest they should themselves be despised by the Indians. At least, this is the only reason they assign for their neglect of those whom they make partners of their beds and mothers of their children.

Both sexes are fond of, and excessively indulgent to, their children. The father never punishes them, and if the mother, more hasty in her temper, sometimes bestows a blow or two on a troublesome child, her heart is instantly softened by the roar which follows, and she mingles her tears with those that streak the smoky face of her darling. It may be fairly said, then, that restraint or punishment forms no part of the education of an Indian child, nor are they early trained to that command over their temper which they exhibit in after years.

The discourse of the parents is never restrained by the presence of their children, ever transaction between the sexes being openly talked of before them.

The Crees having early obtained arms from the European traders, were enabled to make harassing inroads on the lands of their neighbours, and are known to have made war excursions as far to the westward as the Rocky Mountains, and to the northward as far as Mackenzie's River; but their enemies being now as well armed as themselves, the case is much altered.

They show great fortitude in the endurance of hunger, and the other evils incident to a hunter's life; but any unusual accident dispirits them at once, and they seldom venture to meet their enemies in open warfare, or to attack them even by surprise, unless with the advantage of superiority of numbers. Perhaps they are much deteriorated in this respect by their intercourse with Europeans. Their existence at present hangs upon the supplies of ammunition and clothing they receive from the traders, and they deeply feel their dependant situation. But their character has been still more debased by the passion for spirituous liquors, so assiduously fostered among them. To obtain the noxious beverage, they descend to the most humiliating entreaties, and assume an abjectness of behaviour which does not seem natural to them, and of which not a vestige is to be seen in their intercourse with each other. Their character has sunk among the neighbouring nations. They are no longer the warriors who drove before them the inhabitants of the Saskatchawan, and Missinippi. The Cumberland House Crees, in particular, have been long disused to war. Betwixt them and their ancient enemies, the Slave nations, lie the extensive plains of Saskatchawan, inhabited by the powerful Asseeneepoytuck, or Stone Indians, who having whilst yet a small tribe entered the country under the patronage of the Crees, now render back the protection they received.

The manners and customs of the Crees have, probably since their acquaintance with the Europeans, undergone a change at least, equal to that which has taken place in their moral character; and, although we heard of many practices peculiar to them, yet they appeared to be nearly as much honoured in the breach as the observance. We shall, however, briefly notice a few of the most remarkable customs.

When a hunter marries his first wife, he usually takes up his abode in the tent of his father-in-law, and of course hunts for the family; but when he becomes a father, the families are at liberty to separate, or remain together, as their inclinations prompt them. His second wife is for the most part the sister of the first, but not necessarily so, for an Indian or another family often presses his daughter upon a hunter whom he knows to be capable of maintaining her well. The first wife always remains the mistress of the tent, and assumes an authority over the others, which is not in every case quietly submitted to. It may be remarked, that whilst an Indian resides with his wife's family, it is extremely improper for his mother-in-law to speak, or even look at him; and when she has a communication to make, it is the etiquette that she should turn her back upon him, and address him only through the medium of a third person. This singular custom is not very creditable to the Indians, if it really had its origin in the cause which they at present assign for it, namely, that a woman's speaking to her son-in-law is a sure indication of her having conceived a criminal affection for him.

It appears also to have been an ancient practice for an Indian to avoid eating or sitting down in the presence of the father-in-law. We received no account of the origin of this custom, and it is now almost obsolete amongst the Cumberland House Crees, though still partially observed by those who frequent Carlton.

Tattooing is almost universal with the Crees. The women are in general content with having one or two lines drawn from the corners of the mouth towards the angles of the lower jaw; but some of the men have their bodies covered with a great variety of lines and figures. It seems to be considered by most rather as a proof of courage than an ornament, the operation being very painful, and, if the figures are numerous and intricate, lasting several days. The lines on the face are formed by dexterously running an awl under the cuticle, and then drawing a cord, dipped in charcoal and water, through the canal thus formed. The punctures on the body are formed by needles of various sizes set in a frame. A number of hawk bells attached to this frame serve by their noise to cover the suppressed groans of the sufferer, and, probably for the same reason, the process is accompanied with singing. An indelible stain is produced by rubbing a little finely-powdered willow-charcoal into the punctures. A half-breed, whose arm I amputated, declared, that tattooing was not only the most painful operation of the two, but rendered infinitely more difficult to bear by its tediousness, having lasted in his case three days.

A Cree woman, at certain periods, is laid under considerable restraint. They are far, however, from carrying matters to the extremities mentioned by Hearne in his description of the Chipewyans, or Northern Indians. She lives apart from her husband also for two months if she has borne a boy, and for three if she has given birth to a girl.

Many of the Cree hunters are careful to prevent a woman from partaking of the head of a moose-deer, lest it should spoil their future hunts; and for the same reason they avoid bringing it to a fort, fearing lest the white people should give the bones to the dogs.

The games or sports of the Crees are various. One termed the game of the mitten, is played with four balls, three of which are plain, and one marked. These being hid under as many mittens, the opposite party is required to fix on that which is marked. He gives or receives a feather according as he guesses right or wrong. When the feathers, which are ten in number, have all passed into one hand, a new division is made; but when one of the parties obtains possession of them thrice, he seizes on the stakes.

The game of Platter is more intricate, and is played with the claws of a bear, or some other animal, marked with various lines and characters. These dice, which are eight in number, and cut flat at their large end, are shook together in a wooden dish, tossed into the air and caught again. The lines traced on such claws as happen to alight on the platter in an erect position, indicate what number of counters the caster is to receive from his opponent.

They have, however, a much more manly amusement termed the *Cross*, although they do not engage even in it without depositing considerable stakes. An extensive meadow is chosen for this sport, and the articles staked are tied to a post, or deposited in the custody of two old men. The combatants being stripped and painted, and each provided with a kind of battledore or racket, in shape resembling the letter P, with a handle about two feet long and a head loosely wrought with net-work, so as to form a shallow bag, range themselves on different sides. A ball being now tossed up in the middle, each party endeavours to drive it to their respective goals, and much dexterity and agility is displayed in the contest. When a nimble runner gets the ball in his *cross*, he sets off towards the goal with the utmost speed, and is followed by the rest, who endeavour to jostle him and shake it out; but, if hard pressed, he discharges it with a jerk, to be forwarded by his own party, or bandied back by their opponents, until the victory is decided by its passing the goal.

Of the religious opinions of the Cretes, it is difficult to give a correct account, not only because they show a disinclination to enter upon the subject, but because their ancient traditions are mingled with the information they have more recently obtained, by their intercourse with Europeans.

None of them ventured to describe the original formation of the world, but they all spoke of an universal deluge, caused by an attempt of the fish to drown Woesack-ootchacht, a kind of demi-god, with whom they had quarrelled. Having constructed a raft, he embarked with his family and all kinds of birds and beasts. After the flood had continued for some time, he ordered several water-fowl to dive to the bottom; they were all drowned: but a muskrat having been despatched on the same errand, was more successful, and returned with a mouthful of mud, out of which Woesack-ootchacht, imitating the mode in which the rats construct their houses, formed a new earth. First, a small conical hill of mud appeared above the water; by-and-by, its base gradually spreading out, it became an extensive bank, which the rays of the sun at length hardened into firm land. Notwithstanding the power that Woesack-ootchacht here displayed, his person is held in very little reverence by the Indians; and, in return, he seizes every opportunity of tormenting them. His conduct is far from being moral, and his amours, and the disguises he assumes in the prosecution of them, are more various and extraordinary than those of the Grecian Jupiter himself; but as his adventures are more remarkable for their eccentricity than their delicacy, it is better to pass them over in silence. Before we quit him, however, we may remark, that he converses with all kinds of birds and beasts in their own languages, constantly addressing them by the title of brother, but through an inherent suspicion of his intentions, they are seldom willing to admit of his claims of relationship. The Indians make no sacrifices to him, not even to avert his wrath. They pay a kind of worship, however, and make offerings to a being, whom they term *Kepoochikawn*.

This deity is represented sometimes by rude images of the human figure, but more commonly merely by tying the tops of a few willow bushes together; and the offerings to him consist of everything that is valuable to an Indian; yet they treat him with considerable familiarity, interlarding their most solemn speeches with expostulations and threats of neglect, if he fails in complying with their requests. As most of their petitions are for plenty of food, they do not trust entirely to the favour of Kepoochikawn, but endeavour, at the same time, to propitiate the *animal*, an imaginary representative of the whole race of larger quadrupeds that are objects of the chase.

In the month of May, whilst I was at Carlton House, the Cree hunter engaged to attend that post, resolved upon dedicating several articles to Kepoochikawn, and as I had made some inquiries of him respecting their modes of worship, he gave me an invitation to be present. The ceremony took place in a sweating house, or as it may be designated from its more important use, a *temple*, which was erected for the occasion by the worshipper's two wives. It was framed of arch willows, interlaced so as to form a vault capable of containing ten or twelve men, ranged closely side by side, and high enough to admit of their sitting erect. It was very similar in shape to an oven or the kraal of a Hottentot, and was closely covered with moose-skins, except at the east end, which was left open for a door. Near the centre of the building there was a hole in the ground, which contained ten or twelve red-hot stones, having a few leaves of the *taccohaymenan*, a species of *prunus*, strewed around them. When the women had completed the preparations, the hunter made his appearance, perfectly naked, carrying in his hand an image of Kepoochikawn, rudely carved, and about two feet long. He placed his god at the upper end of the sweating-house, with his face towards the door, and proceeded to tie round its neck his offerings, consisting of a cotton handkerchief, a looking-glass, a tin pan, a piece of riband, and a bit of tobacco, which he had procured the same day, at the expense of fifteen or twenty skins. Whilst he was thus occupied, several other Crees, who were encamped in the neighbourhood, having been informed of what was going on, arrived, and stripping a the door of the temple, entered, and ranged themselves on each side; the hunter himself squatted down at the right-hand of Kepoochikawn. The atmosphere of the temple having become so hot that none but zealous worshippers would venture in, the interpreter and myself sat down on the threshold, and the two women remained on the outside as attendants.

The hunter, who throughout officiated as high priest, commenced by making a speech to Kepoochikawn, in which he requested him to be propitious, told him of the value of the things now presented, and cautioned him against ingratitude. This oration was delivered in a monotonous tone, and with great rapidity of utterance, and the speaker retained his squatting posture, but turned his face to his god. At its conclusion, the priest began a hymn, of which the burthen was, 'I will walk with God, I will go with the animal'; and, at the end of each stanza, the rest joined in an insignificant chorus. He next took up a calumet, filled with a mixture of tobacco and bear-berry leaves, and holding its stem by the middle, in a horizontal position, over the hot stones, turned it slowly in a circular manner, following the course of the sun. Its mouth-piece being then with much formality, held for a few seconds to the face of Kepoochikawn, it was next presented to the earth, having been previously turned a second time over the hot stones; and afterwards, with equal ceremony, pointed in succession to the four quarters of the sky; then drawing a few whiffs from the calumet himself, he handed it to his left-hand neighbour, by whom it was gravely passed round the circle; the interpreter and myself, who were seated at the door, were asked to partake in our turn, but requested to keep the head of the calumet within the threshold of the sweating-house. When the tobacco was exhausted by passing several times round, the hunter made another speech, similar to the former; but was, if possible, still more urgent in his requests. A second hymn followed, and a quantity of water being sprinkled on the hot stones, the attendants were ordered to close the temple, which they did, by very carefully covering it up with moose-skins. We had no means of ascertaining the temperature of the sweating-house; but before it was closed, not only those within, but also the spectators without, were perspiring freely. They continued in the vapour bath for thirty-five minutes, during which time a third speech was made, and a hymn was sung, and water occasionally sprinkled on the stones, which still retained much heat, as was evident from the hissing noise they made. The coverings were then thrown off, and the poor half-stewed worshippers exposed freely to the air; but the kept their squatting postures until a fourth speech was made, in which the deity was strongly reminded of the value of the gifts, and exhorted to take an early opportunity of showing his gratitude. The ceremony concluded by the sweaters scampering down to the river, and plunging into the stream. It may be remarked, that the door of the temple, and, of course, the face of the god, was turned to the rising sun; and the spectators were desired not to block up entirely the front of the building, but to leave a lane for the entrance or exit of some influence of which they could not give me a correct description. Several Indians, who lay on the outside of the sweating-house as spectators, seemed to regard the proceedings with very little awe, and were extremely free in the remarks and jokes they passed upon the condition of the sweaters, and even of Kepoochikawn himself. One of them made a remark, that the shawl would have been much better bestowed upon himself than upon Kepoochikawn, but the same fellow afterwards stripped and joined in the ceremony.

I did not learn that the Indians worship any other god by a specific name. They often refer, however, to the Keetchee-Maneeto, or Great Master of Life; and to an evil spirit, or Maatche-Maneeto. They also speak of Weet-tako, a kind of vampire or devil, into which those who have fed on human flesh are transformed.

Whilst at Carlton, I took an opportunity of asking a communicative old Indian, of the Blackfoot nation, his opinion of a future state; he replied, that they had heard from their fathers, that the souls of the departed have to scramble with great labour up the sides of a steep mountain, upon attaining the summit of which they are rewarded with the prospect of an extensive plain, abounding in all sorts of game, and interspersed here and there with new tents, pitched in agreeable situations. Whilst they are absorbed in the contemplation of this delightful scene, they are descried by the inhabitants of the happy land, who, clothed in new skin-dresses, approach and welcome with every demonstration of kindness those Indians who have led good lives; but the bad Indians, who have imbrued their hands in the blood of their countrymen, are told to return from whence they came, and without more ceremony precipitated down the steep sides of the mountain.

Women, who have been guilty of infanticide, never reach the mountain at all, but are compelled to hover round the seats of their crimes, with branches of trees tied to their legs. The melancholy sounds, which are heard in the still summer evenings, and which the ignorance of the white people considers as the screams of the goat-sucker, are really, according to my informant, the moanings of these unhappy beings.

The Crees have somewhat similar notions, but as they inhabit a country widely different from the mountainous lands of the Blackfoot Indians, the difficulty of their journey lies in walking along a slender and slippery tree, laid as a bridge across a rapid stream of stinking and muddy water. The night owl is regarded by the Crees with the same dread that it has been viewed by other nations. One small species, which is known to them by its melancholy nocturnal hootings, (for as it never appears in the day, few even of the hunters have ever seen it,) is particularly ominous. They call it the *cheepai-peethees*, or death bird, and never fail to whistle when they hear its note. If it does not reply to the whistle by its hootings, the speedy death of the inquirer is augured.

When a Cree dies, that part of his property which he has not given away before his death is burned with him, and his relations take care to place near the grave little heaps of firewood, food, pieces of tobacco, and such things as he is likely to need in his journey. Similar offerings are made when they revisit the grave, and as kettles and other articles of value, are sometimes offered, they are frequently carried off by passengers, yet the relations are not displeased, provided sufficient respect has been shown to the dead, by putting some other article, although of inferior value, in the place of that which has been taken away.

The Crees are wont to celebrate the returns of the seasons by religious festivals, but we are unable to describe the ceremonial in use on these joyous occasions from personal observation. The following brief notice of a feast, which was given by an old Cree chief, according to his annual custom, on the first croaking of the frogs, is drawn up from the information of one of the guests. A large oblong tent, or lodge, was prepared for the important occasion, by the men of the party, none of the women being suffered to interfere. It faced the setting sun, and great care was taken that everything about it should be as neat and clean as possible. Three fireplaces were raised within it, at equal distances, and little holes were dug in the corners to contain the ashes of their pipes. In a recess, at its upper end, one large image of Kepoochikawn, and many smaller ones, were ranged with their faces towards the door. The food was prepared by the chief's wife, and consisted of *marrow* pemmican, berries boiled with fat, and various other delicacies that had been preserved for the occasion.

The preparations being completed, and a slave, whom the chief had taken in war, having warned the guests to the feast by the mysterious word *peenasheway*, they came, dressed out in their best garments, and ranged themselves according to their seniority, the elders seating themselves next the chief at the upper end, and the young men near the door.

The chief commenced by addressing his deities in an appropriate speech, in which he told him, that he had hastened as soon as summer was indicated by the croaking of the frogs to solicit their favour for himself and his young men, and hoped that they would send him a pleasant and plentiful season. His oration was concluded by an invocation to all the animals in the land, and a signal being given to the slave at the door, he invited them severally by their names to come and partake of the feast.

The Cree chief having by this very general invitation displayed his unbounded hospitality, next ordered one of the young men to distribute a mess to each of the guests. This was done in new dishes of birch bark, and the utmost diligence was displayed in emptying them, it being considered extremely improper in a man to leave any part of that which is placed before him on such occasions. It is not inconsistent with good manners, however, but rather considered as a piece of politeness, that a guest who has been too liberally supplied, should hand the surplus to his neighbour. When the viands had disappeared, each filled his calumet and began to smoke with great assiduity, and in the course of the evening several songs were sung to the responsive sounds of the drum, and seeseequay, their usual accompaniments.

The Cree drum is double-headed, but possessing very little depth, it strongly resembles a tambourine in shape. Its want of depth is compensated, however, by its diameter, which frequently exceeds three feet. It is covered with moose-skin parchment, painted with rude figures of men and beasts, having various fantastic additions, and is beat with a stick. The seeseequay is merely a rattle formed by enclosing a few grains of shot in a piece of dried hide. These two instruments are used in all their religious ceremonies, except those which take place in a sweating-house.

A Cree places great reliance on his drum, and I cannot adduce a stronger instance than that of the poor man who is mentioned in a preceding page, as having lost his only child by famine, almost within sight of the fort. Notwithstanding his exhausted state, he travelled with an enormous drum tied to his back.

Many of the Crees make vows to abstain from particular kinds of food, either for a specific time, or for the remainder of their life, esteeming such abstinence to be a certain means of acquiring some supernatural powers, or at least of entailing upon themselves a succession of good fortune.

One of the wives of the Carlton hunter, of whom we have already spoken as the worshipper of Kepoochikawn, made a determination not to eat of the flesh of the

Wawaskeesh, or American stag; but during our abode at the place, she was induced to feed heartily upon it, through the intentional deceit of her husband, who told her that it was buffalo meat. When she had finished her meal, her husband told her of the trick, and seemed to enjoy the terror with which she contemplated the consequences of the involuntary breach of her vow. Vows of this nature are often made by a Cree before he joins a war party, and they sometimes, like the eastern bronzes, walk for a certain number of days on all fours, or impose upon themselves some other penance, equally ridiculous. By such means the Cree warrior becomes *god-like*; but unless he kills an enemy before his return, his newly-acquired powers are estimated to be productive in future of some direful consequence to himself.

As we did not witness any of the Cree dances ourselves, we shall merely mention, that, like the other North American nations, they are accustomed to practise that amusement on meeting with strange tribes, before going to war, and on other solemn occasions.

The habitual intoxication of the Cumberland House Crees has induced such a disregard of personal appearance, that they are squalid and dirty in the extreme; hence a minute description of their clothing would be by no means interesting. We shall, therefore, only remark in a general manner that the dress of the male consists of a blanket thrown over the shoulders, a leathern skirt or jacket, and a piece of cloth tied round the middle. The woman have in addition a long petticoat; and both sexes wear a kind of wide hose, which, reaching from the ankle to the middle of the thigh, are suspended by strings to the girdle. These hose, or as they are termed, *Indian stockings*, are commonly ornamented with beads or ribands, and from their convenience, have been universally adopted by the white residents, as an essential part of their winter clothing. Their shoes, or rather short boots, for they tie round the ankle, are made of soft dressed moose-skins, and during the winter they wrap several pieces of blanket round their feet.

They are fond of European articles of dress, considering it as means to be dressed entirely in leather, and the hunters are generally furnished annually with a *capot* or great coat, and the women with shawls, printed calicoes, and other things very unsuitable to their mode of life, but which they wear in imitation of the wives of the traders; all these articles, however showy they may be at first, are soon reduced to a very filthy condition by the Indian custom of greasing the face and hair with soft fat or marrow, instead of washing them with water. This practice they say preserves the skin soft, and protects it from cold in the winter, and the moschetoes in summer, but it renders their presence disagreeable to the olfactory organs of an European, particularly when they are seated in a close tent and near a hot fire.

The only peculiarity which we observed, in their mode of rearing children consists in the use of a sort of cradle, extremely well adapted to their mode of life. The infant is placed in the bag having its lower extremities wrapt up in soft sphagnum or bog-moss, and may be hung up in the tent, or to the branch of a tree, without the least danger of tumbling out; or in a journey suspended on the mother's back, by a band which crosses the forehead, so as to leave her hands perfectly free. It is one of the neatest articles of furniture they possess, being generally ornamented with beads, and bits of scarlet cloth, but it bears a very strong resemblance in its form to a mummy case.

The sphagnum in which the child is laid, forms a soft elastic bed, which absorbs moisture very readily, and affords such a protection from the cold of a rigorous winter, that its place would be ill supplied by cloth.

The mothers are careful to collect a sufficient quantity in autumn for winter use; but when through accident their stock fails, they have recourse to the soft down of the typha, or reed mace, the dust of rotten wood, or even feathers, although none of these articles are so cleanly, or so easily changed as the sphagnum.

The above is a brief sketch of such parts of the manners, character and customs of the Crees, as we could collect from personal observation, or from the information of the most intelligent half-breeds we met with; and we shall merely add a few remarks on the manner in which the trade is conducted at the different inland posts of the Fur Companies.

The standard of Exchange in all mercantile transactions with the natives is a beaver skin, the relative value of which, as originally established by the traders, differs considerably from the present worth of the articles it represents; but the Indians are averse to change. Three marten, eight musk-rat, or a single lynx, or wolverene skin, are equivalent to one beaver; a silver fox, white fox, or otter, are reckoned two beavers, and a black fox, or large black bear, are equal to four; a mode of reckoning which has very little connexion with the real value of these different furs in the European market. Neither has any attention been paid to the original cost of European articles, in fixing the tariff by which they are sold to the Indians. A coarse butcher's knife is one skin, a woollen blanket or a fathom of coarse cloth, eight, and a fowling-piece fifteen. The Indians receive their principal outfit of clothing and ammunition on credit in the autumn, to be repaid by their winter hunts; the amount intrusted to each of the hunters, varying with their reputations for industry and skill, from twenty to one hundred and fifty skins. The Indians are generally anxious to pay off the debt thus incurred, but their good intentions are often frustrated by the arts of the rival traders. Each of the Companies keeps men constantly employed travelling over the country during the winter, to collect the furs from the different bands of hunters as fast as they are produced. The poor Indian endeavours to behave honestly, and when he has gathered a few skins sends notice to the post from whence he procured his supplies, but if discovered in the meantime by the opposite party, he is seldom proof against the temptation to which he is exposed. However firm he may be inn his denials at first, his resolutions are enfeebled by the sight of a little rum, and when he has tasted the intoxicating beverage, they vanish like smoke, and he brings forth his store of furs, which he has carefully concealed from the scrutinising eyes of his visitors. This mode of carrying on the trade not only causes the amount of furs, collected by either of the two Companies, to depend more upon the activity of their agents, the knowledge they possess of the motions of the Indians, and the quantity of rum they carry, than upon the liberality of the credits they give, but is also productive of an increasing deterioration of the character of the Indians, and will probably, ultimately prove destructive to the fur trade itself. Indeed the evil has already, in part, recoiled upon the traders; for the Indians, long deceived, have become deceivers in their turn, and not unfrequently after having incurred a heavy debt at one post, move off to another, to play the same game. In some cases the rival posts have entered into a mutual agreement, to trade only with the Indians they have respectively fitted out; but such treaties, being seldom rigidly adhered to, prove a fertile subject for disputes, and the differences have been more than once decided by force of arms. To carry on the contest, the two Companies are obliged to employ a great many servants, whom they maintain often with much difficulty, and always at a considerable expense.[1]

There are thirty men belonging to the Hudson's Bay Fort at Cumberland, and nearly as many women and children.

1 As the contending parties have united, the evils mentioned in this and the two preceding pages, are now, in all probability, at an end.

The inhabitants of the North-West Company's House are still more numerous. These large families are fed during the greatest part of the year on fish, which are principally procured at Beaver Lake, about fifty miles distant. The fishery commencing with the first frosts in autumn, continues abundant till January, and the produce is dragged over the snow on sledges, each drawn by three dogs and carrying about two hundred and fifty pounds. The journey to and from the lake occupies five days, and every sledge requires a driver. About three thousand fish, averaging three pounds apiece, were caught by the Hudson's Bay fishermen last season; in addition to which a few sturgeon were occasionally caught in Pine Island Lake; and towards the spring a considerable quantity of moose meat was procured from the Basquiau Hill, sixty or seventy miles distant. The rest of our winter's provision consisted of geese, salted in the autumn, and of dried meats and pemmican, obtained from the provision posts on the plains of the Saskatchawan. A good many potatoes are also raised at this post, and a small supply of tea and sugar is brought from the depôt at York Factory. The provisions obtained from these various sources were amply sufficient in the winter of 1819–20; but through improvidence this post has in former seasons been reduced to great straits.

Many of the labourers, and a great majority of the agents and clerks employed by the two Companies, have Indian or half-breed wives, and the mixed offspring thus produced has become extremely numerous.

These métifs, or, as the Canadians term them, *bois brulés*, are upon the whole a good looking people, and where the experiment has been made, have shown much aptness in learning, and willingness to be taught; they have, however, been sadly neglected. The example of their fathers has released them from the restraint imposed by the Indian opinions of good and bad behaviour; and generally speaking, no pains have been taken to fill the void with better principles. Hence it is not surprising that the males, trained up in a high opinion of the authority and rights of the Company to which their fathers belonged, and unacquainted with the laws of the civilised world, should be ready to engage in any measure whatever, that they are prompted to believe will forward the interests of the cause they espouse. Nor that the girls, taught a certain degree of refinement by the acquisition of an European language, should be inflamed by the unrestrained discourse of their Indian relations, and very early give up all pretensions to chastity. It is, however, but justice to remark that there is a very decided difference in the conduct of the children of the Orkney men employed by the Hudson's Bay Company and those of the Canadian voyagers. Some trouble is occasionally bestowed in teaching the former, and it is not thrown away; but all the good that can be said of the latter is, that they are not quite so licentious as their fathers are.

Many of the half-breeds, both male and female, are brought up amongst, and intermarry with, the Indians; and there are few tents wherein the paler children of such marriages are not to be seen. It has been remarked, I do not know with what truth, that half-breeds show more personal courage than the pure Crees.[1]

The girls at the forts, particularly the daughters of Canadians, are given in marriage very young; they are very frequently wives at twelve years of age, and mothers at fourteen. Nay, more than once, instance came under our observation of the master of a post having permitted a voyager to take to wife a poor child that had scarcely attained the age of ten years. The master of posts and wintering partners of the Companies deemed this criminal indulgence to the vices of their servants necessary to stimulate them to exertion for the interest of their respective concerns. Another practice may also be noticed, as showing the state of moral feeling on these subjects amongst the white residents of the fur countries. It was

1 A singular change takes place in the physical constitution of the Indian females who become inmates of a fort; namely, they bear children more frequently and longer, but, at the same time, are rendered liable to indurations of the mammae and prolapsus of the uterus; evils from which they are, in a great measure, exempt whilst they lead a wandering and laborious life.

not very uncommon, amongst the Canadian voyages, for one woman to be common to, and maintained at the joint expense of, two men; nor for a voyager to sell his wife, either for a season or altogether, for a sum of money, proportioned to her beauty and good qualities, but always inferior to the price of a team of dogs.

The country around Cumberland House is flat and swampy, and is much intersected by small lakes. Limestone is found everywhere under a thin stratum of soil, and it not unfrequently shows itself above the surface. It lies in strata generally horizontal, but in one spot near the fort, dipping to the northward at an angle of 40°. Some portions of this rock contain very perfect shells. With respect to the vegetable productions of the district the *populus trepida*, or aspen, which thrives in moist situations, is perhaps the most abundant tree on the banks of the Saskatchawan, and is much prized as firewood, burning well when cut green. The *populus balsamifera*, or taccamahac, called by the Crees *matheh meteos*, or ugly poplar, in allusion to its rough bark and naked stem, crowned in an aged state with a few distorted branches, is scarcely less plentiful. It is an inferior firewood, and does not burn well, unless when cut in the spring and dried during the summer; but it affords a great quantity of potash. A decoction of its resinous buds has been sometimes used by the Indians with success in cases of *snow-blindness*, but its application to the inflamed eye produces much pain. Of pines, the white spruce is the most common here: the red and black spruce, the balsam of Gilead fir, and Banksian pine, also occur frequently. The larch is found only in swampy spots, and is stunted and unhealthy. The canoe birch attains a considerable size in this latitude, but from the great demand for its wood to make sledges, it has become rare. The alder abounds on the margin of the little grassy lakes, so common in the neighbourhood. A decoction of its inner bark is used as an emetic by the Indians, who also extract from it a yellow dye. A great variety of willows occur on the banks of the streams; and the hazel is met with sparingly in the woods. The sugar maple, elm, ash, and the *arbor vitoe*,[1] termed by the Canadian voyagers *cedar*, grow on various parts of the Saskatchawan; but that river seems to form their northern boundary. Two kinds of prunus also grow here, one of which,[2] a handsome small tree, produces a black fruit, having a very astringent taste, whence the term *choke-cherry* applied to it. The Crees call it *tawquoy-meena*, and esteemed it to be, when dried and bruised, a good addition to pemmican. The other species[3] is a less elegant shrub, but is said to bear a bright red cherry of a pleasant sweet taste. Its Cree name is *passe-awey-meenan*, and it is known to occur as far north as Great Slave Lake.

The most esteemed fruit of the country, however, is the produce of the *aronia ovalis*. Under the name of *meesass-cootoomeena* it is a favourite dish at most of the Indian feasts, and mixed with pemmican it renders that greasy food actually palatable. A great variety of currants and gooseberries are also mentioned by the natives, under the name of *sappoom-meena*, but we only found three species in the neighbourhood of Cumberland House. The strawberry, called by the Crees *otei-meena*, or heart-berry, is found in abundance, and rasps are common on the sandy banks of the rivers. The fruits hitherto mentioned fall in the autumn, but the following berries remained hanging on the bushes in the spring, and are considered as much mellowed by exposure to the colds in winter. The red whortleberry (*vaccinium vitis idea*) is found everywhere, but is most abundant in rocky places. It is aptly termed by the Crees *weesawgum-meena*, sour berry. The common cranberry (*oxycocccos palustris*) is distinguished from the preceding by its growing on moist sphagnous spots, and is hence called *maskoego-meena*, swamp-berry. The American guelder rose, whose fruit so strongly resembles the cranberry,

1 Thuya occidentalis.
2 Prunus Virginiana.
3 Prunus Pensylvanica.

is also common. There are two kinds of it (*virbunum oxycocoos*, and *edule*), one termed by the natives *peepon-meena*, winter-berry, and the other *mongsoa-meena*, moose-berry. There is also a berry of a bluish white colour, the produce of the white cornel tree, which is named *musqua-meena*, bear-berry, because these animals are said to fatten on it. The dwarf Canadian cornel bears a corymb of red berries, which are highly ornamental to the woods throughout the country, but are not otherwise worthy of notice, for they have an insipid farinaceous taste, and are seldom gathered.

The Crees extract some beautiful colours from several of their native vegetables. They dye their porcupine quills a beautiful scarlet with the roots of two species of bed-straw (galium tinctorium and boreale), which they indiscriminately term *sawoyan*. The roots, after being carefully washed are boiled gently in a clean copper kettle, and a quantity of the juice of the moose-berry, strawberry, cranberry, or arctic raspberry, is added together with a few red tufts of pistils of the larch. The porcupine quills are plunged into the liquor before it becomes quite cold, and are soon tinged of a beautiful scarlet. The process sometimes fails, and produces only a dirty brown, a circumstance which ought probably to be ascribed to the use of an undue quantity of acid. They dye black with an ink made of elder bark, and a little bog-iron-ore, dried and pounded, and they have various modes of producing yellow. The deepest colour is obtained from the dried root of a plant which, from their description, appears to be cowbane (*cicuta virosa*). An inferior colour is obtained from the bruised buds of the Dutch myrtle, and they have discovered methods of dyeing with various lichens.

The quadrupeds that are hunted for food in this part of the country are the moose and the reindeer, the former termed by the Crees *mongsoa*, or *moosoa*, the latter *attekh*. The buffalo or bison (*moostoosh*), the red-deer or American stag (*wawaskeeshoo*), the *apeesee-mongsoos*, or jumping deer, the *kinwaithoos*, or long-tailed deer, and the *apistat-choekoos*, a species of antelope; animals that frequent the plains above the forks of the Saskatchawan are not found in the neighbourhood of Cumberland House.

Of fur-bearing animals, various kinds of foxes (*makkee-shewuc*), are found in the district, distinguished by the traders under the names of *black, silver, cross, red*, and *blue* foxes. The two former are considered by the Indians to be the same kind, varying accidentally in the colour of the pelt. The black foxes are very rare, and fetch a high price. The cross and red foxes differ from each other only in colour, being of the same shape and size. Their shades of colour are not disposed in any determinate manner, some individuals approaching in that respect very nearly to the silver fox, others exhibiting ever link of the chain down to a nearly uniform deep or orange-yellow, the distinguishing colour of a pure red fox. It is reported both by Indians and traders that all the varieties have been found in the same litter. The blue fox is seldom seen here, and is supposed to come from the southward. The gray wolf (*mahaygan*) is common here. In the month of March the females frequently entice the domestic dog from the forts, although at other seasons a strong antipathy seemed to subsist between them. Some black wolves are occasionally seen. The black and red varieties of the American bear (*musquah*) are also found near Cumberland House, though not frequently; a black bear often has red cubs, and *vice versâ*. The grizzly bear, so much dreaded by the Indians for its strength and ferocity, inhabits a track of country nearer the Rocky Mountains. It is extraordinary that although I made inquiries extensively amongst the Indians, I met with but one who said that he had killed a she-bear with young in the womb.

The wolverene, in Cree *okeekoohawgees*, or *ommeethatsees*, is an animal of great strength and cunning, and is much hated by the hunters on account of the mischief it does to their marten-traps. The Canadian lynx (*peeshew*) is a timid but well-armed animal, which preys upon the American hare. Its fur is esteemed. The marten (*wapeestan*) is one of the most common furred animals in the country. The fisher, notwithstanding its name, is an inhabitant of the land, living with the common marten principally on mice. It is the *otchoek* of the Crees, and the *pekan* of the Canadians. The mink (*atjackash*) has been often confounded by writers with the fisher. It is a much smaller animal, inhabits the banks of rivers, and swims well; its prey is fish. The otter (*neekeek*) is larger than the English species, and produces a much more valuable fur.

The musk-rat (*watsuss*, or *musquash*) is very abundant in all the small grassy lakes. They build small conical houses with a mixture of hay and earth; those which build early raising their houses on the mud of the marshes, and those which build later in the season founding their habitations upon the surface of the ice itself. The house covers a hole in the ice, which permits them to go into the water in search of the roots on which they feed. In severe winters when the small lakes are frozen to the bottom, and these animals cannot procure their usual food, they prey upon each other. In this way great numbers are destroyed.

The beaver (*ammisk*) furnish the staple fur of the country. Many surprising stories have been told of the sagacity with which this animal suits the form of its habitation, retreats, and dam, to local circumstances; and I compared the account of its manners, given by Cuvier, in his *Régne Animal*, with the reports of the Indians, and found them to agree exactly. They have been often seen in the act of constructing their houses in the moonlight nights, and the observers agree that the stones, wood, or other materials are carried in their teeth, and generally leaning against the shoulder. When they have placed it to their mind, they turn round and give it a smart blow with their flat tail. In the act of diving they give a similar stroke to the surface of the water. They keep their provision of wood under water in front of the house. Their favourite food is the bark of the aspen, birch and willow; they also eat the alder, but seldom touch any of the pine tribe unless from necessity; they are fond of the large roots of the *nuphar lutea*, and grow fat upon it, but it gives their flesh a strong rancid taste. In the season of love their call resembles a groan, that of the male being the hoarsest, but the voice of the young is exactly like the cry of a child. They are very playful, as the following anecdote will show:- One day a gentleman, long resident in this country, espied five young beavers sporting in the water, leaping upon the trunk of a tree, pushing one another off, and playing a thousand interesting tricks. He approached softly under cover of the bushes, and prepared to fire on the unsuspecting creatures, but a nearer approach discovered to him such a similitude betwixt their gestures and the infantile caresses of his own children, that he threw aside his gun. This gentleman's feelings are to be envied, but few traders in fur would have acted so feelingly. The musk-rat frequently inhabits the same lodge with the beaver, and the otter also thrusts himself in occasionally; the latter, however, it not always a civil guest, as he sometimes devours his host.

These are the animals most interesting in an economical point of view. The American hare, and several kinds of grouse and ptarmigan, also contribute towards the support of the natives; and the geese, in their periodical flights in the spring and autumn, likewise prove a valuable resource both to the Indians and white residents; but the principal article of food, after the moose-deer, is fish; indeed, it forms almost the sole support of the traders at some of the posts. The most esteemed fish is the Coregonus albus, the *attihhawmeg* of the Crees, and the *white-fish* of the Americans. Its usual weight is between three and four pounds, but it has been known to reach sixteen or eighteen pounds. Three fish of the ordinary size is the daily allowance to each man at the fort, and is considered as equivalent to two geese or eight pounds of solid moose-meat. The fishery for the attihhawmeg lasts the whole year, but is most productive in the spawning season, from the middle of September to the middle of October. The *ottonneebees* (Coregonus Artedi) closely resembles the last. Three species of carp (Catastomus Hudsonius, C. Forsterianus, and C. Lesuerii), are also found abundantly in all the lakes, their Cree names are *namaypeeth, meethquaw-maypeeth*, and *wapawhawkeeshew*. The *occow*, or river perch, termed also horn-fish, piccarel, or doré, is common, but is not so much esteemed as the attihhawmeg. It attains the length of twenty inches in these lakes. The methy is another common fish; it is the *gadus lota*, or burbot, of Europe. Its length is about two feet, its gullet is capacious, and it preys upon fish large enough to distend its body to nearly twice its proper size. It is never eaten, not even by the dogs unless through necessity, but its liver and roe are considered as delicacies.

The pike is also plentiful, and being readily caught in the winter-time with the hook, is so much prized on that account by the natives as to receive from them the name of *eithinyoo-cannooshoeoo*, or Indian fish. The common trout, or *nammoecous*, grows here to an enormous size, being caught in particular lakes, weighing upwards of sixty pounds; thirty pounds is no uncommon size at Beaver Lake, from whence Cumberland House is supplied. The Hioden clodalis, *oweepeetcheesees*, or gold-eye is a beautiful small fish, which resembles the trout in its habits.

One of the largest fish is the *mathemegh*, cat-fish, or *barbue*. It belongs to the genus *silurus*. It is rare but is highly prized as food.

The sturgeon (Accipenser ruthenus) is also taken in the Saskatchawan and lakes communicating with it, and furnishes an excellent, but rather rich, article of food.

CHAPTER IV

Leave Cumberland House – Mode of Travelling in Winter –
Arrival at Carlton House – Stone Indians – Visit to a Buffalo
Pound – Goitres – Departure from Carlton House – Isle à la
Crosse – Arrival at Fort Chipewyan.

January 18, 1820

This day we set out from Cumberland House; but previously to detailing the events of the journey, it may be proper to describe the necessary equipments of a winter traveller in this region, which I cannot do better than by extracting the following brief, but accurate account of it from Mr. Hood's journal:-

'A snow-shoe is made of two light bars of wood, fastened together at their extremities, and projected into curves by transverse bars. The side bars have been so shaped by a frame, and dried before a fire, that the front part of the shoe turns up, like the prow of a boat, and the part behind terminates in an acute angle; the spaces between the bars are filled up with a fine netting of leathern thongs, except that part behind the main bar, which is occupied by the feet; the netting is there close and strong, and the foot is attached to the main bar by straps passing round the heel but only fixing the toes, so that the heel rises after each step, and the tail of the shoe is dragged on the snow. Between the main bar and another in front of it, a small space is left, permitting the toes to descend a little in the act of raising the heel to make the step forward, which prevents their extremities from chafing. The length of a snow-shoe is from four to six feet and the breadth one foot and a half, or one and three-quarters, being adapted to the size of the wearer. The motion of walking in them is perfectly natural, for one shoe is level with the snow, when the edge of the other is passing over it. It is not easy to use them among bushes, without frequent overthrows, nor to rise afterwards without help. Each shoe weighs about two pounds when unclogged with snow. The northern Indian snow-shoes differ a little from those of the southern Indians, having a greater curvature on the outside of each shoe; one advantage of which is, that when the foot rises the over-balanced side descends and throws off the snow. All the superiority of European art has been unable to improve the native contrivance of this useful machine.

'Sledges are made of two or three flat boards, curving upwards in front, and fastened together by transverse pieces of wood above. They are so thin that, if heavily laden, they bend with the inequalities of the surface over which they pass. The ordinary dog-sledges are eight or ten feet long and very narrow, but the lading is secured to a lacing round the edges. The cariole used by the traders is merely a covering of leather for the lower part of the body, affixed to the common sledge, which is painted and ornamented according to the taste of the proprietor. Besides snow-shoes, each individual carries his blanket, hatchet, steel, flint, and tinder, and generally firearms.'

The general dress of the winter traveller is a *capot*, having a hood to put up under the fur cap in windy weather, or in the woods, to keep the snow from his neck; leathern trowsers and Indian stockings which are closed at the ankles, round the upper part of his *mocassins*, or Indian shoes, to prevent the snow from getting into them. Over these he wears a blanket, or leathern coat, which is secured by a belt round his waist, to which his fire-bag, knife, and hatchet are suspended.

Mr. Back and I were accompanied by the seaman, John Hepburn; we were provided with two carioles and two sledges; their drivers and dogs being furnished in equal proportions by the two Companies. Fifteen days' provision so completely filled the sledges, that it was with difficulty we found room for a small sextant, one suit of clothes, and three changes of linen, together with our bedding. Notwithstanding we thus restricted ourselves, and even loaded the carioles with part of the luggage, instead of embarking in them ourselves, we did not set out without considerable grumbling from the voyagers of both Companies, respecting the overlading of their dogs. However, we left the matter to be settled by our friends at the fort, who were more conversant with winter travelling than ourselves. Indeed the loads appeared to us so great that we should have been inclined to listen to the complaints of the drivers. The weight usually placed upon a sledge, drawn by three dogs, cannot, at the commencement of a journey, be estimated at less than three hundred pounds, which, however, suffers a daily diminution from the consumption of provisions. The sledge itself weighs about thirty pounds. When the snow is hard frozen, or the track well trodden, the rate of travelling is about two miles and a half an hour, including rests, or about fifteen miles a day. If the snow be loose the speed is necessarily much less and the fatigue greater.

At eight in the morning of the 18th, we quitted the fort, and took leave of our hospitable friend, Governor Williams, whose kindness and attention I shall ever remember with gratitude. Dr. Richardson, Mr. Hood, and Mr. Connolly, accompanied us along the Saskatchawan until the snow became too deep for their walking without snow-shoes. We then parted from our associates, with sincere regret at the prospect of a long separation. Being accompanied by Mr. Mackenzie, of the Hudson's Bay Company, who was going to Isle à la Cross, with four sledges under his charge, we formed quite a procession, keeping in an Indian file, on the track of the man who preceded the foremost dogs; but, as the snow was deep, we proceeded slowly on the surface of the river, which is about three hundred and fifty yards wide, for the distance of six miles, which we went this day. Its alluvial banks and islands are clothed with willows. At the place of our encampment we could scarcely find sufficient pine branches to floor 'the hut,' as the Orkney men term the place where travellers rest. Its preparation, however, consists only in clearing away the snow to the ground, and covering that space with pine branches, over which the party spread their blankets and coats, and sleep in warmth and comfort, by keeping a good fire at their feet, without any other canopy than the heaven, even though the thermometer should be far below zero.

The arrival at the place of encampment gives immediate occupation to every one of the party; and it is not until the sleeping-place has been arranged, and a sufficiency of wood collected as fuel for the night, that the fire is allowed to be kindled. The dogs alone remain inactive during this busy scene, being kept harnessed to their burdens until the men have leisure to unstow the sledges, and hang upon the trees every species of provision out of their reach. We had ample experience, before morning, of the necessity of this precaution, as they contrived to steal a considerable part of our stores, almost from underneath Hepburn's head, notwithstanding their having been well fed at supper.

This evening we found the mercury of our thermometer had sunk into the bulb, and was frozen. It rose again into the tube on being held to the fire, but quickly re-descended into the bulb on being removed into the air; we could not, therefore, ascertain by it the temperature of the atmosphere, either then or during our journey. The weather was perfectly clear.

January 19

We rose this morning after the enjoyment of a sound and comfortable repose, and recommenced our journey at sunrise, but made slow progress through the deep snow. The task of beating the track for the dogs was so very fatiguing, that each of the men took the lead in turn, for an hour and a half. The scenery of the banks of the river improved as we advanced today; some firs and poplars were intermixed with the willows. We passed through two creeks, formed by islands, and encamped on a pleasant spot on the north shore, having only made six miles and three-quarters actual distance.

The next day we pursued our course along the river; the dogs had the greatest difficulty in dragging their heavy burdens through the snow. We halted to refresh them at the foot of Sturgeon River, and obtained the latitude 53° 51′ 41″ N. This is a small stream, which issues from a neighbouring lake. We encamped near to Musquito Point, having walked nine miles. The termination of the day's journey was a great relief to me, who had been suffering during the greater part of it, in consequence of my feet having been galled by the snow-shoes; this, however, is an evil which few escape on their initiation to winter travelling. It excites no pity from the more experienced companions of the journey, who travel on as fast as they can, regardless of your pain.

Mr. Isbester, and an Orkney man, joined us from Cumberland House, and brought some pemmican that we had left behind; a supply which was very seasonable after our recent loss. The general occupation of Mr. Isbester during the winter, is to follow or find out the Indians, and collect their furs, and his present journey will appear adventurous to persons accustomed to the certainty of travelling on a well-known road. He was going in search of a band of Indians, of whom no information had been received since last October, and his only guide for finding them was their promise to hunt in a certain quarter; but he looked at the jaunt with indifference, and calculated on meeting them in six or seven days, for which time only he had provision. Few persons in this country suffer more from want of food than those occasionally do who are employed on this service. They are furnished with a sufficiency of provision to serve until they reach the part where the Indians are expected to be; but it frequently occurs that, on their arrival at the spot, they have gone elsewhere, and that a recent fall of snow has hidden their track, in which case the voyagers have to wander about in search of them; and it often happens, when they succeed in finding the Indians, that they are unprovided with meat. Mr. Isbester had been placed in this distressing situation only a few weeks ago, and passed four days without either himself or his dogs tasting food. At length, when he had determined on killing one of the dogs to satisfy his hunger, he happily met with a beaten track, which led him to some Indian lodges, where he obtained food.

The morning of the 21st was cold, but pleasant for travelling. We left Mr. Isbester and his companion, and crossed the peninsula of Musquito Point, to avoid a detour of several miles which the river makes. Though we put up at an early hour, we gained eleven miles this day. Our encampment was at the lower extremity of

Tobin's Falls. The snow being less deep on the rough ice which enclosed this rapid, we proceeded, on the 22nd, at a quicker pace than usual, but at the expense of great suffering to Mr. Back, myself, and Hepburn, whose feet were much galled. After passing Tobin's Falls, the river expands to the breadth of five hundred yards, and its banks are well wooded with pines, poplars, birch, and willow. Many tracks of moose-deer and wolves were observed near the encampment.

On the 23rd the sky was generally overcast, and there were several snow showers. We saw two wolves and some foxes cross the river in the course of the day, and passed many tracks of the moose and red-deer. Soon after we had encamped the snow fell heavily, which was an advantage to us after we had retired to rest, by its affording an additional covering to our blankets. The next morning, at breakfast time, two men arrived from Carlton on their way to Cumberland. Having the benefit of their track, we were enabled, to our great joy, to march at a quick pace without snow-shoes. My only regret was, that the party proceeded too fast to allow of Mr. Back's halting occasionally, to note the bearings of the points, and delineate the course of the river,[1] without being left behind. As the provisions were getting short, I could not therefore, with propriety, check the progress of the party; and, indeed, it appeared to me less necessary, as I understood the river had been carefully surveyed. In the afternoon, we had to resume the incumbrance of the snow-shoes, and to pass over a rugged part where the ice had been piled over a collection of stones. The tracks of animals were very abundant on the river, particularly near the remains of an old establishment, called the Lower Nippéween.

So much snow had fallen on the night of the 24th, that the track we intended to follow was completely covered, and our march today was very fatiguing. We passed the remains of two red-deer, lying at the bases of perpendicular cliffs, from the summits of which they had, probably, been forced by the wolves. These voracious animals who are inferior in speed to the moose or red-deer are said frequently to have recourse to this expedient in places where extensive plains are bounded by precipitous cliffs. Whilst the deer are quietly grazing, the wolves assemble in great numbers, and, forming a crescent, creep slowly towards the herd so as not to alarm them much at first, but when they perceive that they have fairly hemmed in the unsuspecting creatures, and cut off their retreat across the plain, they move more quickly and with hideous yells terrify their prey and urge them to flight by the only open way, which is that towards the precipice; appearing to know that when the herd is once at full speed, it is easily driven over the cliff, the rearmost urging on those that are before. The wolves then descend at their leisure, and feast on the mangled carcasses. One of these animals passed close to the person who was beating the track, but did not offer any violence. We encamped at sunset, after walking thirteen miles.

On the 26th, we were rejoiced at passing the half-way point, between Cumberland and Carlton. The scenery of the river is less pleasing beyond this point, as there is a scarcity of wood. One of our men was despatched after a red-deer that appeared on the bank. He contrived to approach near enough to fire twice, though without success, before the animal moved away. After a fatiguing march of seventeen miles we put up at the Upper Nippé-ween, a deserted establishment; and performed the comfortable operations of shaving and washing for the first time since our departure from Cumberland, the weather having been hitherto too severe. We passed an uncomfortable and sleepless night, and agreed next morning to encamp in future in the open air, as preferable to the imperfect shelter of a deserted house without doors or windows.

1 This was afterwards done by Dr. Richardson during a voyage to Carlton in the spring.

The morning was extremely cold, but fortunately the wind was light, which prevented our feeling it severely; experience indeed had taught us that the sensation of cold depends less upon the state of temperature, than the force of the wind. An attempt was made to obtain the latitude, which failed, in consequence of the screw, that adjusts the telescope of the sextant, being immovably fixed, from the moisture upon it having frozen. The instrument could not be replaced in its case before the ice was thawed by the fire in the evening.

In the course of the day we passed the confluence of the south branch of the Saskatchawan, which rises from the Rocky Mountains near the sources of the northern branch of the Missouri. At Coles Falls, which commence a short distance from the branch, we found the surface of the ice very uneven, and many spots of open water.

We passed the ruins of an establishment, which the traders had been compelled to abandon, in consequence of the intractable conduct and pilfering habits of the Assiné-boine or Stone Indians; and we learned that all the residents at a post on the south branch, had been cut off by the same tribe some years ago. We travelled twelve miles today. The wolves serenaded us through the night with a chorus of their agreeable howling, but none of them ventured near the encampment. But Mr. Back's repose was disturbed by a more serious evil: his buffalo robe caught fire, and the shoes on his feet, being contracted by the heat, gave him such pain, that he jumped up in the cold, and ran into the snow as the only means of obtaining relief.

On the 28th we had a strong and piercing wind from N.W. in our faces, and much snow-drift; we were compelled to walk as quick as we could, and to keep constantly rubbing the exposed parts of the skin, to prevent their being frozen, but some of the party suffered in spite of every precaution. We descried three red-deer on the banks of the river, and were about to send the best marksmen after them, when they espied the party, and ran away. A supply of meat would have been very seasonable, as the men's provision had become scanty, and the dogs were without food, except a little burnt leather. Owing to the scarcity of wood, we had to walk until a late hour, before a good spot for an encampment could be found, and had then attained only eleven miles. The night was miserably cold; our tea froze in the tin pots before we could drink it, and even a mixture of spirits and water became quite thick by congelation; yet, after we lay down to rest, we felt no inconvenience, and heeded not the wolves, though they were howling within view.

The 29th was also very cold, until the sun burst forth, when the travelling became pleasant. The banks of the river are very scantily supplied with wood through the part we passed today. A long track on the south shore, called Holms Plains, is destitute of anything like a tree, and the opposite bank has only stunted willows; but, after walking sixteen miles, we came to a spot better wooded, and encamped opposite to a remarkable place, called by the voyagers 'The Neck of Land.'

A short distance below our encampment, on the peninsula formed by the confluence of the Net-setting river with the Saskatchawan, there stands a representation of Kepoochikawn, which was formerly held in high veneration by the Indians, and is still looked upon with some respect. It is merely a large willow bush, having its tops bound into a bunch. Many offerings of value such as handsome dresses, hatchets, and kettles, used to be made to it, but of late its votaries have been less liberal. It was mentioned to us as a signal instance of its power, that a sacrilegious moose-deer having ventured to crop a few of its tender twigs was found dead at the distance of a few yards. The bush having now grown old and stunted is exempted from similar violations.

On the 30th we directed our course round The Neck of Land, which is well clothed with pines and firs; though the opposite or western bank is nearly destitute of wood. This contrast between the two banks continued until we reached the commencement of what our companions called the Barren Grounds, when both the banks were alike bare. Vast plains extend behind the southern bank, which afford excellent pasturage for the buffalo, and other grazing animals. In the evening we saw a herd of the former, but could not get near to them. After walking fifteen miles we encamped. The men's provision having been entirely expended last night, we shared our small stock with them. The poor dogs had been toiling some days on the most scanty fare; their rapacity, in consequence, was unbounded; they forced open a deal box, containing tea, &c., to get at a small piece of meat which had been incautiously placed in it.

As soon as daylight permitted, the party commenced their march in expectation of reaching Carlton House to breakfast, but we did not arrive before noon, although the track was good. We were received by Mr. Prudens, the gentleman in charge of the post, with that friendly attention which Governor Williams's circular was calculated to ensure at every station; and were soon afterwards regaled with a substantial dish of buffalo steaks, which would have been excellent under any circumstances, but were particularly relished by us, after our travelling fare of dried meat and pemmican, though eaten without either bread or vegetables. After this repast, we had the comfort of changing our travelling dresses, which had been worn for fourteen days; a gratification which can only be truly estimated by those who have been placed under similar circumstances. I was still in too great pain from swellings in the ankles to proceed to La Montée, the North-West Company's establishment, distant about three miles; but Mr. Hallet, the gentleman in charge, came the following morning, and I presented to him the circular from Mr. S. M'Gillivray. He had already been furnished, however, with a copy of it from Mr. Connolly, and was quite prepared to assist us in our advance to the Athabasca.

Mr. Back and I having been very desirous to see some of the Stone Indians, who reside on the plains in this vicinity, learned with regret that a large band of them had left the house on the preceding day; but our curiosity was amply gratified by the appearance of some individuals, on the following and every subsequent day during our stay.

The looks of these people would have prepossessed me in their favour, but for the assurances I had received from the gentlemen of the posts, of their gross and habitual treachery. Their countenances are affable and pleasing, their eyes large and expressive, nose aquiline, teeth white and regular, the forehead bold, the cheek-bones rather high. Their figure is usually good, above the middle size, with slender but well proportional limbs. Their colour is a light copper, and they have a profusion of every black hair, which hangs over the ears, and shades the face. Their dress, which I think extremely neat and convenient, consists of a vest and trowsers of leather fitted to the body; over these a buffalo robe is thrown gracefully. These dresses are in general cleaned with *white-mud*, a sort of marl, though some use *red-earth*, a kind of bog-iron-ore; but this colour neither looks so light, nor forms such an agreeable contrast as the white with the black hair of the robe. Their quiver hangs behind them, and in the hand is carried the bow, with an arrow always ready for attack or defence, and sometimes they have a gun; they also carry a bag containing materials for making a fire, some tobacco, the calumet or pipe, and whatever valuables they possess. This bag is neatly ornamented with porcupine quills. Thus equipped, the Stone Indian bears himself with an air of perfect independence.

The only articles of European commerce they require in exchange for the meat they furnish to the trading post, are tobacco, knives, ammunition, and spirits, and occasionally some beads, but more frequently buttons, which they string in their hair as ornaments. A successful hunter will probably have two or three dozen of them hanging at equal distances on locks of hair, from each side of the forehead. At the end of these locks, small coral bells are sometimes attached, which tinkle at every motion of the head, a noise which seems greatly to delight the wearer; sometimes strings of buttons are bound round the head like a tiara; and a bunch of feathers gracefully crowns the head.

The Stone Indians steal whatever they can, particularly horses; these animals they maintain are common property, sent by the Almighty for the general use of man, and therefore may be taken wherever met with; still they admit the right of the owners to watch them, and to prevent theft if possible. This avowed disposition on their part calls forth the strictest vigilance at the different posts; notwithstanding which the most daring attacks are often made with success, sometimes on parties of three or four, but oftener on individuals. About two years ago a band of them had the audacity to attempt to take away some horses which were grazing before the gate of the N.-W. Company's fort; and, after braving the fire from the few people then at the establishment through the whole day, and returning their shots occasionally, they actually succeeded in their enterprise. One man was killed on each side. They usually strip defenceless persons whom they meet of all their garments, but particularly of those which have buttons, and leave them to travel alone in that state, however severe the weather. If resistance be expected, they not unfrequently murder before they attempt to rob. The traders, when they travel, invariably keep some men on guard to prevent surprise, whilst the others sleep; and often practise the stratagem of lighting a fire at sunset, which they leave burning, and move on after dark to a more distant encampment – yet these precautions do not always baffle the depredators. Such is the description of men whom the traders of this river have constantly to guard against. It must require a long residence among them, and much experience of their manners, to overcome the apprehensions their hostility and threats are calculated to excite. Through fear of having their provisions and supplies entirely cut off, the traders are often obliged to overlook the grossest offences, even murder, though the delinquents present themselves with unblushing effrontery almost immediately after the fact, and perhaps boast of it. They do not, on detection, consider themselves under any obligation to deliver up what they have stolen without receiving an equivalent.

The Stone Indians keep in amity with their neighbours the Crees from motives of interest; and the two tribes unite in determined hostility against the nations dwelling to the westward, which are generally called Slave Indians – a term of reproach applied by the Crees to those tribes against whom they have waged successful wars. The Slave Indians are said greatly to resemble the Stone Indians, being equally desperate and daring in their acts of aggression and dishonesty towards the traders.

These parties go to war almost every summer, and sometimes muster three or four hundred horsemen on each side. Their leaders, in approaching the foe, exercise all the caution of the most skilful generals; and whenever either party considers that it has gained the best ground, or finds it can surprise the other, the attack is made. They advance at once to close quarters, and the slaughter is consequently great, though the battle may be short. The prisoners of either sex are seldom spared, but slain on the spot with wanton cruelty. The dead are scalped, and he is considered the bravest person who bears the greatest number of scalps from the field. These are afterwards attached to his war dress, and worn as proofs of his prowess. The victorious party, during a certain time, blacken their faces and every part of their dress in token of joy, and in that state they often come to the establishment, if near, to testify their delight by dancing and singing, bearing all the horrid insignia of war, to display their individual feats. When in mourning, they completely cover their dress and hair with white mud.

The Crees in the vicinity of Carlton House have the same cast of countenance as those about Cumberland, but are much superior to them in appearance, living in a more abundant country. These men are more docile, tractable, and industrious than the Stone Indians, and bring greater supplies of provision and furs to the posts. Their general mode of dress resembles that of the Stone Indians; but sometimes they wear cloth leggings, blankets, and other useful articles, when they can afford to purchase them. They also decorate their hair with buttons.

The Crees procure guns from the traders, and use them in preference to the bow and arrow; and from them the Stone Indians often get supplied, either by stealth, gaming, or traffic. Like the rest of their nation, these Crees are remarkably fond of spirits, and would make any sacrifice to obtain them. I regretted to find the demand for this pernicious article had greatly increased within the last few years. The following notice of these Indians is extracted from Dr. Richardson's Journal:–

'The Asseenaboine, termed by the Crees Asseeneepoy-tuck, or Stone Indians, are a tribe of Sioux, who speak a dialect of the Iroquois, one of the great divisions under which the American philologists have classed the known dialects of the aborigines of North America. The Stone Indians, or, as they name themselves, *Eascab*, originally entered this part of the country under the protection of the Crees, and in concert with them attacked and drove to the westward the former inhabitants of the banks of the Saskatchawan. They are still the allies of the Crees, but have now become more numerous than their former protectors. They exhibit all the bad qualities ascribed to the Mengwe or Iroquois, the stock whence they are sprung. Of their actual number I could obtain no precise information, but it is very great. The Crees who inhabit the plains, being fur hunters, are better known to the traders.

'They are divided into two distinct bands, the Ammiskwatcheéthinyoowuck or Beaver Hill Crees, who have about forty tents, and the Sacaweé-thinyoowuc, or Thick Wood Crees, who have thirty-five. The tents average nearly ten inmates each, which gives a population of seven hundred and fifty to the whole.

'The nations who were driven to the westward by the Eascab and Crees are termed, in general, by the latter, Yatcheé-thinyoowuc, which has been translated Slave Indians, but more properly signifies Strangers.

'They now inhabit the country around Fort Augustus, and towards the foot of the Rocky Mountains, and have increased in strength until they have become an object of terror to the Eascab themselves. They rear a great number of horses, make use of firearms, and are fond of European articles; in order to purchase which they hunt the beaver and other furred animals, but they depend principally on the buffalo for subsistence.

'They are divided into five nations:- First, the Pawäustic-eythin-yoowuc, or Fall Indians, so named from their former residence on the falls of the Saskatchawan. They are the Minetarres, with whom Captain Lewis's party had a conflict on their return from the Missouri. They have about four hundred and fifty or five hundred tents; their language is very guttural and difficult.

'Second, the Peganoo-eythinyoowuc Pegans, or Muddy River Indians, named in their own language Peganoé-koon, have four hundred tents.

1 'As the subjects may be
interesting to philologists, I
subjoin a few words of the
Blackfoot language:–

Peestãhkan,	tobacco.
Moohksee,	an awl.
Nappœ-oòhkee,	rum.
Cook keet,	give me.
Eeninee,	buffalo.
Pooxãpoot,	come here.
Kat oetsits,	none; I have none.
Keet stã kee,	a beaver.
Naum`,	a bow.
Stoo-an,	a knife.
Sassoopats,	ammunition.
Meenee,	beads.
Poommees,	fat.
Miss ta poot,	keep off.
Saw,	no.
Stwee,	cold; it is cold.
Pennãkomit,	a horse.
Ahseeu,	good.'

'Third, the Meethco-thinyoowuc, or Blood Indians, named by themselves Kainoè-koon, have three hundred tents.

'Fourth, the Cuskoeteh-waw-thésseetuck, or Blackfoot Indians, in their own language Saxoe-koe-koon, have three hundred and fifty tents.

'The last three nations, or tribes, the Pegans, Blood Indians, and Blackfeet speak the same language. It is pronounced in a slow and distinct tone, has much softness, and is easily acquired by their neighbours. I am assured by the best interpreters in the country that it bears no affinity to the Cree, Sioux, or Chipewyan languages.

'Lastly, the Sassees, or Circees, have one hundred and fifty tents; they speak the same language with their neighbours, the Snare Indians, who are a tribe of the extensive family of the Chipewyans.'[1]

On the 6th of February, we accompanied Mr. Prudens on a visit to a Cree encampment and a buffalo pound, about six miles from the house; we found seven tents pitched within a small cluster of pines, which adjoined the pound. The largest, which we entered, belonged to the chief, who was absent, but came in on learning our arrival. The old man (about sixty) welcomed us with a hearty shake of the hand, and the customary salutation of 'What cheer!' an expression which they have gained from the traders. As we had been expected, they had caused the tent to be neatly arranged, fresh grass was spread on the ground, buffalo robes were placed on the side opposite the door for us to sit on, and a kettle was on the fire to boil meat for us.

After a few minutes' conversation, an invitation was given to the chief and his hunters to smoke the calumet with us, as a token of our friendship: this was loudly announced through the camp, and ten men from the other tents immediately joined our party. On their entrance the women and children withdrew, their presence on such occasions being contrary to etiquette. The calumet having been prepared and lighted by Mr. Pruden's clerk, was presented to the chief, who performed the following ceremony before he commenced smoking:- He first pointed the stem to the south, then to the west, north, and east, and afterwards to the heavens, the earth and the fire, as an offering to the presiding spirits;- he took three whiffs only, and then passed the pipe to his next companion, who took the same number of whiffs, and so did each person as it went round. After the calumet had been replenished, the person who then commenced repeated only the latter part of the ceremony, pointing the stem to the heavens, the earth and the fire. Some spirits, mixed with water, were presented to the old man, who, before he drank, demanded a feather, which he dipped into the cup several times, and sprinkled the moisture on the ground, pronouncing each time a prayer. His first address to the Keetchee Manitou, or Great Spirit, was, that buffalo might be abundant everywhere, and that plenty might come into their pound. He next prayed, that the other animals might be numerous, and particularly those which were valuable for their furs, and then implored that the party present might escape the sickness which was at that time prevalent, and be blessed with constant health. Some other supplications followed, which we could not get interpreted without interrupting the whole proceeding; but at every close, the whole Indian party assented by exclaiming Aha; and when he had finished the old man drank a little and passed the cup round. After these ceremonies each person smoked at his leisure, and they engaged in a general conversation, which I regretted not understanding, as it seemed to be very humorous, exciting frequent bursts of laughter. The younger men, in particular, appeared to ridicule the abstinence of one of the party, who neither drank nor smoked. He bore their jeering with perfect composure, and assured them, as I was told, they would be better if they would follow his example. I was happy to learn from Mr. Prudens, but the most cheerful and contented of the tribe.

Four Stone Indians arrived at this time and were invited into the tent, but one only accepted the invitation and partook of the fare. When Mr. Prudens heard the others refuse, he gave immediate directions that our horses should be narrowly watched, as he suspected these fellows wished to carry them off. Having learned that these Crees considered Mr. Back and myself to be war chiefs, possessing great power, and that they expected we should make some address to them, I desired them to be kind to the traders, to be industrious in procuring them provision and furs, and to refrain from stealing their stores and horses; and I assured them, that if I heard of their continuing to behave kindly, I would mention their good conduct in the strongest terms to their Great Father across the sea, (by which appellation they designate the King,) whose favourable consideration they had been taught by the traders to value most highly.

They all promised to follow my advice, and assured me it was not they, but the Stone Indians, who robbed and annoyed the traders. The Stone Indian who was present, heard this accusation against his tribe quite unmoved, but he probably did not understand the whole of the communication. We left them to finish their rum, and went to look round the lodges, and examine the pound.

The greatest proportion of labour, in savage life, falls to the women; we now saw them employed in dressing skins, and conveying wood, water, and provision. As they have often to fetch the meat from some distance, they are assisted in this duty by their dogs, which are not harnessed in sledges, but carry their burthens in a manner peculiarly adapted to this level country. Two long poles are fastened by a collar to the dog's neck; their ends trail on the ground, and are kept at a proper distance by a hoop, which is lashed between them, immediately behind the dog's tail; the hoop is covered with network, upon which the load is placed.

The boys were amusing themselves by shooting arrows at a mark, and thus training to become hunters. The Stone Indians are so expert with the bow and arrow, that they can strike a very small object at a considerable distance, and will shoot with sufficient force to pierce through the body of a buffalo when near.

The buffalo pound was a fenced circular space of about a hundred yards in diameter; the entrance was banked up with snow, to a sufficient height to prevent the retreat of the animals that once have entered. For about a mile on each side of the road leading to the pound, stakes were driven into the ground at nearly equal distances of about twenty yards; these were intended to represent men, and to deter the animals from attempting to break out on either side. Within fifty or sixty yards from the pound, branches of trees were places between these stakes to screen the Indians, who lie down behind them to await the approach of the buffalo.

The principal dexterity in this species of chase is shown by the horsemen, who have to manoeuvre round the herd in the plains so as to urge them to enter the roadway, which is about a quarter of a mile broad. When this has been accomplished, they raise loud shouts, and, pressing close upon the animals, so terrify them that they rush heedlessly forward towards the snare. When they have advanced as far as the men who are lying in ambush, they also rise, and increase the consternation by violent shouting and firing guns. The affrighted beasts having no alternative, run directly to the pound, where they are quickly despatched, either with an arrow or gun.

There was a tree in the centre of the pound, on which the Indians had hung strips of buffalo flesh and pieces of cloth as tributary or grateful offerings to the Great Master of Life; and we were told that they occasionally place a man in the tree to sing to the presiding spirit as the buffaloes are advancing, who must keep his station until the whole that have entered are killed. This species of hunting is very similar to that of taking elephants on the Island of Ceylon, but upon a smaller scale.

The Crees complained to us of the audacity of a party of Stone Indians, who, two nights before, had stripped their revered tree of many of its offerings, and had injured their pound by setting their stakes out of the proper places.

Other modes of killing the buffalo are practised by the Indians with success; of these the hunting them on horseback requires most dexterity. An expert hunter, when well mounted, dashes at the herd, and chooses an individual which he endeavours to separate from the rest. If he succeeds, he contrives to keep him apart by the proper management of his horse, though going at full speed. Whenever he can get sufficiently near for a ball to penetrate the beast's hide, he fires, and seldom fails of bringing the animal down; though of course he cannot rest the piece against the shoulder, nor take a deliberate aim. On this service the hunter is often exposed to considerable danger, from the fall of his horse in the numerous holes which the badgers make in these plains, and also from the rage of the buffalo, which, when closely pressed, often turns suddenly, and, rushing furiously on the horse, frequently succeeds in wounding it, or dismounting the rider. Whenever the animal shows this disposition, which the experienced hunter will readily perceive, he immediately pulls up his horse, and goes off in another direction.

When the buffaloes are on their guard, horses cannot be used in approaching them; but the hunter dismounts at some distance, and crawls in the snow towards the herd, pushing his gun before him. If the buffaloes happen to look towards him, he stops, and keeps quite motionless, until their eyes are turned in another direction; by this cautious proceeding a skilful person will get so near as to be able to kill two or three out of the herd. It will easily be imagined this service cannot be very agreeable when the thermometer stands 30° or 40° below zero, as sometimes happens in this country.

As we were returning from the tents, the dogs that were harnessed to three sledges, in one of which Mr. Back was seated, set off in pursuit of a buffalo-calf. Mr. Back was speedily thrown from his vehicle, and had to join me in my horse-cariole. Mr. Heriot, having gone to recover the dogs, found them lying exhausted beside the calf, which they had baited until it was as exhausted as themselves. Mr. Heriot, to show us the mode of hunting on horseback, or, as the traders term it, running of the buffalo, went in chase of a cow, and killed it after firing three shots.

The buffalo is a huge and shapeless animal, quite devoid of grace or beauty; particularly awkward in running, but by no means slow; when put to his speed, he plunges through the deep snow very expeditiously; the hair is dark brown, very shaggy, curling about the head, neck, and hump, and almost covering the eye, particularly in the bull, which is larger and more unsightly than the cow. The most esteemed part of the animal is the hump, called by the Canadians *bos*, by the Hudson's Bay people the *wig*; it is merely a strong muscle, on which nature at certain seasons forms a considerable quantity of fat. It is attached to the long spinous processes of the first dorsal vertebrae, and seems to be destined to support the enormous head of the animal. The meat which covers the spinal processes themselves, after the wig is removed, is next in esteem for its flavour and juiciness, and is more exclusively termed the hump by the hunters.

The party was prevented from visiting a Stone Indian encampment by a heavy fall of snow, which made it impracticable to go and return the same day. We were dissuaded from sleeping at their tents by the interpreter at the N.W. post, who told us they considered the whooping-cough and measles, under which they were now suffering, to have been introduced by some white people recently arrived in the country, and that he feared those who had lost relatives, imagining we were the persons, might vent their revenge on us. We regretted to learn that these diseases had been so very destructive among the tribes along the Saskatchawan, as to have carried off about three hundred persons, Crees and Asseenaboiines, within the trading circle of these establishments. The interpreter also informed us of another bad trait peculiar to the Stone Indians. Though they receive a visitor kindly at their tents, and treat him very hospitably during his stay, yet it is very probable they will despatch some young men to waylay and rob him in going towards the post: indeed, all the traders assured us it was more necessary to be vigilantly on our guard on the occasion of a visit to them, than at any other time.

Carlton House, (which our observations place in latitude 52° 50′ 47″ N., longitude 106° 12′ 42″ W., variation 20° 44′ 47″ E.,) is pleasantly situated about a quarter of a mile from the river's side on the flat ground under the shelter of the high banks that bound the plains. The land is fertile, and produces, with little trouble, ample returns of wheat, barley, oats, and potatoes. The ground is prepared for the reception of these vegetables about the middle of April, and when Dr. Richardson visited this place on May 10th, the blade of wheat looked strong and healthy. There were only five acres in cultivation at the period of my visit. The prospect from the fort must be pretty in summer, owing to the luxuriant verdure of this fertile soil; but in the uniform and cheerless garb of winter, it has little to gratify the eye.

Beyond the steep bank behind the house, commences the vast plain, whose boundaries are but perfectly known; it extends along the south branch of the Saskatchawan, and towards the sources of the Missouri and Asseenaboine Rivers, being scarcely interrupted through the whole of this great space by hills, or even rising grounds. The excellent pasturage furnishes food in abundance, to a variety of grazing animals, of which the buffalo, red-deer, and a species of antelope, are the most important. Their presence naturally attracts great hordes of wolves, which are of two kinds, the large, and the small. Many bears prowl about the banks of this river in summer; of these the grizzly bear is the most ferocious, and is held in dread both by Indians and Europeans. The traveller, in crossing these plains, not only suffers from the want of food and water, but is also exposed to hazard from his horse stumbling in the numerous badger-holes. In many large districts, the only fuel is the dried dung of the buffalo; and when a thirsty traveller reaches a spring, he has not unfrequently the mortification to find the water salt.

Carlton House, and La Montée, are provision-posts, only an inconsiderable quantity of furs being obtained at either of them. The provisions are procured in the winter season from the Indians, in the form of dried meat and fat, and when converted by mixture into pemmican, furnish the principal support of the voyagers, in their passages to and from the depôts in summer. A considerable quantity of it is also kept for winter use, at most of the fur-posts, as the least bulky article can be taken to a winter journey. The mode of making pemmican is very simple, the meat is dried by the Indians in the sun, or over a fire, and pounded by beating it with stones when spread on a skin. In this state it is brought to the forts, where the admixture of hair is partially sifted out, and a third part of melted fat incorporated with it, partly by turning the two over with a wooden shovel, partly by kneading them together with the hands. The pemmican is then firmly pressed into leathern bags, each capable of containing eighty-five pounds, and being placed in an airy place to cool, is fit for use. It keeps in this state, if not allowed to get wet, very well for one year, and with great care it may be preserved good for two. Between three and four hundred bags were made here by each of the Companies this year.

There were eight men, besides Mr. Prudens and his clerk, belonging to Carlton House. At La Montée there were seventy Canadians and half-breeds, and sixty women and children, who consumed upwards of seven hundred pounds of buffalo meat daily, the allowance per diem for each man being eight pounds: a portion not so extravagant as may at first appear, when allowance is made for bone, and the entire want of farinaceous food or vegetables.

There are other provision post, Fort Augustus and Edmonton farther up the river, from whence some furs are also procured. The Stone Indians have threatened to cut off the supplies in going up to these establishments, to prevent their enemies from obtaining ammunition, and other European articles; but as these menaces have been frequently made without being put in execution, the traders now hear them without any great alarm, though they take every precaution to prevent being surprised. Mr. Back and I were present when an old Cree communicated to Mr. Prudens, that the Indians spoke of killing all the white people in that vicinity this year, which information he received with perfect composure, and was amused, as well as ourselves, with the man's judicious remark which immediately followed, 'A pretty state we shall then be in without the goods you bring us.'

The following remarks on a well-known disease are extracted from Dr. Richardson's Journal:–

'Bronchocele, or Goitre, is a common disorder at Edmonton. I examined several of the individuals afflicted with it, and endeavoured to obtain every information on the subject from the most authentic sources. The following facts may be depended upon. The disorder attacks those only who drink the water of the river. It is indeed in its worst state confined almost entirely to the half-breed women and children, who reside constantly at the fort, and make use of river water, drawn in the winter through a hole cut in the ice. The men, being often from home on journeys through the plain, when their drink is melted snow, are less affected; and, if any of them exhibit during the winter, some incipient symptoms of the complaint, the annual summer voyage to the sea-coast generally effects a cure. The natives who confine themselves to snow-water in the winter, and drink of the small rivulets which flow through the plains in the summer, are exempt from the attacks of this disease.

'These facts are curious, inasmuch as they militate against the generally received opinion that the disease is caused by drinking snow-water; an opinion which seems to have originated from bronchocele being endemial to sub-alpine districts.

'The Saskatchawan, at Edmonton, is clear in the winter, and also in the summer, except during the May and July floods. This distance from the Rocky Mountains (which I suppose to be of primitive formation), is upwards of one hundred and thirty miles. The neighbouring plains are alluvial, the soil is calcareous, and contains numerous travelled fragments of limestone. At a considerable distance below Edmonton, the river, continuing its course through the plains, becomes turbid, and acquires a white colour. In this state it is drunk by the inmates of Carlton House, where the disease is known only by name. It is said that the inhabitants of Rocky Mountain House, sixty miles nearer the source of the river, are more severely affected than those at Edmonton. The same disease occurs near the sources of the Elk and Peace Rivers; but, in those parts of the country which are distant from the Rocky Mountain Chain, it is unknown, although melted snow forms the only drink of the natives for nine months of the year.

'A residence of a single year at Edmonton is sufficient to render a family bronchocelous. Many of the goitres acquire great size. Burnt sponge has been tried, and found to remove the disease, but an exposure to the same cause immediately reproduces it.

'A great proportion of the children of women who have goitres are born idiots, with large heads, and the other distinguishing marks of *cretins*. I could not learn whether it was necessary that both parents should have goitres, to produce cretin children: indeed the want of chastity in the half-breed women would be a bar to the deduction of any inference on this head.'

February 8

Having recovered from the swellings and pains which our late march from Cumberland had occasioned, we prepared for the commencement of our journey to Isle à la Crosse, and requisitions were made on both the establishments for the means of conveyance, and the necessary supply of provisions for the party, which were readily furnished. On the 9th the carioles and sledges were loaded, and sent off after breakfast; but Mr. Back and I remained till the afternoon, as Mr. Prudens had offered that his horses should convey us to the encampment. At three P.M. we parted from our kind host, and in passing through the gate were honoured with a salute of musketry. After riding six miles, we joined the men at their encampment, which was made under the shelter of a few poplars. The dogs had been so much fatigued in wading through the very deep snow with their heavy burdens, having to drag upwards of ninety pounds' weight each, that they could get no farther. Soon after our arrival, the snow began to fall heavily, and it continued through the greater part of the night.

Our next day's march was therefore particularly tedious, the snow being deep, and the route lying across an unvarying level, destitute of wood, except one small cluster of willows. In the afternoon we reached the end of the plain, and came to an elevation, on which poplars, willows, and some pines grew, where we encamped; having travelled ten miles. We crossed three small lakes, two of fresh water and one of salt, near the latter of which we encamped, and were, in consequence, obliged to use for our tea, water made from snow, which has always a disagreeable taste.

We had scarcely ascended the hill on the following morning, when a large herd of red-deer was perceived grazing at a little distance; and though we were amply supplied with provision, our Canadian companions could not resist the temptation of endeavouring to add to our stock. A half-breed hunter was therefore sent after them. He succeeded in wounding one, but not so as to prevent its running off with the herd in a direction wide of our course. A couple of rabbits and brace of wood partridges were shot in the afternoon. There was an agreeable variety of hill and dale in the scenery we passed through today; and sufficient wood for ornament, but not enough to crowd the picture. The valleys were intersected by several small lakes and pools, whose snowy covering was happily contrasted with the dark green of the pine-trees which surrounded them. After ascending a moderately high hill by a winding path through a close wood, we opened suddenly upon Lake Iroquois, and had a full view of its picturesque shores. We crossed it and encamped.

Though the sky was cloudless, yet the weather was warm. We had the gratification of finding a beaten track soon after we started on the morning of the 12th, and were thus enabled to walk briskly. We crossed at least twenty hills, and found a small lake or pool at the foot of each. The destructive ravages of fire were visible during the greater part of the day. The only wood we saw for miles together consisted of pine-trees stript of their branches and bark by this element: in other parts poplars alone were growing, which we have remarked invariably to succeed the pine after a conflagration. We walked twenty miles today, but the direct distance was only sixteen.

The remains of an Indian hut were found in a deep glen, and close to it was placed a pile of wood, which our companions supposed to cover a deposit of provision. Our Canadian voyagers, induced by their insatiable desire of procuring food, proceeded to remove the upper pieces and examine its contents; when, to their surprise, they found the body of a female, clothed in leather, which appeared to have been recently placed there. Her former garments, the materials for making a fire, a fishing line, a hatchet, and a bark dish, were laid beside the corpse. The wood was carefully replaced. A small owl, perched on a tree near the spot, called forth many singular remarks from our companions as to its being a good or bad omen.

We walked the whole of the 13th over flat meadow-land, which is much restored to by the buffalo at all seasons. Some herds of them were seen, which our hunters were too unskilful to approach. In the afternoon we reached the Stinking Lake, which is nearly of an oval form. Its shores are very low and swampy, to which circumstances, and not to the bad quality of the waters, it owes its Indian name. Our observations place its western part in latitude 53° 25′ 24″ N., longitude 107° 18′ 58″ W., variation 20° 32′ 10″ E.

After a march of fifteen miles and a half, we encamped among a few pines, at the only spot where we saw sufficient wood for making our fire during the day. The next morning, about an hour after we had commenced our march, we came upon a beaten track and perceived recent marks of snow-shoes. In a short time an Iroquois joined us, who was residing with a party of Cree Indians, to secure the meat and furs they should collect for the North-West Company. He accompanied us as far as the stage on which his meat was placed, and then gave us a very pressing invitation to halt for the day and partake of his fare; which, as the hour was too early, we declined, much to the annoyance of our Canadian companions, who had been cherishing the prospect of indulging their amazing appetites at this well-furnished store, ever since the man had been with us. He gave them, however, a small supply previous to our parting. The route now crossed some ranges of hills on which fir, birch and poplar grew so thickly that we had much difficulty in getting the sledges through the narrow pathway between them. In the evening we descended from the elevated ground, crossed three swampy meadows, and encamped at their northern extremity within a cluster of large pine-trees, the branches of which were elegantly decorated with abundance of a greenish yellow lichen. Our march was ten miles. The weather was very mild, almost too warm for the exercise we were taking.

We had a strong gale from the N.W. during the night, which subsided as the morning opened. One of the sledges had been so much broken the day before in the woods that we had to divide its cargo among the others. We started after this had been arranged, and finding almost immediately a firm track, soon arrived at some Indian lodges to which it led. The inhabitants were Crees belonging to the posts on the Saskatchawan, from whence they had come to hunt beaver. We made but a short stay, and proceeded through a swamp to Pelican Lake. Our view to the right was bounded by a range of lofty hills, which extended for several miles in a north and south direction, which, it may be remarked, was that of all the hilly land we had passed since quitting the plain.

Pelican Lake is of an irregular form, about six miles from east to west, and eight from north to south; it decreases to the breadth of a mile towards the northern extremity, and is therefore terminated by a creek. We went up this creek for a short distance and then struck into the woods and encamped among a cluster of the firs, which the Canadians term cyprès (*pinus Banksiana*), having come fourteen miles and a half.

February 16

Shortly after commencing the journey today we met an Indian and his family, who had come from the houses at Green Lake; they informed us the track was well beaten the whole way. We therefore put forth out utmost speed in the hope of reaching them by night; but were disappointed, and had to halt at dark about twelve miles from them in a fishermans' hut, which was unoccupied. Frequent showers of snow fell during the day, and the atmosphere was thick and gloomy.

We started at an early hour the following morning and reached the Hudson's Bay Company's post to breakfast, and were received very kindly by Mr. MacFarlane, the gentleman in charge. The other establishment, situated on the opposite side of the river, was under the direction of Mr. Dugald Cameron, one of the partners of the North-West Company, on whom Mr. Back and I called soon after our arrival, and were honoured with a salute of musketry.

These establishments are small, but said to be well situated for procuring furs; as the numerous creeks in their vicinity are much resorted to by the beaver, otter and musquash. The residents usually obtain a superabundant supply of provision. This season, however, they barely had sufficient for their own support, owing to the epidemic which has incapacitated the Indians for hunting. The Green Lake lies nearly north and south, is eighteen miles in length, and does not exceed one mile and a half of breadth in any part. The water is deep, and it is in consequence one of the last lakes in the country that is frozen. Excellent tittameg and trout are caught in it from March to December, but after that time most of the fish remove to some larger lake.

We remained two days awaiting the return of some men who had been sent to the Indian lodges for meat, and who were to go on with us. Mr. Back and I did not need this rest, having completely surmounted the pain occasioned by the snow-shoes. We dined twice with Mr. Cameron and received from him many useful suggestions respecting our future operations. This gentleman, having informed us that provisions would, probably, be very scarce next spring in the Athabasca department, in consequence of the sickness of the Indians during the hunting season, undertook at my request to cause a supply of pemmican to be conveyed from the Saskatchawan to Isle à la Crosse for our use during the winter, and I wrote to apprise Dr. Richardson and Mr. Hood that they would find it at the latter post when they passed; and also to desire them to bring as much as the canoes would stow from Cumberland.

The atmosphere was clear and cold during our stay; observations were obtained at the Hudson's Bay Fort, lat. 54° 16′ 10″ N., long. 107° 29′ 52″ W., var. 22° 6′ 35″ E.

February 20

Having been equipped with carioles, sledges and provisions from the two posts, we this day recommenced our journey, and were much amused by the novelty of the salute given at our departure, the guns being principally fired by the women in the absence of the men. Our course was directed to the end of the lake, and for a short distance along a small river; we then crossed the woods to the Beaver River, which we found to be narrow and very serpentine, having moderately high banks. We encamped about one mile and a half farther up among poplars. The next day we proceeded along the river; it was winding and about two hundred yards broad. We passed the mouths of two rivers whose waters it receives; the latter one, we were informed, is a channel by which the Indians go to the Lesser Slave Lake. The banks of the river became higher as we advanced, and were adorned with pines, poplars and willows.

Though the weather was very cold we travelled more comfortably than at any preceding time since our departure from Cumberland, as we had light carioles, which enabled us to ride nearly the whole day warmly covered up with a buffalo robe. We were joined by Mr. M'Leod, of the North-West Company, who had kindly brought some things from Green Lake, which our sledges could not carry. Pursuing our route along the river we reached at an early hour the upper extremity of the 'Grand Rapid,' where the ice was so rough that the carioles and sledges had to be conveyed across a point of land. Soon after noon we left the river, including N.E., and directed our course N.W., until we reached Long Lake, and encamped at its northern extremity, having come twenty-three miles. This lake is about fourteen miles long, and from three-quarters to one mile and a half broad; its shores and islands low, but well wooded. There were frequent snow-showers during the day.

February 23

The night was very stormy, but the wind became more moderate in the morning. We passed today through several nameless lakes and swamps before we came to Train Lake, which received its name from being the place where the traders procured the birch to make their sledges, or traineaux; but this wood has been all used, and there only remains pines and a few poplars. We met some sledges laden with fish, kindly sent to meet us by Mr. Clark of the Hudson's Bay Company, on hearing of our approach. Towards the evening the weather became much more unpleasant, and we were exposed to a piercingly cold wind and much snowdrift in traversing the Isle à la Crosse Lake; we were, therefore, highly pleased at reaching the Hudson's Bay House by six P.M. We were received in the most friendly manner by MR. Clark and honoured by volleys of musketry. Similar marks of attention were shown to us on the following day by Mr. Bethune, the partner in charge of the North-West Company's fort. I found here the letters which I had addressed from Cumberland in November last to the partners of the North-West Company in the Athabaca, which circumstance convinced me of the necessity of our present journey.

These establishments are situated on the southern side of the lake and close to each other. They are forts of considerable importance, being placed at a point of communication with the English River, the Athabasca and Columbia Districts. The country around them is low and intersected with water, and was formerly much frequented by beavers and otters, which, however, have been so much hunted by the Indians that their number is greatly decreased. The Indians frequenting these forts are the Crees and some Chipewyans; they scarcely ever come except in the spring and autumn; in the former season to bring their winter's collection of furs, and in the latter to get the stores they require.

Three Chipewyan lads came in during our stay to report what furs the band to which they belonged had collected, and to desire they might be sent for; the Indians having declined bringing either furs or meat themselves since the opposition between the Companies commenced. Mr. Back drew the portrait of one of the boys.

Isle à la Crosse Lake receives its name from an island situated near the forts, on which the Indians formerly assembled annually to amuse themselves at the game of the Cross. It is justly celebrated for abundance of the finest tittameg, which weigh from five to fifteen pounds. The residents live principally upon this most delicious fish, which fortunately can be eaten a long time without disrelish. It is plentifully caught with nets throughout the year except for two or three months.

March 4

We witnessed the Aurora Borealis very brilliant for the second time since our departure from Cumberland. A winter encampment is not a favourable situation for viewing this phenomenon, as the trees in general hide the sky. Arrangements had been made for recommencing our journey today, but the wind was stormy, and the snow had drifted too much for travelling with comfort; we therefore stayed and dined with Mr. Bethune, who promised to render every assistance in getting pemmican conveyed to us from the Saskatchawan to be in readiness for our canoes when they might arrive in the spring; Mr. Clark also engaged to procure six bags for us, and to furnish our canoes with any other supplies which might be wanted and could be spared from his post, and to contribute his aid in forwarding the pemmican to the Athabasca, if our canoes could not carry it all.

I feel greatly indebted to this gentleman for much valuable information respecting the country and the Indians residing to the north of Slave Lake, and for furnishing me with a list of stores he supposed we should require. He had resided some years on Mackenzie's River, and had been once so far towards its mouth as to meet the Esquimaux in great numbers. But they assumed such a hostile attitude that he deemed it unadvisable to attempt opening any communication with them, and retreated as speedily as he could.

The observations we obtained here showed that the chronometers had varied their rates a little in consequence of the jolting of the carioles, but their errors and rates were ascertained previous to our departure. We observed the position of this fort to be latitude 55° 25′ 35″ N., longitude 107° 51′ 00″ W., by lunars reduced back from Fort Chipewyan, variation 22° 15′ 48″ W., dip 84° 13′ 35″.

March 5

We recommenced our journey this morning, having been supplied with the means of conveyance by both the Companies in equal proportions. Mr. Clark accompanied us with the intention of going as far as the boundary of his district. This gentleman was an experienced winter traveller, and we derived much benefit from his suggestions; he caused the men to arrange the encampment with more attention to comfort and shelter than our former companions had done. After marching eighteen miles we put up on Gravel Point in the Deep River.

At nine the next morning we came to the commencement of Clear Lake. We crossed its southern extremes and then went over a point of land to Buffalo Lake, and encamped after travelling twenty-six miles. After supper we were entertained till midnight with paddling songs by our Canadians, who required very little stimulus beyond their natural vivacity to afford us this diversion. The next morning we arrived at the establishments which are situated on the western side of the lake near a small stream, called the Beaver River. They were small log buildings, hastily erected last October for the convenience of the Indians who hunt in the vicinity. Mr. Macmurray, a partner in the N.-W. Company, having sent to Isle à la Crosse an invitation to Mr. Back and I, our carioles were driven to his post, and we experienced the kindest reception. These posts are frequented by only a few Indians, Crees, and Chipewyans. The country round is not sufficiently stocked with animals to afford support to many families, and the traders subsist almost entirely in fish caught in the autumn prior to the lake being frozen; but the water being shallow, they remove to a deeper part as soon as the lake is covered with ice. The Aurora Borealis was brilliantly displayed on both the nights we remained here, but particularly on the 7th, when its appearances were most diversified and the motion extremely rapid. Its coruscations occasionally concealed from sight stars of the first magnitude in passing over them, at other times these were faintly discerned through them; once I perceived a stream of light to illumine the under surface of some clouds as it passed along. There was no perceptible noise.

Mr. Macmurray gave a dance to his voyagers and the women; this is a treat which they expect on the arrival of any stranger at the post.

We were presented by this gentleman with the valuable skin of a black fox, which we had entrapped some days before our arrival; it was forwarded to England with other specimens.

Our observations place the North-West Company's House in latitude 55° 53′ 00″ N., longitude 108° 51′ 10″ W., variation 22° 33′ 22″ E.

The shores of Buffalo Lake are of moderate height, and well wooded, but immediately beyond the bank the country is very swampy and intersected with water in every direction. At some distance from the western side there is a conspicuous hill, which we hailed with much pleasure as being the first interruption to the tediously uniform scene we had for some time passed through.

On the 10th we recommenced our journey after breakfast and travelled quickly, as we had the advantage of a well-beaten track. At the end of eighteen miles we entered upon the river 'Loche,' which has a serpentine course, and is confined between alluvial banks that support stunted willows and a few pines; we encamped about three miles farther on; and in the course of the next day's march perceived several holes on the ice, and many unsafe places for the sledges. Our companions said the ice of this river is always in the same insecure state, even during the most severe winter, we crossed a portage and came upon the Methye Lake, and soon afterwards arrived at the trading posts on its western side. These were perfect huts which had been hastily built after the commencement of the last winter. We here saw two hunters who were Chipewyan, half-breeds, and made many inquiries of them respecting the countries we expected to visit, but we found them quite ignorant of every part beyond the Athabasca Lake. They spoke of Mr. Hearne and of his companion Matonnabee, but did not add to our stock of information respecting that journey. It had happened before their birth, but they remembered the expedition of Sir Alexander Mackenzie towards the sea.

This is a picturesque lake about ten miles long and six broad, and receives its name from a species of fish caught in it, but not much esteemed; the residents never eat any part but the liver except through necessity, the dogs dislike even that. The tittameg and trout are also caught in the fall of the year. The position of the houses by our observations is latitude 56° 24′ 20″ N., longitude 109° 23′ 06″ W., variation 22° 50′ 28″ E.

On the 13th we renewed our journey and parted from Mr. Clark, to whom we were much obliged for his hospitality and kindness. We soon reached the Methye Portage, and had a very pleasant ride across it in our carioles. The track was good and led through groups of pines, so happily placed that it would not have required a great stretch of imagination to fancy ourselves in a well-arranged park. We had now to cross a small lake, and then gradually ascend hills beyond it, until we arrived at the summit of a lofty chain of mountains commanding the most picturesque and romantic prospect we had yet seen in this country. Two ranges of high hills run parallel to each other for several miles, until the faint blue haze hides their particular characters, when they slightly change their course and are lost to the view. The space between them is occupied by nearly a level plain through which a river pursues a meandering course, and receives supplies from the creeks and rills issuing from the mountains on each side. The prospect was delightful even amid the snow, and though marked with all the cheerless characters of winter; how much more charming must it be when the trees are in leaf and the ground is arrayed in summer verdure! Some faint idea of the difference was conveyed to my mind by witnessing the effect of the departing rays of a brilliant sun. The distant prospect, however, is surpassed in grandeur by the wild scenery which appeared immediately below our feet. There the eye penetrates into vast ravines two or three hundred feet in depth, that are clothed with trees and lie on either side of the narrow pathway descending to the river over eight successive ridges of hills. At one spot termed the Cockscomb the traveller stands insulated as it were on a small slip, where a false step might precipitate him into the glen. From this place Mr. Back took an interesting and accurate sketch, to allow time for which we encamped early, having come twenty-one miles.

The Methye Portage is about twelve miles in extent, and over this space the canoes and all their cargoes are carried, both in going to and from the Athabasca department. It is part of the range mountains which separates the waters flowing south from those flowing north. According to Sir Alexander Mackenzie, 'this range of hills continues in a S.W. direction until its local height is lost between the Saskatchawan and Elk Rivers, close on the banks of the former, in latitude 53° 36′ N., longitude 113° 45′ W., when it appears to take its course due north.' Observations, taken in the spring by Mr. Hood, place the northside of the portage in latitude 56° 41′ 40″ N., longitude 109° 52′ 15″ W., variation 25° 2′ 30″ E., dip 85° 7′ 27″.

At daylight on the 14th we began to descend the range of hills leading towards the river, and no small care was required to prevent the sledges from being broken in going down these almost perpendicular heights, or being precipitated into the glens on each side. As a precautionary measure the dogs were taken off and the sledges guided by the men, notwithstanding which they descended with amazing rapidity, and the men were thrown into the most ridiculous attitudes in endeavouring to stop them. When we had arrived at the bottom I could not but feel astonished at the laborious task which the voyagers have twice in the year to encounter at this place in conveying their stores backwards and forwards. We went across the Clear Water River, which runs at the bases of these hills, and followed an Indian track along its northern bank, by which we avoided the White Mud and Good Portages. We afterwards followed the river as far as the Pine Portage, when we passed through a very romantic defile of rocks, which presented the appearance of Gothic ruins, and their rude characters were happily contrasted with the softness of the snow and the darker foliage of the pines which crowned their summits. We next crossed the Cascade Portage, which is the last on the way to the Athabasca Lake, and soon afterwards came to some Indian tents, containing five families belonging to the Chipewyan tribe. We smoked the calumet in the chief's tent, whose name was the Thumb, and distributed some tobacco and a weak mixture of spirits and water among the men. They received this civility with much less grace than the Crees, and seemed to consider it a matter of course. There was an utter neglect of cleanliness and a total want of comfort in their tents; and the poor creatures were miserably clothed. Mr. Frazer, who accompanied us from the Methye Lake, accounted for their being in this forlorn condition by explaining that this band of Indians had recently destroyed everything they possessed, as a token of their great grief for the loss of their relatives in the prevailing sickness. It appears that no article is spared by these unhappy men when a near relative dies; their clothes and tents are cut to pieces, their guns broken, and every other weapon rendered useless if some person do not remove these articles from their sight, which is seldom done. Mr. Back sketched one of the children, which delighted the father very much, who charged the boy to be very good, since his picture had been drawn by a great chief. We learned that they prize pictures very highly, and esteem any they can get, however badly executed, as efficient charms. They were unable to give us any information respecting the country beyond the Athabasca Lake, which is the boundary of their peregrinations to the northward. Having been apprised of our coming, they had prepared an encampment for us; but we had witnessed too many proofs of their importunity to expect that we could pass the night near them in any comfort, whilst either spirits, tobacco or sugar remained in our possession; and therefore preferred to go about two miles farther along the river and to encamp among a cluster of fine pine-trees after a journey of sixteen miles.

On the morning of the 15th, in proceeding along the river we perceived a strong smell of sulphur, and on the north shore found a quantity of it scattered, which seemed to have been deposited by some spring in the neighbourhood: it appeared very pure and good. We continued our course the whole day along the river, which is about four hundred yards wide, has some islands, and is confined between low land, extending from the bases of the mountains on each side. We put up at the end of thirteen miles, and were then joined by a Chipewyan, who came, as we supposed, to serve as our guide to Pierre au Calumet, but as none of the party would communicate with our new friend, otherwise than by signs, we waited patiently until the morning to see what he intended to do. The wind blew a gale during the night, and the snow fell heavily. The next day our guide led us to the Pembina River, which comes from the southward, where we found traces of Indians, who appeared to have quitted this station the day before; we had, therefore, the benefit of a good track, which our dogs much required, as they were greatly fatigued, having dragged their loads through very deep snow for the last two days. A moose-deer crossed the river just before the party: this animal is plentiful in the vicinity. We encamped in a pleasant well-sheltered place, having travelled fourteen miles.

A short distance on the following morning brought us to some Indian lodges which belonged to an old Chipewyan chief, named the Sun, and his family, consisting of five hunters, their wives and children. They were delighted to see us, and when the object of our expedition had been explained to them expressed themselves much interested in our progress; but they could not give a particle of information respecting the countries beyond the Athabasca Lake. We smoked with them, and gave each person a glass of mixed spirits and some tobacco. A Canadian servant of the North-West Company, who was residing with them, informed us that this family had lost numerous relatives, and that the destruction of property which had been made after their deaths, was the only cause for the pitiable condition in which we saw them, as the whole family were industrious hunters, and, therefore, were usually better provided with clothes and other useful articles than most of the Indians. We purchased from them a pair of snow-shoes in exchange for some ammunition. The Chipewyans are celebrated for making them good and easy to walk in; we saw some here upwards of six feet long and three broad. With these unwieldy clogs an active hunter, in the spring, when there is a crust on the surface of the snow, will run down a moose or red-deer.

We made very slow progress after leaving this party on account of the deep snow, but continued along the river until we reached its junction with the Athabasca or Elk River. We obtained observations on an island a little below the Forks, which gave, longitude 111° 8′ 42″ W., variation 24° 18′ 20″ E. Very little wood was seen during this day's march. The western shore near the Forks is destitute of trees; it is composed of lofty perpendicular cliffs, which were now covered with snow. The eastern shore supports a few pines.

March 18

Soon after our departure from the encampment we met two men from the establishment at Pierre au Calumet, who gave us correct information of its situation and distance. Having the benefit of their track we marched at a tolerably quick pace, and made twenty-two miles in the course of the day, though the weather was very disagreeable for travelling, being stormy with constant snow. We kept along the river the whole time: its breadth is about two miles. The islands appear better furnished with wood than its banks, the summits of which are almost bare. Soon after we had encamped our Indian guide rejoined us; he had remained behind the day before without consulting us to accompany a friend on a hunting excursion. On his return he made no endeavour to explain the reason of his absence, but sat down coolly and began to prepare his supper. This behaviour made us sensible that little dependence is to be placed on the continuance of an Indian guide when his inclination leads him away.

Early the next morning we sent forward the Indian and a Canadian to apprise the gentleman in charge of Pierre au Calumet of our approach; and, after breakfast, the rest of the party proceeded along the river for that station, which we reached in the afternoon. The senior partner of the North-West Company in the Athabasca department, Mr. John Stuart, was in charge of the post. Though he was quite ignorant until this morning of our being in the country, we found him prepared to receive us with great kindness and ready to afford every information and assistance, agreeably to the desire conveyed in Mr. Simon M'Gillivray's circular letter. This gentleman had twice traversed this continent, and reached the Pacific by the Columbia River; he was, therefore, fully conversant with the different modes of travelling and with the obstacles that may be expected in passing through unfrequented countries. His suggestions and advice were consequently very valuable to us, but not having been to the northward of the Great Slave Lake, he had no knowledge of that line of country except what he had gained from the reports of Indians. He was of opinion, however, that positive information, on which our course of proceedings might safely be determined, could be procured from the Indians that frequent the north side of the lake when they came to the forts in the spring. He recommended my writing to the partner in charge of that department, requesting him to collect all the intelligence he could, and to provide guides and hunters from the tribe best acquainted with the country through which we proposed to travel.

To our great regret Mr. Stuart expressed much doubt as to our prevailing upon any experienced Canadian voyagers to accompany us to the sea, in consequence of their dread of the Esquimaux; who, he informed us, had already destroyed the crew of one canoe, which had been sent under Mr. Livingstone to open a trading communication with those who reside near the mouth of the Mackenzie River; and he also mentioned that the same tribe had driven away the canoes under Mr. Clark's direction, going to them on a similar object, to which circumstance I have alluded in my remarks at Isle à la Crosse.

This was unpleasant information; but we were comforted by Mr. Stuart's assurance that himself and his partners would use every endeavour to remove their fears as well as to promote our views in every other way; and he undertook, as a necessary part of our equipment in the spring, to prepare the bark and other materials for constructing two canoes at this post.

Mr. Stuart informed us that the residents at Fort Chipewyan, from the recent sickness of their Indian hunters, had been reduced to subsist entirely on the produce of their fishing-nets, which did not yield more than a bare sufficiency for their support; and he kindly proposed to us to remain with him until the spring; but, as we were most desirous to gain all the information we could as early as possible, and Mr. Stuart assured us that the addition of three persons would not be materially felt in their large family at Chipewyan, we determined on proceeding thither, and fixed on the 22nd for our departure.

Pierre au Calumet receives its name from the place where the stone is procured, of which many of the pipes used by the Canadians and Indians are made. It is a clayey limestone, impregnated with various shells. The house, which is built on the summit of a steep bank, rising almost perpendicular to the height of one hundred and eighty feet, commands an extensive prospect along this fine river and over the plains which stretch out several miles at the back of it, bounded by hills of considerable height, and apparently better furnished with wood than the neighbourhood of the fort, where the trees grow very scantily. There had been an establishment belonging to the Hudson's Bay Company on the opposite bank of the river, but it was abandoned in December last, the residents not being able to procure provision, from their hunters having been disabled by the epidemic sickness, which has carried off one-third of the Indians in these parts. They belong to the Northern Crees, a name given them from their residing in the Athabasca department. There are now but few families of these men, who, formerly, by their numbers and predatory habits, spread terror among the natives of this part of the country.

There are springs of bituminous matter on several of the islands near these houses; and the stones on the river bank are much impregnated with this useful substance. There is also another place remarkable for the production of a sulphureous salt, which is deposited on the surface of a round-backed hill about half a mile from the beach and on the marshy ground underneath it. We visited these places at a subsequent period of the journey, and descriptions of them will appear in Dr. Richardson's Mineralogical Notices.

The latitude of the North-West Company's House is 57° 24′ 06″ N, but this was the only observation we could obtain, the atmosphere being cloudy. Mr. Stuart had an excellent thermometer, which indicated the lowest state of temperature to be 43° below zero. He told me 45° was the lowest temperature he had ever witnessed at the Athabasca or Great Slave Lake after many years' residence. On the 21st it rose above zero, and at noon attained the height of 43°; the atmosphere was sultry, snow fell constantly, and there was quite an appearance of a change in the season.

On the 22nd we parted from our hospitable friend and recommenced our journey, but under the expectation of seeing him again in May; at which time the partners of the Company usually assemble at Fort Chipewyan, where we hoped the necessary arrangements for our future proceedings would be completed. We encamped at sunset at the end of fourteen miles, having walked the whole way along the river, which preserves nearly a true north course, and is from four hundred to six hundred yards broad. The banks are high and well clothed with the liard, spruce, fir, alder, birch-tree and willows. Having come nineteen miles and a half on the 23rd we encamped among pines of a great height and girth.

Showers of snow fell until noon on the following day, but we continued our journey along the river, whose banks and islands became gradually lower as we advanced and less abundantly supplied with wood except willows. We passed an old Canadian, who was resting his wearied dogs during the heat of the sun. He was carrying meat from some Indian lodges to Fort Chipewyan, having a burden exceeding two hundred and fifty pounds on his sledge, which was dragged by two miserable dogs. He came up to our encampment after dark. We were much amused by the altercation that took place between him and our Canadian companions as to the qualifications of their respective dogs. This, however, is such a general topic of conversation among the voyagers in the encampment that we should not probably have remarked it had not the old man frequently offered to bet the whole of his wages that his two dogs, poor and lean as they were, would drag their load to the Athabasca Lake in less time than any three of theirs. Having expressed our surprise at his apparent temerity, he coolly said the men from the lower countries did not understand the management of their dogs, and that he depended on his superior skill in driving; and we soon gathered from his remarks that the voyagers of the Athabasca department consider themselves very superior to any other. The only reasons which he could assign were, that they had borne their burdens across the terrible Methye Portage, and that they were accustomed to live harder and more precariously.

March 25

Having now the guidance of the old Canadian, we sent forward the Indian and one of our men with letters to the gentleman at the Athabasca Lake. The rest of the party set off afterwards and kept along the river until ten, when we branched off by portages into the Embarras River, the usual channel of communication in canoes with the lake. It is a narrow and serpentine stream, confined between alluvial banks which support pines, poplars and willows. We had not advanced far before we overtook the two men despatched for us this morning. The stormy weather had compelled them to encamp, as there was too much drifting of the snow for any attempt to cross the lake. We were obliged, though most reluctantly, to follow their example; but comforted ourselves with the reflection that this was the first time we had been stopped by the weather during our long journey, which was so near at an end. The gale afterwards increased, the squalls at night became very violent, disburthened the trees of the snow, and gave us the benefit of continual fall of patches from them, in addition to the constant shower. We therefore quickly finished our suppers and retired under the shelter of our blankets.

March 26

The boisterous weather continued through the night, and it was not before six this morning that the wind became apparently moderate and the snow ceased. Two of the Canadians were immediately sent off with letters to the gentlemen at Fort Chipewyan. After breakfast we also started, but our Indian friend, having a great indisposition to move in such weather, remained by the fire. We soon quitted the river, and after crossing a portage, a small lake and a point of land, came to the borders of the Mamma-wee Lake. We then found our error as to the strength of the wind; and that the gale still blew violently, and there was so much drifting of the snow as to cover the distant objects by which our course could be directed. We fortunately got a glimpse through this cloud of a cluster of islands in the direction of the houses, and decided on walking towards them; but in doing this we suffered very much from the cold, and were obliged to halt under the shelter of them and await the arrival of our Indian guide. He conducted us between these islands, over a small lake, and by a swampy river into the Athabasca Lake, from whence the establishments were visible. At four P.M. we had the pleasure of arriving at Fort Chipewyan, and of being received by Messrs. Keith and Black, the partners of the North-West Company in charge, in the most kind and hospitable manner. Thus terminated a winter's journey of eight hundred and fifty-seven miles, in the progress of which there was a great intermixture of agreeable and disagreeable circumstances. Could the amount of each be balanced, I suspect the latter would much preponderate; and amongst these the initiation into walking in snow-shoes must be considered as prominent. The suffering it occasions can be but faintly imagined by a person who thinks upon the inconvenience of marching with a weight of between two and three pounds constantly attached to galled feet and swelled ankles. Perseverance and practice only will enable the novice to surmount this pain.

The next evil is the being constantly exposed to witness the wanton and unnecessary cruelty of the men to their dogs, especially those of the Canadians, who beat them unmercifully, and habitually vent on them the most dreadful and disgusting imprecations. There are other inconveniences which, though keenly felt during the day's journey, are speedily forgotten when stretched out in the encampment before a large fire, you enjoy the social mirth of your companions, who usually pass the evening in recounting their former feats in travelling. At this time the Canadians are always cheerful and merry, and the only bar to their comfort arises from the frequent interruption occasioned by the dogs, who are constantly prowling about the circle and snatching at every kind of food that happens to be within their reach. These useful animals are a comfort to them afterwards by the warmth they impart when lying down by their side or feet, as they usually do. But the greatest gratifications a traveller in these regions enjoys are derived from the hospitable welcome he receives at every trading post, however poor the means of the host may be; and from being disrobed even for a short time of the trappings of a voyager, and experiencing the pleasures of cleanliness.

The following are the estimated distances, in statute miles, which Mr. Back and I had travelled since our departure from Cumberland:

From Cumberland House to Carlton House	263
From Carlton to Isle à la Crosse	230
From Isle à la Crosse to north side of the Methye Portage	124
From the Methye Portage to Fort Chipewyan	240
	857 Miles.

CHAPTER V

Transactions at Fort Chipewyan – Arrival of Dr. Richardson and
Mr. Hood – Preparations for our Journey to the Northward.

March 26, 1820

On the day after our arrival at Fort Chipewyan we called upon Mr. MacDonald, the gentleman in charge of the Hudson's Bay Establishment called Ford Wedderburne, and delivered to him Governor Williams's circular letter, which desired that every assistance should be given to further our progress, and a statement of the requisitions which we should have to make on his post.

Our first object was to obtain some certain information respecting our future route; and accordingly we received from one of the North-West Company's interpreters, named Beaulieu, a half-breed, who had been brought up amongst the Dog-ribbed and Copper Indians, some satisfactory information which we afterwards found tolerably correct, respecting the mode of reaching the Copper-Mine River, which he had descended a considerable way, as well as of the course of that river to its mouth. The Copper Indians, however, he said, would be able to give us more accurate information as to the latter part of its course, as they occasionally pursue it to the sea. He sketched on the floor a representation of the river, and a line of coast according to his idea of it. Just as he had finished, an old Chipewyan Indian named Black Meat, unexpectedly came in, and instantly recognised the plan. He then took the charcoal from Beaulieu, and inserted a track among the sea-coast, which he had followed in returning from a war excursion, made by his tribe against the Esquimaux. He detailed several particulars of the coast and the sea, which he represented as studded with well-wooded islands, and free from ice, close to the shore, in the month of July but not to a great distance. He described two other rivers to the eastward of the Copper-Mine River, which also fall into the Northern Ocean. The Anatessy, which issues from the Contway-to or Rum Lake, and the Thloueeatessy or Fish River, which rises near the eastern boundary of the Great Slave Lake; but he represented both of them as being shallow, and too much interrupted by barriers for being navigated in any other than small Indian canoes.

Having received this satisfactory intelligence, I wrote immediately to Mr. Smith, of the North-West Company, and Mr. M'Vicar, of the Hudson's Bay Company, the gentlemen in charge of the posts at the Great Slave Lake, to communicate the object of the Expedition, and our proposed route; and to solicit any information they possessed, or could collect, from the Indians, relative to the countries we had to pass through, and the best manner of proceeding. As the Copper Indians frequent the establishment on the north side of the lake, I particularly requested them to explain to that tribe the object of our visit, and to endeavour to procure from them some guides and hunters to accompany our party. Two Canadians were sent by Mr. Keith with these letters.

The month of April commenced with fine and clear but extremely cold weather; unfortunately we were still without a thermometer, and could not ascertain the degrees of temperature. The coruscations of the Aurora were very brilliant almost every evening of the first week, and were generally of the most variable kind. On the 3rd they were particularly changeable. The first appearance exhibited three illuminated beams issuing from the horizon in the north, east, and west points, and directed towards the zenith; in a few seconds these disappeared, and a complete circle was displayed, bounding the horizon at an elevation of fifteen degrees. There was quick lateral motion in the attenuated beams of which this zone was composed. Its colour was a pale yellow, with an occasional tinge of red.

On the 8th of April the Indians saw some geese in the vicinity of this lake, but none of the migratory birds appeared near the houses before the 15th, when some swans flew over. These are generally the first that arrive; the weather had been very stormy for the four preceding days, and this in all probability kept the birds from venturing farther north than where the Indians had first seen them.

In the middle of the month the snow began to waste daily, and by degrees it disappeared from the hills and the surface of the lake. On the 17th and 19th the Aurora appeared very brilliant in patches of light, bearing N.W. An old Cree Indian having found a beaver-lodge near to the fort, Mr. Keith, Back, and I, accompanied him to see the method of breaking into it, and their mode of taking those interesting animals. The lodge was constructed on the side of a rock in a small lake, having the entrance into it beneath the ice. The frames were formed of layers of sticks, the interstices being filled with mud, and the outside was plastered with earth and stones, which the frost had so completely consolidated, that to break through required great labour, with the aid of the ice chisel, and the other iron instruments which the beaver hunters use. The chase, however, was unsuccessful, as the beaver had previously vacated the lodge.

On the 21st we observed the first geese that flew near the fort, and some were brought to the house on the 30th, but they were very lean. On the 25th flies were seen sporting in the sun, and on the 26th the Athabasca River having broken up, overflowed the lake along its channel; but except where this water spread, there was no appearance of decay in the ice.

May

During the first part of this month, the wind blew from the N.W., and the sky was cloudy. It generally thawed during the day, but froze at night. On the 2nd the Aurora faintly gleamed through very dense clouds.

We had a long conversation with Mr. Dease of the North-West Company, who had recently arrived from his station at the bottom of the Athabasca Lake. This gentleman, having passed several winters on the Mackenzie's River, and at the posts to the northward of Slave Lake, possessed considerable information respecting the Indians, and those parts of the country to which our inquiries were directed, which he very promptly and kindly communicated. During our conversation, an old Chipewyan Indian, named the Rabbit's Head, entered the room, to whom Mr. Dease referred for information on some point. We found from his answer that he was a step-son of the late chief Matonnabee, who had accompanied Mr. Hearne on his journey to the sea, and that he had himself been of the party, but being then a mere boy, he had forgotten many of the circumstances. He confirmed, however, the leading incidents related by Hearne, and was positive he reached the sea, though he admitted that none of the party had tasted the water. He represented himself to be the only survivor of that party. As he was esteemed a good Indian, I presented him with a medal, which he received gratefully, and concluded a long speech upon the occasion, by assuring me he should preserve it carefully all his life. The old man afterwards became more communicative, and unsolicited began to relate the tradition of his tribe, respecting the discovery of the Copper-Mine, which we thought amusing: and as the subject is somewhat connected with our future researches, I will insert the translation of it which was given at the time by Mr. Dease, though a slight mention of it has been made by Hearne.

'The Chipewyans suppose the Esquimaux originally inhabited some land to the northward which is separated by the sea from this country; and that in the earliest ages of the world a party of these men came over and stole a woman from their tribe, whom they carried to this distant country and kept in a state of slavery. She was very unhappy in her situation, and effected her escape after many years residence among them. The forlorn creature wandered about, for some days, in a state of uncertainty what direction to take, when she chanced to fall upon a beaten path, which she followed and was led to the sea. At the sight of the ocean her hope of being able to return to her native country vanished, and she sat herself down in despair, and wept. A wolf now advanced to caress her, and having licked the tears from her eyes, walked into the water, and she perceived with joy that it did not reach up to the body of the animal; emboldened by this appearance, she instantly arose, provided two sticks to support herself, and determined on following the wolf. The first and second nights she proceeded on, without finding any increase in the depth of the water, and when fatigued, rested herself on the sticks, whose upper ends she fastened together for the purpose. She was alarmed on the third morning, by arriving at a deeper part, but resolved on going forward at any risk, rather than return; and her daring perseverance was crowned with success, by her attaining her native shore on the fifth day. She fortunately came to a part where there was a beaten path, which she knew to be the track made by the reindeer in their migrations. Here she halted and prepared some sort of weapon for killing them; as soon as this was completed, she had the gratification to behold several herds advancing along the road, and had the happiness of killing a sufficient number for her winter's subsistence, which she determined to pass at that place, and therefore formed a house for herself, after the manner she had learned from the Esquimaux. When spring came, and she emerged from her subterraneous dwelling, (for such the Chipewyans suppose it to have been,) she was astonished by observing a glittering appearance on a distant hill, which she knew was not produced by the reflection of the sun, and being at a loss to assign any other cause for it she resolved on going up to the shining object, and then found the hill was entirely composed of copper. She broke off several pieces, and finding it yielded so readily to her beating, it occurred to her that this metal would be very serviceable to her countrymen, if she could find them again. While she was meditating on what was to be done, the thought struck her that it would be advisable to attach as many pieces of copper to her dress as she could, and then proceed into the interior, in search of some inhabitants, who, she supposed, would give her a favourable reception, on account of the treasure she had brought

'It happened that she met her own relations, and the young men, elated with the account she had given of the hill, made her instantly return with them; which she was enabled to do, having taken the precaution of putting up marks to indicate the path. The party reached the spot in safety, but the story had a melancholy catastrophe. The youths overcome by excess of joy, gave loose to their passions, and offered the grossest insults to their benefactress. She powerfully resisted them for some time, and when her strength was failing, fled to the point of the mountain, as the only place of security. The moment she had gained the summit, the earth opened and ingulphed both herself and the mountain, to the utter dismay of the men, who were not more astonished at its sudden disappearance, than sorrowful for this just punishment of their wickedness. Ever since this event, the copper has only been found in small detached pieces on the surface of the earth.'

On the 10th of May we were gratified by the appearance of spring, though the ice remained firm on the lake. The anemone (pulsatilla, pasque flower), appeared this day in flower, the trees began to put forth their leaves, and the musquitoes visited the warm rooms. On the 17th and 18th there were frequent showers of rain, and much thunder and lightning. This moist weather caused the ice to waste so rapidly, that by the 24th it had entirely disappeared from the lake. The gentlemen belonging to both the Companies quickly arrived from the different posts in this department, bringing their winter's collection of furs, which are forwarded from these establishments to the depôts.

I immediately waited on Mr. Colin Robertson, the agent of the Hudson's Company, and communicated to him, as I had done before to the several partners of the North-West Company, our plan, and the requisitions we should have to make on each Company, and I requested of all the gentlemen the favour of their advice and suggestions. As I perceived that the arrangement of their winter accounts, and other business, fully occupied them, I forbore further pressing the subject of our concerns for some days, until there was an appearance of despatching the first brigade of canoes. It then became necessary to urge their attention to them; but it was evident, from the determined commercial opposition, and the total want of intercourse between the two Companies, that we could not expect to receive any cordial advice, or the assurance of the aid of both, without devising some expedient to bring the parties together. I therefore caused a tent to be pitched at a distance from both establishments, and solicited the gentlemen of both Companies to meet Mr. Back and myself there, for the purpose of affording us their combined assistance.

With this request they immediately complied; and on May 25th we were joined at the tent by Mr. Stuart and Mr. Grant, of the North-West Company, and Mr. Colin Robertson, of the Hudson's Bay Company, all of whom kindly gave very satisfactory answers to a series of questions which we had drawn up for the occasion, and promised all the aid in their power.

Furnished with the information thus obtained, we proceeded to make some arrangements respecting the obtaining of men, and the stores we should require for their equipment, as well as for presents to the Indians; and on the following day a requisition was made on he Companies for eight men each, and whatever useful stores they could supply. We learned with regret, that, in consequence of the recent lavish expenditure of their goods in support of the opposition, their supply to us would, of necessity, be very limited. The men, too, were backward in offering their services, who demanded a much higher rate of wages than I considered it proper to grant.

June 3

Mr. Smith, a partner of the North-West Company, arrived from the Great Slave Lake, bearing the welcome news that the principal chief of the Copper Indians had received the communication of our arrival with joy, and given all the intelligence he possessed respecting the route to the sea-coast by the Copper-Mine River; and that he and a party of his men, at the instance of Mr. Wentzel, a clerk of the North-West Company, whom they wished might go along with them, had engaged to accompany the Expedition as guides and hunters. They were to wait our arrival at Fort Providence, on the north side of the Slave Lake. Their information coincided with that given by Beaulieu. They had no doubt of our being able to obtain the means of subsistence in travelling to the coast. This agreeable intelligence had a happy effect upon the Canadian voyagers, many of their fears being removed: several of them seemed now disposed to volunteer; and indeed, on the same evening, two men from the North-West Company offered themselves and were accepted.

June 5

This day Mr. Back and I went over to Fort Wedderburne, to see Mr. Robertson respecting his quota of men. We learned from him that, notwithstanding his endeavours to persuade them, his most experienced voyagers still declined engaging without very exorbitant wages. After some hesitation, however, six men engaged with us, who were represented to be active and steady; and I also got Mr. Robertson's permission for St. Germain, an interpreter belonging to this Company, to accompany us from Slave Lake if he should choose. The bow-men and steersmen were to receive one thousand six hundred livres Halifax per annum, and the middle men one thousand two hundred, exclusive of their necessary equipments; and they stipulated that their wages should be continued until their arrival in Montreal, or their rejoining the service of their present employers.

I delivered to Mr. Robertson an official request, that the stores we had left at York Factory and the Rock Depôt, with some other supplies, might be forwarded to Slave Lake by the first brigade of canoes which should come in. He also took charge of my letters addressed to the Admiralty. Five men afterwards engaged from the North-West Company for the same wages, and under the same stipulations as the others, besides an interpreter for the Copper Indians; but this man required three thousand livres Halifax currency, which we were obliged to give him, as his services were indispensable.

The extreme scarcity of provision at the posts rendered it necessary to despatch all our men to the Man-ma-wee Lake, where they might procure their own subsistence by fishing. The women and children resident at the fort were also sent away for the same purpose; and no other families were permitted to remain at the houses after the departure of the canoes, than those belonging to the men who were required to carry on the daily duty.

The large party of officers and men, which had assembled here from the different posts in the department, was again quickly dispersed. The first brigade of canoes, laden with furs, was despatched to the depôt on May 30th, and the others follows in two or three days afterwards. Mr. Stuart, the senior partner of the North-West Company, quitted us for the same destination on June 4th; Mr. Robertson, for his depôt, on the next day; and on the 9th we parted with our friend Mr. Keith, to whose unremitting kindness we felt much indebted. I intrusted to his care a box containing some drawings by Mr. Back, the map of our route from Cumberland House, and the skin of a black beaver, (presented to the Expedition by Mr. Smith,) with my official letters, addressed to the Under Secretary of State. I wrote by each of these gentlemen to inform Dr. Richardson and Mr. Hood of the scarcity of stores at these posts, and to request them to procure all they possibly could on their route. Mr. Smith was left in charge of this post during the summer; this gentleman soon evinced his desire to further our progress, by directing a new canoe to be built for our use, which was commenced immediately.

June 21

This day an opportunity offered of sending letters to the Great Slave Lake; and I profited by it, to request Mr. Wentzel would accompany the Expedition agreeably to the desire of the Copper Indians, communicating to him that I had received permission for him to do so from the partners of the North-West Company. Should he be disposed to comply with my invitation, I desired that he would go over to Fort Providence, and remain near the Indians whom he had engaged for our service. I feared lest they should become impatient at our unexpected delay, and, with the usual fickleness of the Indian character, remove from the establishment before we could arrive. It had been my intention to go to them myself, could the articles, with which they expected to be presented on my arrival, have been provided at these establishments; but as they could not be procured, I was compelled to defer my visit until our canoes should arrive. Mr. Smith supposed that my appearance amongst them, without the means of satisfying any of their desires, would give them an unfavourable impression respecting the Expedition, which would make them indifferent to exertion, if it did not even cause them to withdraw from their engagements.

The establishments at this place, Forts Chipewyan and Wedderburne, the chief posts of the Companies in this department, are conveniently situated for communicating with the Slave and Peace Rivers, from whence the canoes assemble in the spring and autumn; on the first occasion they bring the collection of furs which has been made at the different outposts during the winter; and at the latter season they receive a supply of stores for the equipment of the Indians in their vicinity. Fort Wedderburne is a small house, which was constructed on Coal Island about five years ago, when the Hudson's Bay Company recommenced trading in this part of the country. Fort Chipewyan has been built many years, and is an establishment of very considerable extent, conspicuously situated on a rocky point of the northern shore; it has a tower which can be seen at a considerable distance. This addition was made about eight years ago, to watch the motions of the Indians, who intended, as it was then reported, to destroy the house and all its inhabitants. They had been instigated to this rash design by the delusive stories of one among them, who had acquired great influence over his companions by his supposed skill in necromancy. This fellow had prophesied that there would soon be a complete change in the face of their country; that fertility and plenty would succeed to the present sterility; and that the present race of white inhabitants, unless they became subservient to the Indians, would be removed, and their place be filled by other traders, who would supply their wants in every possible manner. The poor deluded wretches, imagining they would hasten this happy change by destroying their present traders, of whose submission there was no prospect, threatened to extirpate them. None of these menaces, however, were put in execution. They were probably deterred from the attempt by perceiving that most vigilant guard was kept against them.

The portion of this extensive lake which is near the establishments, is called 'The Lake of the Hills,' not improperly, as the northern shore and the islands are high and rocky. The south side, however, is quite level, consisting of alluvial land, subject to be flooded, lying betwixt the different mouths of the Elk River, and much intersected by water. The rocks of the northern shore are composed of syenite over which the soil is thinly spread; it is, however, sufficient to support a variety of firs and poplars, and many shrubs, lichens and mosses. The trees were now in full foliage, the plants generally in flower, and the whole scene quite enlivening. There can scarcely be a higher gratification than that which is enjoyed in this country in witnessing the rapid change which takes place in the course of a few days in the spring; scarcely does the snow disappear from the ground, before the trees are clothed with thick foliage, the shrubs open their leaves, and put forth their variegated flowers, and the whole prospect becomes animating. The spaces between the rocky hills, being for the most part swampy, support willows and a few poplars. These spots are the favourite resort of the musquitoes, which incessantly torment the unfortunate persons who have to pass through them.

Some of the hills attain an elevation of five or six hundred feet, at the distance of a mile from the house; and from their summits a very picturesque view is commanded of the lake, and of the surrounding country. The land above the Great Point at the confluence of the main stream of the Elk River is six or seven hundred feet high, and stretches in a southern direction behind Pierre au Calumet. Opposite to that establishment, on the west side of the river, at some distance in the interior, the Bark Mountain rises and ranges to the N.W., until it reaches Clear Lake, about thirty miles to the southward of these forts, and then goes to the south-westward. The Cree Indians generally procure from this range their provision, as well as the bark for making their canoes. There is another range of hills on the south shore, which runs towards the Peace River.

The residents of these establishments depend for subsistence almost entirely on the fish which this lake affords; they are usually caught in sufficient abundance throughout the winter, though at the distance of eighteen miles from the houses; on the thawing of the ice, the fish remove into some smaller lakes, and the rivers on the south shore. Though they are nearer to the forts than in winter, it frequently happens that high winds prevent the canoes from transporting them thither, and the residents are kept in consequence without a supply of food for two or three days together. The fish caught in the net are the attih-hawmegh, trout, carp, methye, and pike.[1]

The traders also get supplied by the hunters with buffalo and moose-deer meat, (which animals are found at some distance from the forts,) but the greater part of it is either in a dried state, or pounded ready for making pemmican; and is required for the men whom they keep travelling during the winter to collect the furs from the Indians, and for the crews of canoes on their outward passage to the depôts in spring. There was a great want of provision this season, and both the Companies had much difficulty to provide a bare sufficiency for their different brigades of canoes. Mr. Smith assured me that after the canoes had been despatched he had only five hundred pounds of meat remaining for the use of the men who might travel from the post during the summer, and that five years preceding, there had been thirty thousand pounds in store under similar circumstances. He ascribed this amazing difference more to the indolent habits which the Indians had acquired since the commercial struggle commenced, than to their recent sickness, mentioning in confirmation of his opinion that they could now, by the produce of little exertion, obtain whatever they demanded from either establishment.

1 See page 62.

At the opening of the water in spring, the Indians resort to the establishments to settle their accounts with the traders, and to procure the necessaries they require for the summer. This meeting is generally a scene of much riot and confusion, as the hunters receive such quantities of spirits as to keep them in a state of intoxication for several days. This spring, however, owing to the great deficiency of spirits, we had the gratification of seeing them generally sober. They belong to the great family of the Chipewyan, or Northern, Indians; dialects of their language being spoken in the Peace and Mackenzie's Rivers, and by the populous tribes in New Caledonia, as ascertained by Sir Alexander Mackenzie in his journey to the Pacific. They style themselves generally *Dinneh* men, or Indians, but each tribe, or horde, adds some distinctive epithet taken from the name of the river, or lake, on which they hunt, or the district from which they last migrated. Those who come to Fort Chipewyan term themselves Saw-eessaw-dinneh, (Indians from the rising sun, or Eastern Indians,) their original hunting grounds being between the Athabasca and Great Slave Lakes, and Churchill River. This district, more particularly termed the Chipewyan lands, or *barren country*, is frequented by numerous herds of reindeer, which furnish easy subsistence, and clothing to the Indians; but the traders endeavour to keep them in the parts to the westward where the beavers resort. There are about one hundred and sixty hunters who carry their furs to the Great Slave Lake, forty to Hay River, and two hundred and forty to Fort Chipewyan. A few Northern Indians also resort to the posts at the bottom of the Lake of the Hills, on Red Deer Lake, and to Churchill. The distance, however, of the latter post from their hunting grounds, and the sufferings to which they are exposed in going thither from want of food, have induced those who were formerly accustomed to visit it, to convey their furs to some nearer station.

These people are so minutely described by Hearne and Mackenzie, that little can be added by a passing stranger, whose observations were made during short interviews, and when they were at the forts, where they lay aside many of their distinguishing characteristics, and strive to imitate the manners of the voyagers and traders.

The Chipewyans are by no means prepossessing in appearance: they have broad faces, projecting cheek-bones and wide nostrils; but they have generally good teeth, and fine eyes. When at the fort they imitate the dress of the Canadians, except that, instead of trowsers, they prefer the Indian stockings, which only reach from the thigh to the ankle, and in place of the waistband they have a piece of cloth round the middle which hangs down loosely before and behind. Their hunting dress consists of a leathern shirt and stockings, over which a blanket is thrown, the head being covered with a fur cap or band. Their manner is reserved, and their habits are selfish; they beg with unceasing importunity for everything they see. I never saw men who either received or bestowed a gift with such bad grace; they almost snatch the thing from you in the one instance, and throw it at you in the other. It could not be expected that such men should display in their tents the amiable hospitality which prevails generally amongst the Indians of this country. A stranger may go away hungry from their lodges, unless he possesses sufficient impudence to thrust, uninvited, his knife into the kettle, and help himself. The owner, indeed, never deigns to take any notice of such an act of rudeness, except by a frown, it being beneath the dignity of a hunter, to make disturbance about a piece of meat.

As some relief to the darker shades of their character it should be stated that instances of theft are extremely rare amongst them. They profess strong affection for their children, and some regard for their relations, who are often numerous, as they trace very far the ties of consanguinity. A curious instance of the former was mentioned to us, and so well authenticated, that I shall venture to give it in the words of Dr. Richardson's Journal.

'A young Chipewyan had separated from the rest of his band for the purpose of trenching beaver, when his wife, who was his sole companion, and in her first pregnancy was seized with the pains of labour. She died on the third day after she had given birth to a boy. The husband was inconsolable, and vowed in his anguish never to take another woman to wife, but his grief was soon in some degree absorbed in anxiety for the fate of his infant son. To preserve its life he descended to the office of nurse, so degrading in the eyes of a Chipewyan, as partaking of the duties of a woman. He swaddled it in soft moss, fed it with broth made from the flesh of deer, and to still its cries applies it to his breast, praying earnestly to the great Master of Life, to assist his endeavours. The force of the powerful passion by which he was actuated produced the same effect in his case, as it has done in some others which are recorded: a flow of milk actually took place from his breast. He succeeded in rearing his child, taught him to be a hunter, and when he attained the age of manhood, chose him a wife from the tribe. The old man kept his vow in never taking a second wife himself, but he delighted in tending his son's children, and when his daughter-in-law used to interfere, saying, that it was not the occupation of a man, he was wont to reply, that he had promised to the great Master of Life, if his child were spared, never to be proud, like the other Indians. He used to mention, too, as a certain proof of the approbation of Providence, that although he was always obliged to carry his child on his back while hunting, yet that it never roused a moose by its cries, being always particularly still at those times. Our informant[1] added that he had often seen this Indian in his old age, and that his left breast, even then, retained the unusual size it had acquired in his occupation of nurse.'

We had proof of their sensibility towards their relations, in their declining to pitch their tents where they had been accustomed for many years, alleging a fear of being reminded of the happy hours they had formerly spent there, in the society of the affectionate relatives whom the sickness had recently carried off. The change of situation, however, had not the effect of relieving them from sorrowful impressions, and they occasionally indulged in very loud lamentations, as they sat in groups, within and without their tents. Unfortunately, the spreading of a severe dysentery amongst them, at this time, gave occasion for the renewal of their grief. The medicinal charms of drumming and singing were plentifully applied, and once they had recourse to conjuring over a sick person. I was informed, however, that the Northern Indians do not make this expedient for the cure of a patient so often as the Crees; but when they do, the conjuror is most assiduous, and suffers great personal fatigue. Particular persons only are trained in the mysteries of the art of conjuring, to procure the recovery of the sick, or to disclose future events.

On extraordinary occasions the man remains in his narrow conjuring tent for days without eating, before he can determine the matter to his satisfaction. When he is consulted about the sick, the patient is shut up with him; but on other occasions he is alone, and the poor creature often works his mind up to a pitch of illusion that can scarcely be imagined by one who has not witnessed it. His deluded companions seat themselves round his tent, and await his communication with earnest anxiety, yet during the progress of his manoeuvres, they often venture to question him, as to the disposition of the Great Spirit.

1 Mr. Wentzel.

These artful fellows usually gain complete ascendancy over the minds of their companions. They are supported by voluntary contributions of provision, that their minds may not be diverted by the labour of hunting from the peculiar duties of their profession.

The chiefs among the Chipewyans are now totally without power. The presents of a flag, and a gaudy dress, still bestowed upon them by the traders, do not procure for them any respect or obedience, except from the youths of their own families. This is to be attributed mainly to their living at peace with their neighbours, and to the facility which the young men find in getting their wants supplied independent of the recommendation of the chiefs, which was formerly required. In war excursions, boldness and intrepidity would still command respect and procure authority; but the influence thus acquired would, probably, cease with the occasion that called it forth. The traders, however, endeavour to support their authority by continuing towards them the accustomed marks of respect, hoisting the flag and firing a salute of musketry on their entering the fort.

The chief halts at a distance from the house, and despatches one of his young men to announce his approach, and to bring his flat, which is carried before him when he arrives. The messenger carries back to him some vermilion to ornament the faces of his party, together with a looking-glass and comb, some tobacco, and a few rounds of ammunition, that they may return the salute. These men paint round the eyes, the forehead, and the cheekbones.

The Northern Indians evince no little vanity, by assuming to themselves the comprehensive title of 'The People,' whilst they designate all other nations by the name of their particular country. If men were seen at a distance, and a Chipewyan was asked who those persons were, he would answer, The People, if he recognised them to belong to his tribe, and never Chipewyans; but he would give them their respective names, if they were Europeans, Canadians, or Cree Indians.

As they suppose their ancestors to come originally from the east, those who happen to be born in the eastern part of their territory are considered to be of the purest race. I have been informed, that all the Indians who trade at the different posts in the north-west parts of America, imagine that their forefathers came from the east, except the Dog-ribs, who reside between the Copper Indian Islands and the Mackenzie's River, and who deduce their origin from the west, which is the more remarkable, as they speak a dialect of the Chipewyan language. I could gather no information respecting their religious opinions, except that they have a tradition of the deluge.

The Chipewyans are considered to be less expert hunters than the Crees, which probably arises from their residing much on the barren lands, where the reindeer are so numerous that little skill is requisite. A good hunter, however, is highly esteemed among them. The facility of procuring goods, since the commercial opposition commenced, has given great encouragement to their native indolence of disposition, as is manifested by the difference in the amount of their collections of furs and provision between the late and former years. From six to eight hundred packs of furs used formerly to be sent from this department, now the return seldom exceeds half that amount. The decrease in the provision has been already mentioned.

The Northern Indians suppose that they originally sprang from a dog; and about five years ago, a superstitious fanatic so strongly impressed upon their minds the impropriety of employing these animals, to which they were related, for purposes of labour, that they universally resolved against using them any more, and strange as it may seem destroyed them. They now have to drag everything themselves on sledges. This laborious task falls most heavily on women; nothing can more shock the feelings of a person accustomed to civilised life, than to witness the state of their degradation. When a party is on a march the women have to drag the tent, the meat, and whatever the hunter possesses, whilst he only carries his gun and medicine case. In the evening they form the encampment, cut wood, fetch water, and prepare the supper; and then, perhaps, are not permitted to partake of the fare until the men have finished. A successful hunter sometimes has two or three wives; whoever happens to be the favourite, assumes authority over the others, and has the management of the tent. These men usually treat their wives unkindly, and even with harshness; except, indeed, when they are about to increase the family, and then they show them much indulgence.

Hearne charges the Chipewyans with the dreadful practice of abandoning, in extremity, their aged and sick people. The only instance that came under our personal notice was attended with some palliating circumstances:- An old woman arrived at Fort Chipewyan, during our residence, with her son, a little boy, about ten years old, both of whom had been deserted by their relations, and left in an encampment, when much reduced by sickness: two or three days after their departure the woman gained a little strength, and with the assistance of the boy, was enabled to paddle a canoe to the fishing station of this post, where they were supported for some days, until they were enabled to proceed in search of some other relations, who, they expected, would treat them with more kindness. I learned, that the woman bore an extremely bad character, having even been guilty of infanticide, and that her companions considered her offences merited the desertion.

This tribe, since its present intimate connexion with the traders, has discontinued its war excursions against the Esquimaux, but they still speak of that nation in terms of the most inveterate hatred. We have only conversed with four men who have been engaged in any of those expeditions; all these confirm the statements of Black Meat respecting the sea-coast. Our observations concerning the half-breed population in this vicinity, coincided so exactly with those which have been given of similar persons in Dr. Richardson's account of the Crees, that any statement respecting them at this place is unnecessary. Both the Companies have wisely prohibited their servants from intermarrying with pure Indian women, which was formerly the cause of many quarrels with the tribes.

The weather was extremely variable during the month of June; we scarcely had two clear days in succession, and the showers of rain were frequent; the winds were often strong, and generally blowing from the north-east quarter. On the evening of the 16th the Aurora Borealis was visible, but after that date the nights were too light for our discerning it.

The musquitoes swarmed in great numbers about the house, and tormented us so incessantly by their stings, that we were compelled to keep our rooms constantly filled with smoke, which is the only means of driving them away: the weather indeed was now warm. Having received one of Dolland's eighteen-inch spirit thermometers from Mr. Stuart, which he had the kindness to send us from his post at Pierre au Calumet, after he had learned that ours had been rendered useless, I observed the temperature, at noon, on the 25th of June, to be 63°.

On the following morning we made an excursion, accompanied by Mr. Smith, round the fishing stations on the south side of the lake, for the purpose of visiting our men; we passed several groups of women and children belonging to both the forts, posted wherever they could find a sufficiently dry spot for an encampment. At length we came to our men, pitched upon a narrow strip of land, situated between two rivers. Though the portion of dry ground did not exceed fifty yards, yet they appeared to be living very comfortably, having formed huts with the canoe's sail and covering, and were amply supported by the fish their nets daily furnished. They sometimes had a change in their fare, by procuring a few ducks and other water-fowl, which resort in great abundance to the marshes, by which they were surrounded.

July 2

The canoe, which was ordered to be built for our use, was finished. As it was constructed after the manner described by Hearne and several of the American travellers, a detail of the process will be unnecessary. Its extreme length was thirty-two feet six inches, including the bow and stern pieces, its greatest breadth was four feet ten inches, but it was only two feet nine inches forward where the bowman sat, and two feet four inches behind where the steersman was placed; and its depth was one foot eleven and a quarter inches. There were seventy-three hoops of thin cedar, and a layer of slender laths of the same wood within the frame. These feeble vessels of bark will carry twenty-five pieces of goods, each weighing ninety pounds, exclusive of the necessary provision and baggage for the crew of five or six men, amounting in the whole to about three thousand three hundred pounds' weight. This great lading they annually carry between the depôts and the posts in the interior; and it rarely happens that any accidents occur, if they be managed by experienced bowmen and steersmen, on whose skill the safety of the canoe entirely depends in the rapids and difficult places. When a total portage is made, these two men carry the canoe, and they often run with it, though its weight is estimated at about three hundred pounds, exclusive of the poles and oars, which are occasionally left in where the distance is short.

On the 5th, we made an excursion for the purpose of trying our canoe. A heavy gale came on in the evening, which caused a great swell in the lake, and in crossing the waves we had the satisfaction to find that our birchen vessel proved an excellent sea-boat.

July 7

This morning some men, and their families, who had been sent off to search for Indians with whom they intended to pass the summer, returned to the fort in consequence of a serious accident having befallen their canoe in the Red Deer River; when they were in the act of hauling up a strong rapid, the line broke, the canoe was overturned, and two of the party narrowly escaped drowning; fortunately the women and children happened to be on shore, or in all probability they would have perished in the confusion of the scene. Nearly all their stores, their guns and fishing nets, were lost, and they could not procure any other food for the last four days than some unripe berries.

Some gentlemen arrived in the evening with a party of Chipewyan Indians, from Hay River, a post between the Peace River and the Great Slave Lake. These men gave distressing accounts of sickness among their relatives, and the Indians in general along the Peace River, and they said many of them have died. The disease was described as dysentery. On the 10th and 11th we had very sultry weather, and were dreadfully tormented by musquitoes. The highest temperature was 73°.

This morning Mr. Back and I had the sincere gratification of welcoming our long-separated friends, Dr. Richardson and Mr. Hood, who arrived in perfect health with two canoes, having made a very expeditious journey from Cumberland, notwithstanding they were detained near three days in consequence of the melancholy loss of one of their bowmen, by the upsetting of a canoe in a strong rapid; but, as the occurrences of this journey, together with the mention of some other circumstances that happened previous to their departure from Cumberland, which have been extracted from Mr. Hood's narrative, will appear in the following chapter, it will be unnecessary to enter further into these points now.

The zeal and talent displayed by Dr. Richardson and Mr. Hood, in the discharge of their several duties since my separation from them, drew forth my highest approbation. These gentlemen had brought all the stores they could procure from the establishments of Cumberland and Isle à la Crosse; and at the latter place they had received ten bags of pemmican from the North-West Company, which proved to be mouldy, and so totally unfit for use, that it was left at the Methye Portage. They got none from the Hudson's Bay post. The voyagers belonging to that Company, being destitute of provision, had eaten what was intended for us. In consequence of these untoward circumstances, the canoes arrived with only one day's supply of this most essential article. The prospect of having to commence our journey from hence, almost destitute of provision, and scantily supplied with stores, was distressing to us, and very encouraging to the men. It was evident, however, that any unnecessary delay here would have been very imprudent, as Fort Chipewyan did not, at the present time, furnish the means of subsistence for so large a party, much less there was a prospect of our receiving a supply to carry us forward. We therefore hastened to make the necessary arrangements for our speedy departure. All the stores were demanded that could possibly be spared from both the establishments; and we rejoiced to find that when this collection was added to the articles that had been brought up by the canoes, we had a sufficient quantity of clothing for the equipment of the men who had been engaged here, as well as to furnish a present to the Indians, besides some few goods for the winter's consumption; but we could not procure any ammunition, which was the most essential article, or spirits, and but little tobacco.

We then made a final arrangement respecting the voyagers, who were to accompany the party; and, fortunately, there was no difficulty in doing this, as Dr. Richardson and Mr. Hood had taken the very judicious precaution of bringing up ten men from Cumberland, who were engaged to proceed forward if their services were required. The Canadians, whom they brought, were most desirous of being continued, and we felt sincere pleasure in being able to keep men who were so zealous in the cause, and who had given proofs of their activity on their recent passage to this place, by discharging those men who were less willing to undertake the journey; of these, three were Englishmen, one American, and three Canadians. When the numbers were completed, which we had been recommended by the traders to take as a protection against the Esquimaux, we had sixteen Canadian voyagers, and our worthy and only English attendant John Hepburn, besides the two interpreters whom we were to receive at the Great Slave Lake; we were also accompanied by a Chipewyan woman. An equipment of goods was given to each of the men who had been engaged at this place, similar to what had been furnished to the others at Cumberland; and when this distribution had been made, the remainder were made up into bales, preparatory to our departure on the following day. We were cheerfully assisted in these and all our occupations by Mr. Smith, who evinced an anxious desire to supply our wants as far as his means permitted.

Mr. Hood having brought up the dipping needle from Cumberland House, we ascertained the dip to be 85° 23′ 42″, and the difference produced by reversing the face of the instrument was 6° 2′ 10″. The intensity of the magnetic force was also observed. Several observations had been procured on both sides of the moon during our residence at Fort Chipewyan, the result of which gave for its longitude 111° 18′ 20″ W., its latitude was observed to be 58° 42′ 38″ N., and the variation of the compass 22° 49′ 32″ E. Fresh rates were procured for the chronometers and their errors determined for Greenwich time, by which the survey to the northward was carried on.

CHAPTER VI

Mr. Hood's journey to the Basquiau Hill – Sojourns with an
Indian Party – His Journey to Chipewyan.

March, 1820

Being desirous of obtaining a drawing of a moose-deer, and also of making some observation on the height of the Aurora, I set out on the 23rd to pass a few days at the Basquiau Hill. Two men accompanied me, with dogs and sledges, who were going to the hill for meat. We found the Saskatchawan open and we were obliged to follow it several miles to the eastward. We did not, then, cross it without wading in water, which had overflowed the ice; and our snow-shoes were encumbered with a heavy weight for the remainder of the day. On the south bank of the Saskatchawan were some poplars ten or twelve feet in circumference at the root. Beyond the river, we traversed an extensive swamp, bounded by woods. In the evening we crossed the Swan Lake, about six miles in breadth, and eight in length, and halted on its south side for the night, twenty-four miles S.S.W. of Cumberland House.

At four in the morning of the 24th we continued the journey, and crossed some creeks in the woods, and another large swamp. These swamps are covered with water in summer to the depth of several feet, which arises from the melted snow from the higher grounds. The tracks of foxes, wolves, wolverenes and martens, were very numerous. The people employed in carrying meat set traps on their way out, and take possession of their captures at their return, for which they receive a sum from the Company, proportioned to the value of the fur.

In the evening we crossed the Goose Lake, which is a little longer than Swan Lake, and afterwards the river Sepanach, a branch of the Saskatchawan, forming an island extending thirty miles above, and forty below Cumberland House. We turned to the westward on the Root River, which enters the Sepanach, and halted on its banks, having made in direct distance not more than twenty miles since the 23rd.

We passed the Shoal Lake on the 25th, and then marched twelve miles through woods and swamps to a hunting tent of the Indians. It was situated in a grove of large poplars, and would have been no unpleasant residence if we could have avoided the smoke. A heavy gale from the westward, with snow, confined us for several days to this tent. On the 30th two Indians arrived, one of whom, named the Warrior, was well known at the House. We endeavoured to prevail upon them to set out in quest of moose, which they agreed to do on receiving some rum. Promises were of no avail; the smallest present gratification is preferred to the certainty of ample reward at another period; an unfailing indication of strong animal passions, and a weak understanding. On our compliance with their demand they departed.

The next day I went to the Warrior's tent, distant about eleven miles. The country was materially changed: the pine had disappeared, and gentle slopes, with clumps of large poplars, formed some pleasing groups: willows were scattered over the swamps. When I entered the tent, the Indians spread a buffalo robe before the fire, and desired me to sit down. Some were eating, others sleeping, many of them without any covering except the breech cloth and a blanket over the shoulders; a state in which they love to indulge themselves till hunger drives them forth to the chase. Besides the Warrior's family, there was that of another hunter named *Long-legs*, whose bad success in hunting had reduced him to the necessity of feeding on moose leather for three weeks, when he was compassionately relieved by the Warrior. I was an unwilling witness of the preparation of my dinner by the Indian women. They cut into pieces a portion of fat meat, using for that purpose a knife and their teeth. It was boiled in a kettle, and served in a platter made of birch bark, from which, being dirty, they had peeled the surface. However, the flavour of good moose meat will survive any process that it undergoes in their hands, except smoking.

Having provided myself with some drawing materials, I amused the Indians with a sketch of the interior of the tent and its inhabitants. An old woman, who was relating with great volubility an account of some quarrel with the traders at Cumberland House, broke off from her narration when she perceived my design; supposing, perhaps, that I was employing some charm against her; for the Indians have been taught a supernatural dread of particular pictures. One of the young men drew, with a piece of charcoal, a figure resembling a frog, on the side of the tent, and by significantly pointing at me, excited peals of merriment from his companions. The caricature was comic; but I soon fixed their attention by producing my pocket compass and affecting it with a knife. They have great curiosity, which might easily be directed to the attainment of useful knowledge. As the dirt accumulated about these people was visibly of a communicative nature, I removed at night into the open air, where the thermometer fell to 15° below zero, although it was the next day 60° above it.

In the morning the Warrior and his companion arrived; I found that, instead of hunting, they had passed the whole time in a drunken fit, at a short distance from the tent. In reply to our angry questions, the Warrior held out an empty vessel, as if to demand the payment of a debt, before he entered into any new negotiation. Not being inclined to starve his family, we set out for another Indian tent, ten miles to the southward, but we found only the frame, or tent poles, standing, when we reached the spot. The men, by digging where the fire-place had been, ascertained that the Indians had quitted it the day before; and as their marches are short, when encumbered with the women and baggage we sought out their track, and followed it. At an abrupt angle of it, which was obscured by trees, the men suddenly disappeared; and hastening forward to discover the cause, I perceived them both still rolling at the foot of a steep cliff, over which they had been dragged while endeavouring to stop the descent of their sledges. The dogs were gazing silently, with the wreck of their harness about them, and the sledges deeply buried in the snow. The effects of this accident did not detain us long, and we proceeded afterwards with greater caution.

The air was warm at noon, and the solitary but sweet notes of the jay, the earliest spring bird, were in every wood. Late in the evening we descried the ravens wheeling in circles round a small grove of poplars, and according to our expectations found the Indians encamped there.

The men were absent hunting, and returned unsuccessful. They had been several days without provisions, and thinking that I could depend upon the continuance of their exertions, I gave them a little rum; the next day they set out, and at midnight they swept by us with their dogs in close pursuit.

In the morning we found that a moose had eaten the bark of a tree near our fire. The hunters, however, again failed; and they attributed the extreme difficulty of approaching the chase to the calmness of the weather, which enabled it to hear them at a great distance.

They concluded, as usual, when labouring under any affliction, that they were tormented by the evil spirit; and assembled to beat a large tambourine, and sing an address to the Manito, or deity, praying for relief, according to the explanation which I received; but their prayer consisted of only three words, constantly repeated. One of the hunters yet remained abroad; and as the wind rose at noon, we had hopes that he was successful. In the evening he made his appearance, and announcing that he had killed a large moose, immediately secured the reward which had been promised.

The tidings were received with apparent indifference by people whose lives are alternate changes from the extremity of want to abundance. But as their countenances seldom betray their emotions, it cannot be determined whether their apathy is real or affected. However, the women prepared their sledges and dogs, with the design of dismembering, and bringing home, the carcass: a proceeding to which, in their necessitous condition, I could have had neither reasonable nor available objections, without giving them a substitute. By much solicitation I obtained an audience, and offered them our own provisions, on condition of their suspending the work of destruction till the next day. They agreed to the proposition, and we set out with some Indians for the place where the animal was lying. The night advancing, we were separated by a snow-storm, and not being skilful enough to follow tracks which were so speedily filled up, I was bewildered for several hours in the woods, when I met with an Indian, who led me back at such a pace that I was always in the rear, to his infinite diversion. The Indians are vain of their local knowledge, which is certainly very wonderful. Our companions had taken out the entrails and young of the moose, which they buried in the snow.

The Indians then returned to the tents, and one of my men accompanied them; he was the person charged with the management of the trade at the hunting tent; and he observed, that the opportunity of making a bargain with the Indians, while they were drinking, was too advantageous to be lost.

It remained for us to prevent the wolves from mangling the moose; for which purpose we wrapped ourselves in blankets between its feet, and placed the hatchets within our reach. The night was stormy, and apprehension kept me long awake; but finding my companion in so deep a sleep, that nothing could have roused him, except the actual gripe of a wolf, I thought it advisable to imitate his example, as much as was in my power, rather than bear the burthen of anxiety alone. At daylight we shook off the snow, which was heaped upon us, and endeavoured to kindle a fire; but the violence of the storm defeated all our attempts. At length two Indians arrived, with whose assistance we succeeded, and they took possession of it, to show their sense of our obligations to them. We were ashamed of the scene before us; the entrails of the moose and its young, which had been buried at our feet, bore testimony to the nocturnal revel of the wolves, during the time we had slept. This was a fresh subject of derision for the Indians, whose appetites, however, would not suffer them to waste long upon us a time so precious. They soon finished what the wolves had begun, and with as little aid from the art of cookery, eating both the young moose, and the contents of the paunch, raw.

I had scarcely secured myself by a lodge of branches from the snow, and placed the moose in a position for my sketch, when we were stormed by a troop of women and children, with their sledges and dogs. We obtained another short respite from the Indians, but our blows could not drive, nor their caresses entice, the hungry dogs from the tempting feast before them.

I had not finished my sketch before the impatient crowd tore the moose to pieces, and loaded their sledges with meat. On our way to the tent, a black wolf rushed out upon an Indian, who happened to pass near its den. It was shot; and the Indians carried away three black whelps, to improve the breed of their dogs. I purchased one of them, intending to send it to England, but it perished for want of proper nourishment.

The latitude of these tents was 53° 12′ 46″ N., and longitude by chronometers 103° 13′ 10″ W. On the 5th of April we set out for the hunting tent by our former track, and arrived there in the evening.

As the increasing warmth of the weather had threatened to interrupt communication by removing the ice, orders had been sent from Cumberland House to the people at the tent to quit it without delay; which we did on the 7th. Some altitudes of the Aurora were obtained.

We had a fine view, at sunrise, of the Basquiau Hill, skirting half the horizon with its white sides, chequered by forests of pine. It is seen from Pine Island lake, at the distance of fifty miles; and cannot, therefore, be less than three-fourths of a mile in perpendicular height; probably the greatest elevation between the Atlantic Ocean and the Rocky Mountains.

A small stream runs near the hunting tent, strongly impregnated with salt. There are several salt springs about it, which are not frozen during the winter.

The surface of the snow, thawing in the sun, and freezing at night, had become a strong crust, which sometimes gave way in a circle round our feet, immersing us in the soft snow beneath. The people were afflicted with snow blindness; a kind of ophthalmia occasioned by the reflection of the sun's rays in the spring.

The miseries endured during the first journey of this nature are so great, that nothing could induce the sufferer to undertake a second, while under the influence of present pain. He feels his frame crushed by unaccountable pressure, he drags a galling and stubborn weight at his feet, and his track is marked with blood. The dazzling scene around him affords no rest to his eye, no objection to divert his attention from his own agonising sensations. When he arises from sleep, half his body seems dead, till quickened into feeling by the irritation of his sores. But fortunately for him, no evil makes an impression so evanescent as pain. It cannot be wholly banished, nor recalled by the force of reality, by any act of the mind, either to affect our determinations, or to sympathise with another. The traveller soon forgets his sufferings, and at every future journey their recurrence is attended with diminished acuteness.

It was not before the 10th or 12th of April, that the return of the swans, geese and ducks, gave certain indications of the advance of spring. The juice of the maple-tree began to flow, and the women repaired to the woods for the purpose of collecting it. This tree which abounds to the southward, is not, I believe, found to the northward of the Saskatchawan. The Indians obtain the sap by making incisions into the tree. They boil it down, and evaporate the water, skimming off the impurities. They are so fond of sweets that after this simple process, they set an extravagant price upon it.

On the 15th fell the first shower of rain we had seen for six months, and on the 17th the thermometer rose to 77° in the shade. The whole face of the country was deluged by the melted snow. All the nameless heaps of dirt, accumulated in the winter, now floated over the very thresholds, and the long-imprisoned scents dilated into vapours so penetrating, that no retreat was any security from them. The flood descended into the cedar below our house, and destroyed a quantity of powder and tea; a loss irreparable in our situation.

The noise made by the frogs which this inundation produced, is almost incredible. There is strong reason to believe that they outlive the severity of winter. They have often been found frozen and revived by warmth, nor is it possible that the multitude which incessantly filled our ears with its discordant tones could have been matured in two or three days.

The fishermen at Beaver Lake, and the other detached parties were ordered to return to the post. The expedients to which the poor people were reduced, to cross a country so beset with waters, presented many uncouth spectacles. The inexperienced were glad to compromise, with the loss of property, for the safety of their persons, and astride upon ill-balanced rafts with which they struggled to be uppermost, exhibited a ludicrous picture of distress. Happy were they who could patch up an old canoe, though obliged to bear it half the way on their shoulders, through miry bogs and interwoven willows. But the veteran trader, wedged in a box of skin, with his wife, children, dogs, and furs, wheeled triumphantly through the current, and deposited his heterogeneous cargo safely on the shore. The woods re-echoed with the return of their exiled tenants. An hundred tribes, as gaily dressed as any burnished natives of the south, greeted our eyes in our accustomed walks, and their voices, though unmusical, were the sweetest that ever saluted our ears.

From the 19th to the 26th the snow once more blighted the resuscitating verdure, but a single day was sufficient to remove it. On the 28th the Saskatchawan swept away the ice which had adhered to its banks, and on the morrow a boat came down from Carlton House with provisions. We received such accounts of the state of vegetation at that place, that Dr. Richardson determined to visit it, in order to collect botanical specimens, as the period at which the ice was expected to admit of the continuation of our journey was still distant. Accordingly he embarked on the 1st of May.

In the course of the month the ice gradually wore away from the south side of the lake, but the great mass of it still hung to the north side with some snow visible on its surface. By the 21st the elevated grounds were perfectly dry, and teeming with the fragrant offspring of the season. When the snow melted, the earth was covered with the fallen leaves of the last year, and already it was green with the strawberry plant, and the bursting buds of the gooseberry, raspberry, and rose bushes, soon variegated by the rose and the blossoms of the choke cherry. The gifts of nature are disregarded and undervalued till they are withdrawn, and in the hideous regions of the Arctic Zone, she would make a convert of him for whom the gardens of Europe had no charms, or the mild beauties of a southern climate had bloomed in vain.

Mr. Williams found a delightful occupation in his agricultural pursuits. The horses were brought to the plough, and fields of wheat, barley, and Indian corn, promised to reward his labours. His dairy furnished us with all the luxuries of an English farm.

On the 25th the ice departed from Pine Island Lake. We were, however, informed that Beaver Lake, which was likewise in our route, would not afford a passage before the 4th of June. According to directions left by Mr. Franklin, applications were made to the chiefs of the Hudson's Bay and North-West

Companies' posts, for two canoes, with their crews, and a supply of stores, for the use of the Expedition. They were not in a condition to comply with this request till the arrival of their respective returns from Isle à la Crosse and the Saskatchawan departments. Of the six men whom we brought from England, the most serviceable, John Hepburn, had accompanied Mr. Franklink, and only one other desired to prosecute the journey with us. Mr. Franklin had made arrangements with Mr. Williams for the employment of the remaining five men in bringing to Cumberland House the ammunition, tobacco, etc., left at York Fort, which stores were, if possible, to be sent after us in the summer. On the 30th Dr. Richardson returned from Carlton House, and on the 31st the boats arrived belonging to the Hudson's Bay Company's Saskatchawan department. We obtained a canoe and two more volunteers. On the 1st of June the Saskatchawan, swelled by the melting of the snow near the Rocky Mountains, rose twelve feet, and the current of the little rivers bounding Pine Island ran back into the lake, which it filled with mud.

On the 5th the North-West Company's people arrived, and Mr. Connolly furnished us with a canoe and five Canadians. They were engaged to attend us till Mr. Franklin should think fit to discharge them, and bound under the usual penalties in case of disobedience, or other improper conduct. These poor people entertained such dread of a ship of war, that they stipulated not to be embarked in Lieutenant Parry's vessels, if we should find them on the coast; a condition with which they would gladly have dispensed, had that desirable event taken place. As we required a Canadian foreman and steersman for the other canoe, we were compelled to wait for the appearance of the Isle à la Crosse canoes under Mr. Clark.

On the 8th Mr. Williams embarked for York Fort. He gave us a circular letter addressed to the chiefs of the Hudson's Bay Company's posts, directing them to afford us all possible assistance on our route, and he promised to exert every endeavour to forward the Esquimaux interpreter, upon whom the success of our journey so much depended. He was accompanied by eight boats. With him we sent our collections of plants, minerals, charts, and drawings, to be transmitted to England by the Hudson's Bay ships. After this period, our detention, though short, cost us more vexation than the whole time we had passed at Cumberland House, because every hour of the short summer was invaluable to us. On the 11th Mr. Clark arrived, and completed our crews. – He brought letters from Mr. Franklin, dated March 28th, at Fort Chipewyan, where he was engaged procuring hunters and interpreters. A heavy storm of wind and rain from the north-east again delayed us till the morning of the 13th. The account we had received at York Factory of the numerous stores at Cumberland House proved to be very erroneous. The most material stores we received did not amount, in addition to our own, to more than two barrels of powder, a keg of spirits, and two pieces of tobacco, with pemmican for sixteen days.

The crew of Dr. Richardson's canoe consisted of three Englishmen and three Canadians, and the other carried five Canadians; both were deeply laden and the waves ran high on the lake. No person in our party being well acquainted with the rivers to the northward, Mr. Connolly gave us a pilot, on condition that we should exchange him when we met with the Athabasca brigade of canoes. At four A.M. we embarked. We soon found that birchen-bark canoes were not calculated to brave rough weather on a large lake, for we were compelled to land on the opposite border, to free them from the weather which had already saturated their cargoes. The wind became more moderate, and we were enabled, after traversing a chain of smaller lakes, to enter the mouth of the Sturgeon River, at sunset, where we encamped.

The lading of the canoes is always, if possible, carried on shore at night, and the canoes taken out of the water. The following evening we reached Beaver Lake, and landed to repair some damages sustained by the canoes. A round stone will displace the lading of a canoe, without doing any injury, but a slight blow against a sharp corner penetrates the bark. For the purpose of repairing it, a small quantity of gum or pitch, bark and pine roots, are embarked, and the business is so expeditiously performed, that the speed of the canoe amply compensates for every delay. The Sturgeon River is justly called by the Canadians La Riviére Maligne, from its numerous and dangerous rapids. Against the strength of a rapid it is impossible to effect any progress by paddling, and the canoes are tracked, or if the bank will not admit it, propelled with poles, in the management of which the Canadians show with great dexterity. Their simultaneous motions were strongly contrasted with the awkward confusion of the inexperienced Englishmen, deafened by the torrent, who sustained the blame of every accident which occurred.

At sunset we encamped on an island in Beaver Lake, and at four A.M., the next morning, passed the first portage in the Ridge River. Beaver Lake is twelve miles in length, and six in breadth. The flat limestone country rises into bold rocks on its banks, and at the mouth of the Ridge River, the limestone discontinues. The lake is very deep, and has already been noticed for the number and excellence of its fish. The Ridge River is rapid and shallow. We had emerged from the muddy channels through an alluvial soil, and the primitive rocks interrupted our way with frequent portages, through the whole route to Isle à la Crosse Lake. At two P.M. we passed the mouth of the Hay River, running from the westward; and the ridge above its confluence takes the name of the Great River, which rises at the height of land called Frog Portage.

The thermometer was this day 100° in the sun, and the heat was extremely oppressive, from our constant exposure to it. We crossed three portages in the Great River, and encamped at the last; here we met the director of the North-West Company's affairs in the north, Mr. Stuart, on his way to Fort William, in a light canoe. He had left the Athabasca Lake only thirteen days, and brought letters from Mr. Franklin, who desired that we would endeavour to collect stores of every kind at Isle à la Crosse, and added a favourable account of the country, to the northward of the Slave Lake.

On the 16th, at three A.M., we continued our course, the river increasing to the breadth of half a mile, with many rapids between the rocky islands. The banks were luxuriantly clothed with pines, poplars, and birch trees, of the largest size: but the different shades of green were undistinguishable at a distance, and the glow of autumnal colours was wanting to render the variety beautiful.

Having crossed two portages at the different extremities of the Island Lake, we ran under sail through two extensive sheets of water, called the Heron and Pelican Lakes; the former of which is fifteen miles in length, and the latter five; but its extent to the southward has not been explored. An intricate channel, with four small portages, conducted us to the Woody Lake. Its borders were, indeed, walls of pines, hiding the face of steep and high rocks; and we wandered in search of a landing-place till ten P.M., when we were forced to take shelter from an impending storm on a small island where we wedged ourselves between the trees. But though we secured the canoes, we incurred a personal evil of much greater magnitude, in the torments inflicted by the musquitoes, a plague which had grown upon us since our departure from Cumberland House, and which infested us during the whole summer; we found no relief from their attacks by exposing ourselves to the utmost violence of the wind and rain. Our last resource was to plunge ourselves in the water, and from this uncomfortable situation we gladly escaped at day-light, and hoisted our sails.

The Woody Lake is thirteen miles in length, and a small grassy channel at its north-western extremity, leads to the Frog Portage, the source of the waters descending by Beaver Lake to the Saskatchawan. The distance to the Missinippi, or Churchill River, is only three hundred and eighty yards; and as its course crosses the height nearly at right angles to the direction of the Great River, it would be superfluous to compute the elevation at this place. The portage is in latitude 55° 26′ 0″ N., and longitude 103° 34′ 50″ W. Its name, according to Sir Alexander Mackenzie, is derived from the Crees having left suspended a stretched frog's skin, in derision of the Northern Indian mode of dressing the beaver.

The part of the Missinippi, in which we embarked, we should have mistaken for a lake, had it not been for the rapidity of the current against which we made our way. At four P.M. we passed a long portage occasioned by a ledge of rocks, three hundred yards in length, over which the river falls seven or eight feet. After crossing another portage we encamped.

On the 18th we had rain, wind, and thunder, the whole day; but this weather was much preferable to the heat we had borne hitherto. We passed three portages, and, at six P.M., encamped on the north bank. Below the third portage is the mouth of the Rapid River, flowing from a large lake to the southward, on which a post was formerly maintained by the North-West Company. Next morning we found ourselves involved in a confused mass of islands, through the openings of which we could not discern the shore. The guide's knowledge of the river did not extend beyond the last portage, and our perplexity continued, till we observed some foam floating on the water, and took the direction from which it came. The noise of a heavy fall, at the Mountain Portage, reached our ears, at the distance of four miles, and we arrived there at eight A.M. The portage was a difficult ascent over a rocky island, between which and the main shore were two cataracts and a third in sight above them, making another portage. We surprised a large brown bear which immediately retreated into the woods. To the northward of the second portage we again found the channels intricate, but the shores being sometimes visible, we ventured to proceed. The character of the country was new and more interesting than before. The mountainous and strong elevations receded from the bank, and the woods crept through their openings to the valleys behind; the adventurous pine alone ascending their bases, and braving storms unfelt below.

At noon we landed at the Otter Portage, where the river ran with great velocity for half a mile, among large stones. Having carried across the principal part of the cargo, the people attempted to track the canoes along the edge of the rapid. With the first they succeeded, but the other, in which were the foreman and steersman, was overset and swept away by the current. An account of this misfortune was speedily conveyed to the upper end of the portage, and the men launched the remaining canoe into the rapid, though wholly unacquainted with the dangers of it. The descent was quickly accomplished, and they perceived the bottom of the lost canoe above water in a little bay, whither it had been whirled by the eddy. One man had reached the bank, but no traces could be found of the foreman, Louis Saint Jean. We saved the canoe, out of which two guns and a case of preserved meats had been thrown into the rapid.[1] So early a disaster deeply affected the spirits of the Canadians, and their natural vivacity gave way to melancholy forebodings, while they erected a wooden cross in the rocks near the spot where their companion perished.

1 Mr. Hood himself was the first to leap into the canoe and incite the men to follow him, and shoot the rapid to save the lives of their companions. – Dr. RICHARDSON'S Journal.

The loss of this man's services, and the necessity of procuring a guide, determined us to wait for the arrival of the North-West Company's people from Fort Chipewyan, and we encamped accordingly. The canoe was much shattered, but as the gunwales were not broken, we easily repaired it. In the evening a N.W. canoe arrived, with two of the partners. They gave us an account of Mr. Franklin's proceedings and referred us to the brigade following them for a guide.

During the 20th it rained heavily, and we passed the day in anxious suspense confined to our tents. A black bear came to the bank on the opposite side of the river, and on seeing us glided behind the trees.

Late on the 21st, Mr. Robertson, of the Hudson's Bay Company, arrived, and furnished us with a guide, but desired that he might be exchanged when we met the northern canoes. We took advantage of the remainder of the day, to cross the next portage, which was three-fourths of a mile in length.

On the 22nd we crossed three small portages, and encamped at the fourth. At one of them we passed some of the Hudson's Bay Company's canoes, and our application to them was unsuccessful. We began to suspect that Isle à la Crosse was the nearest place at which we might hope for assistance. However, on the morning of the 23rd, as we were about to embark, we encountered the last brigades of canoes belonging to both the Companies, and obtained a guide and foreman from them. Thus completely equipped, we entered the Black Bear Island Lake, the navigation of which requires a very experienced pilot. Its length is twenty-two miles, and its breadth varies from three to five, yet it is so choked with islands, that no channel is to be found through it, exceeding a mile in breadth. At sunset we landed, and encamped on an island, and at six A.M. on the 24th, left the lake and crossed three portages into another, which has, probably, several communications with the last, as that by which we passed is too narrow to convey the whole body of the Missinippi. At one of these portages called the Pin Portage is a rapid, about ten yards in length, with a descent of ten or twelve feet, and beset with rocks. Light canoes sometimes venture down this fatal gulf, to avoid the portage, unappalled by the warning crosses which overhang the brink, the mournful records of former failures.

The Hudson's Bay Company's people whom we passed on the 23rd, going to the rock house with their furs, were badly provided with food, of which we saw distressing proofs at every portage behind them. They had stripped the birch trees of their rind to procure the soft pulpy vessels in contact with the wood, which are sweet, but very insufficient to satisfy a craving appetite.

The lake to the westward of the Pin Portage, is called Sandfly Lake; it is seven miles long; and a wide channel connects it with the Serpent Lake, the extent of which to the southward we could not discern. There is nothing remarkable in this chain of lakes, except their shapes, being rocky basins filled by the waters of the Missinippi, insulating the massy eminences, and meandering with almost imperceptible current between them. From the Serpent to the Sandy Lake, it is again confined in a narrow space by the approach of its winding banks, and on the 26th we were some hours employed in traversing a series of shallow rapids, where it was necessary to lighten the canoes. Having missed the path through the woods, we walked two miles in the water upon sharp stones, from which some of us were incessantly slipping into deep holes, and floundering in vain for footing at the bottom; a scene highly diverting, notwithstanding our fatigue. We were detained in Sandy Lake, till one P.M., by a strong gale, when the wind becoming moderate we crossed five miles to the mouth of the river, and at four P.M. left the main branch of it, and entered a little rivulet called the Grassy River, running through an extensive reedy swamp. It is the nest of innumerable ducks, which rear their young, among the long rushes, in security from beasts of prey. At sunset we encamped on the banks of the main branch.

At three A.M. June 28th, we embarked in a thick fog occasioned by a fall of the temperature of the air ten degrees below that of the water. Having crossed Knee Lake, which is nine miles in length, and a portage at its western extremity, we entered Primeau Lake, with a strong and favourable wind, by the aid of which we ran nineteen miles through it, and encamped at the river's mouth. It is shaped like the barb of an arrow, with the point towards the north, and its greatest breadth is about four miles.

During the night, a torrent of rain washed us from our beds, accompanied with the loudest thunder I ever heard. This weather continued during the 29th, and often compelled us to land, and turn the canoes up, to prevent them from filling. We passed one portage, and the confluence of a river, said to afford, by other rivers beyond a height of land, a shorter but more difficult route to the Athabasca Lake than that which is generally pursued.

On the 28th we crossed the last portage, and at ten A.M. entered the Isle à la Crosse Lake. Its long succession of woody points, both banks stretching towards the south, till their forms were lost in the haze of the horizon, was a grateful prospect to us, after our bewildered and interrupted voyage in the Missinippi. The gale wafted us with unusual speed, and as the lake increased in breadth, the waves swelled to a dangerous height. A canoe running before the wind is very liable to burst asunder, when on the top of a wave, so that part of the bottom is out of the water; for there is nothing to support the weight of its heavy cargo but the bark, and the slight gunwales attached to it.

On making known our exigencies to the gentlemen in charge of the Hudson's Bay and North-West Companies' forts, they made up an assortment of stores, amounting to five bales; for four of which we were indebted to Mr. M'Leod of the North-West Company, who shared with us the ammunition absolutely required for the support of his post; receiving in exchange an order for the same quantity upon the cargo which we expected to follow us from York Factory. We had heard from Mr. Stuart that Fort Chipewyan was too much impoverished to supply the wants of the Expedition, and we found Isle à la Crosse in the same condition; which, indeed, we might have foreseen, from the exhausted state of Cumberland House, but could not have provided against. We never had heard before our departure from York that the posts in the interior only received annually the stores necessary for the consumption of a single year. It was fortunate for us that Mr. Franklin had desired ten bags of pemmican to be sent from the Saskatchawan across the plains to Isle à la Crosse for our use. This resource was untouched, but we could not embark more than five pieces in our own canoes. However, Mr. M'Leod agreed to send a canoe after us to the Methye Portage, with the pemmican, and we calculated that the diminution of our provision would there enable us to receive it.

The Beaver River enters this lake on the S.E. side, and another river which has not been named, on the S.W. Both these rivers are branches of the Missinippi, as it is the only outlet from the lake. The banks appeared to be rocky, and the beach in many places sandy, but its waters are yellow and muddy. It produces a variety of fish, among which its white-fish are esteemed the best in the country. The only birds visible at this season, are common to every part of the Missinippi; gulls, ducks, pigeons, goatsuckers, and the raven; and geese and swans pay a momentary visit in passing to the north and returning.

There was little in the forts differing from the establishments that we had before seen. The ground on which they are erected is sandy, and favourable to cultivation. Curiosity, however, was satisfied by the first experiment, and utility alone has been unable to extend it. Isle à la Crosse is frequented by the Crees and the Chipewyans. It is not the dread of the Indians, but of one another, that has brought the rival Companies so close together at every trading post; each party seeking to prevent the other from engaging the affections of the natives, and monopolising the trade. Whenever a settlement is made by the one, the other immediately follows, without considering the eligibility of the place; for it may injure its opponent, though it cannot benefit itself, and that advantage which is the first object of all other commercial bodies, becomes but the second with the fur traders.

On the evening of the 30th we embarked, and entered a wide channel to the northward of the forts, and extending towards the north-west. It gradually decreased in breadth till it became a river, which is the third fork of the Missinippi, and its current being almost insensible, we entered the Clear Lake at ten A.M. on the 1st of July. Of this lake, which is very large, no part is known except the south border, but its extend would lead us to conclude, that its evaporation must be supplied by another river to the northward, especially as the small channel that communicates with Buffalo Lake is motionless. The existence of such a river is asserted by the Indians, and a shorter passage might be found by it across the height of land to Clear Water River, than the portage from the Methye Lake.

In Buffalo Lake, the wind was too strong for us to proceed, and we therefore encamped upon a gravel beach thrown up by the waves. We embarked at three A.M. July 2nd, and at four P.M. entered the mouth of the Methye River. The lake is thirty-four miles in length, and fourteen in breadth. It is probably very deep, for we saw no islands on this wide expanse, except at the borders. On the south-west side were two forts, belonging to the Companies, and near them a solitary hill seven or eight hundred feet high. At eight P.M. we encamped in the Methye River, at the confluence of the river Pembina. A route has been explored by it to the Red Willow River, across the height of land, but the difficulties of it were so great that the ordinary route is preferred.

On the 3rd we passed through the Methye River, and encamped on the borders of the Methye Lake. The soil from Isle à la Crosse to this place is sandy, with some portion of clay, and the trees numerous; but the Methye River is stony, and so shallow, that to lighten the canoes, we made two portages of five and two miles. The paths were overflowed with cold spring water, and barricadoed by fallen trees; we should have been contented to immerse ourselves wholly had the puddle been sufficiently deep, for the musquitoes devoured every part that was exposed to them.

On the 4th we crossed the Methye Lake, and landed at the portage on the north-west side, in one of the sources of the Missinippi. The lake is seventeen miles in length, with a large island in the middle. We proceeded to the north side of the portage with two men, carrying a tent and some instruments, leaving the canoes and cargoes to be transported by daily journeys of two or three miles. The distance is fourteen statute miles, and there are two small lakes about five miles from the north side. Several species of fish were found in them, though they have no known communication with any other body of water, being situated on the elevation of the height. The road was a gentle ascent, miry from the late rainy weather, and shaded by pines, poplars, birches, and cypresses, which terminated our view. On the north side we discovered through an opening in the trees, that we were on a hill eight or nine hundred feet high, and at the edge of a steep descent. We were prepared to expect an extensive prospect, but the magnificent scene before us was so superior to what the nature of the country had promised, that it banished even our sense of suffering from the musquitoes, which hovered in clouds about our heads. Two parallel chains of hills extended towards the setting sun, their various projecting outlines exhibiting the several gradations of distance, and the opposite bases closing at the horizon. On the nearest eminence, the objects were clearly defined by their dark shadows; the yellow rays blended their softening hues with brilliant green on the next, and beyond it all distinction melted into gray and purple. In the long valley between, the smooth and colourless Clear Water River wound its spiral course, broken and shattered by encroaching woods. An exuberance of rich herbage covered the soil, and lofty trees climbed the precipice at our feet, hiding its brink with their summits. Impatient as we were, and blinded with pain, we paid a tribute of admiration, which this beautiful landscape is capable of exciting, unaided by the borrowed charms of a calm atmosphere, glowing with the vivid tints of evening.

We descended to the banks of the Clear Water River, and having encamped, the two men returned to assist their companions. We had sometimes before procured a little rest, by closing the tent, and burning wood, or flashing gunpowder within, the smoke driving the musquitoes into the crannies of the ground. But this remedy was now ineffectual, though we employed it so perseveringly, as to hazard suffocation: they swarmed under our blankets, goring us with their envenomed trunks, and steeping our clothes in blood. We rose at daylight in a fever, and our misery was unmitigated during our whole stay.

The musquitoes of America resemble, in shape, those of Africa and Europe, but differ essentially in size and other particulars. There are two distinct species, the largest of which is brown, and the smallest black. Where they are bred cannot easily be determined, for they are numerous in every soil. They make their first appearance in May, and the cold destroys them in September; in July they are most voracious; and fortunately for the traders, the journeys from the trading posts to the factories are generally concluded at that period. The food of the musquito is blood, which it can extract by penetrating the hide of a buffalo; and if it is not disturbed, it gorges itself so as to swell its body into a transparent globe. The wound does not swell, like that of the African musquito, but it is infinitely more painful; and when multiplied a hundred fold, and continued for so many successive days, it becomes an evil of such magnitude, that cold, famine, and every other concomitant of an inhospitable climate, must yield the pre-eminence to it. It chases the buffalo to the plains, irritating him to madness; and the reindeer to the sea-shore, from which they do not return till the scourge has ceased.

On the 6th the thermometer was 106° in the sun, and on the 7th 110°. The musquitoes sought the shade in the heat of the day. It was some satisfaction to us to see the havoc made among them by a large and beautiful species of dragon-fly, called the musquito hawk, which wheeled through their retreats, swallowing their pray without a momentary diminution of speed. But the temporary relief that we had hoped for was only an exchange of tormentors: our new assailant, the horse-fly, or bull-dog, ranged in the hottest glare of the sun, and carried off a portion of flesh at each attack. Another noxious insect, the smallest, but not the least formidable, was the sand-fly known in Canada by the name of the *brulot*. To such annoyance all travellers must submit, and it would be unworthy to complain of that grievance in the pursuit of knowledge, which is endured for the sake of profit. This detail of it has only been as an excuse for the scantiness of our observations on the most interesting part of the country through which we passed.

The north side of the Methye Portage is in latitude 56° 41′ 40″ N. and longitude 109° 52′ 0″ W. It is, of course, one hundred and twenty-four miles from Isle à la Crosse, and considered as a branch of the Missinippi, five hundred and ninety-two miles from the Frog Portage. The Clear Water River passing through the valley, described above, evidently rises not far to the eastward. The height, computed by the same mode as that of the Echiamamis, by allowing a foot for each mile of distance, and six feet on an average, for each fall and rapid, is two thousand four hundred and sixty-seven feet above the level of the sea, admitting it to be nine hundred feet above the Clear Water River. The country, in a line between it and the mouth of Mackenzie's River, is a continual descent, although to the eastward of that line, there may be several heights between it and the Arctic Sea. To the eastward, the lands descend to Hudson's Bay; and to the westward also, till the Athabasca River cuts through it, from whence it ascends to the Rocky Mountains. Daring was the spirit of enterprise that first led Commerce, with her cumbrous train, from the waters of Hudson's Bay to those of the Arctic Sea, across and obstacle to navigation so stupendous as this; and persevering has been the industry which drew riches from a source so remote.

On the 8th two men arrived, and informed us that they had brought us our ten bags of pemmican from Isle à la Crosse, but that they were found to be rotten. Thus were we unexpectedly deprived of the most essential of our stores, for we knew Fort Chipewyan to be destitute of provisions, and that Mr. Franklin depended upon us for a supply, whereas, enough did not remain for our own use. On the 9th, the canoes and cargoes reached the north side of the portage. Our people had selected two bags of pemmican less mouldy than the rest, which they left on the beach. Its decay was caused by some defect in the mode of mixing it.

On the 10th, we embarked in the Clear Water River, and proceeded down the current. The hills, the banks, and bed of the river, were composed of fine yellow sand, with some limestone rocks. The surface soil was alluvial. At eight A.M. we passed a portage on which the limestone rocks were singularly scattered through the woods, bearing the appearance of houses and turrets overgrown with moss. The earth emitted a hollow sound, and the river was divided by rocks into narrow crooked channels, every object indicating that some convulsion had disturbed the general order of nature at this place. We had passed a portage above it, and after two long portages below it we encamped. Near the last was a small stream so strongly impregnated with sulphur, as to taint the air to a great distance around it. We sat two brown bears on the hills in the course of the day.

At daylight, on the 11th, we embarked. The hills continued on both sides of the mouth of the river, varying from eight hundred to one thousand feet in height. They declined to the banks in long green slopes, diversified by woody mounds and copses. The pines were not here in thick impenetrable masses, but perched aloft in single groups on the heights, or shrouded by the livelier hues of the poplar and willow.

We passed the mouth of the Red Willow River on the south bank, flowing through a deep ravine. It is the continuation of the route by the Pembina, before mentioned. At noon we entered the majestic Athabasca or Elk River. Its junction with the Clear Water River is called the Forks. Its banks were inaccessible cliffs, apparently of clay and stones, about two hundred feet high, and its windings in the south were encircled by high mountains. Its breadth exceeded half a mile and was swelled to a mile in many places by long muddy islands in the middle covered with trees. No more portages interrupted our course, but a swift current hurried us towards the quarter in which our anticipated discoveries were to commence. The passing cliffs returned a loud confusion of echoes to the sprightly canoe song, and the dashing paddles; and the eagles, watching with half-closed eyes on the pine-tops, started from their airy nest, and prepared their drowsy pinions for the flight.

About twenty miles from the Forks are some salt pits and plains, said to be very extensive. The height of the banks was reduced to twenty or thirty feet, and the hills ranged themselves at an increased distance from the banks in the same variety as those of the Clear Water River. At sunset we encamped on a small sandy island, but the next morning made a speedy retreat to the canoes, the water having nearly overflown our encampment. We passed two deserted settlements of the fur traders on opposite banks, at a place called Pierre au Calumet. Beyond it the hills disappeared, and the banks were no longer visible above the trees. The river carries away yearly large portions of soil, which increases its breadth, and diminishes its depth, rendering the water so muddy as to be scarcely drinkable. Whole forests of timber are drifted down the stream, and choke up the channels between the islands at its mouth. We observed the traces of herds of buffaloes, where they had crossed the river, the trees being trodden down and strewed, as if by a whirlwind.

At four P.M. we left the main branch of the Athabasca, entering a small river, called the Embarras. It is narrow and muddy, with pines of an enormous size on its banks. Some of them are two hundred feet high, and three or four feet in diameter. At nine P.M. we landed and encamped; but finding ourselves in a nest of musquitoes, we continued our journey before daybreak; and at eight A.M., emerged into the Athabasca Lake. A strong wind agitated this sea of fresh water, which, however, we crossed without any accident, and landed on the north side of it, at Fort Chipewyan; where we had the satisfaction of finding our companions in good health, and of experiencing that sympathy in our anxiety on the state of affairs, which was only to be expected from those who were to share our future fortunes.

CHAPTER VII

July 18, 1820

Early this morning the stores were distributed to the three canoes. Our stock of provision unfortunately did not amount to more than sufficient for one day's consumption, exclusive of two barrels of flour, three cases of preserved meats, some chocolate, arrowroot, and portable soup, which we had brought from England, and intended to reserve for our journey to the coast the next season. Seventy pounds of moose meat and a little barley were all that Mr. Smith was enabled to give us. It was gratifying, however, to perceive that this scarcity of food did not depress the spirits of our Canadian companions, who cheerfully loaded their canoes, and embarked in high glee after they had received the customary dram. At noon we bade farewell to our kind friend Mr. Smith. The crews commenced a lively paddling song on quitting the shore, which was continued until we had lost sight of the houses. We soon reached the western boundary of the lake, and at two entered the Stony River, one of the discharges of the Athabasca Lake into the Slave Lake, and having a favouring current passed swiftly along. This narrow stream is confined between low swampy banks, which support willows, dwarf birch, and alder. At five we passed its conflux with the Peace River. The Slave River, formed by the union of these streams, is about three-quarters of a mile wide. We descended this magnificent river with much rapidity, and after passing through several narrow channels, formed by an assemblage of islands, crossed a spot where the waters had a violent whirling motion, which, when the river is low, is said to subside into a dangerous rapid; on the present occasion no other inconvenience was felt than the inability of steering the canoes, which were whirled about in every direction by the eddies, until the current carried them beyond their influence. We encamped at seven on the swampy bank of the river, but had scarcely pitched the tents before we were visited by a terrible thunder-storm; the rain fell in torrents, and the violence of the wind caused the river to overflow its banks, so that we were completely flooded. Swarms of musquitoes succeeded the storm, and their tormenting stings, superadded to other incon-veniences, induced us to embark, and, after taking a hasty supper, to pursue our voyage down the stream during the night.

At six on the following morning we passed the Reindeer Islands, and at ten reached the entrance of the Dog River, where we halted to set the fishing nets. These were examined in the evening, but to our mortification we obtained only four small trout, and were compelled to issue part of our preserved meats for supper. The latitude of the mouth of Dog River was observed, 59° 52′ 16″ N.

The nets were taken up at daylight, but they furnished only a solitary spike. We lost no time in embarking, and crossed the crooked channel of the Dog Rapid, when two of the canoes came in such violent contact with each other, that the sternmost had its bow broken off. We were fortunately near the shore, or the disabled canoe would have sunk. The injury being repaired in two hours, we again embarked, and having descended another rapid, arrived at the Cassette Portage of four hundred and sixty paces, over which the cargoes and canoes were carried in about twenty-six minutes. We next passed through a narrow channel full of rapids, crossed the Portage d'Embarras of seventy yards; and the portage of the Little Rock, of three hundred yards, at which another accident happened to one of the canoes, by the bowman slipping and letting it fall upon a rock, and breaking it in two. Two hours were occupied in sewing the detached pieces together, and covering the seam with pitch; but this being done it was as effective as before. After leaving this place we soon came to the next portage, of two hundred and seventy-three paces; and shortly afterwards to the Mountain Portage, of one hundred and twenty: which is appropriately named, as the path leads over the summit of a high hill. This elevated situation commands a very grand and picturesque view, for some miles along the river, which at this part is about a mile wide.

We next crossed a portage of one hundred and twenty yards; and then the Pelican Portage, of eight hundred paces. Mr. Back took an accurate sketch of the interesting scenery which the river presents at this place. After descending six miles farther we came to the last portage on the route to Slave Lake which we crossed, and encamped in its lower end. It is called 'The Portage of the Drowned,' and it received that name from a melancholy accident which took place many years ago. Two canoes arrived at the upper end of the portage, in one of which there was an experienced guide. This man judging from the height of the river, deemed it practicable to shoot the rapid, and determined upon trying it. He accordingly placed himself in the bow of his canoe, having previously agreed, that if the passage was found easy, he should, on reaching the bottom of the rapid, fire a musket, as a signal for the other canoe to follow. The rapid proved dangerous and called forth all the skill of the guide, and the utmost exertion of his crew, and they narrowly escaped destruction. Just as they were loading, an unfortunate fellow seizing the loaded fowling-piece, fired at a duck which rose at the instant. The guide anticipating the consequences, ran with the utmost haste to the other end of the portage, but he was too late: the other canoe had pushed off, and he arrived only to witness the fate of his comrades. They got alarmed in the middle of the rapid, the canoe was upset, and every man perished.

The various rapids we passed this day, are produced by an assemblage of islands and rocky ledges, which obstruct the river, and divide it into many narrow channels. Two of these channels are rendered still more difficult by accumulations of drift timber; a circumstance which has given a name to one of the portages. The rocks which compose the bed of the river, and the numerous islands, belong to the granite formation. The distance made today was thirteen miles.

July 21

We embarked at four A.M. and pursued our course down the river. The rocks ceased at the last portage; and below it the banks are composed of alluvial soil, which is held together by the roots of trees and shrubs that crown their summits. The river is about a mile wide, and the current is greatly diminished. At eight we landed at the mouth of the Salt River, and pitched our tents, intending to remain there that and the next day for the purpose of fishing. After breakfast, which made another inroad on our preserved meats, we proceeded up the river in a light canoe, to visit the salt springs, leaving a party behind to attend the nets. This river is about one hundred yards wide at its mouth. Its waters did not become brackish until we had ascended it seven or eight miles; but when we had passed several rivulets of fresh water which flowed in, the main stream became very salt, at the same time contracting its width to fifteen or twenty yards. At a distance of twenty-two miles, including the windings of the river, the plains commence. Having pitched the tent at this spot, we set out to visit the principal springs, and had walked about three miles when the musquitoes compelled us to give up our project. We did not see the termination of the plains towards the east, but on the north and west they are bounded by an even ridge, about six or seven hundred feet in height. Several salt springs issue from the foot of this ridge, and spread their waters over the plain, which consists of tenacious clay. During the summer much evaporation takes place, and large heaps of salt are left behind crystallised in the form of cubes. Some beds of grayish compact gypsum were exposed on the sides of the hills.

The next morning after filling some casks with salt for our use during winter, we embarked to return, and had descended the river a few miles, when turning round a point, we perceived a buffalo plunge into the river before us. Eager to secure so valuable a prize, we instantly opened a fire upon him from four muskets, and in a few minutes he fell, but not before he had received fourteen balls. The carcass was towed to the bank, and the canoe speedily laden with meat. After this piece of good fortune, we descended the stream merrily, our voyages chanting their liveliest songs. On arrival at the mouth of the river, we found that our nets had not produced more than enough to supply a scanty meal to the men whom we had left behind, but this was now of little importance, as the acquisition of meat we had made would enable us to proceed without more delay to Slave Lake. The *poisson inconnu* mentioned by Mackenzie, is found here. It is a species of the Genus Salmo, and is said by the Indians to ascend from the Arctic Sea, but being unable to pass the cascade of the Slave River, is not found higher than this place. In the evening a violent thunderstorm came on with heavy rain, thermometer 70°.

At a very early hour on the following morning we embarked, and continued to paddle against a very strong wind and high waves, under the shelter of the bank of the rivers, until two P.M., when having arrived at a more exposed part of the stream, the canoes took in so much water that we were obliged to disembark on a small island. The river here is from one mile and a quarter to one mile and three-quarters wide. Its banks are of moderate height, sandy, and well wooded.

July 24

We made more progress notwithstanding the continuance of the wind. The course of the river is very winding, making in one place a circuit of seven or eight miles round a peninsula, which is joined to the west bank by a narrow isthmus. Near the foot of this elbow, a long island occupies the centre of the river, which it divides into two channels. The longitude was obtained near to it 113° 25′ 36″, and variation 27° 25′ 14″ N., and the latitude 60° 54′ 52″ N., about four miles farther down. We passed the mouth of a broad channel leading to the north-east, termed La Grande Rivière de Jean, one of the two large branches by which the river pours its waters into the Great Slave Lake; the flooded *delta* at the mouth of the river is intersected by several smaller channels, through one of which, called the Channel of the Scaffold, we pursued our voyage on the following morning, and by eight A.M. reached the establishment of the North-West Company on Moose-Deer Island. We found letters from Mr. Wentzel, dated Fort Providence, a station to the north side of the lake, which communicated to us, that there was an Indian guide waiting for us at that post; but, that the chief and the hunters, who were to accompany the party, had gone to a short distance to hunt, having become impatient at our delay.

Soon after landing, I visited the Hudson's Bay post on the same island, and engaged Pierre St. Germain, an interpreter for Copper Indians. We regretted to find the posts of both the Companies extremely bare of provision; but as the gentlemen in charge had despatched men on the preceding evening, to a band of Indians, in search of meat, and they promised to furnish us with whatever should be brought, it was deemed advisable to wait for their return, as the smallest supply was now of importance to us. Advantage was taken of the delay to repair effectually the canoe which had been broken in the Dog Rapid. On the next evening the men arrived with the meat, and enabled Mr. M'Leod, of the North-West Company, to furnish us with our four hundred pounds of dried provisions. Mr. M'Vicar, of the Hudson's Bay Company, also supplied one hundred and fifty pounds. This quantity we considered would be sufficient, until we could join the hunters. We also obtained three fishing-nets, a gun, and a pair of pistols, which were all the stores these posts could furnish, although the gentlemen in charge were much disposed to assist us.

Moose-Deer Island is about a mile in diameter, and rises towards the centre about three hundred feet above the lake. Its soil is in general sandy, in some parts swampy. The varieties of the northern berries grow abundantly on it. The North-West Company's fort is in latitude 61° 11′ 8″ N.; longitude 113° 51′ 37″ W., being two hundred and sixty statute miles distant from Fort Chipewyan, by the river course. The variation of the compass is 25° 40′ 47″ E. The houses of the two Companies are small, and have a bleak northern aspect. There are vast accumulations of drift wood on the shores of the lake, brought down by the river, which afford plenty of fuel. The inhabitants live principally on the fish, which the lake at certain seasons furnishes in great abundance; of these, the white fish, trout, and *poisson inconnu* are considered the best. They also procure moose, buffalo, and reindeer meat occasionally from their hunters; but these animals are generally found at the distance of several days' walk from the forts. The Indians who trade here are Chipewyans. Beavers, martens, foxes, and musk-rats, are caught in numbers in the vicinity of this great body of water. The musquitoes here were still a serious annoyance to us, but less numerous than before. They were in some degree replaced by a small sandfly, whose bite is succeeded by a copious flow of blood, and considerable swelling, but is attended with incomparably less irritation, than the puncture of the musquito.

On the 27th of July we embarked at four A.M., and proceeded along the south shore of the lake, through a narrow channel, formed by some islands, beyond the confluence of the principal branch of the Slave River; and as far as Stony Island, where we breakfasted. This island is merely a rock of gneiss, that rises forty or fifty feet above the lake, and is precipitous on the north side. As the day was fine, and the lake smooth, we ventured upon paddling across to the Rein-Deer Islands, which were distant about thirteen miles in a northern direction, instead of pursuing the usual track by keeping farther along the south shore which inclines to the eastward from this point. These islands are numerous, and consist of granite, rising from one hundred to two hundred feet above the water. They are for the most part naked; but towards the centres of the larger ones, there is a little soil, and a few groves of pines. At seven in the evening we landed upon one of them, and encamped. On the following morning we ran before a strong breeze, and a heavy swell, for some hours, but at length were obliged to seek shelter on a large island adjoining to Isle à la Cache of Mackenzie, where the following observations were obtained: latitude 61° 50′ 18″ N., longitude 113° 21′ 40″ W., and variation 31° 2′ 06″ E.

The wind and swell having subsided in the afternoon, we re-embarked and steered towards the western point of the Big-Island of Mackenzie, and when four miles distant from it, had forty-two fathoms soundings. Passing between this island and a promontory of the main shore, termed Big Cape, we entered into a deep bay, which receives the waters from several rivers that come from the northward; and we immediately perceived a decrease in the temperature of the waters from 59° to 48°. We coasted along the eastern side of the bay, its western shore being always visible, but the canoes were exposed to the hazard of being broken by the numerous sunken rocks, which were scattered in our track. We encamped for the night on a rocky island, and by eight A.M. on the following morning, arrived at Fort Providence, which is situated twenty-one miles from the entrance of the bay. The post is exclusively occupied by the North-West Company, the Hudson's Bay Company having no settlement to the northward of Great Slave Lake. We found Mr. Wentzel and our interpreter Jean Baptise Adam here, with one of the Indian guides; but the chief of the tribe and his hunters were encamped with their families, some miles from the fort, in a good situation for fishing. Our arrival was announced to him by a fire on the top of a hill, and before night a messenger came to communicate his intention of seeing us next morning. The customary present, of tobacco and some other articles, was immediately sent to him.

Mr. Wentzel prepared me for the first conference with the Indians by mentioning all the information they had already given him. The duties allotted to this gentleman were, the management of the Indians, the superintendence of the Canadian voyagers, the obtaining, and the general distribution, of the provision, and the issue of the other stores. These services he was well qualified to perform, having been accustomed to execute similar duties, during a residence of upwards of twenty years in this country. We also deemed Mr. Wentzel to be a great acquisition to our party, as a check on the interpreters, he being one of the few traders who speak the Chipewyan language.

As we were informed that external appearances made lasting impressions on the Indians, we prepared for the interview by decorating ourselves in uniform, and suspending a medal round each of our necks. Our tents had been previously pitched and over one of them a silken union flag was hoisted. Soon after noon, on July 30th, several Indian canoes were seen advancing in a regular line, and on their approach, the chief was discovered in the headmost, which was paddled by two men. On landing at the fort, the chief assumed a very grave aspect, and walked up to Mr. Wentzel with a measured and dignified step, looking neither to the right nor to the left at the persons who had assembled on the beach to witness his debarkation, but preserving the same immovability of countenance until he reached the hall, and was introduced to the officers. When he had smoked his pipe, drank a small portion of spirits and water himself, and issued a glass to each of his companions, who had seated themselves on the floor, he commenced his harangue, by mentioning the circumstances that led to his agreeing to accompany the Expedition, an engagement which he was quite prepared to fulfil. He was rejoiced, he said, to see such great chiefs on his lands; his tribe were poor, but they loved white men who had been their benefactors; and he hoped that our visit would be productive of much good to them. The report which preceded our arrival, he said, had caused much grief to him. It was at first rumoured that a great medicine chief accompanied us, who was able to restore the dead to life; at this he rejoiced; the prospect of again seeing his departed relatives had enlivened his spirits, but his first communication with Mr. Wentzel had removed these vain hopes, and he felt as if his friends had a second time been torn from him. He now wished to be informed exactly of the nature of our Expedition.

In reply to this speech, which I understood had been prepared for many days, I endeavoured to explain the objects of our mission in a manner best calculated to ensure his exertions in our service. With this view, I told him that we were sent out by the greatest chief in the world, who was the sovereign also of the trading companies in the country; that he was the friend of peace, and had the interest of every nation at heart. Having learned that his children in the north were much in want of articles of merchandise, in consequence of the extreme length and difficulty of the present route, he had sent us to search for a passage by the sea, which if found, would enable large vessels to transport great quantities of goods more easily to their lands. That we had not come for the purpose of traffic, but solely to make discoveries for their benefit, as well as that of every other people. That we had been directed to inquire into the nature of all the productions of the countries we might pass through, and particularly respecting their inhabitants. That we desired the assistance of the Indians in guiding us, and providing us with food; finally, that we were most positively enjoined by the great chief to recommend that hostilities should cease throughout the country; and especially between the Indians and the Esquimaux, whom he considered his children, in common with other natives; and by way of enforcing the latter point more strongly, I assured him that a forfeiture of all the advantages which might be anticipated from the Expedition would be a certain consequence if any quarrel arose between his party and the Esquimaux. I also communicated to him that, owing to the distance we had travelled, we had now few more stores than was necessary for the use of our own party, a part of these, however, should be forthwith presented to him; on his return he and his party should be remunerated with cloth, ammunition, and tobacco, and some useful iron materials, besides having their debts to the North-West Company discharged.

The chief, whose name is Akaitcho or Big-foot, replied by a renewal of his assurances, that he and his party would attend to us to the end of our journey, and that they would do their utmost to provide use with the means of subsistence. He admitted that his tribe had made war upon the Esquimaux, but said they were now desirous of peace, and unanimous in their opinion as to the necessity of all who accompanied us abstaining from every act of enmity against that nation. He added, however, that the Esquimaux were very treacherous, and therefore recommended that we should advance towards them with caution.

The communications which the chief and the guides then gave respecting the route to the Copper-Mine River, and its course to the sea, coincided in every material point with the statements which were made by Boileau and Black Meat at

Chipewyan, but they differed in their descriptions of the coast. The information, however, collected from both sources was very vague and unsatisfactory. None of his tribe had been more than three days' march along the sea-coast to the eastward of the river's mouth.

As the water was unusually high this season, the Indian guides recommended our going by a shorter route to the Copper-Mine River than that they had first proposed to Mr. Wentzel, and they assigned as a reason for the change, that the reindeer would be sooner found upon this track. They then drew a chart of the proposed route on the floor with charcoal, exhibiting a chain of twenty-five small lakes extending towards the north, about one-half of them connected by a river which flows into Slave Lake, near Fort Providence. One of the guides, named Keskarrah, drew the Copper-Mine River, running through the Upper Lake, in a westerly direction towards the Great Bear Lake, and then northerly to the sea. The other guide drew the river in a straight line to the sea from the above-mentioned place, but, after some dispute, admitted the correctness of the first delineation. The latter was elder brother to Akaitcho, and he said that he had accompanied Mr. Hearne on his journey, and though very young at the time, still remembered many of the circumstances, and particularly the massacre committed by the Indians on the Esquimaux.

They pointed out another lake to the southward of the river, about three days' journey distant from it, on which the chief proposed the next winter's establishment should be formed, as the reindeer would pass there in the autumn and spring. Its waters contained fish, and there was a sufficiency of wood for building as well as for the winter's consumption. These were important considerations, and determined me in pursuing the route they now proposed. They could not inform us what time we should take in reaching the lake, until they saw our manner of travelling in the large canoes, but they supposed we might be about twenty days, in which case I entertained the hope that if we could then procure provision we should have time to descend the Copper-Mine River for a considerable distance if not to the sea itself, and return to the lake before the winter set in.

It may here be proper to mention that it had been my original plan to descend the Mackenzie's River, and to cross the Great Bear Lake, from the eastern side of which, Boileau informed me, there is a communication with the Copper-Mine River by four small lakes and portages; but, under our present circumstances, this course could not be followed, because it would remove us too far from the establishments at the Great Slave Lake, to receive the supplies of ammunition and some other stores in the winter which were absolutely necessary for the prosecution of our journey, or to get the Esquimaux interpreter, whom we expected. If I had not deemed these circumstances paramount I should have preferred the route by Bear Lake.

Akaitcho and the guides having communicated all the information they possessed on the different points to which our questions had been directed, I placed my medal round the neck of the chief, and the officers presented theirs to an elder brother of his and the two guides, communicating to them that these marks of distinction were given as tokens of our friendship and as pledges of the sincerity of our professions. Being conferred in the presence of all the hunters their acquisition was highly gratifying to them, but they studiously avoided any great expression of joy, because such an exposure would have been unbecoming the dignity which the senior Indians assume during a conference. They assured us, however, of their being duly sensible of these tokens of our regard, and that they should be preserved during their lives with the utmost care. The chief evinced much penetration and intelligence during the whole of this conversation, which gave us a favourable opinion of his intellectual powers. He made many inquiries respecting the Discovery ships, under the command of Captain Parry, which had been mentioned to him, and asked why a passage had not been discovered long ago, if one existed. It may be stated that we gave a faithful explanation to all his inquiries, which policy would have prompted us to do if a love of truth had not; for whenever these northern nations detect a falsehood in the dealings of the traders, they make it an unceasing subject of reproach, and their confidence is irrecoverably lost.

We presented to the chief, the two guides, and the seven hunters, who had engaged to accompany us, some cloth, blankets, tobacco, knives, daggers, besides other useful iron materials, and a gun to each; also a keg of very weak spirits and water, which they kept until the evening, as they had to try their guns before dark, and make the necessary preparations for commencing the journey on the morrow. They, however, did not leave us so soon, as the chief was desirous of being present, with his party, at the dance, which was given in the evening to our Canadian voyagers. They were highly entertained by the vivacity and agility displayed by our companions in their singing and dancing: and especially by their imitating the gestures of a Canadian, who placed himself in the most ludicrous postures; and, whenever this was done, the gravity of the chief gave way to violent bursts of laughter. In return for the gratification Akaitcho had enjoyed, he desired his young men exhibit the Dog-Rib Indian dance; and immediately they ranged themselves in a circle, and, keeping their legs widely separated, began to jump simultaneously sideways; their bodies were bent, their hands placed on their hips, and they uttered forcibly the interjection *tsa* at each jump. Devoid as were their attitudes of grace, and their music of harmony, we were much amused by the novelty of the exhibition.

In the midst of this scene an untoward accident occurred, which for a time interrupted our amusements. The tent in which Dr. Richardson and I lodged, having caught fire from some embers that had been placed in it to expel the musquitoes, was entirely burnt. Hepburn, who was sleeping within it, close to some powder, most providentially awoke in time to throw it clear of the flame, and rescue the baggage, before any material injury had been received. We dreaded the consequences of this disaster upon the fickle minds of the Indians, and wished it not to be communicated to them. The chief, however, was soon informed of it by one of his people, and expressed his desire that no further misfortune should be concealed from him. We found that he was most concerned to hear that the flag had been burnt, but we removed his anxiety on that point, by the assurance that it could easily be repaired. We were advised by Mr. Wentzel to recommence the dancing after this event, lest the Indians should imagine, by our putting a stop to it, that we considered the circumstance as an unfavourable commencement of our undertaking. We were, however, deeply impressed with a grateful sense of the Divine Providence, in averting the threatened destruction of our stores, which would have been fatal to every prospect of proceeding forward this season.

August 1

This morning the Indians set out, intending to wait for us at the mouth of the Yellow-Knife River. We remained behind to pack our stores, in bales of eighty pounds each, an operation which could not be done in the presence of these Indians, as they are in the habit of begging for everything they see. Our stores consisted of two barrels of gunpowder, one hundred and fifty pounds of ball and small shot, four fowling-pieces, a few old trading guns, eight pistols, twenty-four Indian daggers, some packages of knives, chisels, nails, and fastenings for a boat; a few yards of cloth, some blankets, needles, looking-glasses, and beads; together with nine fishing-nets, having meshes of different sizes. Our provision was two casks of flour, two hundred dried reindeer tongues, some dried moose-meat, portable soup, and arrowroot, sufficient in the whole for ten day's consumption, besides two cases of chocolate, and two canisters of tea. We engaged another Canadian voyager at this place, and the Expedition then consisted of twenty-eight persons, including the officers, and the wives of three of our voyagers, who were brought for the purpose of making shoes and clothes for the men at the winter establishment; there were also three children, belonging to two of these women.[1]

Our observations place Fort Providence in latitude 62° 17′ 19″ N., longitude 114° 9′ 27″ W.; the variation of the compass is 33° 35′ 55″ E., and the dip of the needle 86° 38′ 02″. It is distant from Moose-Deer Island sixty-six geographic miles. This is the last establishment of the traders in this direction, but the North-West Company have two to the northward of it, on the Mackenzie River. It has been erected for the convenience of the Copper and Dog-Rib Indians, who generally bring such a quantity of reindeer meat that the residents are enabled, out of their superabundance, to send annually some provision to the fort at Moose-Deer Island. They also occasionally procure moose and buffalo meat, but these animals are not numerous on this side of the lake. Few furs are collected. *Les poissons inconnus*, trout, pike, carp, and white-fish are very plentiful, and on these the residents principally subsist. Their great supply of fish is procured in the latter part of September and the beginning of October, but there are a few taken daily in the nets during the winter. The surrounding country consists almost entirely of coarse grained granite, frequently enclosing large masses of red-dish felspar. These rocks form hills which attain an elevation of three hundred or four hundred feet, about a mile behind the house; their surface is generally naked, but in the valleys between them grow a few spruce, aspen, and birch trees, together with a variety of shrubs and berry-bearing plants.

On the afternoon of the 2nd of August we commenced our journey, having, in addition to our three canoes, a smaller one to convey the women; we were all in high spirits, being heartily glad that the time had at length arrived when our course was to be directed towards the Copper-Mine River, and through a line of country which had not been previously visited by any European. We proceeded to the northward, along the eastern side of a deep bay of the lake, passing through various channels, formed by an assemblage of rocky islands; and, at sunset, encamped on a projecting point of the north main shore, eight miles from Fort Providence. To the westward of this arm, or bay, of the lake, there is another deep bay, that receives the waters of a river, which communicates with Great Marten Lake, where the North-West Company had once a post established. The eastern shores of the Great Slave Lake are very imperfectly known: none of the traders have visited them, and the Indians give such loose and unsatisfactory accounts, that no estimation can be formed of its extent in that direction. These men say there is a communication from its eastern extremity by a chain of lakes, with a shallow river, which discharges its waters into the sea. This stream they call the Thlouee-tessy, and report it to be navigable for Indian canoes only. The forms of the south and western shores are better known from the survey of Sir Alexander Mackenzie, and in consequence of the canoes having to pass and repass along these borders annually, between Moose-Deer Island and Mackenzie's River. Our observations made the breadth of the lake, between Stony Island, and the north main shore, sixty

1 The following is the list of the officers and men who composed the Expedition on its departure from Fort Providence:

John Franklin, Lieutenant of the Royal Navy and Commander.

John Richardson, M.D., Surgeon of the Royal Navy.

Mr. George Back, of the Royal Navy, Admiralty Midshipman.

Mr. Robert Hood, of the Royal Navy, Admiralty Midshipman.

Mr. Frederick Wentzel, Clerk of the North-West Company.

John Hepburn, English seaman.

Canadian Voyagers

Joseph Peltier,

Matthew Pelonquin, dit Crèdit,

Solomon Belanger,

Joseph Benoit,

Joseph Gagné,

Pierre Dumas,

Joseph Forcier,

Ignace Perrault,

Francois Samandré,

Gabriel Beauparlant,

Vincenza Fontano,

Registe Vaillant,

Jean Baptiste Parent,

Jean Baptiste Belanger,

Jean Baptiste Belleau,

Emanuel Cournoyée

Michel Teroahauté, an Iroquois.

Interpreters

Pierre St. Germain,

Jean Baptiste Adam,

Chipewyan Bois Brulés.

miles less than it is laid down in Arrowsmith's map; and there is also a considerable difference in the longitude of the eastern side of the bay, which we entered.

This lake, owing to its great depth, is seldom completely frozen over before the last week in November, and the ice, which is generally seven feet thick, breaks up about the middle of June, three weeks later than that of the Slave River. The only known outlet to this vast body of water, which receives so many streams on its north and south shores, is the Mackenzie River.

August 3

We embarked at three A.M. and proceeded to the entrance of the Yellow-Knife River of the traders, which is called by the natives Beg-ho-lo-dessy; or, River of the Toothless Fish. We found Akaitcho, and the hunters with their families, encamped here. There were also several other Indians of his tribe, who intended to accompany us some distance into the interior. This party was quickly in motion after our arrival, and we were soon surrounded by a fleet of seventeen Indian canoes. In company with them we paddled up the river, which is one hundred and fifty yards wide, and, in an hour, came to a cascade of five feet, where we were compelled to make a portage of one hundred and fifty-eight yards. We next crossed a dilatation of the river, about six miles in length, upon which the name of Lake Prosperous was bestowed. Its shores, though scantily supplied with wood, are very picturesque.

Akaitcho caused himself to be paddled by his slave, a young man, of the Dog-Rib nation, whom he had taken by force from his friends; when he thought himself, however, out of reach of our observation, he laid aside a good deal of his state, and assisted in the labour; and after a few days' further acquaintance with us, he did not hesitate to paddle in our presence, or even carry his canoe on the portages. Several of the canoes were managed by women, who proved to be noisy companions, for they quarrelled frequently, and the weakest was generally profuse in her lamentations, which were not at all diminished when the husband attempted to settle the difference by a few blows from his paddle.

An observation, near the centre of the lake, gave 114° 13′ 39″ W., and 33° 8′ 06″ E., variation.

Leaving the lake, we ascended a very strong rapid, and arrived at a range of three steep cascades, situated in the bend of the river. Here we made a portage of one thousand three hundred yards over a rocky hill, which received the name of the Bowstring Portage, from its shape. We found that the Indians had greatly the advantage of us in this operation; the men carried their small canoes, the women and children the clothes and provisions, and at the end of the portage they were ready to embark; whilst it was necessary for our people to return four times, before they could transport the weighty cargo with which we were burdened. After passing through another expansion of the river, and over the Steep Portage of one hundred and fifteen yards, we encamped on a small rocky isle, just large enough to hold our party, and the Indians took possession of an adjoining rock. We were now thirty miles from Fort Providence.

As soon as the tents were pitched, the officers and men were divided into watches for the night; a precaution intended to be taken throughout the journey, not merely to prevent our being surprised by strangers, but also to show our companions that we were constantly on our guard. The chief, who suffered nothing to escape his observation, remarked, 'that he should sleep without anxiety among the Esquimaux, for he perceived no enemy could surprise us.'

After supper we retired to rest, but our sleep was soon interrupted by the Indians joining in loud lamentations over a sick child, whom they supposed to be dying. Dr. Richardson, however, immediately went to the boy, and administered some medicine which relieved his pain, and put a stop to their mourning. The temperatures, this day, were at four A.M. 54°, three P.M. 72°, at seven P.M. 65°.

On the 4th we crossed a small lake, and passed in succession over the Blue Berry Cascade, and Double Fall Portages, where the river falls over ridges of rocks that completely obstruct the passages for canoes. We came to three strong rapids beyond these barriers, which were surmounted by the aid of the poles and lines, and then to a bend of the river in which the cascades were so frequent, that to avoid them we carried the canoes into a chain of small lakes. We entered them by a portage of nine hundred and fifty paces, and during the afternoon traversed three other grassy lakes and encamped on the banks of the river, at the end of the Yellow-Knife Portage, of three hundred and fifty paces. This day's work was very laborious to our men. Akaitcho, however, had directed his party to assist them in carrying their burdens on the portages, which they did cheerfully. This morning Mr. Back caught several fish with a fly, a method of fishing entirely new to the Indians; and they were not more delighted than astonished at his skill and success. The extremes of temperature today were 54° and 65°.

On August 5th we continued the ascent of the river, which varied much in breadth as did the current in rapidity. It flows between high rocky banks on which there is sufficient soil to support pines, birch, and poplars. Five portages were crossed, then the Rocky Lake, and we finished our labours at the end of the sixth portage. The issue of dried meat for breakfast this morning had exhausted all our stock; and no other provision remained but the portable soups, and a few pounds of preserved meat. At the recommendation of Akaitcho, the hunters were furnished with ammunition, and desired to go forward as speedily as possible to the part where the reindeer were expected to be found; and to return to us with any provision they could procure. He also assured us that in our advance towards them we should come to some lakes abounding in fish. Many of the Indians being likewise in distress for food, decided on separating from us, and going on at a quicker pace than we could travel.

Akaitcho himself was always furnished with a portion at our meals, as a token of regard which the traders have taught the chiefs to expect, and which we willingly paid.

The next morning we crossed a small lake and a portage, before we entered the river; shortly afterwards, the canoes and cargoes were carried a mile along its banks, to avoid three very strong rapids, and over another portage into a narrow lake; we encamped on an island in the middle of it, to set the nets; but they only yielded a few fish, and we had a very scanty supper, as it was necessary to deal out our provision sparingly. The longitude 114° 27′ 03″ W. and variation 33° 00′ 04″ E., were observed.

We had the mortification of finding the nets entirely empty next morning, an untoward circumstance that discouraged our voyagers very much; and they complained of being unable to support the fatigue to which they were daily exposed, on their present scanty fare. We had seen with regret that the portages were more frequent as we advanced to the northward, and feared that their strength would fail, if provision were not soon obtained. We embarked at six, proceeded to the head of the lake, and crossed a portage of two thousand five hundred paces, leading over ridges of sand-hills, which nourished pines of a larger size than we had lately seen.

This conducted us to Mossy Lake, whence we regained the river, after traversing another portage. The Birch and Poplar Portages next followed, and beyond these we came to a part where the river takes a great circuit, and its course is interrupted by several heavy falls. The guide, therefore, advised us to quit it, and proceed through a chain of nine lakes extending to the north-east, which we did, and encamped on Icy Portage, where the nets were set. The bottom of the valley, through which the track across this portage led, was covered with ice four or five feet thick, that remains of a large iceberg, which is annually formed there, by the snow drifting into the valley, and becoming consolidated into ice by the overflowing of some springs that are warm enough to resist the winter's cold. The latitude is 63° 22′ 15″ N., longitude 114° 15′ 30″ W.

We were alarmed in the night by our fire communicating to the dry moss, which, spreading by the force of a strong wind, encircled the encampment and threatened destruction to our canoes and baggage. The watch immediately aroused all the men, who quickly removed whatever could be injured to a distant part, and afterward succeeded in extinguishing the flame.

August 8

During this day we crossed five portages, passing over a very bad road. The men were quite exhausted with fatigue by five P.M., when we were obliged to encamp on the borders of the fifth lake, in which the fishing-nets were set. We began this evening to issue some portable soup and arrowroot, which our companions relished very much; but this food is too unsubstantial to support their vigour under their daily exhausting labour, and we could not furnish them with a sufficient quantity even of this to satisfy their desires. We commenced our labours on the next day in a very wet uncomfortable state, as it had rained through the night until four A.M. The fifth grassy lake was crossed, and four others, with their intervening portages, and we returned to the river by a portage of one thousand four hundred and fifteen paces. The width of the stream here is about one hundred yards, its banks are moderately high and scantily covered with wood. We afterwards twice carried the cargoes along its banks to avoid a very stony rapid, and then crossed the first Carp Portage in longitude 114° 2′ 01″ W., variation of the compass 32° 30′ 40″ E., and encamped on the borders of Lower Carp Lake.

The chief having told us that this was a good lake for fishing, we determined on halting for a day or two to recruit our men, of whom three were lame, and several others had swelled legs. The chief himself went forward to look after the hunters, and promised to make a fire as a signal if they had killed any reindeer. All the Indians had left us in the course of yesterday and today to seek these animals, except the guide Keskarrah.

August 10

The nets furnishing only four carp, we embarked for the purpose of searching for a better spot, and encamped again on the shores of the same lake. The spirits of the men were much revived by seeing some recent traces of reindeer at this place, which circumstance caused them to cherish the hope of soon getting a supply of meat from the hunters. They were also gratified by finding abundance of blue berries near the encampment, which made an agreeable and substantial addition to their otherwise scanty fare. We were teased by sand-flies this evening, although the thermometer did not rise above 45°. The country through which we had travelled for some days consists principally of granite, intermixed in some spots with mica-slate, often passing into clay-slate. But the borders of Lower Carp Lake, where the gneiss formation prevails, are composed of hills, having less altitude, fewer precipices, and more rounded summits. The valleys are less fertile, containing a gravelly soil and fewer trees; so that the country has throughout a more barren aspect.

August 11

Having caught sufficient trout, white-fish, and carp, yesterday and this morning, to afford the party two hearty meals, and the men having recovered from their fatigue, we proceeded on our journey, crossed the Upper Carp Portage, and embarked on the lake of that name, where we had the gratification of paddling for ten miles. We put up at its termination to fish, by the advice of our guide, and the following observations were then taken: longitude 113° 46′ 35″ W., variation of the compass 36° 45′ 30″ E., dip 87° 11′ 48″. At this place we first perceived the north end of our dipping-needle to pass the perpendicular line when the instrument was faced to the west.

We had scarcely quitted the encampment next day before an Indian met us, with the agreeable communication that the hunters had made several fires, which were certain indications of their having killed reindeer. This intelligence inspired our companions with fresh energy, and they quickly traversed the next portage, and paddled through the Reindeer Lake; at the north side of it we found the canoes of our hunters, and learned from our guide that the Indians usually leave their canoes here, as the water communication on their hunting grounds is bad. The Yellow-Knife River had now dwindled into an insignificant rivulet, and we could not trace it beyond the next lake, except as a mere brook. The latitude of its source 64° 1′ 30″ N., longitude 113° 36′ 00″ W., and its length is one hundred and fifty-six statute miles. Though this river is of sufficient breadth and depth for navigating in canoes, yet I conceive its course is to much interrupted by cascades and rapids for its ever being used as a channel for the conveyance of merchandise. Whilst the crews were employed in making a portage over the foot of Prospect Hill, we ascended to the top of it, and as it is the highest ground in the neighbourhood, its summit, which is about five hundred feet above the water, commands an extensive view.

Akaitcho, who was here with his family, pointed out to us the smoke of the distant fires which the hunters had made. The prospect is agreeably diversified by an inter-mixture of hill and valley, and the appearance of twelve lakes in different directions. On the borders of these lakes a few thin pine groves occur, but the country in general is destitute of almost every vegetable, except a few berry-bearing shrubs and lichens, and has a very barren aspect. The hills are composed of gneiss, but their acclivities are covered with a coarse gravelly soil. There are many large loose stones both on their sides and summits composed of the same materials as the solid rock.

We crossed another lake in the evening, encamped, and set the nets. The chief made a large fire to announce our situation to the hunters.

August 13

We caught twenty fish in the morning, but they were small, and furnished but a scanty breakfast for the party. Whilst this meal was preparing, our Canadian voyagers, who had been for some days past murmuring at their meagre diet, and striving to get the whole of our little provision to consume at once, broke out into open discontent, and several of them threatened they would not proceed forward unless more food was given to them. This conduct was the more unpardonable, as they saw we were rapidly approaching the fires of the hunters, and that provision might soon be expected. I, therefore, felt the duty incumbent on me to address them in the strongest manner on the danger of insubordination, and to assure them of my determination to inflict the heaviest punishment on any that should persist in their refusal to go on, or in any other way attempt to retard the Expedition. I considered this decisive step necessary, having learned from the gentlemen, most intimately acquainted with the character of the Canadian voyagers, that they invariably try how far they can impose upon every new master, and that they will continue to be disobedient and intractable if they once gain any ascendency over him. I must admit, however, that the present hardships of our companions were of a kind which few could support without murmuring, and no one could witness without a sincere pity for their sufferings.

After this discussion we went forward until sunset. In the course of the day we crossed seven lakes and as many portages. Just as we had encamped we were delighted to see four of the hunters arrive with the flesh of two reindeer. This seasonable supply, though only sufficient for this evening's and the next day's consumption, instantly revived the spirits of our companions, and they immediately forgot all their cares. As we did not, after this period, experience any deficiency of food during this journey, they worked extremely well, and never again reflected upon us as they had done before, for rashly bringing them into an inhospitable country, where the means of subsistence could not be procured.

Several blue fish, resembling the grayling, were caught in a stream which flows out of Hunter's Lake. It is remarkable for the largeness of the dorsal fin and the beauty of its colours.

August 14

Having crossed the Hunter's Portage, we entered the Lake of the same name, in latitude 64° 6' 47" N., longitude 113° 25' 00" W.; but soon quitted it by desire of the Indian guide, and diverged more to the eastward that we might get into the line upon which our hunters had gone. This was the only consideration that could have induced us to remove to a chain of small lakes connected by long portages. We crossed three of these, and then were obliged to encamp to rest the men. The country is bare of wood except a few dwarf birch bushes, which grow near the borders of the lakes, and here and there a few stunted pines; and our fuel principally consisted of the roots of decayed pines, which we had some difficulty to collect in sufficient quantity for cooking. When this material is wanting, the reindeer lichen and other mosses that grow in profusion on the gravelly acclivities of the hills are used as substitutes. Three more of the hunters arrived with meat this evening, which supply came very opportunely as our nets were unproductive. At eight P.M., a faint Aurora Borealis appeared to the southward, the night was cold, the wind strong from N.W.

We were detained some time in the following morning before the fishing-nets, which had sunk in the night, could be recovered.

After starting we first crossed the Orkney Lake, then a portage which brought us to Sandy Lake, and here we missed one of our barrels of powder, which the steersman of the canoe then recollected had been left the day before. He and two other men were sent back to search for it, in the small canoe. The rest of the party proceeded to the portage on the north side of the Grizzle-Bear Lake, where the hunters had made a deposit of meat, and there encamped to await their return, which happened at nine P.M., with the powder. We perceived from the direction of this lake, that considerable labour would have been spared if we had continued our course yesterday instead of striking off at the guide's suggestion, as the bottom of this lake cannot be far separated from either Hunter's Lake or the one to the westward of it. The chief and all the Indians went off to hunt, accompanied by Pierre St. Germain, the interpreter. They returned at night, bringing some meat, and reported that they had put the carcasses of several reindeer *en cache*. These were sent for early next morning, and as the weather was unusually warm, the thermometer at noon being 77°, we remained stationary all day, that the women might prepare the meat for keeping, by stripping the flesh from the bones and drying it in the sun over a slow fire. The hunters were again successful, and by the evening we had collected the carcasses of seventeen deer. As this was a sufficient store to serve us until we arrived at Winter Lake, the chief proposed that he and his hunters should proceed to that place and collect some provision against our arrival. He also requested that we would allow him to be absent ten days to provide his family with clothing, as the skin of the reindeer is unfit for that purpose after the month of September. We could not refuse to grant such a reasonable request, but caused St. Germain to accompany him, that his absence might not exceed the appointed time. Previous to his departure the chief warned us to be constantly on our guard against the grizzly bears, which he described as being numerous in this vicinity, and very ferocious; one had been seen this day by an Indian, to which circumstance the lake owes its appellation. We afterwards learned that the only bear in this part of the country is the brown bear, and that this by no means possesses the ferocity which the Indians, with their usual love of exaggeration, ascribe to it. The fierce grizzly bear, which frequents the course of the Missouri, is not found on the barren grounds.

The shores of this lake and the neighbouring hills are principally composed of sand and grave; they are much varied in their outline and present some picturesque scenery.

The following observations were taken here: latitude 64° 15′ 17″ N., longitude 113° 2″ 39″ W.; variation of the compass 36° 50′ 47″ E.; and dip of the needle 87° 20′ 35″.

On August the 17th, having finished drying the meat, which had been retarded by the heavy showers of rain that fell in the morning, we embarked at one P.M. and crossed two lakes and two portages. The last of these was two thousand and sixty-paces long, and very rugged, so that the men were much fatigued. On the next day we received the flesh of four reindeer by the small canoe which had been sent for it, and heard that the hunters had killed several more deer on our route. We saw many of these animals as we passed along; and our companions, delighted with the prospect of having food in abundance, now began to accompany their paddling with singing, which they had discontinued ever since our provisions became scarce. We passed from one small lake to another over four portages, then crossed a lake about six miles in diameter, and encamped on its border, where, finding pines, we enjoyed the luxury of a good fire, which we had not done for some days. At ten P.M. the Aurora Borealis appeared very brilliant in an arch across the zenith, from north-west to south-east, which afterwards gave place to a beautiful corona borealis.

August 19

After crossing a portage of five hundred and ninety five paces, a small lake and another portage of two thousand paces, which occupied the crews seven hours, we embarked on a small stream, running towards the north-west, which carried us to the lake, where Akaitcho proposed that we should pass the winter. The officers ascended several of the loftiest hills in the course of the day, prompted by a natural anxiety to examine the spot which was to be their residence for many months. The prospect, however, was not then the most agreeable, as the borders of the lake seemed to be scantily furnished with wood, and that of a kind too small for the purposes of building.

We perceived the smoke of a distant fire which the Indians suppose had been made by some of the Dog-Ribbed tribe, who occasionally visit this part of the country.

Embarking at seven next morning, we paddled to the western extremity of the lake, and there found a small river, which flows out of it to the S.W. To avoid a strong rapid at its commencement, we made a portage, and then crossed to the north bank of the river, where the Indians recommended that the winter establishment should be erected, and we soon found that the situation they had chosen possessed all the advantages we could desire. The trees were numerous, and of a far greater size than we had supposed them to be in a distant view, some of the pines being thirty or forty feet high, and two feet in diameter at the root. We determined on placing the house on the summit of the bank, which commands a beautiful prospect of the surrounding country. The view in the front is bounded at the distance of three miles by round-backed hills; to the eastward and westward lie the Winter and Round-rock Lakes, which are connected by the Winter River, whose banks are well clothed with pines, and ornamented with a profusion of mosses, lichens, and shrubs.

In the afternoon we read divine service, and offered our thanksgiving to the Almighty for His goodness in having brought us thus far on our journey; a duty which we never neglected, when stationary on the Sabbath.

The united length of the portages we had crossed, since leaving Fort Providence, is twenty-one statute miles and a half; and as our men had to traverse each portage four times, with a load of one hundred and eighty pounds, and return three times light, they walked in the whole upwards of one hundred and fifty miles. The total length of our voyage from Chipewyan is five hundred and fifty-three miles.[1]

A fire was made on the south side of the river to inform the chief of our arrival, which spreading before a strong wind, caught the whole wood, and we were completely enveloped in a cloud of smoke for the three following days.

On the next morning our voyagers were divided into two parties, the one to cut the wood for the building of a storehouse, and the other to fetch the meat as the hunters procured it. An interpreter was sent with Keskarrah, the guide, to search for the Indians who had made the fire seen on Saturday, from whom we might obtain some supplies of provision. An Indian was also despatched to Akaitcho, with directions for him to come to this place directly, and bring whatever provision he had, as we were desirous of proceeding, without delay, to the Copper-Mine River. In the evening our men brought in the carcasses of seven reindeer, which two hunters had shot yesterday, and the women commenced drying the meat for our journey. We also obtained a good supply of fish from our nets today.

A heavy rain, on the 23rd, prevented the men from working, either at the building, or going for meat; but on the next day the weather was fine, and they renewed their labours. The thermometer that day did not rise higher than 42°, and it fell to 31° before midnight. On the morning of the 25th, we were surprised by some early symptoms of the approach of winter; the small pools were frozen over,

1	Statute Miles
Stony and Slave Rivers	260
Slave River	107
Yellow-Knife River	156.5
Barren country between the source of the Yellow-Knife River and Fort Enterprise	29.5
	553

and a flock of geese passed to the southward. In the afternoon, however, a fog came on, which afterwards changed into rain, and the ice quickly disappeared. We suffered great anxiety all the next day respecting John Hepburn, who had gone to hunt before sunrise on the 25th, and had been absent ever since. About four hours after his departure the wind changed, and a dense fog obscured every mark by which his course to the tents could be directed, and we thought it probable he had been wandering in an opposite direction to our situation, as the two hunters, who had been sent to look for him, returned at sunset without having seen him. Akaitcho arrived with his party, and we were greatly disappointed at finding they had stored up only fifteen reindeer for us. St. Germain informed us, that having heard of the death of the chief's brother-in-law, they had spent several days in bewailing his loss, instead of hunting. We learned also, that the decease of this man had caused another party of the tribe, who had been sent by Mr. Wentzel to prepare provision for us on the banks of the Copper-Mine River, to remove to the shores of the Great Bear Lake, distant from our proposed route. Mortifying as these circumstances were, they produced less painful sensations than we experienced in the evening, by the refusal of Akaitcho to accompany us in the proposed descent of the Copper-Mine River. When Mr. Wentzel, by my direction, communicated to him my intention of proceeding at once on that service, he desired a conference with me upon the subject, which being immediately granted, he began by stating that the very attempt would be rash and dangerous, as the weather was cold, the leaves were falling, some geese had passed to the southward, and the winter would shortly set in; and that, as he considered the lives of all who went on such a journey would be forfeited, he neither would go himself, nor permit his hunters to accompany us. He said there was no wood within eleven days' march, during which time we could not have any fire, as the moss, which the Indians use in their summer excursions, would be too wet for burning, in consequence of the recent rains; that we should be forty days in descending the Copper-Mine River, six of which would be expended in getting to its banks, and that we might be blocked up by the ice in the next moon; and during the whole journey the party must experience great sufferings for want of food, as the reindeer had already left the river.

He was now reminded that these statements were very different from the account he had given, both at Fort Providence and on the route hither; and that up to this moment we had been encouraged by his conversation to expect that the party might descend the Copper-Mine River accompanied by the Indians. He replied, that at the former place he had been unacquainted with our slow mode of travelling, and that the alteration in his opinion arose from the advance of winter.

We now informed him that we were provided with instruments by which we could ascertain the state of the air and water, and that we did not imagine the winter to be so near as he supposed; however, we promised to return on discovering the first change in the season. He was also told that all the baggage being left behind, our canoes would now of course travel infinitely more expeditiously than anything he had hitherto witnessed. Akaitcho appeared to feel hurt that we should continue to press the matter further, and answered with some warmth: 'Well, I have said everything I can urge to dissuade you from going on this service, on which, it seems you wish to sacrifice your own lives, as well as the Indians who might attend you: however, if after all I have said you are determined to go, some of my young men shall join the party, because it shall not be said that we permitted you to die alone after having brought you hither; but from the moment they embark in the canoes, I and my relatives shall lament them as dead.'

We could only reply to this forcible appeal, by assuring him and the Indians who were seated around him, that we felt the most anxious solicitude for the safety of every individual, and that it was far from our intention to proceed without considering every argument for and against the proposed journey.

We next informed him that it would be very desirable to see the river at any rate, that we might give some positive information about its situation and size, in our next letters to the Great Chief; and that we were very anxious to get on its banks, for the purpose of observing an eclipse of the sun, which we described to him, and said would happen in a few days. He received this communication with more temper than the preceding, though he immediately assigned as a reason for his declining to go, that 'the Indians must now procure a sufficient quantity of deer-skins for winter clothing for themselves, and dresses for the Canadians, who would need them if they had to travel in the winter.' Finding him so averse to proceed, and feeling at the same time how essential his continuance with us was, not only to our future success, but even to our existence during the winter, I closed the conversation here, intending to propose to him next morning some modification of the plan, which might meet his approbation. Soon after we were gone, however, he informed Mr. Wentzel, with whom he was in the habit of speaking confidentially, that as his advice was neglected, his presence was useless, and he should, therefore, return to Fort Providence with his hunters after he had collected some winter provision for us. Mr. Wentzel having reported this to me, the night was passed in great anxiety, and after weighing all the arguments that presented themselves to my mind, I came reluctantly to the determination of relinquishing the intention of going any distance down the river this season. I had considered that could we ascertain what were the impediments to the navigation of the Copper-Mine River, and whether drift timber existed where the country was naked, our operations next season would be much facilitated; but we had also cherished the hope of reaching the sea this year, for the Indians in their conversations with us had only spoken of two great rapids as likely to obstruct us. This was a hope extremely painful to give up; for, in the event of success, we should have ascertained whether the sea was clear of ice, and navigable for canoes; have learned the disposition of the Esquimaux; and might have obtained other information that would have had great influence on our future proceedings.

I must confess, however, that my opinion of the probability of our being able to attain so great a desideratum this season had been somewhat altered by the recent changes in the weather, although, had the chief been willing to accompany us with his party, I should have made the attempt; with the intention, however, of returning immediately upon the first decided appearance of winter.

On the morning of August 27th, having communicated my sentiments to the officers on the subject of the conference last evening, they all agreed that the descent to the sea this season could not be attempted, without hazarding a complete rupture with the Indians; but they thought that a party should be sent to ascertain the distance and size of the Copper-Mine River. These opinions being in conformity with my own, I determined in despatching Messrs. Back and Hood on that service, in a light canoe, as soon as possible.

We witnessed this morning an instance of the versatility of our Indian companions, which gave us much uneasiness, as it regarded the safety of our faithful attendant Hepburn. When they heard, on their arrival last night, of his having been so long absent, they expressed the greatest solicitude about him, and the whole party immediately volunteered to go in search of him as soon as daylight permitted. Their resolutions, however, seem to have been changed, in consequence of the subsequent conversation we had with the chief, and we found all of them indisposed to proceed on that errand this morning; and it was only by much entreaty, that three of the hunters and a boy were prevailed upon to go. They fortunately succeeded in their search, and we were infinitely rejoiced to see Hepburn return with them in the afternoon, though much jaded by the fatigue he had undergone. He had got bewildered, as we had conjectured, in the foggy weather on the 25th, and had been wandering about ever since, except during half an hour that he slept yesterday. He had eaten only a partridge and some berries, for his anxiety of mind had deprived him of appetite; and of a deer which he had shot, he took only the tongue, and the skin to protect himself from the wind and rain. This anxiety, we learned from him, was occasioned by the fear that the party which was about to descend the Copper-Mine River, might be detained until he was found, or that it might have departed without him. He did not entertain any dread of the white bears, of whose numbers and ferocious attacks the Indians had been constantly speaking, since we had entered the barren grounds. Our fears for his safety, however, were in a considerable degree excited by the accounts we had received of these animals. Having made a hearty supper he retired to rest, slept soundly, and arose next morning in perfect health.

On the 28th of August Akaitcho was informed of our intention to send a party to the river, and of the reasons for doing so, of which he approved, when he found that I had relinquished the idea of going myself, in compliance with the desire which he and the Indians had expressed; and he immediately said two of the hunters should go to provide them with food on the journey, and to serve as guides. During this conversation we gathered from him, for the first time, that there might still be some of his tribe near to the river, from whom the party could get provision. Our next object was to despatch the Indians to their hunting-ground to collect provision for us, and to procure the fat of the deer for our use during the winter, and for making the pemmican we should require in the spring. They were therefore furnished with some ammunition, clothing, and other necessary articles, and directed to take their departure as soon as possible.

Akaitcho came into our tent this evening at supper, and made several pertinent enquiries respecting the eclipse, of which we had spoken last night. He desired to know the effect that would be produced, and the cause of it, which we endeavoured to explain; and having gained this information, he sent for several of his companions, that they might also have it repeated to them. They were most astonished at our knowing the time at which this event should happen, and remarked that this knowledge was a striking proof of the superiority of the whites over the Indians. We took advantage of this occasion to speak to them respecting the Supreme Being, who ordered all the operations of nature, and to impress on their minds the necessity of paying strict attention to their moral duties, in obedience to His will. They readily assented to all these points, and Akaitcho assured us that both himself and his young men would exert themselves in obtaining provision for us, in return for the interesting communications we had just made to them.

Having received a supply of dried meat from the Indian lodges, we were enabled to equip the party for the Copper-Mine River, and at nine A.M., on the 29th, Mr. Back and Mr. Hood embarked on that service in a light canoe, with St. Germain, eight Canadians and one Indian. We could not furnish them with more than eight days' provision, which, with their blankets, two tents, and a few instruments, composed their lading. Mr. Back, who had charge of the party, was directed to proceed to the river, and if, when he arrived at its banks, the weather should continue to be mild, and the temperature of the water was not lower than

40°, he might embark, and descend the stream for a few days to gain some knowledge of its course, but he was not to go so far as to risk his being able to return to this place in a fortnight with the canoe. But, if the weather should be severe, and the temperature of the water below 40°, he was not to embark, but return immediately, and endeavour to ascertain the best track for our goods to be conveyed thither next spring.

We had seen that the water decreases rapidly in temperature at this season, and I feared that, if he embarked to descend the river when it was below 40°, the canoe might be frozen in, and the crew have to walk back in very severe weather.

As soon as the canoe had started, Akaitcho and the Indians took their departure also, except two of the hunters, who stayed behind to kill deer in our neighbourhood, and old Keskarrah and his family, who remained as our guests.

The fishing-nets were this day transferred from the river in which they had been set since our arrival to Winter Lake, whither the fish had removed, and the fishermen built a log-hut on its borders to reside in, that they might attend more closely to their occupation.

The month of September commenced with very disagreeable weather. The temperature of the atmosphere ranged between 39° and 31° during the first three days, and that of the water in the river decreased from 49° to 44°. Several reindeer and a large flight of white geese passed to the southward. These circumstances led us to fear for the comfort, if not for the safety, of our absent friends. On the 4th of September we commenced building our dwelling-house, having cut sufficient wood for the frame of it.

In the afternoon of September the 6th, we removed our tent to the summit of a hill, about three miles distant, for the better observing the eclipse, which was calculated to occur on the next morning. We were prevented, however, from witnessing it by a heavy snow-storm, and the only observation we could then make was to examine whether the temperature of the atmosphere altered during the eclipse, but we found that both the mercurial and spirit thermometers remained steadily at 30° for a quarter of an hour previous to its commencement, during its continuance, and for half an hour subsequent to its termination; we remarked the wind increased very much, and the snow fell in heavier flakes just after the estimated time of its commencement. This boisterous weather continued until three P.M., when the wind abated, and the snow changed to rain.

As there was now no immediate reason for my remaining on the spot, the eclipse being over, and the Indians having removed to their hunting grounds, Dr. Richardson and I determined on taking a pedestrian excursion to the Copper-Mine River, leaving Mr. Wentzel in charge of the men, and to superintend the buildings. On the morning of September the 9th we commenced our journey, under the guidance of old Keskarrah, and accompanied by John Hepburn and Samandré, who carried our blankets, cooking utensils, hatchets, and a small supply of dried meat. Our guide led us from the top of one hill to the top of another, making as straight a course to the northward as the numerous lakes, with which the country is intersected, would permit. At noon we reached a remarkable hill, with precipitous sides, named by the Copper Indians the Dog-Rib Rock, and its latitude, 64° 34' 52" S., was obtained. The canoe-track passes to the eastward of this rock, but we kept to the westward, as being the more direct course. From the time we quitted the banks of the Winter River we saw only a few detached clumps of trees; but after we passed the Dog-Rib Rock even these disappeared, and we travelled through a naked country. In the course of the afternoon Keskarrah killed a reindeer, and loaded himself with its head and skin, and our men also carried off a few pounds of its flesh for supper; but their loads were altogether too great to permit them to take much additional weight. Keskarrah offered to us as a great treat the raw marrow from the hind legs of the animal, of which all the party ate except myself, and thought it very good. I was also of the same opinion, when I subsequently conquered my then too fastidious taste. We halted for the night on the borders of a small lake, which washed the base of a ridge of sand-hills, about three hundred feet high, having walked in direct distance sixteen miles.

There were four ancient pine-trees here which did not exceed six or seven feet in height, but whose branches spread themselves out for several yards, and we gladly cropped a few twigs to make a bed and to protect us from the frozen ground, still white from a fall of snow which took place in the afternoon. We were about to cut down one of these trees for firewood, but our guide solicited us to spare them, and made us understand by signs that they had been long serviceable to his nation, and that we ought to content ourselves with a few of the smaller branches. As soon as we comprehended his request we complied with it, and our attendants having, with some trouble, grubbed up a sufficient quantity of the roots of the dwarf birch to make a fire, we were enabled to prepare a comfortable supper of reindeer's meat, which we despatched with the appetites which travelling in this country never fails to ensure. We then stretched ourselves out on the pine brush, and covered by a single blanket, enjoyed a night of sound repose. The small quantity of bed-clothes we carried induced us to sleep without undressing. Old Keskarrah followed a different plan; he stripped himself to the skin, and having toasted his body for a short time over the embers of the fire, he crept under his deer-skin and rags, previously spread out as smoothly as possible, and coiling himself up in a circular form, fell asleep instantly. This custom of undressing to the skin even when lying in the open air is common to all the Indian tribes. The thermometer at sunset stood at 29°.

Resuming our journey next morning we pursued a northerly course, but had to make a considerable circuit round the western ends of two lakes whose eastern extremities were hidden from our view. The march was very uncomfortable as the wind was cold, and there was a constant fall of snow until noon; our guide too persisted in taking us over the summit of every hill that lay in the route, so that we had the full benefit of the breeze.

We forded two streams in the afternoon flowing between small lakes, and being wet, did not much relish having to halt, whilst Keskarrah pursued a herd of reindeer; but there was no alternative, as he set off and followed them without consulting our wishes. The old man loaded himself with the skin, and some meat of the animal he killed, in addition to his former burden; but after walking two miles, finding his charge too heavy for his strength, he spread the skin on the rock, and deposited the meat under some stones, intending to pick them up on our return.

We put up at sunset on the borders of a large lake, having come twelve miles. A few dwarf birches afforded us but a scanty fire, yet being sheltered from the wind by a sandy bank, we passed the night comfortably, though the temperature was 30°. A number of geese passed over us to the southward. We set off early next morning, and marched at a tolerably quick pace. The atmosphere was quite foggy, and our view was limited to a short distance. At noon, the sun shone forth for a few minutes, and the latitude 64° 57′ 7″ was observed. The small streams that we had hitherto crossed run uniformly to the southward.

At the end of sixteen miles and a half we encamped amongst a few dwarf pines, and were much rejoiced at having a good fire, as the nights was very stormy and cold. The thermometer fluctuated this day between 31° and 35°. Though the following morning was foggy and rainy, we were not sorry to quit the cold and uncomfortable beds of rock upon which we had slept, and commence our journey at an early hour. After walking about three miles, we passed over a steep sandy ridge, and found the course of the rivulets running towards the north and north-west. Our progress was slow in the early part of the morning, and we were detained for two hours on the summit of a hill exposed to a very cold wind, whilst our guide went in an unsuccessful pursuit of some reindeer. After walking a few miles farther, the fog cleared away, and Keskarrah pointed out the Copper-Mine River at a distance, and we pushed towards it with all the speed we could put forth. At noon we arrived at an arm of Point Lake, an extensive expansion of the river, and observed the latitude 65° 9′ 06″ N. We continued our walk along the south end of this arm for about a mile farther, and then halted to breakfast amidst a cluster of pines. Here the longitude, 112° 57′ 25″, was observed. After breakfast we set out and walked along the east-side of the arm towards the main body of the lake, leaving Samandré to prepare an encampment amongst the pines against our return. We found the main channel deep, its banks high and rocky, and the valleys on its borders interspersed with cluster of spruce-trees. The latter circumstance was a source of much gratification to us. The temperature of its surface water was 41°, that of the air being 43°. Having gained all the information we could collect from our guide and from personal observation, we retraced our steps to the encampment; and on the way back Hepburn and Keskarrah shot several waveys (*anas hyperborea*) which afforded us a seasonable supply, our stock of provision being nearly exhausted. These birds were feeding in large flocks on the crow-berries, which grew plentifully on the sides of the hills. We reached the encampment after dark, found a comfortable hut prepared for our reception, made an excellent supper, and slept soundly though it snowed hard the whole night.

The hills in this neighbourhood are higher than those about Fort Enterprise; they stand, however, in the same detached manner, without forming connected ranged; and the bottom of every valley is occupied, either by a small lake or a stony marsh. On the borders of such of these lakes as communicate with the Copper-Mine River, there are a few groves of spruce-trees, generally growing on accumulations of sand, on the acclivities of the hills.

We did not quit the encampment on the morning of September 13th until nine o'clock, in consequence of a constant fall of snow; but at that hour we set out on our return to Fort Enterprise, and taking a route somewhat different from the one by which we came, kept to the eastward of a chain of lakes. Soon after noon the weather became extremely disagreeable; a cold northerly gale came on, attended by snow and sleet; and the temperature fell very soon from 43° to 34°. The waveys, alarmed at the sudden change, flew over our heads in great numbers to a milder climate. We walked as quickly as possible to get a place that would furnish some fuel and shelter; but the fog occasioned us to make frequent halts, from the inability of our guide to trace his way. At length we came to a spot which afforded us plenty of dwarf birches, but they were so much frozen, and the snow fell so thick, that upwards of two hours were wasted in endeavouring to make a fire; during which time our clothes were freezing upon us. At length our efforts were crowned with success, and after a good supper, we laid, or rather sat down to sleep; for the nature of the ground obliged us to pass the night in a demi-erect position, with our backs against at bank of earth. The thermometer was 16° at six P.M.

After enjoying a more comfortable night's rest than we had expected, we set off at daybreak: the thermometer then standing at 18°. The ground was covered with snow, the small lakes were frozen, and the whole scene had a wintry appearance. We got on but slowly at first, owing to an old sprained ankle, which had been very troublesome to me for the last three days, and was this morning excessively painful. In fording a rivulet, however, the application of cold water gave me immediate relief, and I walked with ease the remainder of the day. In the afternoon we rejoined our track outwards and came to the place where Keskarrah had made his deposit of provision, which proved a very acceptable supply, as our stock was exhausted. We then crossed some sand hills, and encamped amidst a few small pines, having walked thirteen miles.

The comfort of a good fire made us soon insensible to the fatigue we had experienced through the day, in marching over the rugged stones, whose surface was rendered slippery by the frost. The thermometer at seven P.M. stood at 27°.

We set off at sunrise next morning, and our provision being expended pushed on as fast as we could to Fort Enterprise, where we arrived at eight P.M., almost exhausted by a harassing day's march of twenty-two miles. A substantial supper of reindeer steaks soon restored our vigour. We had the happiness of meeting our friends Mr. Back and Mr. Hood, who had returned from their excursion on the day succeeding what on which we set out; and I received from them the following account of their journey.

They proceeded up the Winter River to the north end of the Little Marten Lake, and then the guide, being unacquainted with the route by water to the Copper-Mine River, proposed that the canoe should be left. Upon this they ascended the loftiest hill in the neighbourhood, to examine whether they could discover any large lakes, or water communication in the direction where the guide described the river to be. They only saw a small rivulet, which was too shallow for the canoe, and also wide of the course; and as they perceived the crew would have to carry it over a rugged hilly track, they judiciously decided on leaving it, and proceeding forward on foot. Having deposited the canoe among a few dwarf birch bushes, they commenced their march, carrying their tents, blankets, cooking utensils, and a part of the dried meat. St. Germain, however, had previously delineated with charcoal, a man and a house on a piece of bark, which he placed over the canoe and the few things that were left, to point out to the Dog-Ribs that they belonged to white people.

The party reached the shores of Point Lake, through which the Copper-Mine River runs, on the 1st of September. The next day was too stormy for them to march, but on the 3rd, they proceeded along its shores to the westward, round a mountainous promontory, and perceiving the course of the lake extending to the W.N.W., they encamped near some pines, and then enjoyed the luxury of a good fire, for the first time since their departure from us. The temperature of the water in the lake was 35°, and of the air 32°, but the latter fell to 20° in the course of that night. As their principal object was to ascertain whether any arm of the lake branched nearer to Fort Enterprise than the part they had fallen upon, to which the transport of our goods could be more easily made next spring, they returned on its borders to the eastward, being satisfied, by the appearance of the mountains between south and west, that no further examination was necessary in that direction; and they continued their march until the 6th at noon, without finding any part of the lake inclining nearer the fort. They therefore encamped to observe the eclipse, which was to take place on the following morning; but a violent snow-storm rendering the observation impossible, they commenced their return, and after a comfortless and laborious march regained their canoe on the 10th, and embarking in it, arrived the same evening at the house.

Point Lake varied, as far as they traced, from one to three miles in width. Its main course was nearly east and west, but several arms branched off in different directions. I was much pleased with the able manner in which these officers executed the service they had been despatched upon, and was gratified to learn from them, that their companions had conducted themselves extremely well, and borne the fatigues of their journey most cheerfully. They scarcely ever had more than sufficient fuel to boil the kettle; and were generally obliged to lie down in their wet clothes, and consequently, suffered much from cold.

The distance which the parties travelled, in their journey to and from Point Lake, may be estimated at one hundred and ten statute miles, which being added to the distances given in the preceding pages, amount to one thousand five hundred and twenty miles that the Expedition travelled in 1820, up to the time of its residence at Fort Enterprise.

CHAPTER VIII

Transactions at Fort Enterprise – Mr. Back's Narrative of his
Journey to Chipewyan, and Return.

September, 1820

During our little expedition to the Copper-Mine River, Mr. Wentzel had made great progress in the erection of our winter-house, having nearly roofed it in. But before proceeding to give an account of a ten months' residence at this place, henceforth designated Fort Enterprise, I may premise, that I shall omit many of the ordinary occurrences of a North American winter, as they have been already detailed in so able and interesting a manner by Ellis,[1] and confine myself principally to the circumstances which had an influence on our progress in the ensuing summer. The observations on the magnetic needle, the temperature of the atmosphere, the Aurora Borealis, and other meteorological phenomena, together with the mineralogical and botanical notices, being less interesting to the general reader, are omitted in this edition.

The men continued to work diligently at the house, and by the 30th of September had nearly completed it for our reception, when a heavy fall of rain washed the greater part of the mud off the roof. This rain was remarked by the Indians as unusual, after what they had deemed so decided a commencement of winter in the early part of the month. The mean temperature for the month was 33¾°, but the thermometer had sunk as low as 16°, and on one occasion rose to 53°.

Besides the party constantly employed at the house, two men were appointed to fish, and others were occasionally sent for meat, as the hunters procured it. This latter employment, although extremely laborious, was always relished by the Canadians, as they never failed to use a prescriptive right of helping themselves to the fattest and most delicate parts of the deer. Towards the end of the month, the reindeer began to quit the barren grounds, and came into the vicinity of the house, on their way to the woods; and the success of the hunters being consequently great, the necessity of sending for the meat considerably retarded the building of the house. In the meantime we resided in our canvas tents, which proved very cold habitations, although we maintained a fire in front of them, and also endeavoured to protect ourselves from the piercing winds by a barricade of pine branches.

On the 6th of October, the house being completed, we struck our tents, and removed into it. It was merely a log building, fifty feet long, and twenty-four wide, divided into a hall, three bed rooms and a kitchen. The walls and roof were plastered with clay, the floors laid with planks rudely squared with the hatchet, and the windows closed with parchment of deer-skin. The clay which, from the coldness of the weather, required to be tempered before the fire with hot water,

1 Voyage to Hudson's Bay in the *Dobbs* and *California*

froze as it was daubed on, and afterwards cracked in such a manner as to admit the wind from every quarter; yet, compared with the tents, our new habitation appeared comfortable; and having filled our capacious clay-built chimney with fagots, we spent a cheerful evening before the invigorating blaze. The change was peculiarly beneficial to Dr. Richardson, who having in one of his excursions incautiously laid down on the frozen side of a hill when heated with walking, had caught a severe inflammatory sore throat, which became daily worse whilst we remained in the tents, but began to mend soon after he was enabled to confine himself to the more equable warmth of the house. We took up our abode at first on the floor, but our working party, who bad shown such skill as house carpenters, soon proved themselves to be, with the same tools, (the hatchet and crooked knife,) excellent cabinet makers, and daily added a table, chair, or bedstead to the comforts of our establishment. The crooked knife generally made of an old file, bent and Tempered by heat, serves an Indian or Canadian voyager for plane, chisel, and auger. With it the snow-shoe and canoe-timbers are fashioned, the deals of their sledges reduced to the requisite thinness and polish, and their wooden bowls and spoons hollowed out. Indeed, though not quite so requisite for existence as the hatchet, yet without its aid there would be little comfort in these wilds.

On the 7th we were gratified by a sight of the sun, after it had been obscured for twelve days. On this and several following days the meridian sun melted the light covering of snow or hoar frost on the lichens, which clothe the barren grounds, and rendered them so tender as to attract great herds of reindeer to our neighbourhood. On the morning of the 10th I estimated the numbers I saw during a short walk, at upwards of two thousand. They form into herds of different sizes, from ten to a hundred, according as their fears or accident induce them to unite or separate.

The females being at this time more lean and active, usually lead the van. The haunches of the males are now covered to the depth of two inches or more with fat, which is beginning to get red and high flavoured, and is considered a sure indication of the commencement of the rutting season. Their horns, which in the middle of August were yet tender, have now attained their proper size, and are beginning to lose their hairy covering which hangs from them in ragged filaments. The horns of the reindeer vary, not only with its sex and age, but are otherwise so uncertain in their growth, that they are never alike in any two individuals. The old males shed theirs about the end of December; the females retain them until the disappearance of the snow enables them to frequent the barren grounds, which may be stated to be about the middle or end of May, soon after which period they proceed towards the sea-coast and drop their young. The young males lose their horns about the same time with the females or a little earlier, some of them as early as April. The hair of the reindeer falls in July, and is succeeded by a short thick coat of mingled clove, deep reddish, and yellowish browns; the belly and under parts of the neck, etc., remaining white. As the winter approaches the hair becomes longer, and lighter in its colours, and it begins to loosen in May, being then much worn on the sides, from the animal rubbing itself against trees and stones. It becomes grayish and almost white before it is completely shed. The Indians form their robes of the skins procured in autumn, when the hair is short. Towards the spring the larvæ of the œstrus attaining a large size, produce so many perforations in the skins, that they are good for nothing. The cicatrices only of these holes are to be seen in August, but a fresh set of ova have in the mean time been deposited.[1]

The reindeer retire from the sea-coast in July and August, rut in October on the verge of the barren grounds, and shelter themselves in the woods during the

1 "It is worthy of remark, that in the month of May a very great number of large larvae exist under the mucous membrane at the root of the tongue and posterior part of the nares and pharynx. The Indians consider them to belong to the same species with the œstrus, that deposits its ova under the skin: to us the larvae of the former appeared more flattened than those of the latter. Specimens of both kinds, preserved in spirits, were destroyed by the frequent falls they received on the portages." – Dr. RICHARDSON'S Journal.

winter. They are often induced by a few fine days in winter to pay a transitory visit to their favourite pastures in the barren country, but their principal movement to the northward commences generally in the end of April, when the snow first begins to melt on the sides of the hills, and early in May, when large patches of the ground are visible, they are on the banks of the Copper-Mine River. The females take the lead in this spring migration, and bring forth their young on the sea-coast about the end of May or beginning of June. There are certain spots or passes well known to the Indians, through which the deer invariably pass in their migrations to and from the coast, and it has been observed that they always travel against the wind. The principal food of the reindeer in the barren grounds, consists of the *cetraria nivalis* and *cucullata, cenomyce rangiferina, cornicularia ochrileuca,* and other lichens, and they also eat the hay or dry grass which is found in the swamps in autumn. In the woods they feed on the different lichens which hang from the trees. They are accustomed to gnaw their fallen antlers, and are said also to devour mice.

The weight of a full grown barren-ground deer, exclusive of the offal, varies from ninety to one hundred and thirty Pounds. There is, however, a much larger kind found in the woody parts of the country, whose carcass weighs from two hundred to two hundred and forty pounds. This kind never leaves the woods, but its skin is as much perforated by the gad-fly as that of the others; a presumptive proof that the smaller species are not driven to the sea-coast solely by the attacks of that insect. There are a few reindeer occasionally killed in the spring, whose skins are entire, and these are always fat, whereas the others are lean at that season. This insect likewise infests the red-deer (*wawaskeesh*), but its ova are not found in the skin of the moose or buffalo, nor, as we have been informed, of the sheep and goat that inhabit the Rocky Mountains, although the reindeer found in those parts, (which are of an unusually large kind,) are as much tormented by them as the barren ground variety.

The herds of reindeer are attended in their migrations by bands of wolves, which destroy a great many of them. The Copper Indians kill the reindeer in the summer with the gun, or taking advantage of a favourable disposition of the ground, they enclose a herd upon a neck of land, and drive them into a lake, where they fall an easy prey; but in the rutting season and in the spring, when they are numerous on the skirts of the woods, they catch them in snares. The snares are simple nooses, formed in a rope made of twisted sinew, which are placed in the aperture of a slight hedge, constructed of the branches of trees. This hedge is so disposed as to form several winding compartments, and although it is by no means strong, yet the deer seldom attempt to break through it. The herd is led into the labyrinth by two converging rows of poles, and one is generally caught at each of the openings by the noose placed there. The hunter, too, lying in ambush, stabs some of them with his bayonet as they pass by, and the whole herd frequently becomes his prey. Where wood is scarce, a piece of turf turned up answers the purpose of a pole to conduct them towards the snares.

The reindeer has a quick eye, but the hunter by keeping to leeward and using a little caution, may approach very near; their apprehensions being much more easily roused by the smell than the sight of any unusual object. Indeed their curiosity often causes them to come close up and wheel around the hunter; thus affording him a good opportunity of singling out the fattest of the herd, and upon these occasions they often become so confused by the shouts and gestures of their enemy, that they run backwards and forwards with great rapidity, but without the power of making their escape.

The Copper Indians find by experience that a white dress attracts them most readily, and they often succeed in bringing them within shot, by kneeling and vibrating the gun from side to side, in imitation of the motion of a deer's horns when he is in the act of rubbing his head against a stone.

The Dog-Rib Indians have a mode of killing these animals, which though simple, is very successful. It was thus described by Mr. Wentzel, who resided long amongst that people. The hunters go in pairs, the foremost man carrying in one hand the horns and part of the skin of the head of a deer, and in the other a small bundle of twigs, against which he, from time to time, rubs the horns, imitating the gestures peculiar to the animal. His comrade follows treading exactly in his footsteps, and holding the guns of both in a horizontal position, so that the muzzles project under the arms of him who carries the head. Both hunters have a fillet of white skin round their foreheads, and the foremost has a strip of the same kind round his wrists. They approach the herd by degrees, raising their legs very slowly, but setting them down somewhat suddenly, after the manner of a deer, and always taking care to lift their right or left feet simultaneously. If any of the herd leave off feeding to gaze upon this extraordinary phenomenon, it instantly stops, and the head begins to play its part by licking its shoulders, and performing other necessary movements. In this way the hunters attain the very centre of the herd without exciting suspicion, and have leisure to single out the fattest. The hindmost man then pushes forward his comrade's gun, the head it dropt, and they both fire nearly at the same instant. The herd scampers off, the hunters trot after them; in a short time the poor animals halt to ascertain the cause of their terror, their foes stop at the same instant, and having loaded as they ran, greet the grazers with a second fatal discharge. The consternation of the deer increases, they run to and fro in the utmost confusion, and sometimes a great part of the herd is destroyed within the space of a few hundred yards. A party who had been sent to Akaitcho returned, bringing three hundred and seventy pounds of dried meat, and of two hundred and twenty pounds of suet, together with the unpleasant information, that a still larger quantity of the latter article had been found and carried off, as he supposed, by some Dog-Ribs, who had passed that way.

The weather becoming daily colder, all the lakes in the neighbourhood of the house were completely, and the river partially, frozen over by the middle of the month. The reindeer now began to quit us for more southerly and better-sheltered pastures. Indeed, their longer residence in our neighbourhood would have been of little service to us, for our ammunition was almost completely expended, though we had dealt it of late with a very sparing hand to the Indians. We had, however, already secured in the storehouse the carcasses of one hundred deer, together with one thousand pounds of suet, and some dried meat; and had, moreover, eighty deer stowed up at various distances from the house. The necessity of employing the men to build a house for themselves, before the weather became too severe, obliged us to put the latter *en cache,* as the voyagers term it, instead of adopting the more safe plan of bringing them to the house. Putting a deer *en cache,* means merely protecting it against the wolves, and in still more destructive wolverenes, by heavy loads of wood or stones; the latter animal, however, sometimes digs underneath the pile, and renders the precautions abortive. On the 18th, Mr Back and Mr. Wentzel set out for Fort Providence, accompanied by Beauparlant, Belanger, and two Indians, Akalyazza and Thoolezzeh, with their wives, the Little Forehead, and the Smiling Marten. Mr. Back had volunteered to go and make the necessary arrangements for transporting the stores we expected from Cumberland House, and to endeavour

CAPT^N FRANKLIN, R.N. F.R.S.

*Commander of the Land Arctic Expedition
with Earl Enterprise in the back ground*

This engraved 1824 portrait of Franklin captures the friendly nature of the man. Franklin's rugged determination and drive are not captured by the relaxed pose, but the scientific tools of the explorer, his surveying instruments, are symbols not only of his accomplishment but also of Britain's technological prowess as a counter to nature. Franklin's first overland expedition, and his final expedition in search of the Northwest Passage clearly show how easily nature overpowered "modern" technology. (Bridgeman Art Library).

Jane Griffin, Lady Franklin as depicted in this 1816 portrait. Lady Jane married John Franklin in 1828 and was his second wife; his first Eleanor Porden, had died in 1825. When there was no news of his final expedition she persistently lobbied the Admiralty to rescue her husband, spending £3000 of her own money sponsoring four expeditions to the region. It was not until 1859 that she received confirmation that her husband was dead. (National Portrait Gallery).

The *Trent* among ice floes, June 7 1818, during Lieutenant John Franklin's first voyage to the Polar Seas. Although the ice floes halted the 1818 exploration several valuable charts were made which would benefit later expeditions. Taken from Murray Smith's *Arctic Expeditions* of 1877. (Mary Evans Picture Library).

The Arctic Council of explorers consisted of experts in the field. These included Sir John Franklin (second from left), Sir George Back, Sir William Parry, Sir James Ross and Sir John Barrow. (National Maritime Museum, Greenwich).

Drawn by Lieut Hood, R.N.

PORTRAIT OF AKAITCHO AND HIS SON.

Published March 1823, by John Murray, London.

Franklin's first overland expedition relied heavily on the native peoples of the regions he explored. Akaitchoo, chief of the Yellowknife Indians, agreed to guide Franklin and his small expedition north, and in July 1821, delivered the British and their voyageurs to the Coppermine River delta. When the expedition met with disaster on their return, George Back was able to reach Akaitchoo and his people. Their "most friendly hospitality and all sorts of personal attention," as Franklin later noted, nursed the survivors back to health. Lt. Hood drew this painting of Akaitchoo and his son. (Bridgeman Art Library).

The compass is an essential tool for the mariner and the explorer. Rather than carry a large boat compass, Franklin carried this pocket compass on his first overland expedition of 1819-1822. After the expedition, Franklin presented the compass to Hudson Bay Company chaplain John R. West. (National Maritime Museum, Greenwich).

Engraving of a Buffalo Pound based on a drawing made by Lieutenant George Back R.N. for the original edition of John Franklin's *Narrative of a Journey to the Shores of the Polar Sea in the years 1819-22*. (Bridgeman Art Library).

While John Franklin's overland party struggled to reach the shores of the "Polar Sea", another expedition, commanded by William Edward Parry, sailed through Lancaster Sound and deep into the heart of the Canadian Arctic. In this scene, from Parry's *Journal of a Voyage*, his ships *Hecla* and *Griper* pass the entrance to Lancaster Sound while the waves crash against the icy shores. (Vancouver Maritime Museum).

Establishing camp while underway in March 1820, the Franklin expedition gathers wood while the commander rests under a tree, writing in his journal. A cook pot hangs over the fire – food is not yet a problem for the explorers. By the next year, many of the men were dying in a desperate race for food, shelter and life itself. (Bridgeman Art Library).

Capt.ⁿ W. E. Parry. R. L..

Commander of the Polar Expedition

1819—20.

Captain Sir William Edward Parry, like his contemporary John Franklin, was a veteran Arctic explorer. Parry's luck was better than Franklin's. Joining John Ross's Baffin Bay expedition in 1818, Parry disagreed with his former commander that the bay held no entrance to the Northwest Passage. In three separate expeditions, in conjunction with Franklin on land, Parry probed the Arctic for the passage between 1819 and 1827, mapping tremendous areas of the north. His third expedition nearly ended in disaster when the ice crushed his ship, HMS *Fury*, but Parry managed to extract his second ship, HMS *Hecla*, and all of his men from the Arctic. After a fourth expedition, seeking to sail to the North Pole, Parry retired from exploration, never to try his luck in the dangerous Arctic again. (National Maritime Museum, Greenwich).

Drawn by Lieut. Back. R.N.

In an age before cameras, early explorers captured scenes of distant lands and strange peoples by sketching or painting. Robert Hood and George Back both created a rich record of Franklin's first overland expedition. Back's fascination with the native peoples he encountered on the expedition inspired this portrait of a "Stone Indian." (Bridgeman Art Library).

Based on a painting by Robert Hood, this engraving shows the interior of a Cree Indian tent visited by the first overland expedition on March 25 1820. (Bridgeman Art Library).

Parry's crew was the first British expedition to winter in the deep Arctic. Anchored at Winter Harbour, on Melville Island, the ships froze into the ice. Within the relative comfort of *Hecla* and *Griper*, and supported by canned provisions, the crews survived the long twilight of winter. They covered the decks with canvas and surrounded the hulls with ice and snow for insulation. Meanwhile, further south, Franklin's men fought the cold and starvation. (Vancouver Maritime Museum).

This mitt, made out of a Hudson's Bay Company trade blanket, belonged to Franklin. Made by one of the groups of the native peoples the overland expeditions encountered, it is a striking reminder of the merging of two technologies and cultures on the Canadian frontier. (National Maritime Museum, Greenwich).

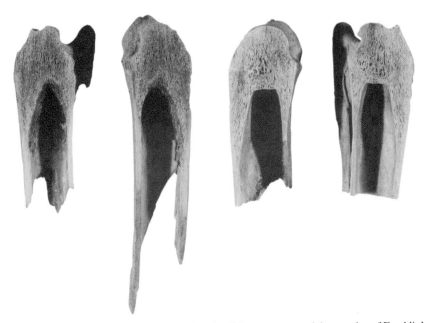

In August 1970, Canadian archaeologist Timothy C. Losey excavated the remains of Franklin's Fort Enterprise. There, at the site of the final drama of the ill-fated overland expedition, Losey and his team uncovered the remains of the fort's buildings, buttons, gunflints, shot, nails and other fragmented artifacts – and these evocative traces of starvation. Split open, smashed, burnt and reamed out for their marrow, these caribou bones joined half-rotten hides and leather moccasins as food for the desperate explorers. (Dr. Timothy C. Losey).

Midshipman George Back collected these beaded moccasins during Franklin's first overland expedition. Back, fascinated with the landscape and the people, collected a number of items and kept a detailed notebook that he filled with paintings. Back's close relationship with the native peoples was a determining factor in the rescue of the first overland expedition when Back and his native guides raced ahead of the other starving explorers to seek food and assistance. (National Maritime Museum, Greenwich).

CAPTAIN FRANKLIN, R.N.

COMMANDER OF THE EXPEDITION TO THE MOUTH OF THE COPPER-MINE RIVER

AND SHORES OF THE POLAR SEA.

ENGRAVED BY W.T FRY. FROM AN ORIGINAL DRAWING BY T WAGEMAN.

London Published for the New European Magazine by John Low Jun! 32 Cornhill 1st April 1823.

"Captain Franklin, R.N., Commander of the Expedition to the Mouth of the Copper Mine River and Shores of the Polar Sea." Safely back in England, the "man who ate his boots" posed for his portrait in April 1823. This engraving, by William Thomas Fry, is based on a painting by Thomas Charles Wageman. (National Maritime Museum, Greenwich).

The routes of John Franklin's two overland expeditions to the shores of the Arctic Ocean, 1819-1821 and 1825-1827. (Map by Eric Leinberger, from *Across the Top of the World*, by James P. Delgado)

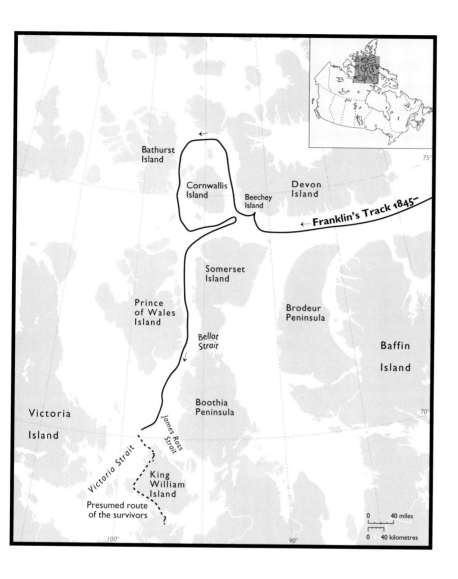

Bathurst
Island

Cornwallis
Island

Beechey
Island

Devon
Island

← Franklin's Track 1845

75°

Somerset
Island

Prince
of Wales
Island

Brodeur
Peninsula

Bellot
Strait

Baffin

Island

James Ross Strait

Boothia
Peninsula

Victoria

Island

70°

Victoria Strait

King
William
Island

Presumed route
of the survivors
?

0   40 miles

0   40 kilometres

100°

90°

Reconstructed from the brief note left by F.R.M. Crozier and James Fitzjames in a cairn
close to the end of the final Franklin expedition, this map shows the route of *Erebus* and
Terror on that ill-fated foray into the Northwest Passage. (Map by Eric Leinberger, from
Across the Top of the World, by James P. Delgado).

British explorers in the Arctic were fascinated by both the landscape and the people. George Francis Lyon, sailing with William Edward Parry on a voyage north of Hudson Bay in HMS *Hecla* and HMS *Fury* from 1821 to 1823, was one of them. Lyon captured this scene of the interior of an igloo. A young mother has pulled up her parka to nurse an infant, interrupting her preparations for a meal. The snow platform near her has pieces of meat and entrails, with a stone *ulu* (knife) stuck into the snow. The soapstone cooking pots and the *kudlik* (lamp) all have food or fat in them. (Bridgeman Art Library).

The exterior of Eskimo snow huts as Franklin would have found them. The snow huts could be quite complex in construction, often including the long entrance tunnel, depicted here, designed to keep out snow and cold air. Individual igloos could be linked together with tunnels to create a self contained community. (Mary Evans Picture Library).

Card engraving from November 1823 depicting Captain Parry seeking the Northwest Passage. (National Maritime Museum, Greenwich).

The situation of the ships *Hecla* and *Fury* off Fury beach on August 1 1825. During Parry's third voyage of polar exploration *Fury* suffered severe damage after being pushed ashore by ice. When it became clear that the ship could not be repaired Parry abandoned *Fury* after transferring the stores and crew to the *Hecla*. (National Maritime Museum, Greenwich).

CAPT^N JOHN FRANKLIN, R.N.

Published by John Murray, London, 1828.

After his third voyage of exploration, 1825-27, Franklin was knighted and posted to the Mediterranean and then went to Tasmania as lieutenant-governor. Returning to England in 1843 he was desperate to lead another expedition to the Arctic which, it was hoped, would eventually find the elusive northwest-passage. (National Maritime Museum, Greenwich).

Contemporary engraving of HMS *Fury* and *Hecla* sailing through young ice in September 1824. Converted from Royal Navy bomb vessels, which were chosen for their strong construction, they were typical of the kind of ship favoured by the Admiralty for Arctic exploration. (National Maritime Museum, Greenwich).

HMS *Erebus* and HMS *Terror*, wintering in the Arctic ice, 1846-1847. In this imagined scene, painted by Allen Young, a member of F.L. McClintock's Franklin search party aboard the yacht *Fox*, 1857-1859, the *Erebus* and *Terror* are moored close to each other, just before disaster set in and the crews abandoned the ships. (Vancouver Maritime Museum).

"They Forged the Last Link with their Lives". This painting by Thomas Smith captures the late Victorian romantic fascination with the destruction of the final Franklin expedition. Facing death after completing the discovery of the Northwest Passage, Franklin's men quietly die at their posts. The reality of the expedition's end was less heroic as the crew split into different groups, some resorting to cannibalism. (National Maritime Museum, Greenwich).

This somewhat imaginative Victorian scene depicts the moment when McClintock's search expedition discovered the abandoned boat on King William Island, along with the skeletons of two of the dead crew. The image of the boat, still filled with equipment, supplies and the bodies of the dead, fired the imagination and inspired "They Forged the Last Link with their Lives". (Vancouver Maritime Museum).

The only known photographic image of Sir John Franklin, this daguerreotype view was taken aboard HMS *Erebus* in 1845. Franklin, suffering from a cold, hated the photograph. It is a striking contrast to the heroic paintings and engravings of the explorer. Franklin's Guelphic Order of Hanover, a blurred image around his breast, was later retrieved from the Inuit by F.L. McClintock in 1859. It was McClintock who brought definitive news back to England of Franklin's death in 1847 and the fatal end of the expedition. (National Maritime Museum, Greenwich).

In 1858 the yacht *Fox*, under the command of Captain Francis Leopold McClintock, was dispatched by Lady Franklin to search for Sir John. McClintock discovered two cairns containing the last reports left by the ill fated expedition confirming the death of Franklin. (Mary Evans Picture Library).

These relics of Franklin's last expedition were found in June 1859 by McClintock's search mission scattered around a cairn at Victory Point. They include a medicine chest, the contents of which indicated that Franklin's men had suffered from scurvy, snow blindness, bronchitis and frostbite before they eventually perished. (Mary Evans Picture Library).

This official form, used by Her Majesty's ships to report their position, is the only substantive written account of Franklin's last Arctic expedition. Initially completed on May 24, 1847 and left in a cairn on King William Island, it was used again to note the abandonment of *Erebus* and *Terror*:

"H.M. Ships *Terror* and *Erebus* were deserted on the 2nd April, 5 leagues NNW of this, having been beset since 12th September 1846. The officers & crew consisting of 105 souls under the command of Captain F.R.M. Crozier, landed here.

Sir John Franklin died on the 11th June, 1847 and the total loss by deaths in the expedition has been to this date 9 officers and 15 men."

(From Peterson, *Den Sidste Franklin-Expedition*)).

The cenotaph monument to Sir John Franklin at Westminster Abbey in London includes a bust of the lost explorer, with his usual, kindly expression, one of his ships, beset in the ice, never to be free again, and the famous epitaph by Franklin's nephew, Alfred, Lord Tennyson:

> Not Here: The White North has thy bones; and Thou,
> Heroic Sailor Soul,
> Art Passing on Thine Happier Voyage Now
> Toward No Earthly Pole.

(The Dean and Chapter of Westminster, Box 11(1)).

to obtain some additional supplies from the establishments at Slave Lake. If any accident should have prevented the arrival of our stores, and the establishments at Moose-Deer Island should be unable to supply the deficiency he was, if he found himself equal to the task, to proceed to Chipewyan. Ammunition was essential to our existence, and a considerable supply of tobacco was also requisite, not only for the comfort of the Canadians, who use it largely, and had stipulated for it in their engagements, but also as a means of preserving the friendship of the Indians. Blankets, cloth, and iron-work, were scarcely less indispensable to equip our men for the advance next season.

Mr. Wentzel accompanied Mr. Back, to assist him in obtaining from the traders, on the score of old friendship, that which they might be inclined to deny to our necessities. I forwarded by them letters to the Colonial Office and Admiralty, detailing the proceedings of the Expedition up to this period.

On the 22nd we were surprised by a visit from a dog; the poor animal was in low condition, and much fatigued. Our Indians discovered by marks on his ears that he belonged to the Dog-Ribs. This tribe, unlike the Chipewyans and Copper Indians, had preserved that useful associate of man, although from their frequent intercourse with the latter people, they were not ignorant of the prediction alluded to in a former page. One of our interpreters was immediately despatched, with an Indian, to endeavour to trace out the Dog-Ribs, whom he supposed might be concealed in the neighbourhood from their dread of the Copper Indians; although we had no doubt of their coming to us, were they aware of our being here. The interpreter, however, returned without having discovered any traces of strange Indians; a circumstance which led us to conclude, that the dog had strayed from his masters a considerable time before.

Towards the end of the month the men completed their house, and took up their abode in it. It was thirty-four feet long and eighteen feet wide; was divided into two apartments, and was placed at right angles to the officers' dwelling, and facing the storehouse: the three buildings forming three sides of a quadrangle.

On the 26th Akaitcho and his party arrived, the hunting in this neighbourhood being terminated for the season, by the deer having retired southward to the shelter of the woods.

The arrival of this large party was a serious inconvenience to us, from our being compelled to issue them daily rates of provision from the store. The want of ammunition prevented us from equipping and sending them to the woods to hunt; and although they are accustomed to subsist themselves for a considerable part of the year by fishing, or snaring the deer, without having recourse to firearms, yet on the present occasion, they felt little inclined to do so, and gave scope to their natural love of ease, as long as our storehouse seemed to be well stocked. Nevertheless, as they were conscious of impairing our future resources, they did not fail, occasionally, to remind us that it was not their fault, to express an ardent desire to go hunting, and to request a supply of ammunition, although they knew that it was not in our power to give it.

The summer birds had by this time entirely deserted us, leaving, for our winter companions, the raven, cinereous crow, ptarmigan, and snow-bird. The last of the water-fowl that quitted us was a species of diver, of the same size with the *colymbus arcticus*, but differing from it in the arrangement of the white spots on its plumage, and in having a yellowish white bill. This bird was occasionally caught in our fishing-nets.

The thermometer during the month of October, at Fort Enterprise, never rose above 37°, or fell below 5°; the mean temperature for the month was 23°.

In the beginning of October a party had been sent to the westward to search for birch to make snow-shoe frames, and the Indian women were afterwards employed in netting the shoes and preparing leather for winter clothing to the men. Robes of reindeer skins were also obtained from the Indians, and issued to the men who were to travel, as they were not only a great deal lighter than blankets, but also much warmer, and altogether better adapted for a winter in this climate They are, however, unfit for summer use, as the least moisture causes the skin to spoil, and lose its hair. It requires the skins of seven deer to make one robe. The finest are made of the skins of young fawns.

The fishing, having failed as the weather became more severe, was given up on the 5th. It had procured us about one thousand two hundred *white fish*, from two to three pounds each. There are two other species of *Coregoni* in Winter Lake, *Black's grayling* and the *round fish*; and a few *trout, pike, methye,* and *red carp*, were also occasionally obtained from the nets. It may be worthy of notice here, that the fish froze as they were taken out of the nets, in a short time became a solid mass of ice, and by a blow or two of the hatchet were easily split open, when the intestines might be removed in one lump. If in this completely frozen state they were thawed before the fire, they recovered their animation. This was particularly the case with the carp, and we had occasion to observe it repeatedly, as Dr. Richardson occupied himself with examining the structure of the different species of fish, and was, always in the winter, under the necessity of thawing them before he could cut them. We have seen a carp recover so far as to leap about with much vigour, after it had been frozen for thirty-six hours.

From the 12th to the 16th we had fine, and for the season, warm weather; and the deer, which had not been seen since the 26th of October, reappeared in the neighbourhood of the house, to the surprise of the Indians, who attributed their return to the barren grounds to the unusual mildness of the season. On this occasion, by melting some of our pewter cups, we managed to furnish five balls to each of the hunters, but they were all expended unsuccessfully, except by Akaitcho, who killed two deer.

By the middle of the month Winter River was firmly frozen over, except the small rapid at its commencement, which remained open all the winter. The ice on the lake was now nearly two feet thick. After the 16th we had a succession of cold, snowy, and windy weather. We had become anxious to hear of the arrival of Mr. Back and his party at Fort Providence. The Indians, who had calculated the period at which a messenger ought to have returned from thence to be already passed, became impatient when it had elapsed, and with their usual love of evil augury tormented us by their melancholy forebodings. At one time they conjectured that the whole party had fallen through the ice; at another, that they had been waylaid oil by the Dog-Ribs. In vain did we urge the improbability of the former accident, or the peaceable character of the Dog-Ribs, so little in conformity with the latter. "The ice at this season was deceitful," they said "and the Dog-Ribs, though unwarlike, were treacherous." These assertions, so often repeated, had some effect upon the spirits of our Canadian voyagers, who seldom weigh any opinion they adopt; but we persisted in treating their fears as chimerical, for had we seemed to listen to them for a moment, it is more than probable that the whole of our Indians would have gone to Fort Providence in search of supplies, and we should have found it extremely difficult to have recovered them.

The matter was put to rest by the appearance of Belanger on the morning of the 23rd, and the Indians, now running into the opposite extreme, were disposed to give us more credit for our judgment than we deserved. They had had a tedious and fatiguing journey to Fort Providence, and for some days were destitute of provisions.

Belanger arrived alone; he had walked constantly for the last six-and-thirty hours, leaving his Indian companions encamped at the last woods, they being unwilling to accompany him across the barren grounds during the storm that had prevailed for several days, and blew with unusual violence on the morning of his arrival. His locks were matted with snow, and he was incrusted with ice from head to foot, so that we scarcely recognised him when he burst in upon us. We welcomed him with the usual shake of the hand, but were unable to give him the glass of rum which every voyager receives on his arrival at a trading post.

As soon as his packet was thawed, we eagerly opened it to obtain our English letters. The latest were dated on the preceding April. They came by way of Canada, and were brought up in September to Slave Lake by the North-West Company's canoes.

We were not so fortunate with regard to our stores; of ten pieces, or bales of 90 lbs. weight, which had been sent from York Factory by Governor Williams, five of the most essential had been left at the Grand Rapid on the Saskatchawan, owing, as far as we could judge from the accounts that reached us, to the misconduct of the officer to whom they were intrusted, and who was ordered to convey them to Cumberland House. Being overtaken by some of their taking half of his charge as it was intended for the service of Government. The North-West gentlemen objected, that their canoes had already got a cargo in, and that they had been requested to convey our stores from Cumberland House only, where they had a canoe waiting for the purpose. The Hudson's Bay officer upon this deposited our ammunition and tobacco upon the beach, and departed without any regard to the serious consequences that might result to us from the want of them. The Indians, who assembled at the opening of the packet, and sat in silence watching our countenances, were necessarily made acquainted with the non-arrival of our stores, and bore the intelligence with unexpected tranquillity. We took care, however, in our communications with them to dwell upon the more agreeable parts of our intelligence, and they seemed to receive particular pleasure on being informed of the arrival of two Esquimaux interpreters at Slave Lake, on their way to join the party. The circumstance not only quieted their fears of opposition from the Esquimaux on our descent to the sea next season, but also afforded a substantial proof of our influence in being able to bring two people of that nation from such a distance.

Akaitcho, who is a man of great penetration and shrewdness, duly appreciated these circumstances; indeed he has often surprised us by his correct judgment of the character of individuals amongst the traders of our own party, although his knowledge of their opinions was, in most instances, obtained through the imperfect medium of interpretation. He was an attentive observer, however, of every action, and steadily compared their conduct with their pretensions.

By the newspapers we learned the demise of our revered and lamented sovereign George III., and the proclamation of George IV. We concealed this intelligence from the Indians, lest the death of their Great Father might lead them to suppose that we should be unable to fulfil our promises to them.

The Indians who had left Fort Providence with Belanger arrived the day after him, and, amongst other intelligence, informed Akaitcho of some reports they had heard to our disadvantage. They stated that Mr. Weeks, the gentleman in charge of Fort Providence, had told them, that so far from our being what we represented ourselves to be, the officers of a great King, we were merely a set of dependant wretches, whose only aim was to obtain subsistence for a season in the plentiful country of the Copper Indians; that, out of charity we had been supplied with a portion of goods by the trading Companies, but that there was not the smallest probability of our being able to reward the Indians when their term of service was completed. Akaitcho, with great good sense, instantly came to have the matter explained, stating at the same time, that he could not credit it. I then pointed out to him that Mr. Wentzel, with whom they had long been accustomed to trade, had pledged the credit of his Company for the stipulated rewards to the party that accompanied us, and that the trading debts due by Akaitcho, and his party had already been remitted, which was of itself a sufficient proof of our influence with the North-West Company. I also reminded Akaitcho, that our having caused the Esquimaux to be brought up at a great expense, was evidence of our future intentions, and informed him that I should write to Mr. Smith, the senior trader in the department, on the subject, when I had no doubt that a satisfactory explanation would be given. The Indians retired from the conference apparently satisfied, but this business was in the end productive of much inconvenience to us, and proved very detrimental to the progress of the Expedition. In conjunction also with other intelligence conveyed in Mr. Back's letters respecting the disposition of the traders towards us, particularly a statement of Mr. Weeks, that he had been desired not to assist us with supplies from his post, it was productive of much present uneasiness to me.

On the 28th St. Germain, the interpreter, set out with eight Canadian voyagers and four Indian hunters to bring up our stores from Fort Providence. I wrote by him to Mr. Smith, at Moose-Deer Island, and Mr. Keith, at Chipewyan, both of the North-West Company, urging them in the strongest manner to comply with requisition for stores which Mr. Back would present. I also informed Mr. Simpson, principal agent in the Athabasca for the Hudson's Bay Company, who had proffered every assistance in his power, that we should gladly avail ourselves of the kind intentions expressed in a letter which I had received from him.

We also sent a number of broken axes to Slave Lake to be repaired. The dog that came to us on the 22nd of October, and had become very familiar, followed the party. We were in hopes that it might prove of some use in dragging their loads, but we afterwards learned, that on the evening after their departure from the house, they had the cruelty to kill and eat it, although they had no reason to apprehend a scarcity of provision. A dog is considered to be delicate eating by the voyagers.

The mean temperature of the air for November was −0.7°. The greatest heat observed was 25° above, and the least 31° below, zero.

On the 1st of December the sky was clear, a slight appearance of stratus only being visible near the horizon; but a kind of snow fell at intervals in the forenoon, its particles so minute as to be observed only in the sunshine. Towards noon the snow became more apparent, and the two limbs of a prismatic arch were visible, one on each side of the sun near its place in the heavens, the centre being deficient. We have frequently observed this descent of minute icy spiculæ when the sky appears perfectly clear, and could even perceive that its silent but continued action, added to the snowy covering of the ground.

Having received one hundred balls from Fort Providence by Belanger, we distributed them amongst the Indians, informing the leader at the same time, that the residence of so large a party as his at the house, amounting, with women and children, to forty souls, was producing a serious reduction in our stock of provision. He acknowledged the justice of the statement, and promised to remove as soon as his party had prepared snow-shoes and sledges for themselves. Under one pretext or other, however, their departure was delayed until the 10th of the month, when they left us, having previously received one of our fishing-nets, and all the ammunition we possessed. The leader left his aged mother and two female attendants to our care, requesting that if she died during his absence, she might be buried at a distance from the fort, that he might not be reminded of his loss when he visited us.

Keskarrah, the guide, also remained behind, with his wife and daughter. The old man has become too feeble to hunt, and his time is almost entirely occupied in attendance upon his wife, who has been long affected with an ulcer on the face, which has nearly destroyed her nose.

Lately he made an offering to the water spirits, whose wrath he apprehended to be the cause of her malady. It consisted of a knife, a piece of tobacco, and some other trifling articles, which were tied up in a small bundle, and committed to the rapid with a long prayer. He does not trust entirely, however, to the relenting of the spirits for his wife's cure, but comes daily to Dr. Richardson for medicine.

Upon one occasion he received the medicine from the Doctor with such formality, and wrapped it up in his reindeer robe with such extraordinary carefulness, that it excited the involuntary laughter of Mr. Hood and myself. The old man smiled in his turn, and as he always seemed proud of the familiar way in which we were accustomed to joke with him, we thought no more upon the subject. But lie unfortunately mentioned the circumstance to his wife, who imagined in consequence, that the drug was not productive of its usual good effects, and they immediately came to the conclusion that some bad medicine had been intentionally given to them. The distress produced by this idea, was in proportion to their former faith in the potency of the remedy, and the night was spent in singing and groaning. Next morning the whole family were crying in concert, and it was not until the evening of the second day that we succeeded in pacifying them. The old woman began to feel better, and her faith in the medicine was renewed.

While speaking of this family, I may remark that the daughter, whom we designated Green-stockings from her dress, is considered by her tribe to be a great beauty. Mr. Hood drew an accurate portrait of her, although her mother was averse to her sitting for it. She was afraid, she said, that her daughter's likeness would induce the Great Chief who resided in England to send for the original. The young lady, however, was undeterred by any such fear. She has already been an object of contest between her countrymen, and although under sixteen years of age, has belonged successively to two husbands, and would probably have been the wife of many more, if her mother had not required her services as a nurse.

The weather during this month was the coldest we experienced during our residence in America. The thermometer sunk on one occasion to 57° below zero, and never rose beyond 6° above it; the mean for the month was −29.7°. During these intense colds, however, the atmosphere was generally calm, and the wood-cutters and others went about their ordinary occupations without using any extraordinary precautions, yet without feeling any bad effects. They had their reindeer shirts on, leathern mittens lined with blankets, and furred caps; but none of them used any defence for the face, or needed any. Indeed we have already mentioned that the heat is abstracted most rapidly from the body during strong breezes, and most of those who have perished from cold in this country, have fallen a sacrifice to their being overtaken on a lake or other unsheltered place, by a storm of wind. The intense colds were, however, detrimental to us in another way. The trees froze to their very centres and became as hard as stones, and more difficult to cut. Some of the axes were broken daily, and by the end of the month we had only one left that was fit for felling trees. By intrusting it only to one of the party who had been bred a carpenter, and who could use it with dexterity, it was fortunately preserved until the arrival of our men with others from Fort Providence.

A thermometer, hung in our bedroom at the distance of sixteen feet from the fire, but exposed to its direct radiation, stood even in the daytime occasionally at 15° below zero, and was observed more than once previous to the kindling of the fire in the morning, to be as low as 40° below zero. On two of these occasions the chronometers 2149 and 2151, which during the night lay under Mr. Hood's and Dr. Richardson's pillows, stopped while they were dressing themselves.

The rapid at the commencement of the river remained open in the severest weather, although it was somewhat contracted in width. Its temperature was 32°, as was the surface of the river opposite the house, about a quarter of a mile lower down, tried at a hole in the ice, through which water was drawn for domestic purposes. The river here was two fathoms and a half deep, and the temperature at its bottom was at least 42° above zero. This fact was ascertained by a spirit thermometer; in which, probably, from some irregularity in the tube, a small portion of the coloured liquid usually remained at 42° when the column was made to descend rapidly. In the present instance the thermometer standing at 47° below zero, with no portion of the fluid in the upper part of the tube, was let down slowly into the water, but drawn cautiously and rapidly up again, when a red drop at +42° indicated that the fluid had risen to that point or above it. At this period the daily visits of the sun were very short, and owing to the obliquity of his rays, afforded us little warmth or light. It is half-past eleven before he peeps over a small ridge of hills opposite to the house, and he sinks in the horizon at half-past two. On the 28th Mr. Hood, in order to attain an approximation to the quantity of terrestrial refraction, observed the sun's meridian altitude when the thermometer stood at 46° below zero, at the imminent hazard of having his fingers frozen.

He found the sextant had changed its error considerably, and that the glasses had lost their parallelism from the contraction of the brass. In measuring the error he perceived that the diameter of the sun's image was considerably short of twice the semi-diameter; a proof of the uncertainty of celestial observations made during these intense frosts. The results of this and another similar observation are given at the bottom of the page.[1]

The Aurora appeared with more or less brilliancy on twenty-eight nights of this month, and we were also gratified by the resplendent beauty of the moon, which for many days together performed its circle round the heavens, shining with undiminished lustre, and scarcely disappearing below the horizon during the twenty-four hours.

During many nights there was a halo round the moon, although the stars shone brightly, and the atmosphere appeared otherwise clear. The same phenomenon was observed round the candles, even in our bedrooms; the diameter of the halo increasing as the observer receded from the light. These halos, both round the moon and candles, occasionally exhibited faintly some of the prismatic colours.

As it may be interesting to the reader to know how we passed our time at this season of the year, I shall mention briefly, that a considerable portion of it was occupied in writing up our journals. Some newspapers and magazines, that we had received from England with our letters, were read again and again, and commented upon at our meals; and we often exercised ourselves with conjecturing the changes that might take place in the world before we could hear from it again. The probability of our receiving letters, and the period of their arrival, were calculated to a nicety. We occasionally paid the woodmen a visit, or took a walk for a mile or two on the river.

In the evenings we joined the men in the hall, and took part in their games, which generally continued to a late hour; in short, we never found the time to hang heavy upon our hands; and the peculiar occupations of each of the officers afforded them more employment than might at first be supposed. I re-calculated the observations made on our route; Mr. Hood protracted the charts, and made those drawings of birds, plants and fishes, which cannot appear in this work, but which have been the admiration of every one who has seen them. Each of the party sedulously and separately recorded their observations on the Aurora; and Dr. Richardson contrived to obtain, from under the snow, specimens of most of the lichens in the neighbourhood, and to make himself acquainted with the mineralogy of the surrounding country.

The Sabbath was always a day of rest with us; the woodmen were required to provide for the exigencies of that day on Saturday, and the party were dressed in their best attire. Divine service was regularly performed, and the Canadians attended, and behaved with great decorum, although they were all Roman Catholics, and but little acquainted with the language in which the prayers were read. I regretted much that we had not a French Prayer-Book, but the Lord's Prayer and Creed were always read to them in their own language.

Our diet consisted almost entirely of reindeer meat, varied twice a week by fish, and occasionally by a little flour, but we had no vegetables of any description. On the Sunday mornings we drank a cup of chocolate, but our greatest luxury was tea (without sugar), of which we regularly partook twice a day. With reindeer's fat, and strips of cotton shirts, we formed candles; and Hepburn acquired considerable skill in the manufacture of soap, from the wood-ashes, fat and salt. The formation of soap was considered as rather a mysterious operation by our Canadians, and, in their hands, was always supposed to fail if a woman approached the kettle in which the ley was boiling. Such are our simple domestic details.

On the 30th, two hunters came from the leader, to convey ammunition to him, as soon as our men should bring it from Fort Providence.

The men, at this time, coated the walls of the house on the outside with a thin mixture of clay and water, which formed a crust of ice, that, for some days proved impervious to the air; the dryness of the atmosphere, however, was such, that the ice in a short time evaporated, and gave admission to the wind as before. It is a general custom at the forts to give this sort of coating to the walls at Christmas time. When it was gone, we attempted to remedy its defect, by heaping up snow against the walls.

January 1, 1821

This morning our men assembled, and greeted us with the customary salutation on the commencement of the new year. That they might enjoy a holyday, they had yesterday collected double the usual quantity of firewood, and we anxiously expected the return of the men from Fort Providence, with some additions to their comforts. We had stronger hope of their arrival before the evening, as we knew that every voyager uses his utmost endeavour to reach a post upon, or previous to, the *jour de l'an*, that he may partake of the wonted festivities. It forms, as Christmas is said to have done among our forefathers, the theme of their conversation for months before and after the period of its arrival. On the present

Temperature of the air – 41°. Wind north, a light breeze, a large halo visible about the sun. January 15th, 1821. – Observed an apparent meridian altitude [.] lower limb 4°, 24′ 57″. [.] apparent diameter 31′ 5″. For apparent altitude 4° 24′ 57″, the mean refraction is 10′ 58″ (Mackay's Tables), and the true, found as detailed above, is 14′ 39″, which, increasing in the same ratio as that of the atmosphere at a mean state of temperature, is 43′ 57″ at the horizon. But the difference of refraction between the tipper and lower limbs increasing also in that ratio, gives 48′ 30″ for the horizontal refraction.

'Temperature of the air -35°, a light air from the westward, very clear.

'The extreme coldness of the weather rendered these operations difficult and dangerous; yet I think the observations may be depended upon within 30″, as will appear by their approximate results in calculating the horizontal refraction; for it must be considered that an error of 30″, in the refraction in altitude, would make a difference of several minutes in the horizontal refraction.' – Mr HOOD's Journal.

occasion we could only treat them with a little flour and fat; these were both considered as great luxuries, but still the feast was defective from the want of rum, although we promised them a little when it should arrive.

The early part of January proved mild, the thermometer rose to 20° above zero, and we were surprised by the appearance of a kind of damp fog approaching very nearly to rain. The Indians expressed their astonishment at this circumstance, and declared the present to be one of the warmest winters they had ever experienced. Some of them reported that it had actually rained in the woody parts of the country. In the latter part of the month, however, the thermometer again descended to – 49°, and the mean temperature for the month proved to be – 15.6°. Owing to the fogs that obscured the sky the Aurora was visible only upon eighteen nights in the month.

On the 15th seven of our men arrived from Fort Providence with two kegs of rum, one barrel of powder, sixty pounds of ball, two rolls of tobacco, and some clothing. They had been twenty-one days on their march from Slave Lake, and the labour they underwent was sufficiently evinced by their sledge-collars having worn out the shoulders of their coats. Their loads weighed from sixty to ninety pounds each, exclusive of their bedding and provisions, which at starting must have been at least as much more. We were much rejoiced at their arrival, and proceeded forthwith to pierce the spirit cask, and issue to each of the household the portion of rum which had been promised on the first day of the year. The spirits, which were proof, were frozen, but after standing at the fire for some time they flowed out with the consistency of honey. The temperature of the liquid, even in this state, was so low as instantly to convert into ice the moisture which condensed on the surface of the dram-glass. The fingers also adhered to the glass, and would, doubtless, have been speedily frozen had they been kept in contact with it; yet each of the voyagers swallowed his dram without experiencing the slightest inconvenience, or complaining of toothache.

After the men had retired, an Indian, who had accompanied them from Fort Providence, informed me that they had broached the cask on their way up and spent two days in drinking. This instance of breach of trust was excessively distressing to me; I felt for their privations and fatigues, and was disposed to seize every opportunity of alleviating them, but this, combined with many instances of petty dishonesty with regard to meat, showed how little confidence could be put in a Canadian voyager when food or spirits were in question. We had been indeed made acquainted with their character on these points by the traders; but we thought that when they saw their officers living under equal if not greater privations than themselves, they would have been prompted by some degree of generous feeling to abstain from those depredations which, under ordinary circumstances, they would scarcely have blushed to be detected in.

As they were pretty well aware that such a circumstance could not long be concealed from us, one of them – the next morning with an artful apology for the conduct. He stated that as they knew it was my intention to treat them with a dram on the commencement of the new year, they had helped themselves to a small quantity on that day, trusting to my goodness for forgiveness; and being unwilling to act harshly at this period, I did forgive them after admonishing them to be very circumspect in their future conduct.

The ammunition, and a small present of rum, were sent to Akaitcho.

On the 18th Vaillant, the woodman, had the misfortune to break his axe. This would have been a serious evil a few weeks sooner, but we had just received some others from Slave Lake.

On the 27th Mr. Wentzel and St. Germain arrived with the two Esquimaux, Tattannœuck and Hœootœrock (the belly and the ear). The English names, which were bestowed upon them at Fort Churchill in commemoration of the months of their arrival there, are Augustus and Junius. The former speaks English.

We now learned that Mr. Back proceeded with Beauparant to Fort Chipewyan, on the 24th of December, to pro-cure stores, having previously discharged J. Belleau from our service at his own request, and according to my directions. I was the more induced to comply with this man's desire of leaving us, as he proved to be too weak to perform the duty of a bowman which he had undertaken.

Four dogs were brought up by this party, and proved a great relief to our wood-haulers during the remainder of he season.

By the arrival of Mr. Wentzel, who is an excellent musician, and assisted us (*Con amore*) in our attempts to muse the men, we were enabled to gratify the whole establishment with an occasional dance. Of this amusement the voyagers were very fond, and not the less so, as it was now and then accompanied by a dram as long as our rum lasted.

On the 5th of February, two Canadians came from Akaitcho for fresh supplies of ammunition. We were mortified to learn that he had received some further unpleasant reports concerning us from Fort Providence, and that his faith in our good intentions was somewhat shaken. He expressed himself dissatisfied with the quantity of ammunition we had sent him, accused us of an intention of endeavouring to degrade him in the eyes of his tribe, and informed us that Mr. Weeks had refused to pay some notes for trifling quantities of goods and ammunition that had been given to the hunters who accompanied our men to Slave Lake.

Some powder and shot, and a keg of diluted spirits were sent to him with the strongest assurances of our regard.

On the 12th, another party of six men was sent to Fort Providence, to bring up the remaining stores. St. Germain went to Akaitcho for the purpose of sending two of his hunters to join this party on its route.

On comparing the language of our two Esquimaux with a copy of St. John's Gospel, printed for the use of the Moravian Missionary Settlements on the Labrador coast, it appeared that the Esquimaux who resort to Churchill speak a language essentially the same with those who frequent the Labrador coast. The Red Knives, too, recognise the expression *Teyma*, used by the Esquimaux when they accost strangers in a friendly manner, as similarly pronounced by Augustus, and those of his race who frequent the mouth of the Copper-Mine River.

The tribe to which Augustus belongs resides generally a little to the northward of Churchill. In the spring, before the ice quits the shores, they kill seal, but during winter they frequent the borders of the large lakes near the coast, where they obtain fish, reindeer, and musk-oxen.

There are eighty-four grown men in the tribe, only seven of whom are aged. Six chiefs have each two wives; the rest of the men have only one; so that the number of married people may amount to one hundred and seventy. He could give me no certain data whereby I might estimate the number of children.

Two great chiefs, or *Achhaiyoot*, have complete authority in directing the movements of the party, and in distributing provisions. The *Attoogawnœuck*, or lesser chiefs, are respected principally as senior men. The tribe seldom suffers from want of food, if the chief moves to the different stations at the proper season. They seem to follow the eastern custom respecting marriage. As soon as a girl is born, the young lad who wishes to have her for a wife goes to her father's tent, and proffers himself. If accepted, a promise is given which is considered binding, and the girl is delivered to her betrothed husband at the proper age.

They consider their progenitors to have come from the moon. Augustus has no other idea of a Deity than some confused notions which he has obtained at Churchill.

When any of the tribe are dangerously ill, a conjurer is sent for, and the bearer of the message carries a suitable present to induce his attendance. Upon his arrival he encloses himself in the tent with the sick man, and sings over him for days together without tasting food; but Augustus, as well as the rest of the uninitiated, are ignorant of the purport of his songs, and of the nature of the Being to whom they are addressed. The conjurers practise a good deal of jugglery in swallowing knives, firing bullets through their bodies, etc., but they are at these times generally secluded from view, and the bystanders believe their assertions, without requiring to be eye-witnesses of the fact. Sixteen men and three women amongst Augustus' tribe are acquainted with the mysteries of the art. The skill of the latter is exerted only on their own sex.

Upon the map being spread before Augustus, he soon comprehended it, and recognised Chesterfield Inlet to be "the opening into which salt waters enter at spring tides, and which receives a river at its upper end." He termed it *Kannœuck Kleenœuck*. He has never been farther north himself than Marble Island, which he distinguishes as being the spot where the large ships were wrecked, alluding to the disastrous termination of Barlow and Knight's Voyage of Discovery.[1] He says, however, that Esqulmaux of three different tribes have traded with his countrymen, and that they described themselves as having come across land from a northern sea. One tribe, who named themselves *Ahwhacknanhelett*, he supposes may come from Repulse Bay; another, designated *Ootkooseekkalingmœoot*, or Stone-Kettle Esquimaux, reside more to the westward; and the third, the *Kang-orr-mœoot*, or White Goose Esquimaux, describe themselves as coming from a great distance, and mentioned that a party of Indians had killed several of their tribe in the summer preceding their visit. Upon comparing the dates of this murder with that of tile last massacre which the Copper Indians have perpetrated on these harmless and defenceless people, they appear to differ two years; but the lapse of time is so inaccurately recorded, that this difference in their accounts is not sufficient to destroy their identity; besides, the Chipewyans, the only other Indians who could possibly have committed the deed, have long since ceased to go to war. If this massacre should be the one mentioned by the Copper Indians, the Kang-orr-mœoot must reside near the mouth of the Anatessy, or River of Strangers.

The winter habitations of the Esquimaux who visit Churchill are built of snow, and judging from one constructed by Augustus to-day, they are very comfortable dwellings. Having selected a spot on the river, where the snow was about two feet deep, and sufficiently compact, he commenced by tracing out a circle twelve feet in diameter. The snow in the interior of the circle was next divided with a broad knife, having a long handle, into slabs three feet long, six inches thick, and two feet deep, being the thickness of the layer of snow. These slabs were tenacious enough to admit of being moved about without breaking or even losing the sharpness of their angles, and they had a slight degree of curvature, corresponding with that of the circle from which they were cut. They were piled upon each other exactly like courses of hewn stone around the circle which was traced out, and care was taken to smooth the beds of the different courses with the knife, and to cut them so as to give the wall a slight inclination inwards, by which contrivance the building acquired the properties of a dome. The dome was closed somewhat suddenly and

1 See Introduction to HEARNE'S *Journey*, page xxiv

flatly by cutting the upper slabs in a wedge-form, instead of the more rectangular shape of those below. The roof was about eight feet high, and the last aperture was shut up by a small conical piece. The whole was built from within, and each slab was cut so that it retained its position without requiring support until another was placed beside it, the lightness of the slabs greatly facilitating the operation. When the building was covered in, a little loose snow was thrown over it, to dose up every chink, and a low door was cut through the walls with a knife. A bed-place was next formed and neatly faced up with slabs of snow, which was then covered with a thin layer of pine branches, to prevent them from melting by the heat of the body. At each end of the bed a pillar of snow was erected to place a lamp upon, and lastly, a porch was built before the door, and a piece of clear ice was placed in an aperture cut in the wall for a window.

The purity of the material of which the house was framed, the elegance of its construction, and the translucency of its walls, which transmitted a very pleasant light, gave it an appearance far superior to a marble building, and one might survey it with feelings somewhat akin to those produced by the contemplation of a Grecian temple, reared by Phidias; both are triumphs of art, inimitable in their kinds.

Annexed there is a plan of a complete Esquimaux snow-house and kitchen and other apartments, copied from a sketch made by Augustus, with the names of the different places affixed. The only fireplace is in the kitchen, the heat of the lamps sufficing to keep the other apartments warm.

Several deer were killed near the house, and we received some supplies from Akaitcho. Parties were also employed in bringing in the meat that was placed *en cache* in the early part of the winter. More than one half of these *caches*, however, had been destroyed by the wolves and wolverenes; a circumstance which, in conjunction with the empty state of our storehouse, led us to fear that we should be much straitened for provisions before the arrival of any considerable number of reindeer in this neighbourhood.

A good many ptarmigan were seen at this time, and the women caught some in snares, but not in sufficient quantity to make any further alteration in the rations of deers' meat that were daily issued. They had already been reduced from eight, to the short allowance of five pounds.

Many wolves prowled nightly about the house, and even ventured upon the roof of the kitchen, which is a low building, in search of food; Keskarrah shot a very large white one, of which a beautiful and correct drawing was made by Mr. Hood.

The temperature in February was considerably lower than in the preceding month, although not so low as in December, the mean being −25.3°. The greatest temperature 1° above zero, and the lowest 51° below.

On the 5th of March the people returned from Slave Lake, bringing the remainder of our stores, consisting of a cask of flour, thirty-six pounds of sugar, a roll of tobacco, and forty pounds of powder. I received a letter from Mr. Weeks, wherein he denied that he had ever circulated any reports to our disadvantage; and stated that he had done everything in his power to assist us, and even discouraged Akaitcho from leaving us, when he had sent him a message, saying, that he wished to do so, if he was sure of being well received at Fort Providence.

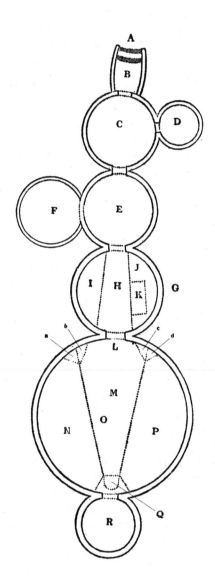

A. *Ablokeyt*, steps.
B. *Pahlœuk*, porch.
C. *Wadl-leek*, passage.
D. *Haddnœweek,* for the reception of the sweepings of the house.
E. *Tokheuook*, antechamber, or passage.
F. *Annarrœartoweek.*
G. *Eegah*, cooking-house.
H *Eegah-natkah*, passage.
I. *Keidgewack,* for piling wood upon.
J. *Keek kloweyt*, cooking side.
K. *Keek loot*, fireplace built of stone.
L. *Kattack*, door.
M. *Nattœuck*, clear space in the apartment.
    a. d. *Eekput*, a kind of shelf where the candle stands; and b. c. a pit where they throw their hones, and other offal of their provision.
N. *Eegl-luck,* bed-place.
O. *Eegleeteoet,* bed-side or sitting place.
P. bed-place, as on the other aide.
Q. *Kietgn-nok*, small pantry.
R. *Hoergloack,* storehouse for provisions.

We mentioned the contents of the letter to the Indians, who were at the house at the time, when one of the hunters, who had attended the men on their journey, stated that he had heard many of the reports against us from Mr. Weeks himself, and expressed his surprise that he should venture to deny them. St. Germain soon afterwards arrived from Akaitcho, and informed us that he left him in good humour, and, apparently, not harbouring the slightest idea of quitting us.

On the 12th we sent four men to Fort Providence; and on the 17th Mr. Back arrived from Fort Chipewyan, having performed, since he left us, a journey of more than one thousand miles on foot. I had every reason to be much pleased with his conduct on this arduous undertaking; but his exertions may be best estimated by the perusal of the following narrative.

"On quitting Fort Enterprise, with Mr. Wentzel and two Canadians, accompanied by two hunters and their wives, our route lay across the barren hills. We saw during the day a number of deer, and occasionally a solitary white wolf; and in the evening halted near a small knot of pines. Owing to the slow progress made by the wives of the hunters, we only travelled the first day a distance of seven miles and a half. During the night we had a glimpse of the fantastic beauties of the Aurora Borealis, and were somewhat annoyed by the wolves, whose nightly howling interrupted our repose. Early the next morning we continued our march, sometimes crossing small lakes (which were just frozen enough to bear us), and at other times going large circuits, in order to avoid those which were open. The walking was extremely bad throughout the day; for independent of the general unevenness of the ground, and the numberless large stones which lay scattered in every direction, the unusual warmth of the weather had dissolved the snow, which not only kept us constantly wet, but deprived us of a firm footing, so that the men, with their heavy burdens, were in momentary apprehension of falling. In the afternoon a fine herd of deer was descried, and the Indians, who are always anxious for the chase, and can hardly be restrained from pursuing every animal they see, set out immediately. It was late when they returned, having had good success, and bringing with them five tongues, and the shoulder of a deer. We made about twelve miles this day. The night was fine, and the Aurora Borealis so vivid, that we imagined, more than once, that we heard a rustling noise like that of autumnal leaves stirred by the wind; but after two hours of attentive listening, we were not entirely convinced of the fact. The coruscations were not so bright, nor the transition from one shape and colour to another so rapid, as they sometimes are; otherwise, I have no doubt, from the midnight silence which prevailed, that we should have ascertained this yet undecided point.

"The morning of the 20th was so extremely hazy that we could not see ten yards before us; it was, therefore, late when we started, and during our journey the hunters complained of the weather, and feared they should lose the track of our route. Towards the evening it became so thick that we could not proceed; consequently, we halted in a small wood, situated in a valley, having only completed a distance of six miles.

"The scenery consisted of high hills, which were almost destitute of trees, and lakes appeared in the valleys. The cracking of the ice was so loud during the night as to resemble thunder, and the wolves howled around us. We were now at the commencement of the woods, and at an early hour, on the 21st, continued our journey over high hills for three miles, when the appearance of some deer caused us to halt, and nearly the remainder of the day was passed in hunting them. In the evening we stopped within sight of Prospect Hill, having killed and concealed six deer. A considerable quantity of snow fell during the night.

"The surrounding country was extremely rugged; the hills divided by deep ravines, and the valleys covered with broken masses of rocks and stones; yet the deer fly (as it were) over these impediments with apparent ease, seldom making a false step, and springing from crag to crag with all the confidence of the mountain goat. After passing Reindeer Lake, (where the ice was so thin as to bend at every step for nine miles,) we halted, perfectly satisfied with our escape from sinking into the water. While some of the party were forming the encampment one of the hunters killed a deer, a part of which was concealed to be ready for use on our return. This evening we halted in a wood near the canoe track, after having travelled a distance of nine miles. The wind was S.E. and the night cloudy, with wind and rain.

"On the 24th and 25th we underwent some fatigue from being obliged to go round the lakes, which lay across our route, and were not sufficiently frozen to bear us. Several rivulets appeared to empty themselves into the lakes, no animals were killed, and few tracks seen. The scenery consisted of barren rocks and high hills, covered with lofty pine, birch, and larch trees.

October 26

'We continued our journey, sometimes on frozen lakes, and at other times on high craggy rocks. When we were on the lakes we were much impeded in our journey by different parts which were unfrozen. There was a visible increase of wood, consisting of birch and larch, as we inclined to the southward. About ten A.M. we passed Icy Portage, where we saw various tracks of the moose, bear and otter; and after a most harassing march through thick woods and over fallen trees, we halted a mile to the westward of Fishing Lake; our provisions were now almost expended; the weather was cloudy with snow.

'On the 27th we crossed two lakes, and performed a circuitous route, frequently crossing high hills to avoid those lakes which were not frozen; during the day one Of the women made a hole through the ice, and caught a fine pike, which she gave to us; the Indians would not partake of it, from the idea (as we afterwards learnt), that we should not have sufficient for ourselves: 'We are accustomed to starvation,' said they, 'but you are not.' In the evening, we halted near Rocky Lake. I accompanied one of the Indians to the summit of a hill, where he showed me a dark horizontal cloud, extending to a considerable distance along the mountains in the perspective, which he said was occasioned by the Great Slave Lake, and was considered a good guide to all the hunters in the vicinity. On our return we saw two untenanted bears' dens.

"The night was cloudy with heavy snow, yet the following morning we continued our tedious march; many of the lakes remained still open, and the rocks were high and covered with snow, which continued to fall all day, consequently we effected but a trifling distance, and that too with much difficulty. In the evening we halted; having only performed about seven miles. One of the Indians gave us a fish which he had caught, though he had nothing for himself; and it was with much trouble that he could be prevailed upon to partake of it. The night was again cloudy with snow. On the 29th we set out through deep snow and thick woods; and after crossing two small lakes stopped to breakfast, sending the women on before, as they had already complained of lameness, and could not keep pace with the party. It was not long before we overtook them on the banks of a small lake, which though infinitely less in magnitude than many we bad passed, yet had not a particle of ice on its surface. It was shoal, had no visible current, and was surrounded by hills. We had nothing to eat, and were not very near an establishment where food could be procured; however, as we proceeded, the lakes were frozen, and we quickened our pace, stopping but twice for the hunters to smoke. Nevertheless the distance we completed was but trifling, and at night we halted near a lake, the men being tired, and much bruised from constantly falling amongst thick broken wood and loose stones concealed under the snow. The night was blowing and hazy with snow.

'On the 30th we set out with the expectation of gaining the Slave Lake in the evening; but our progress was again impeded by the same causes as before, so that the whole day was spent in forcing our way through thick woods and over snow-covered swamps. We had to walk over pointed and loose rocks, which sliding from wider our feet, made our path dangerous, and often threw us down several feet on sharp-edged stones lying beneath the snow. Once we had to climb a towering, and almost perpendicular, rock, which not only detained us, but was the cause of great anxiety for the safety of the women, who being heavily laden with furs, and one of them with a child at her back, could not exert themselves with the activity which such a task required. Fortunately nothing serious occurred, though one of them once fell with considerable violence. During the day one of the hunters broke through the ice, but was soon extricated; when it became dark we halted near the Bow String Portage, greatly disappointed at not having reached the lake. The weather was cloudy, accompanied with thick mist and snow. The Indians expected to have found here a bear in its den, and to have made a hearty meal of its flesh indeed it had been the subject of conversation all day, and they had even gone so far as to divide it, frequently asking me what part I preferred; but when we came to the spot – oh ! lamentable ! it had already fallen a prey to the devouring appetites of some more fortunate hunters, who had only left sufficient evidence that such a thing had once existed, and we had merely the consolation of realising an old proverb. One of our men, however, caught a fish which, with the assistance of some weed scraped from the rocks, (*tripe de roche,*) which forms a glutinous substance, made us a tolerable supper; it was not of the most choice kind, yet good enough for hungry men. While we were eating it I perceived one of the women busily employed scraping an old skin, the contents of which her husband presented us with. They consisted of pounded meat, fat, and a greater proportion of Indians' and deers' hair than either; and though such a mixture may not appear very alluring to an English stomach, it was thought a great luxury after three days' privation in these cheerless regions of America. Indeed had it not been for the precaution and generosity of the Indians, we must have gone without sustenance until we reached the fort.

"On the 1st of November our men began to make a raft to enable us to cross a river which was not even frozen at the edges. It was soon finished, and three of us embarked, being seated up to the ankles in water. We each took a pine branch for a paddle, and made an effort to gain the opposite shore, in which, after some time, (and not without strong apprehensions of drifting into the Slave Lake,) we succeeded. In two hours the whole party was over, with a comfortable addition to it in the shape of some fine fish, which the Indians had caught: of course we did not forget to take these friends with us, and after passing several lakes, to one of which we saw no termination, we halted within eight miles to the fort. The Great Slave Lake was not frozen.

"In crossing a narrow branch of the lake I fell through the ice, but received no injury; and at noon we arrived at Fort Providence, and were received by Mr. Weeks, a clerk of the North-West Company, in charge of the establishment. I found several packets of letters for the officers, which I was desirous of sending to them immediately; but as the Indians and their wives complained of illness and inability to return without rest, a flagon of mixed spirits was given them, and their sorrows were soon forgotten. In a quarter of an hour they pronounced themselves excellent hunters, and capable of going anywhere; however, their boasting ceased with the last drop of the bottle, when a crying scene took place, which would have continued half the night, had not the magic of an additional quantity of spirits dried their tears, and once more turned their mourning into joy. It was a satisfaction to me to behold these poor creatures enjoying themselves, for they had behaved in the most exemplary and active manner towards the party, and with a generosity and sympathy seldom found even in the more civilised parts of the world and the attention and affection which they manifested towards their wives, evinced a benevolence of disposition and goodness of nature which could not fail to secure the approbation of the most indifferent observer.

"The accounts I here received of our goods were of so unsatisfactory a nature, that I determined to proceed, as soon as the lake was frozen, to Moose-Deer Island, or if necessary to the Athabasca Lake, both to inform myself of the unceremonious and negligent manner in which the Expedition had been treated, and to obtain a sufficient supply of ammunition and other stores, to enable it to leave its present situation, and proceed for the attainment of its ultimate object.

November 9

"I despatched to Fort Enterprise one of the men, with the letters and a hundred musket-balls, which Mr. Weeks lent me on condition that they should be returned the first opportunity. An Indian and his wife accompanied the messenger. Lieutenant Franklin was made acquainted with the exact state of things; and I awaited with much impatience the freezing of the lake.

November 16

"A band of Slave Indians came to the fort with a few furs and some bear's grease. Though we had not seen any of them, it appeared that they had received information of our being in the country, and knew the precise situation of our house, which they would have visited long ago, but from the fear of being pillaged by the Copper Indians. I questioned the chief about the Great Bear and Marten Lakes, their distance from Fort Enterprise, etc.; but his answers were so vague and unsatisfactory that they were not worth attention; his description of Bouleau's Route, (which he said was the shortest and best, and abundant in animals,) was very defective, though the relative points were sufficiently characteristic, had we not possessed a better route. He had never been at the sea; and knew nothing about the mouth of the Copper-Mine River. In the evening he made his young men dance, and sometimes accompanied them himself. They had four feathers in each hand. One commenced moving in a circular form, lifting both feet at the same time, similar to jumping sideways. After a short time a second and third joined, and afterwards the whole band was dancing, some in a state of nudity, others half dressed, singing an unmusical wild air with (I suppose,) appropriate words; the particular sounds of which were, ha! ha! ha! uttered vociferously, and with great distortion of countenance, and peculiar attitude of body, the feathers being always kept in a tremulous motion. The ensuing day I made the chief acquainted with the object of our mission, and recommended him to keep at peace with his neighbouring tribes, and to conduct himself with attention and friendship towards the whites. I then gave him a medal, telling him it was the picture of the King, whom they emphatically term ' their Great Father.'

November 18

"We observed two mock moons at equal distances from the central one; and the whole were en-circled by a halo: the colour of the inner edge of the large circle was a light red, inclining to a faint purple.

November 20

"Two parhelia were observable with a halo; the colours of the inner edge of the circle were a bright carmine and red lake, intermingled with a rich yellow, forming a purplish orange; the outer edge was pale gamboge.

December 5

"A man was sent some distance on the lake to see if it was sufficiently frozen for us to cross. I need scarcely mention my satisfaction when he returned with the pleasing information that it was.

December 7

"I quitted Fort Providence, being accompanied by Mr. Wentzel, Beauparlant, and two other Canadians, provided with dogs and sledges. We proceeded along the borders of the lake, occasionally crossing deep bays; and at dusk encamped at the *Gros Cap*, having proceeded twenty-five miles.

December 8

"We set out on the lake with an excessively cold north-west wind, and were frequently interrupted by large pieces of ice which had been thrown up by the violence of the waves during the progress of congelation, and at dusk we encamped on the Reindeer Islands.

"The night was fine, with a faint Aurora Borealis. Next day the wind was so keen, that the men proposed conveying me in a sledge that I might be the less exposed, to which, after some hesitation, I consented. Accordingly a reindeer skin and a blanket were laid along the sledge, and in these I was wrapped tight up to the chin, and lashed to the vehicle, just leaving sufficient play for my head to perceive when I was about to be upset on some rough projecting piece of ice. Thus equipped, we set off before the wind (a favourable circumstance on the lake), and went on very well until noon; when the ice being driven up in ridges, in such a manner as to obstruct us very much, I was released; and I confess not unwillingly, though I had to walk the remainder of the day.

"There are large openings in many parts where the ice had separated; and in attempting to cross one of them, the dogs fell into the water, and were saved with difficulty. The poor animals suffered dreadfully from the cold, and narrowly escaped being frozen to death. We had quickened our pace towards the close of the day, but could not get sight of the land; and it was not till the sun had set that we perceived it about four miles to our left, which obliged us to turn back, and head the wind. It was then so cold, that two of the party were frozen almost immediately about the face and ears. I escaped, from having the good fortune to possess a pair of gloves made of rabbits' skin, with which I kept constantly chafing the places which began to be affected. At six P.M. we arrived at the fishing-huts near Stony Island, and remained the night there. The Canadians were not a little surprised at seeing us whom they had already given up for lost – nor less so at the manner by which we had come – for they all affirmed, that the lake near them was quite free from ice the day before.

December 10

"At an early hour we quitted the huts, lashed on sledges as before, with some little addition to our party; and at three hours thirty minutes P.M. arrived at the North-West Fort on Moose-Deer Island, where I was received by Mr. Smith, with whom. I had been acquainted at the Athabasca. He said he partly expected me. The same evening I visited Messrs. M'Vicar and M'Aulay at Hudson's Bay Fort, when I found the reports concerning our goods were but too true, there being in reality but five packages for us. I also was informed that two Esquimaux, Augustus the chief, and Junius his servant, who had been sent from Fort Churchill by Governor Williams, to serve in the capacity of interpreters to the Expedition, were at the fort. These men were short of stature but muscular, apparently good-natured, and perfectly acquainted with the purpose for which they were intended. They had built themselves a snow-house on an adjacent island, where they used frequently to sleep. The following day I examined the pieces, and to my great disappointment found them to consist of three kegs of spirits, already adulterated by the voyagers who had brought them; a keg of flour, and thirty-five pounds of sugar, instead of sixty. The ammunition and tobacco, the two greatest requisites, were left behind.

"I lost no time in making a demand from both parties; and though their united list did not furnish the half of what was required, yet it is possible that everything was given by them which could be spared consistently with their separate interests, particularly by Mr. M'Vicar, who in many articles gave me the whole he had in his possession. These things were sent away immediately for Fort Enterprise, when an interpreter arrived with letters from Lieutenant Franklin, which referred to a series of injurious reports said to have been propagated against us by some one at Fort Providence.

"Finding a sufficiency of goods could not be provided at Moose-Deer Island, I determined to proceed to the Athabasca Lake, and ascertain the inclinations of the gentlemen there. With this view I communicated my intentions to both parties; but could only get dogs enough from the North-West Company to carry the necessary provisions for the journey. Indeed Mr. Smith informed me plainly he was of opinion that nothing could be spared at Fort Chipewyan; that goods had never been transported so long a journey in the winter season, and that the same dogs could not possibly go and return; besides, it was very doubtful if I could be provided with dogs there; and finally, that the distance was great, and would take sixteen days to perform it. He added that the provisions would be mouldy and bad, and that from having to walk constantly on snow-shoes, I should suffer a great deal of misery and fatigue. Notwithstanding these assertions, on the 23rd of December I left the fort, with Beauparlant and a Bois-brulé, each having a sledge drawn by dogs, laden with pemmican. We crossed an arm of the lake, and entered the Little Buffalo River, which is connected with the Salt River, and is about fifty yards wide at its junction with the lake-the water is brackish. This route is usually taken in the winter, as it cuts off a large angle in going to the Great Slave River. In the afternoon we passed two empty fishing-huts, and in the evening encamped amongst some high pines on the banks of the river, having had several snow-showers during the day, which considerably impeded the dogs, so that we had not proceeded more than fifteen miles.

December 24 and 25

"We continued along the river, frequently making small portages to avoid going round the points, and passed some small canoes, which the Indians had left for the winter. The snow was so deep that the dogs were obliged to stop every ten minutes to rest; and the cold so excessive, that both the men were badly frozen on both sides of the face and chin. At length, having come to a long meadow, which the dogs could not cross that night, we halted in an adjoining wood, and were presently joined by a Canadian, who was on his return to the fort, and who treated us with some fresh meat in exchange for pemmican. During the latter part of the day we had seen tracks of the moose, buffalo, and marten.

December 26

"The weather was so cold that we were compelled to run to prevent ourselves from freezing; our route lay across some large meadows which appeared to abound in animals, though the Indians around Slave Lake are in a state of great want. About noon we passed a sulphur-stream, which ran into the river; it appeared to come from a plain about fifty yards distant. There were no rocks near it, and the soil through which it took its course was composed of a reddish clay. I was much galled by the strings of the snow-shoes during the day, and once got a severe fall, occasioned by the dogs running over one of my feet, and dragging me some distance, my snow-shoe having become entangled with the sledge. In the evening we lost our way, from the great similarity of appearance in the country, and it was dark before we found it again, when we halted in a thick wood, after having come about sixteen miles from the last encampment. Much snow fell during the night.

"At an early hour on the 27th of December, we continued our journey over the surface of a long but narrow lake, and then through a wood, which brought us to the *grand detour* on the Slave River. The weather was extremely cloudy, with occasional falls of snow, which tended greatly to impede our progress, from its gathering in lumps between the dogs' toes; and though they did not go very fast, yet my left knee pained me so much, that I found it difficult to keep up with them. At three P.M. we halted within nine miles of the Salt River, and made a hearty meal of mouldy pemmican.

December 28 and 29

"We had much difficulty in proceeding, owing to the poor dogs being quite worn out, and their feet perfectly raw. We endeavoured to tie shoes on them, to afford them some little relief, but they continually came off when amongst deep snow, so that it occupied one person entirely to look after them. In this state they were hardly of any use among the steep ascents of the portages, when we were obliged to drag the sledges ourselves. We found a few of the rapids entirely frozen. Those that were not had holes and large spaces about them, from whence issued a thick vapour, and in passing this we found it particularly cold; but what appeared most curious was the number of small fountains which rose through the ice, and often rendered it doubtful which way we should take. I was much disappointed at finding several falls (which I had intended to sketch) frozen almost even with the upper and lower parts of the stream; the ice was connected by a thin arch, and the rushing of the water underneath might be heard at a considerable distance. On the banks of these rapids there was a constant overflowing of the water, but in such small quantities as to freeze before it had reached the surface of the central ice, so that we passed between two ridges of icicles, the transparency of which was beautifully contrasted by the flakes of snow and the dark green branches of the overhanging pine.

"Beauparlant complained bitterly of the cold whilst among the rapids, but no sooner had he reached the upper part of the river than he found the change of the temperature so great, that he vented his indignation against the heat. – 'Mais c'est terrible,' said he, to be frozen and sun-burnt in the same day. The poor fellow, who had been a long time in the country, regarded it as the most severe punishment that could have been inflicted on him, and would willingly have given a part of his wages rather than this disgrace had happened; for there is a pride amongst 'Old Voyagers,' which makes them consider the state of being frost-bitten as effeminate, and only excusable in a 'Pork-eater,' or one newly come into the country. I was greatly fatigued, and suffered acute pains in the knees and legs, both of which were much swollen when we halted a little above the Dog River.

December 30 and 31

"Our journey these days was by far the most annoying we had yet experienced; but, independent of the vast masses of ice that were piled on one another, as well as the numerous open places about the rapids (and they did not a little impede us), there was a strong gale from the north-west, and so dreadfully keen, that our time was occupied in rubbing the frozen parts of the face, and in attempting to warm the hands, in order to be prepared for the next operation. Scarcely was one place cured by constant friction than another was frozen; and though there was nothing pleasant about it, yet it was laughable enough to observe the dexterity which was used in changing the position of the hand from the face to the mitten, and *vice versâ*. One of the men was severely affected, the whole side of his face being nearly raw. Towards sunset I suffered so much in my knee and ankle, from a recent sprain, that it was with difficulty I could proceed with snow-shoes to the encampment on the Stony Islands. But in this point I was not singular: for Beauparlant was almost as bad, and without the same cause.

January 1, 1821

"We set out with a quick step, the wind still blowing fresh from the north-west, which seemed in some measure to invigorate the dogs; for towards sunset they left me considerably behind. Indeed my legs and ankles were now so swelled, that it was excessive pain to drag the snow-shoes after me. At night we halted on the banks of Stony River, when I gave the men a glass of grog, to commemorate the new year; and the next day, January 2, we arrived at Fort Chipewyan, after a journey of ten days and four hours – the shortest time in which the distance had been performed at the same season. I found Messrs. G. Keith and S. M'Gillivray in charge of the fort, who were not a little surprised to see me. The commencement of the new year is the rejoicing season of the Canadians, when they are generally intoxicated for some days. I postponed making any demand till this time of festivity should cease; but on the same day I went over to the Hudson's Bay fort, and delivered Lieutenant Franklin's letters to Mr. Simpson. If they were astonished on one side to see me, the amazement was still greater on the other; for reports were so far in advance, that we were said to have already fallen by the spears of the Esquimaux.

January 3

"I made a demand from both parties for supplies; such as ammunition, gun-flints, axes, files, clothing, tobacco and spirits. I stated to them our extreme necessity, and that without their assistance the Expedition must be arrested in its progress. The answer from the North-West gentlemen was satisfactory enough; but on the Hudson's Bay side I was told, 'that any further assistance this season entirely depended on the arrival of supplies expected in a few weeks from a distant establishment.' I remained at Fort Chipewyan five weeks, during which time some laden sledges did arrive, but I could not obtain any addition to the few articles I had procured at first. A packet of letters for us, from England, having arrived, I made preparations for my return, but not before I had requested both Companies to send next year, from the depôts, a quantity of goods for our use, specified in lists furnished to them.

"The weather, during my abode at Chipewyan, was generally mild, with occasional heavy storms, most of which were anticipated by the activity of the Aurora Borealis; and this I observed had been the case between Fort Providence and the Athabasca in December and January, though not invariably so in other parts of the country. One of the partners of the North-West Company related to me the following singular story: – 'He was travelling in a canoe in the English River, and had landed near the Kettle Fall, when the coruscations of the Aurora Borealis were so vivid and low that the Canadians fell on their faces, and began praying and crying, fearing they should be killed; he himself threw away his gun and knife, that they might not attract the flashes, for they were within two feet from the earth, flitting along with incredible swiftness, and moving parallel to its surface. They continued for upwards of five minutes, as near as he could judge, and made a loud rustling noise, like the waving of a flag in a strong breeze. After they had ceased, the sky became clear, with little wind.'

February 9

"Having got everything arranged, and had a hearty breakfast with a *coupe de l'eau de vie*, (a custom amongst the traders,) I took my departure, or rather attempted to do so, for on going to the gate there was a long range of women, who came to bid me farewell. They were all dressed (after the manner of the country) in blue or green cloth, with their hair fresh greased, separated before, and falling down behind, not in careless tresses, but in a good sound tail, fastened with black tape or riband. This was considered a great compliment, and the ceremony consisted in embracing the whole party.

"I had with me four sledges, laden with goods for the Expedition, and a fifth belonging to the Hudson's Bay Company. We returned exactly by the same route, suffering no other inconvenience but that arising from the chafing of the snow-shoe, and bad weather. Some Indians, whom we met on the banks of the Little Buffalo River, were rather surprised at seeing us, for they had heard that we were on an island, which was surrounded by Esquimaux. The dogs were almost worn out, and their feet raw, when, on February the 20th, we arrived at Moose-Deer Island with our goods all in good order. Towards the end of the month two of our men arrived with letters from Lieutenant Franklin, containing some fresh demands, the major part of which I was fortunate enough to procure without the least trouble. Having arranged the accounts and receipts between the Companies and the Expedition, and sent everything before me to Fort Providence, I prepared for my departure; and it is but justice to the gentlemen of both parties at Moose-Deer Island to remark, that they afforded the means of forwarding our stores in the most cheerful and pleasant manner.

March 5

"I took leave of the gentlemen at the forts, and, in the afternoon, got to the fisheries near Stony Island, where I found Mr. M'Vicar, who was kind enough to have a house ready for my reception; and I was not a little gratified at perceiving a pleasant-looking girl employed in roasting a fine joint, and afterwards arranging the table with all the dexterity of an accomplished servant.

March 6

"We set out at daylight, and breakfasted at the Reindeer Islands. As the day advanced, the heat became so oppressive, that each pulled off his coat and ran till sunset, when we halted with two men, who were on their return to Moose-Deer Island. There was a beautiful Aurora Borealis in the night; it rose about N.b.W., and divided into three bars, diverging at equal distances as far as the zenith, and then converging until they met in the opposite horizon; there were some flashes at right angles to the bars.

March 7

"We arrived at Fort Providence, and found our stores safe and in good order. There being no certainty when the Indian, who was to accompany me to our house, would arrive, and my impatience to join my companions increasing as I approached it, after making the necessary arrangements with Mr. Weeks respecting our stores, on March the 10th I quitted the fort, with two of our men, who had each a couple of dogs and a sledge laden with provision. On the 13th we met the Indian, near Icy Portage, who was sent to guide me back. On the 14th we killed a deer, and gave the dogs a good feed; and, on the 17th, at an early hour, we arrived at Fort Enterprise, having travelled about eighteen miles a day. I had the pleasure of meeting my friends all in good health, after an absence of nearly five months, during which time I had travelled one thousand one hundred and four miles, on snow-shoes, and had no other covering at night, in the woods, than a blanket and deer-skin, with the thermometer frequently at −40°, and once at − 57°; and sometimes passing two or three days without tasting food."

CHAPTER IX

Continuation of Proceedings at Fort Enterprise – Some Account
of the Copper Indians – Preparations for the Journey to the
Northward

March 18, 1821

I SHALL now give a brief account of the Copper Indians, termed by the Chipewyans, *Tantsawhot-dinneh,* or Birch-rind Indians. They were originally a tribe of the Chipewyans, and, according to their own account, inhabited the south side of Great Slave Lake, at no very distant period. Their language, traditions, and customs, are essentially the same with those of the Chipewyans, but in personal character they have greatly the advantage of that people; owing, probably, to local causes, or perhaps to their procuring their food more easily and in greater abundance. They hold women in the same low estimation as the Chipewyans do, looking upon them as a kind of property, which the stronger may take from the weaker, whenever there is just reason for quarrelling, if the parties are of their own nation, or whenever they meet, if the weaker party are Dog-Ribs or other strangers.

They suffer, however, the kinder affections to show them-selves occasionally; they, in general, live happily with their wives, the women are contented with their lot, and we witnessed several instances of strong attachment. Of their kindness to strangers we are fully qualified to speak; their love of property, attention to their interests, and fears for the future, made them occasionally clamorous and unsteady; but their delicate and humane attention to us, in a season of great distress, at a future period, are indelibly engraven on our memories. Of their notions of a Deity, or future state, we never could obtain any satisfactory account; they were unwilling, perhaps, to expose their opinions to the chance of ridicule. Akaitcho generally evaded our questions on these points, but expressed a desire to learn from us, and regularly attended Divine Service during his residence at the fort, behaving with the utmost decorum.

This leader, indeed, and many others of his tribe, possess a laudable curiosity, which might easily be directed to the most important ends; and I believe, that a well-conducted Christian mission to this quarter would not fail of producing the happiest effect. Old Keskarrah alone used boldly to express his disbelief of a Supreme Deity, and state that he could not credit the existence of a Being, whose power was said to extend everywhere, but whom he had not yet seen, although he was now an old man. The aged sceptic is not a little conceited, as the following exordium to one of his speeches evinces: "It is very strange that I never meet with any one who is equal in sense to myself." The same old man, in one of his communicative moods, related to us the following tradition. The earth had been formed, but continued enveloped in total darkness, when a bear and a squirrel met on the shores of a lake; a dispute arose as to their respective powers, which they agreed to settle by running in opposite directions round the lake, and whichever arrived first at the starting point, was to evince his superiority by some signal act of power. The squirrel beat, ran up a tree, and loudly demanded light, which instantly beaming forth, discovered a bird dispelling the gloom with its wings; the bird was afterwards recognised to be a crow. The squirrel next broke a piece of bark from the tree, endowed it with the power of floating, and said, "Behold the 'material which shall afford the future inhabitants of the earth the means of traversing the waters."

The Indians are not the first people who have ascribed the origin of nautics to the ingenuity of the squirrel. The Copper Indians consider the bear, otter, and other animals of prey, or rather some kind of spirits which assume the forms of these creatures, as their constant enemies, and the cause of every misfortune they endure; and in seasons of difficulty or sickness they alternately deprecate and abuse them.

Few of this nation have more than one wife at a time, and none but the leaders have more than two. Akaitcho has three, and the mother of his only son is the favourite. They frequently marry two sisters, and there is no prohibition to the intermarriage of cousins, but a man is restricted from marrying his niece.

The last war excursion they made against the Esquimaux was ten years ago, when they destroyed about thirty per-sons, at the mouth of what they term Stony-Point River, not far from the mouth of the Copper-Mine River. They now seem desirous of being on friendly terms with that persecuted nation, and hope, through our means, to establish a lucrative commerce with them. Indeed, the Copper Indians are sensible of the advantages that would accrue to them, were they made the carriers of goods between the traders and Esquimaux.

At the time of Hearne's visit, the Copper Indians being unsupplied with firearms, were oppressed by the Chipewyans; but even that traveller had occasion to praise their kindness of heart. Since they have received arms from the traders, the Chipewyans are fearful of venturing upon their lands; and all of that nation, who frequent the shores of Great Slave Lake, hold the name of Akaitcho in great respect. The Chipewyans have no leader of equal authority amongst themselves.

The number of the Copper Indians may be one hundred and ninety souls, viz., eighty men and boys, and one hundred and ten women and young children. There are forty-five hunters in the tribe. The adherents of Akaitcho amount to about forty men and boys; the rest follow a number of minor chiefs.

For the following notices of the nations on Mackenzie's River, we are principally indebted to Mr. Wentzel, who resided for many years in that quarter.

The *Thlingcha-dinneh,* or Dog-Ribs, or, as they are sometimes termed after the Crees, who formerly warred against them, *Slaves,* inhabit the country to the westward of the Copper Indians, as far as Mackenzie's River. They are of a mild, hospitable, but rather indolent, disposition; spend much of their time in amusements, and are fond of singing and dancing. In this respect, and in another, they differ very widely from most of the other aborigines of North America. I allude to their kind treatment of the women. The men do the laborious work, whilst their wives employ themselves in ornamenting their dresses with quill-work, and in other occupations suited to their sex. Mr. Wentzel has often known the young married men to bring specimens of their wives' needle-work to the forts, and exhibit them with much pride. Kind treatment of the fair sex being usually considered as an indication of considerable progress in civilisation, it might be worth while to inquire how it happens that this tribe has stept so far beyond its neighbours. It has bad, undoubtedly, the same common origin with the Chipewyans, for their languages differ only in accent, and their mode of life is essentially the same. We have not sufficient data to prosecute the inquiry with any hope of success, but we may recall to the reader's memory what was formerly mentioned, that the Dog-Ribs say they came from the westward, whilst the Chipewyans say that they migrated from the eastward.

When bands of Dog-Ribs meet each other after a long absence, they perform a kind of dance. A piece of ground is cleared for the purpose, if in winter of the snow, or if in summer of the bushes; and the dance frequently lasts for two or three days, the parties relieving each other as they get tired. The two bands commence the dance with their backs turned to each other, the individuals following one another in Indian file, and holding the bow in the left hand, and an arrow in the right. They approach obliquely, after many turns, and when the two lines are closely back to back, they feign to see each other for the first time, and the bow is instantly transferred to the right hand, and the arrow to the left, signifying that it is not their intention to employ them against their friends. At a fort they use feathers instead of bows. The dance is accompanied with a song. These people are the dancing-masters of the country. The Copper Indians have neither dance nor music but what they borrow from them. On our first interview with Akaitcho, at Fort Providence, he treated us, as has already been mentioned, with a representation of the Dog-Rib dance; and Mr. Back, during his winter journey, had an opportunity of observing it performed by tile Dog-Ribs themselves.

The chief tribe of the Dog-Rib nation, termed Horn Mountain Indians, inhabit the country betwixt Great Bear Lake, and the west end of Great Slave Lake. They muster about two hundred men and boys capable of pursuing the chase. Small detachments of the nation frequent Marten Lake, and hunt during the summer in the neighbourhood of Fort Enterprise. Indeed this part of the country was formerly exclusively theirs, and most of the lakes and remarkable hills bear the names which they imposed upon them. As the Copper Indians generally pillage them of their women and furs when they meet, they endeavour to avoid them, and visit their ancient quarters on the barren grounds only by stealth.

Immediately to the northward of the Dog-Ribs, on the north side of Bear Lake River, are the *Kawcho-dinneh*, or Hare Indians, who also speak a dialect of the Chipewyan language, and have much of the same manners with the Dog-Ribs, but are considered both by them and by the Copper Indians, to be great conjurers. These people report that in their hunting excursions to the northward of Great Bear Lake they meet small parties of Esquimaux.

Immediately to the northward of the Hare Indians, on both banks of Mackenzie's River, are the *Tykolhee-dinneh*, Loucheux, Squint-Eyes, or Quarrellers. They speak a language distinct from the Chipewyan. They war often with the Esquimaux at the mouth of Mackenzie's River, but have occasionally some peaceable intercourse with them, and it would appear that they find no difficulty in understanding each other, there being considerable similarity in their languages. Their dress also resembles the Esquimaux, and differs from that of the other inhabitants of Mackenzie's River. The Tykothee-dinneh trade with Fort Good-Hope, situated a considerable distance below the confluence of Bear Lake River with Mackenzie's River, and as the traders suppose, within three days' march of the Arctic Sea. It is the most northern establishment of the North-West Company, and some small pieces of Russian copper coin once made their way thither across the continent from the westward. Blue or white beads are almost the only articles of European manufacture coveted by the Loucheux. They perforate the septum of the nose, and insert in the opening three small shells, which they procure at a high price from the Esquimaux.

On the west bank of Mackenzie's River there are several tribes who speak dialects of the Chipewyan language, that have not hitherto been mentioned. The first met with, on tracing the river to the southward from Fort Good-Hope, are the *Ambawtawhoot-dinneh,* or Sheep Indians. They inhabit the Rocky Mountains near the sources of the Dawhoot-dinneh River which flows into Mackenzie's, and are but little known to the traders. Some of them have visited Fort Good-Hope. A report of their being cannibals may have originated in an imperfect knowledge of them.

Some distance to the southward of this people are the Rocky Mountain Indians, a small tribe which musters about forty men and boys capable of pursuing the chase. They differ but little from the next we are about to mention, the *Edchawtawhoot-dinneh*, Strong-bow, Beaver, or Thick-wood Indians, who frequent the *Rivière aux Liards*, or south branch of Mackenzie's River. The Strong-bows resemble the Dog-Ribs somewhat in their disposition; but when they meet they assume a considerable degree of superiority over the latter, who meekly submit to the haughtiness of their neighbours. Until the year 1813, when a small party of them, from some unfortunate provocation, destroyed Fort Nelson on the *Rivière aux Liards*, and murdered its inmates, the Strong-bows were considered to be a friendly and quiet tribe, and esteemed as excellent hunters. They take their names, in the first instance, from their dogs. A young man is the father of a certain dog, but when he is married, and has a son, he styles himself the father of the boy. The women have a habit of reproving the dogs very tenderly when they observe them fighting. – "Are you not ashamed," say they, "are you not ashamed to quarrel with your little brother?" The dogs appear to understand the reproof, and sneak off.

The Strong-bows, and Rocky Mountain Indians, have a tradition in common with the Dog-Ribs, that they came originally from the westward, from a level country, where there was no winter, which produced trees, and large fruits, now unknown to them. It was inhabited also by many strange animals, amongst which there was a small one whose visage bore a striking resemblance to the human countenance. During their residence in this land, their ancestors were visited by a man who healed the sick, raised the dead, and performed many other miracles, enjoining them at the same time to lead good lives, and not to eat of the entrails of animals, nor to use the brains for dressing skins until after the third day; and never to leave the skulls of deer upon the ground within the reach of dogs and wolves, but to hang them carefully upon trees. No one knew from whence this good man came, or whither he went. They were driven from that land by the rising of the waters, and following the tracks of animals on the seashore, they directed their course to the northward. At length they came to a strait, which they crossed upon a raft, but the sea has since frozen, and they have never been able to return. These traditions are unknown to the Chipewyans.

The number of men and boys of the Strong-bow nation who are capable of hunting, may amount to seventy.

There are some other tribes who also speak dialects of the Chipewyan, upon the upper branches of the Rivière aux Liards, such as the *Nohhannies* and the *Tsillawdaw-hoot-dinneh,* or Brushwood Indians. They are but little known, but the latter are supposed occasionally to visit some of the establishments on Peace River.

Having now communicated as briefly as I could the principal facts that came to our knowledge regarding the Indians in this quarter, I shall resume the narrative of events at Fort Enterprise. – The month of March proved fine. The thermometer rose once to 24° above zero, and fell upon another day 49° below zero, but the mean was −11½°.

On the 23rd the last of our winter's stock of deer's meat was expended, and we were compelled to issue a little pounded meat which we had reserved for making pemmican for summer use. Our nets, which were set under the ice on the 15th, produced only two or three small fish daily. Amongst these was the round fish, a species of Coregonus, which we had not previously seen.

On the following day two Indians came with a message from the Hook, the chief next to Akaitcho in authority amongst the Copper Indians. His band was between West Marten and Great Bear Lakes, and he offered to provide a quantity of dried meat for us on the banks of the Copper-Mine River in the beginning of summer, provided we sent him goods and ammunition. It was in his power to do this without inconvenience, as he generally spends the summer months on the banks of the river, near the Copper Mountain; but we had no goods to spare, and I could not venture to send any part of our small stock of ammunition until I saw what the necessities of our own party required. I told them, however, that I would gladly receive either provisions or leather when we met, and would pay for them by notes on the North-West Company's post; but to prevent any misunderstanding with Mr. Weeks, I requested them to take their winter's collection of furs to Fort Providence before they went to the Copper-Mine River. They assured me that the Hook would watch anxiously for our passing, as he was unwell, and wished to consult the doctor.

Several circumstances having come lately to my knowledge that led me to suspect the fidelity of our interpreters, they were examined upon this subject. It appeared that in their intercourse with the Indians they had contracted very fearful ideas of the danger of our enterprise, which augmented as the time of our departure drew near, and had not hesitated to express their dislike to the journey in strong terms amongst the Canadians, who are accustomed to pay much deference to the opinions of an interpreter. But this was not all; I had reason to suspect they had endeavoured to damp the exertions of the Indians, with the hope that the want of provision in the spring would put an end to our progress at once. St. Germain, in particular, had behaved in a very equivocal way, since his journey to Slave Lake. He denied the principal parts of the charge in a very dogged manner, but acknowledged he had told the leader that we had not paid him the attention which a chief like him ought to have received; and that we had put a great affront on him in sending him only a small quantity of rum. An artful man like St. Germain, possessing a flow of language, and capable of saying even what he confessed, had the means of poisoning the minds of the Indians without committing himself by any direct assertion; and it is to be remarked, that unless Mr. Wentzel had possessed a knowledge of the Copper Indian language, we should not have learned what we did.

Although perfectly convinced of his baseness, I could not dispense with his services; and had no other resource but to give him a serious admonition, and desire him to return to his duty; after endeavouring to work upon his fears by an assurance that I would certainly convey him to England for trial, if the Expedition should be stopped through his fault. He replied, "It is immaterial to me where I lose my life, whether in England, or in accompanying you to the sea, for the whole party will perish." After this discussion, however, he was more circumspect in his conduct.

On the 28th we received a small supply of meat from the Indian lodges. They had now moved into a lake, about twelve miles from us, in expectation of the deer coming soon to the northward.

On the 29th Akaitcho arrived at the house, having been sent for to make some arrangements respecting the procuring of provision, and that we might learn what his sentiments were with regard to accompanying us on our future journey. Next morning we had a conference, which I commenced by showing him the charts and drawings that were prepared to be sent to England, and explaining fully our future intentions. He appeared much pleased at this mark of attention, and, when his curiosity was satisfied, began his speech by saying, that "although a vast number of idle rumours had been floating about the barren grounds during the winter," he was convinced that the representations made to him at Fort Providence regarding the purport of the Expedition were perfectly correct. I next pointed out to him the necessity of our proceeding with as little delay as possible during the short period of the year that was fit for our operations, and that to do so it was requisite we should have a large supply of provisions at starting. He instantly admitted the force of these observations, and promised that he and his young men should do their utmost to comply with our desires: and afterwards, in answer to my questions, informed us that he would accompany the Expedition to the mouth of the Copper-Mine River, or, if we did not meet with Esquimaux there, for some distance along the coast; he was anxious, he said, to have an amicable interview with that people; and he further requested, that, in the event of our meeting with Dog-Ribs on the Copper-Mine River, we should use our influence to persuade them to live on friendly terms with his tribe. We were highly pleased to find his sentiments so favourable to our views, and, after making some minor arrangements, we parted, mutually content. He left us on the morning of the 31st, accompanied by Augustus, who, at his request, went to reside for a few days at his lodge.

On the 4th of April our men arrived with the last supply of goods from Fort Providence, the fruits of Mr. Back's arduous journey to the Athabasca Lake; and on the 17th Belanger *le gros* and Belanger *le rouge*, for so our men discriminated them, set out for Slave Lake, with a box containing the journals of the officers, charts, drawings, observations, and letters addressed to the Secretary of State for Colonial Affairs. 'They also conveyed a letter for Governor Williams, in which I requested that he would, if possible, send a schooner to Wager Bay with provisions and clothing to meet the exigencies of the party, should they succeed in reaching that part of the coast.

Connoyer, who was much tormented with biliary calculi, and had done little or no duty all the winter, was discharged at the same time, and sent down in company with an Indian named the Belly.

The commencement of April was fine, and for several days a considerable thaw took place in the heat of the sun, which laying bare some of the lichens on the sides of the hills, produced a consequent movement of the reindeer to the northward, and induced the Indians to believe that the spring was already commencing. Many of them, therefore, quitted the woods, and set their snares on the barren grounds near Fort Enterprise. Two or three days of cold weather, however, towards the middle of the month, damped their hopes, and they began to say that another moon must elapse before the arrival of the wished-for season. In the meantime their premature departure from the woods, caused them to suffer from want of food, and we were in some degree involved in their distress. We received no supplies from the hunters, our nets produced but very few fish, and the pounded meat which we had intended to keep for summer use was nearly expended. Our meals at this period were always scanty, and we were occasionally restricted to one in the day.

The Indian families about the house, consisting principally of women and children, suffered most. I had often requested them to move to Akaitcho's lodge, where they were more certain of receiving supplies; but as most of them were sick or infirm, they did not like to quit the house, where they daily received medicines from Dr. Richardson, to encounter the fatigue of following the movements of a hunting camp. They cleared away the snow on the site of the autumn encampments to look for bones, deer's feet, bits of hide, and other offal. When we beheld them gnawing the pieces of hide, and pounding the bones, for the purpose of extracting some nourishment from them by boiling, we regretted our inability to relieve them, but little thought that we should ourselves be afterwards driven to the necessity of eagerly collecting these same bones a second time from the dunghill.

At this time, to divert the attention of the men from their wants, we encouraged the practice of sliding down the steep bank of the river upon sledges. These vehicles descended the snowy bank with much velocity, and ran a great distance upon the ice. The officers joined in the sport, and the numerous overturns we experienced formed no small share of the amusement of the party; but on one occasion, when I had been thrown from my seat and almost buried in the snow, a fat Indian woman drove her sledge over me, and sprained my knee severely.

On the 18th at eight in the evening a beautiful halo appeared round the sun when it was about 8° high. The colours were prismatic, and very bright, the red next the sun.

On the 21st the ice in the river was measured and found to be five feet thick, and in setting the nets in Round Rock Lake, it was there ascertained to be six feet and a half thick, the water being six fathoms deep. The stomachs of some fish were at this time opened by Dr. Richardson, and found filled with insects which appear to exist in abundance under the ice during the winter.

On the 22nd a moose-deer was killed at the distance of forty-five miles; St. Germain went for it with a dog-sledge and returned with unusual expedition on the morning of the third day. This supply was soon exhausted, and we passed the 27th without eating, with the prospect of fasting a day or two longer, when old Keskarrah entered with the unexpected intelligence of having killed a deer. It was divided betwixt our own family and the Indians, and during the night a seasonable supply arrived from Akaitcho. Augustus returned with the men who brought it, much pleased with the attention he had received from the Indians during his visit to Akaitcho.

Next day Mr. Wentzel set out with every man that we could spare from the fort, for the purpose of bringing meat from the Indians as fast as it could be procured. Dr. Richardson followed them two days afterwards, to collect specimens of the rocks in that part of the country. On the same day the two Belangers arrived from Fort Providence, having been only five days on the march from thence.

The highest temperature in April was +40°, the lowest – 32°, the mean + 4°.6. The temperature of the rapid, examined on the 30th by Messrs. Back and Hood, was 32 at the surface, 33° at the bottom.

On the 7th of May, Dr. Richardson returned. He informed me that the reindeer were again advancing to the northward, but that the leader had been joined by several families of old people, and that the daily consumption of provision at the Indian tents was consequently great. This information excited apprehensions of being very scantily provided when the period of our departure should arrive.

The weather in the beginning of May was fine and warm. On the 2nd some patches of sandy ground near the house were cleared of snow. On the 7th the sides of the hills began to appear bare, and on the 8th a large house-fly was seen. This interesting event spread cheerfulness through our residence and formed a topic of conversation for the rest of the day.

On the 9th the approach of spring was still more agreeably confirmed by the appearance of a merganser and two gulls, and some loons, or arctic divers, at the rapid. This day, to reduce the labour of dragging meat to the house, the women and children and all the men, except four, were sent to live at the Indian tents.

The blue-berries, crow-berries, eye-berries, and cranberries, which had been covered, and protected by the snow during the winter, might at this time be gathered in abundance, and proved indeed a valuable resource. The ground continued frozen, but the heat of the sun had a visible effect on vegetation; the sap thawed in the pine-trees, and Dr. Richardson informed me that the mosses were beginning to shoot, and the calyptræ of some of the junger- manniæ already visible.

On the 11th Mr. Wentzel returned from the Indian lodges, having made the necessary arrangements with Akaitcho for the drying of meat for summer use, the bringing fresh meat to the fort and the procuring a sufficient quantity of the resin of the spruce fir, or as it is termed by the voyagers gum, for repairing the canoes previous to starting, and during the voyage. By my desire, he had promised payment to the Indian women who should bring in any of the latter article, and had sent several of our own men to the woods to search for it. At this time I communicated to Mr. Wentzel the mode in which I meant to conduct the journey of the approaching summer. Upon our arrival at the sea, I proposed to reduce the party to what would be sufficient to man two canoes, in order to lessen the consumption of provisions during our voyage, or journey along the coast; and as Mr. Wentzel had expressed a desire of proceeding no farther than the mouth of the Copper-Mine River, which was seconded by the Indians, who wished him to return with them, I readily relieved his anxiety on this subject; the more so as I thought he might render greater service to us by making deposits of provision at certain points, than by accompanying us through a country which was unknown to him, and amongst a people with whom he was totally unacquainted. My intentions were explained to him in detail, but they were of course to be modified by circumstances.

On the 14th a robin (*turdus migratorius*) appeared; this bird is hailed by the natives as the infallible precursor of warm weather. Ducks and geese were also seen in numbers, and the reindeer advanced to the northward. The merganser, (*mergus serrator*,) which preys upon small fish, was the first of the duck tribe that appeared; next came the teal, (*anus crecca*,) which lives upon small insects that abound in the waters at this season; and lastly the goose, which feeds upon berries and herbage. Geese appear at Cumberland House, in latitude 54°, usually about the 12th of April; at Fort Chipewyan, in latitude 59°, on the 25th of April; at Slave Lake, in latitude 61°, on the 1st of May; and at Fort Enterprise, in latitude 64° 28′, on the 12th or 14th of the same month.

On the 16th a minor chief amongst the Copper Indians, attended by his son, arrived from Fort Providence to consult Dr. Richardson. He was affected with snow-blindness, which was soon relieved by the dropping of a little laudanum into his eyes twice a day. Most of our own men had been lately troubled with this complaint, but it always yielded in twenty or thirty hours to the same remedy.

On the 21st all our men returned from the Indians, and Akaitcho was on his way to the fort. In the afternoon two of his young men arrived to announce his visit, and to request that he might be received with a salute and other marks of respect that he had been accustomed to on visiting Fort Providence in the spring. I complied with his desire although I regretted the expenditure of ammunition, and sent the young man away with the customary present of powder to enable him to return the salute, some tobacco, vermilion to paint their faces, a comb and a looking-glass.

At eleven Akaitcho arrived; at the first notice of his appearance the flag was hoisted at the fort, and upon his nearer approach, a number of muskets were fired by a party of our people, and returned by his young men. Akaitcho, preceded by his standard-bearer, led the party, and advanced with a slow and stately step to the door where Mr. Wentzel and I received him. The faces of the party were daubed with vermilion, the old men having a spot on the right cheek, the young ones on the left. Akaitcho himself was not painted. On entering he sat down on a chest, the rest placed themselves in a circle on the floor. The pipe was passed once or twice round, and in the meantime a bowl of spirits and water, and a present considerable for our circumstances of cloth, blankets, capots, shirts, etc., was placed on the floor for the chief's acceptance, and distribution amongst his people. Akaitcho then commenced his speech, but I regret to say, that it was very discouraging, and indicated that he had parted with his good humour, at least since his March visit. He first inquired, whether, in the event of a passage by sea being discovered, we should come to his lands in any ship that might be sent? And being answered, that it was probable but not quite certain, that some one amongst us might come; he expressed a hope that some suitable present should be forwarded to himself and nation; "for," said he, "the great Chief who commands where all the goods come from, must see from the drawings and descriptions of us and our country that we are a miserable people." I assured him that he would be remembered, provided he faithfully fulfilled his engagement with us.

He next complained of the non-payment of my notes by Mr. Weeks, from which he apprehended that his own reward would be withheld. "If," said he, "your notes to such a trifling amount are not accepted, whilst you are within such a short distance, and can hold communication with the fort, it is not probable that the large reward which has been promised to myself and party, will be paid when you are far distant, on your way to your own country. It really appears to me," he continued, "as if both the Companies consider your party as a third company, hostile to their interests, and that neither of them will pay the notes you give to the Indians".

Afterwards, in the course of a long conference, he enumerated many other grounds of dissatisfaction; the principal of which were our want of attention to him as chief, the weakness of the rum formerly sent to him, the smallness of the present now offered, and the want of the chief's clothing, which he had been accustomed to receive at Fort Providence every spring. He concluded, by refusing to receive the goods now laid before him.

In reply to these complaints it was stated that Mr. Weeks's conduct could not be properly discussed at such a distance from his fort; that no dependence ought to be placed on the vague reports that floated through the Indian territory; that, for our part, although we had heard many stories to his (Akaitcho's) disadvantage, we discredited them all; that the rum we had sent him, being what the great men in England were accustomed to drink, was of a milder kind, but, in fact, stronger than what he had been accustomed to receive; and that the distance we had come, and the speed with which we travelled, precluded us from bringing large quantities of goods like the traders; that this had been fully explained to him when he agreed to accompany us; and that, in consideration of his not receiving his usual spring outfit, his debts to the Company had been cancelled, and a present, much greater than any he had ever received before, ordered to be got ready for his return. He was further informed, that we were much disappointed in not receiving any dried meat from him, an article indispensable for our summer voyage, and which, he had led us to believe, there was no difficulty in procuring; and that, in fact, his complaints were so groundless, in comparison with the real injury we sustained from the want of supplies, that we were led to believe they were preferred solely for the purpose of cloaking his own want of attention to the terms of his engagement. He then shifted his ground, and stated, that if we endeavoured to make a voyage along the sea-coast we should inevitably perish; and he advised us strongly against persisting in the attempt. This part of his harangue being an exact transcript of the sentiments formerly expressed by our interpreters, induced us to conclude that they had prompted his present line of conduct, by telling him, that we had goods or rum concealed. He afterwards received a portion of our dinner, in the manner he had been accustomed to do, and seemed inclined to make up matters with us in the course of the evening, provided we added to the present offered to him. Being told, however, that this was impossible, since we had already offered him all the rum we had, and every article of goods we could spare from our own equipment, his obstinacy was a little shaken, and he made some concessions, but deferred giving a final answer, until the arrival of Humpy, his elder brother. The young men, however, did not choose to wait so long, and at night came for the rum, which we judged to be a great step towards a reconciliation.

St. Germain, the most intelligent of our two interpreters, and the one who had most influence with the Indians, being attributed to the unguarded conversations he had held with them, and which he had in part acknowledged, exerted himself much, on the following day, in bringing about a change in their sentiments, and with some success. The young men, though they declined hunting, conducted them-selves with the same good humour and freedom as formerly. Akaitcho being, as he said, ashamed to show himself, kept close in his tent all day.

On the 24th, one of the women who accompanied us from Athabasca, was sent down to Fort Providence, under charge of the old chief, who came some days before for medicine for his eyes. Angelique and Roulante, the other two women, having families, preferred accompanying the Indians during their summer hunt. On the 25th, clothing, and other necessary articles, were issued to the Canadians as their equipment for the ensuing voyage. Two or three blankets, some cloth, iron work, and trinkets were reserved for distribution amongst the Esquimaux on the sea-coast. Laced dresses were given to Augustus and Junius. It is impossible to describe the joy that took possession of the latter on the receipt of this present. The happy little fellow burst into extatic laughter, as he surveyed the different articles of his gay habiliments.[1]

In the afternoon Humpy, the leader's elder brother; Annœthai-yazzeh, another of his brothers; and one of our guides, arrived with the remainder of Akaitcho's band; as also Long-legs, brother to the Hook, with three of his band. There were now in the encampment thirty hunters, thirty-one women, and sixty children, in all one hundred and twenty-one of the Copper Indian or Red-Knife tribe. The rest of the nation were with the Hook on the lower part of the Copper-Mine River.

Annœthai-yazzeh is remarkable amongst the Indians for the number of his descendants; he has eighteen children living by two wives, of whom sixteen were at the fort at this time.

In the evening we had another formidable conference. The former complaints were reiterated, and we parted about midnight, without any satisfactory answer to my questions, as to when Akaitcho would proceed towards the river, and where he meant to make provision for our march. I was somewhat pleased, however, to find that Humpy and Annœthai-yazzeh censured their brother's conduct, and accused him of avarice.

1 These men kept their dresses, and delighted in them. An Indian chief, on the other hand, only appears once before the donor in the dress of ceremony which he receives, and then transfers it to some favourite in the tribe whom he desires to reward by this "robe of honour."

On the 26th the canoes were removed from the places where they had been deposited, as we judged that the heat of the atmosphere was now so great, as to admit of their being repaired, without risk of cracking the bark. We were rejoiced to find that two of them had suffered little injury from the frost during the winter. The bark of the third was considerably rent, but it was still capable of repair.

The Indians sat in conference in their tents all the morning; and in the afternoon, came into the house charged with fresh matter for discussion.

Soon after they had seated themselves, and the room was filled with the customary volume of smoke from their calumets, the goods which had been laid aside, were again presented to the leader; but he at once refused to distribute so small a quantity amongst his men, and complained that there were neither blankets, kettles, nor daggers, amongst them; and in the warmth of his anger, he charged Mr. Wentzel with having advised the distribution of all our goods to the Canadians, and thus defrauding the Indians of what was intended for them. Mr. Wentzel, of course, immediately repelled this injurious accusation, and on, and reminded Akaitcho again, that he had been told, on engaging to accompany us, that he was not to expect any goods until his return. This he denied with an effrontery that surprised us all, when Humpy, who was present at our first interview at Fort Providence, declared that he heard us say, that no goods could be taken for the supply of the Indians on the voyage; and the first guide added, "I do not expect anything here, I have promised to accompany the white people to the sea, and I will, therefore, go, confidently relying upon receiving the stipulated reward on my return." Akaitcho did not seem prepared to hear such declarations from his brothers, and instantly changing the subject, began to descant upon the treatment he had received from the traders in his concerns with them, with an asperity of language that bore more the appearance of menace than complaint. I immediately refused to discuss this topic, as foreign to our present business, and desired Akaitcho to recall to memory, that he had told me on our first meeting, that he considered me the father of every person attached to the Expedition, in which character it was surely my duty to provide for the comfort and safety of the Canadians as well as the Indians. The voyagers, he knew, had a long journey to perform, and would in all probability, be exposed to much suffering from cold on a coast destitute of wood; and, therefore, required a greater provision of clothing than was necessary for the Indians, who, by returning immediately from the mouth of the river, would reach Fort Providence in August, and obtain their promised rewards. Most of the Indians appeared to assent to this argument, but Akaitcho said, "I perceive the traders have deceived you; you should have brought more goods, but I do not blame you." I then told him, that I had brought from England only ammunition, tobacco, and spirits; and that being ignorant what other articles the Indians required, we were dependent on the traders for supplies; but he must be aware, that every endeavour had been used on our parts to procure them, as was evinced by Mr. Back's journey to Fort Chipewyan. With respect to the ammunition and tobacco, we had been as much disappointed as themselves in not receiving them, but this was to be attributed to the neglect of those to whom they had been intrusted. This explanation seemed to satisfy him. After some minutes of reflection, his countenance became more cheerful, and he made inquiry, whether his party might go to either of the trading posts they chose on their return, and whether the Hudson's Bay Company were rich, for they had been represented to him as a poor people? I answered him, that we really knew nothing about the wealth of either Company, having never concerned ourselves with trade, but that all the traders appeared to us to be respectable. Our thoughts, I added, are fixed solely on the accomplishment of the objects for which we came to the country. Our success depends much on your furnishing us with provision speedily, that we may have all the summer to work; and if we succeed a ship will soon bring goods in abundance to the mouth of the Copper-Mine River. The Indians talked together for a short time after this conversation, and then the leader made an application for two or three kettles and some blankets, to be added to the present to his young men; we were unable to spare him any kettles, but the officers promised to give a blanket each from their own beds.

Dinner was now brought in, and relieved us for a time from their importunity. The leading men, as usual, received each a portion from the table. When the conversation was resumed, the chief renewed his solicitations for goods, but it was now too palpable to be mistaken, that he aimed at getting everything he possibly could, and leaving us without the means of making any presents to the Esquimaux, or other Indians we might meet. I resolved, therefore, on steadily refusing every request; and when he perceived that he could extort nothing more, he rose in an angry manner, and addressing his young men, said: "There are too few goods for me to distribute; those that mean to follow the white people to the sea may take them."

This was an incautious speech, as it rendered it necessary for his party to display their sentiments. The guides, and most of the hunters, declared their readiness to go, and came forward to receive a portion of the present, which was no inconsiderable assortment. This relieved a weight of anxiety from my mind, and I did not much regard the leader's retiring in a very dissatisfied mood.

The hunters then applied to Mr. Wentzel for ammunition, that they might hunt in the morning, and it was cheerfully given to them.

The officers and men amused themselves at prison-bars, and other Canadian games till two o'clock in the morning, and we were happy to observe the Indians sitting in groups enjoying the sport. We were desirous of filling up the leisure moments of the Canadians with amusements, not only for the purpose of enlivening their spirits, but also to prevent them from conversing upon our differences with the Indians, which they must have observed. The exercise was also in a peculiar manner serviceable to Mr. Hood. Ever ardent in his pursuits, he had, through close attention to his drawings and other avocations, confined himself too much to the house in winter, and his health was impaired by his sedentary habits. I could only take the part of a spectator in these amusements, being still lame from the hurt formerly alluded to.

The sun now sank for so short a time below the horizon, that there was more light at midnight, than we enjoyed on some days at noon in the winter-time.

On the 27th the hunters brought in two reindeer. Many of the Indians attended divine service this day, and were attentive spectators of our addresses to the Almighty.

On the 28th I had a conversation with Long-legs, whose arrival two days before has been mentioned. I acquainted him with the objects of our Expedition, and our desire of promoting peace between his nation and the Esquimaux, and learned from him, that his brother the Hook was by this time on the Copper-Mine River with his party; and that, although he had little ammunition, yet it was possible he might have some provision collected before our arrival at his tents. I then decorated him with a medal similar to those given to the other chiefs. He was highly pleased with this mark of our regard, and promised to do everything for us in his power. Akaitcho came in during the latter part of our conversation, with a very cheerful countenance. Jealousy of the Hook, and a knowledge that the sentiments of the young men differed from his own, with respect to the recent discussions, had combined to produce this change in his conduct, and next morning he took an opportunity of telling me that I must not think the worse of him for his importunities. It was their custom, he said, to do so, however strange it might appear to us, and he, as the leader of his party, had to beg for them all; but as he saw we had not deceived him by concealing any of our goods, and that we really had nothing left, he should ask for no more. He then told me that he would set out for the river as soon as the state of the country admitted of travelling. The snow, he remarked, was still too deep for sledges to the northward, and the moss too wet to make fires. He was seconded in this opinion by Long-legs, whom I was the more inclined to believe, knowing that he was anxious to rejoin his family as soon as possible.

Akaitcho now accepted the dress he had formerly refused, and next day clothed himself in another new suit, which he had received from us in the autumn. Ever since his arrival at the fort, he had dressed meanly, and pleaded poverty; but, perceiving that nothing more could be gained by such conduct, he thought proper to show some of his riches to the strangers who were daily arriving. In the afternoon, however, he made another, though a covert, attack upon us. He informed me that two old men had just arrived at the encampment with a little pounded meat which they wished to barter. It was evident that his intention was merely to discover whether we had any goods remaining or not. I told him that we had nothing at present to give for meat, however much we stood in need of it, but that we would pay for it by notes on the North-West Company, in any kind of goods they pleased. After much artful circumlocution, and repeated assurances of the necessities of the men who owned the meat, he introduced them, and they readily agreed to give us the provision on our own terms.

I have deemed it my duty to give the details of these tedious conversations, to point out to future travellers, the art with which these Indians pursue their objects, their avaricious nature, and the little reliance that can be placed upon them when their interests jar with their promises. In these respects they agree with other tribes of northern Indians; but as has been already mentioned, their dispositions are not cruel, and their hearts are readily moved by the cry of distress.

The average temperature for May was nearly 32°, the greatest heat was 68°, the lowest 8°.

We had constant daylight at the end of the month, and geese and ducks were abundant, indeed rather too much so, for our hunters were apt to waste upon them the ammunition that was given to them for killing deer. Uncertain as to the length of time that it might be required to last, we did not deem a goose of equal value with the charge it cost to procure it.

Dr. Richardson and Mr. Back having visited the country to the northward of the Slave Rock, and reported that they thought we might travel over it, I signified my intention of sending the first party off on Monday the 4th of June. I was anxious to get the Indians to move on before, but they lingered about the house, evidently with the intention of picking up such articles as we might deem unnecessary to take. When Akaitcho was made acquainted with my purpose of sending away a party of men, he came to inform me that he would appoint two hunters to accompany them, and at the same time requested that Dr. Richardson, or as he called him, the Medicine Chief, might be sent with his own band. These Indians set a great value upon medicine, and made many demands upon Dr. Richardson on the prospect of his departure. He had to make up little packets, of the different articles in his chest, not only for the leader, but for each of the minor chiefs, who carefully placed them in their medicine bags, noting in their memories the directions he gave for their use. The readiness with which their requests for medical assistance were complied with, was considered by them as a strong mark of our good intentions towards them; and the leader often remarked, that they owed much to our kindness in that respect; that formerly numbers had died every year, but that not a life had been lost since our arrival amongst them. In the present instance, however, the leader's request could not be complied with. Dr. Richardson had volunteered to conduct the first party to the Copper-Mine River, whilst the rest of the officers remained with me to the last moment, to complete our astronomical observations at the house. He, therefore, informed the leader that he would remain stationary at Point Lake until the arrival of the whole party, where he might be easily consulted if any of his people fell sick, as it was in the neighbourhood of their hunting grounds.

On the 2nd the stores were packed up in proper sized bales for the journey. I had intended to send the canoes by the first party, but they were not yet repaired, the weather not being sufficiently warm for the men to work constantly at them, without the hazard of breaking the bark. This day one of the new trading guns, which we had recently received from Fort Chipewyan, burst in the hands of a young Indian; fortunately, however, without doing him any material injury. This was the sixth accident of the kind which had occurred since our departure from Slave Lake. Surely this deficiency in the quality of the guns, which hazards the lives of so many poor Indians, requires the serious consideration of the principals of the trading Companies.

On the 4th, at three in the morning, the party under the charge of Dr. Richardson started. It consisted of fifteen voyagers, three of them conducting dog sledges, Baldhead and Basil, two Indian hunters with their wives, Akaiyazzeh a sick Indian and his wife, together with Angelique and Roulante; so that the party amounted to twenty-three exclusive of children.

The burdens of the men were about eighty pounds each, exclusive of their personal baggage, which amounted to nearly as much more. Most of them dragged their loads upon sledges, but a few preferred carrying them on their backs. They set off in high spirits.

After breakfast the Indians struck their tents, and the women, the boys, and the old men who had to drag sledges, took their departure. It was three P.M., however, before Akaitcho and the hunters left us. We issued thirty balls to the leader, and twenty to each of the hunters and guides with a proportionate quantity of powder, and gave them directions to make all the provision they could on their way to Point Lake. I then desired Mr. Wentzel to inform Akaitcho, in the presence of the other Indians, that I wished a deposit of provision to be made at this place previous to next September, as a resource should we return this way. Lie and the guides not only promised to see this done, but suggested that it would be more secure if placed in the cellar, or in Mr. Wentzel's room. The Dog-Ribs, they said, would respect anything that was in the house, as knowing it to belong to the white people. At the close of this conversation Akaitcho exclaimed with a smile, "I see now that you have really no goods left, (the rooms and stores being completely stripped,) and therefore I shall not trouble you any more, but use my best endeavours to prepare provision for you, and I think if the animals are tolerably numerous, we may get plenty before you can embark on the river.

Whilst the Indians were packing up this morning, one of the women absconded. She belongs to the Dog-Rib tribe, and had been taken by force from her relations by her present husband, who treated her very harshly. The fellow was in my room when his mother announced the departure of his wife, and received the intelligence with great composure, as well as the seasonable reproof of Akaitcho. "You are rightly served," said the chief to him," and will now have to carry all your things yourself, instead of having a wife to drag them." One hunter remained after the departure of the other Indians.

On the 5th the Dog-Rib woman presented herself on a hill at some distance from the house, but was afraid to approach us, until the interpreter went and told her that neither we nor the Indian who remained with us, would prevent her from going where she pleased. Upon this she came to solicit a fire-steel and kettle. She was at first low-spirited, from the non-arrival of a countrywoman who had promised to elope with her, but had probably been too narrowly watched. The Indian hunter, however, having given her some directions as to the proper mode of joining her own tribe, she became more composed, and ultimately agreed to adopt his advice of proceeding at once to Fort Providence, instead of wandering about the country all summer in search of them, at the imminent hazard of being starved.

On the 7th the wind, shifting to the southward, dispersed the clouds which had obscured the sky for several days, and produced a change of temperature under which the snow rapidly disappeared. The thermometer rose to 73° many flies came forth, musquitoes showed themselves for the first time, and one swallow made its appearance. We were the more gratified with these indications of summer, that St. Germain was enabled to commence the repair of the canoes, and before night had completed the two which had received the least injury. Augustus killed two deer today.

On the 10th the dip of the magnetic needle being observed, showed a decrease of 22′ 44″ since last autumn. The repairs of the third canoe were finished this evening.

The snow was now confined to the bases of the hills, and our Indian hunter told us the season was early. The operations of nature, however, seemed to us very tardy. We were eager to be gone, and dreaded the lapse of summer, before the Indians would allow it had begun.

On the 11th the geese and ducks had left the vicinity of Fort Enterprise, and proceeded to the northward. Some young ravens and whiskey-johns made their appearance at this time.

On the 12th Winter River was nearly cleared of ice, and on the 13th the men returned, having left Dr. Richardson on the borders of Point Lake. Dr. Richardson informed me by letter that the snow was deeper in many parts near his encampment than it had been at any time last winter near Fort Enterprise, and that the ice on Point Lake had scarcely begun to decay. Although the voyagers were much fatigued on their arrival, and had eaten nothing for the last twenty-four hours, they were very cheerful, and expressed a desire to start with the remainder of the stores next morning. The Dog-Rib woman, who had lingered about the house since the 6th of June, took alarm at the approach of our men, thinking, perhaps, that they were accompanied by Indians, and ran off. She was now provided with a hatchet, kettle, and fire-steel, and would probably go at once to Fort Providence, in the expectation of meeting with some of her countrymen before the end of summer.

CHAPTER X

Departure from Fort Enterprise-Navigation of the Copper-Mine River – Visit to the Copper Mountain – Interview with the Esquimaux – Departure of the Indian Hunters-Arrangements made with them for our Return.

June 14, 1821[1]

The trains for the canoes having been finished during the night, the party attached to them commenced their journey at ten this morning. Each canoe was dragged by four men assisted by two dogs. They took the route of Winter Lake, with the intention of following, although more circuitous, the watercourse as far as practicable, it being safer for the canoes than travelling over land. After their departure, the remaining stores, the instruments, and our small stock of dried meat, amounting only to eighty pounds, were distributed equally among Hepburn, three Canadians, and the two Esquimaux; with this party and two Indian hunters, we quitted Fort Enterprise, most sincerely rejoicing that the long-wished-for day had arrived, when we were to proceed towards the final object of the Expedition.

We left in one of the rooms a box, containing a journal of the occurrences up to this date, the charts and some drawings, which was to be conveyed to Fort Chipewyan by Mr. Wentzel, on his return from the sea, and thence to be sent to England. The room was blocked up, and by the advice of Mr. Wentzel, a drawing representing a man holding a dagger in a threatening attitude, was affixed to the door, to deter any Indians from breaking it open. We directed our course towards the Dog-Rib Rock, but as our companions were loaded with the weight of near one hundred and eighty pounds each, we of necessity proceeded at a slow pace. The day was extremely warm, and the musquitoes, whose attacks had hitherto been feeble, issued forth in swarms from the marshes, and were very tormenting. Having walked five miles we encamped near a small cluster of pines about two miles from the Dog-Rib Rock. The canoe party had not been seen since they set out. Our hunters went forward to Marten Lake, intending to wait for -us at a place where two deer were deposited. At nine P.M. the temperature of the air was 63°.

We resumed our march at an early hour, and crossed several lakes which lay in our course, as the ice enabled the men to drag their burdens on trains formed of sticks and deers' horns, with more ease than they could carry them on their backs. We were kept constantly wet by this operation, as the ice had broken near the shores of the lakes, but this was little regarded as the day was unusually warm: the temperature at two P.M. being at 82½°. At Marten Lake we joined the canoe party, and encamped with them. We had the mortification of learning from our hunters that the meat they had put *en cache* here had been destroyed by the wolverenes, and we had in consequence to furnish the supper from our scanty stock of dried meat.

1 It will be seen hereafter that I had the misfortune to lose my portfolio containing my journals from Fort Enterprise to the 14th of September. But the loss had been amply redeemed by my brother officers' journals from which the narrative up to that period has been chiefly compiled.

The wind changed from S. E. to N.E. in the evening, and the weather became very cold, the thermometer being at 43° at nine P.M.. The few dwarf birches we could collect afforded fire insufficient to keep us warm, and we retired under the covering of our blankets as soon as the supper was despatched. The N.E. breeze rendered the night so extremely cold, that we procured but little sleep, having neither fire nor shelter; for though we carried our tents, we had been forced to leave the tent-poles which we could not now replace; we therefore gladly recommenced the journey at five in the morning, and travelled through the remaining part of the lake on the ice. Its surface being quite smooth, the canoes were dragged along expeditiously by the dogs, and the rest of the party had to walk very quick to keep pace with them, which occasioned many severe falls. By the time we had reached the end of the lake, the wind had increased to a perfect gale, and the atmosphere was so cold that we could not proceed farther with the canoes without the risk of breaking the bark, and seriously injuring them: we therefore crossed Winter River in them, and put up in a well-sheltered place on a ridge of sand hills; but as the stock of provision was scanty, we determined on proceeding as quick as possible, and leaving the canoe party under the charge of Mr. Wentzel. We parted from them in the afternoon, and first directed our course towards a range of hills, where we expected to find Antonio Fontano, who had separated from us in the morning. In crossing towards these hills I fell through the ice into the lake, with my bundle on my shoulders, but was soon extricated without any injury; and Mr. Back, who left us to go in search of the straggler, met with a similar accident in the evening. We put up on a ridge of sand hills, where we found some pines, and made a large fire to apprise Mr Back and Fontano of our position. St. Germain having killed a deer in the afternoon, we received an acceptable supply of meat. The night was stormy and very cold.

At five the next morning, our men were sent in different directions after our absent companions; but as the weather was foggy, we despaired of finding them, unless they should chance to hear the muskets our people were desired to fire. They returned, however, at ten, bringing intelligence of them. I went immediately with Hepburn to join Mr. Back, and directed Mr. Hood to proceed with the Canadians, and halt with them at the spot where the hunters had killed a deer. Though Mr. Back was much fatigued he set off with me immediately, and in the evening we rejoined our friends on the borders of the Big Lake. The Indians informed us that Fontano only remained a few hours with them, and then continued his journey. We had to oppose a violent gale and frequent snow-storms through the day, which unseasonable weather caused the temperature to descend below the freezing-point this evening. The situation of our encampment being bleak, and our fuel stunted green willows, we passed a very cold and uncomfortable night.

June 18

Though the breeze was moderate this morning, the air was piercingly keen. When on the point of starting, we perceived Mr. Wentzel's party coming, and awaited his arrival to learn whether the canoes had received any injury during the severe weather of yesterday. Finding they had not, we proceeded to get upon the ice on the lake, which could not be effected without walking up to the waist in water, for some distance from its borders. We had not the command of our feet in this situation, and the men fell often' poor Junius broke through the ice with his heavy burden on his back, but fortunately was not hurt.

This lake is extensive, and large arms branch from its main course in different directions. At these parts we crossed the projecting points of land, and on each occasion had to wade as before, which so wearied every one, that we rejoiced when we reached its north side and encamped, though our resting-place was a bare rock. We had the happiness of finding Fontao at this place. The poor fellow had passed the three preceding days without tasting food, and was exhausted by anxiety and hunger. His sufferings were considered to have been a sufficient punishment for his imprudent conduct in separating from us, and I only admonished him to be more cautious in future.

Having received information that the hunters had killed a deer, we sent three men to fetch the meat, which was distributed between our party and the canoe-men who had been encamped near to us. The thermometer at three P.M. was 56°, at nine 34°.

We commenced the following day by crossing a lake about four miles in length, and then passed over a succession of rugged hills for nearly the same distance. The men being anxious to reach some pine-trees, which they had seen on their former journey, walked at a quick pace, though they were suffering from swelled legs and rheumatic pains; we could not, however, attain the desired point, and therefore encamped on the declivity of a hill, which sheltered us from the wind; and used the reindeer moss for fuel, which afforded us more warmth than we expected. Several patches of snow were yet remaining on the surrounding hills. The thermometer varied today between 55° and 45°.

On the 20th of June we began our march by crossing a small lake, not without much risk, as the surface of the ice was covered with water to the depth of two feet, and there were many holes into which we slipped, in spite of our efforts to avoid them. A few of the men, being fearful of attempting the traverse with their heavy loads, walked round the eastern end of the lake. The parties met on the sandy ridge, which separates the streams that fall into Winter Lake from those that flow to the northward; and here we killed three deer. Near the base of this ridge we crossed a small but rapid stream, in which there is a remarkable cascade of about fifty feet. Some Indians joined us here, and gave information respecting the situation of Dr. Richardson's tent, which our hunters considered was sufficient for our guidance, and therefore proceeded as quickly as they could. We marched a few miles farther in the evening, and encamped among some pines; but the comfort of a good fire did not compensate for the torment we suffered from the host of musquitoes at this spot. The temperature was 52°.

We set off next morning at a very early hour. The men took the course of Point Lake, that they might use their sledges, but the officers pursued the nearest route by land to Dr. Richardson's tent, which we reached at eleven A.M. It was on the western side of an arm of the lake, and near the part through which the Copper-Mine River runs. Our men arrived soon after us, and in the evening Mr. Wentzel and his party, with the canoes in excellent condition. They were much jaded by their fatiguing journey and several were lame from swellings of the lower extremities. The ice on the lake was still six or seven feet thick, and there was no appearance of its decay except near the edges; and as it was evident that, by remaining here until it should be removed, we might lose every prospect of success in our undertaking, I determined on dragging our stores along its surface, until we should come to a part of the river where we could embark; and directions were given this evening for each man to prepare a train for the conveyance of his portion of the stores. I may remark here, as a proof of the strong effect of radiation from the earth in melting the ice, that the largest holes in the ice were always formed at the base of the high and steep cliffs, which abound on the borders of this lake.

We found Akaitcho and the hunters encamped here, but their families, and the rest of the tribe, had gone off two days before to the Beth-see-to, a large lake to the northward, where they intended passing the summer. Long-legs and Keskarrah had departed, to desire the Hook to collect as much meat as he could against our arrival at his lodge. We were extremely distressed to learn from Dr. Richardson, that Akaitcho and his party had expended all the ammunition they had received at Fort Enterprise, without having contributed any supply of provision. The Doctor had, however, through the assistance of two hunters he kept with him, prepared two hundred pounds of dried meat, which was now our sole dependance for the journey. On the following morning I represented to Akaitcho that we had been greatly disappointed by his conduct, which was so opposite to the promise of exertion he had made, on quitting Fort Enterprise. He offered many excuses, but finding they were not satisfactory, admitted that the greater part of the ammunition had been given to those who accompanied the women to the Beth-see-to, and promised to behave better in future. I then told him, that I intended in future to give them ammunition only in proportion to the meat which was brought in, and that we should commence upon that plan, by supplying him with fifteen balls, and each of the hunters with ten.

The number of our hunters was now reduced to five, as two of the most active declined going any farther, their father, who thought himself dying, having solicited them to remain and close his eyes. These five were furnished with ammunition, and sent forward to hunt on the south border of the lake, with directions to place any meat they might procure near the edge of the lake, and set up marks to guide us to the spots. Akaitcho, his brother, the guide, and three other men, remained to accompany us. We were much surprised to perceive an extraordinary difference in climate in so short an advance to the northward as fifty miles. The snow here was lying in large patches on the hills. The dwarf-birch and willows were only just beginning to open their buds, which had burst forth at Fort Enterprise many days before our departure. Vegetation seemed to be three weeks or a month later here than at that place. We had heavy showers of rain through the night of the 22nd, which melted the snow, and visibly wasted the ice.

On the 23rd, the men were busily employed in making their trains, and in pounding the meat for pemmican. The situation of the encampment was ascertained, latitude 65° 12′ 40″ N., longitude 113° 8′ 25″ W., and the variation 43° 4′ 20″ E. The arrangements being completed, we purposed commencing our journey next morning, but the weather was too stormy to venture upon the lake with the canoes. In the afternoon a heavy fall of snow took place, succeeded by sleet and rain. The north-east gale continued, but the thermometer rose to 39°.

June 25

The wind having abated in the night, we prepared for starting at an early hour. The three canoes were mounted on sledges, and nine men were appointed to conduct them, having the assistance of two dogs to each canoe. The stores and provisions were distributed equally among the rest of our men, except a few small articles which the Indians carried. The provision consisted of only two bags of pemmican, two of pounded meat, five of suet, and two small bundles of dried provision, together with fresh meat sufficient for our supper at night. It was gratifying to witness the readiness with which the men prepared for and commenced a journey, which threatened to be so very laborious, as each of them had to drag upwards of one hundred and eighty pounds on his sledge.

Our course led down the main channel of the lake, which varied in breadth from half a mile to three miles; but we proceeded at a slow pace, as the snow, which fell last night, and still lay on the ice, very much impeded the sledges. Many extensive arms branched off on the north side of this channel, and it was bounded on the south by a chain of lofty islands. The hills on both sides rose to six or seven hundred feet, and high steep cliffs were numerous. Clusters of pines were occasionally seen in the valleys. We put up, at eight P.M., in a spot which afforded us but a few twigs for fuel. The party was much fatigued, and several of the men were affected by an inflammation on the inside of the thigh attended with hardness and swelling. The distance made today was six miles.

We started at ten next morning. The day was extremely hot, and the men were soon jaded; their lameness increased very much, and some not previously affected began to complain. The dogs too showed symptoms of great weakness, and one of them stretched himself obstinately on the ice, and was obliged to be released from the harness. We were, therefore, compelled to encamp at an early hour, having come only four miles. The sufferings of the people in this early stage of our journey were truly discouraging to them, and very distressing to us, whose situation was comparatively easy. I, therefore, determined on leaving the third canoe, which had been principally carried to provide against any accident to the others. We should thus gain three men, to lighten the loads of those who were most lame, and an additional dog for each of the other canoes. It was accordingly properly secured on a stage erected for the purpose near the encampment. Dried meat was issued for supper, but in the course of the evening the Indians killed two deer, for which we immediately sent.

The channel of the lake through which we had passed today was bounded on both sides by islands of consider-able height, presenting bold and rugged scenery. We were informed by our guide, that a large body of the lake lees to the northward of a long island which we passed.

Another deer was killed next morning, but as the men breakfasted off it before they started, the additional weight was not materially felt. The burdens of the men being considerably lightened by the arrangements of last evening, the party walked at the rate of one mile and three quarters an hour until the afternoon, when our pace was slackened, as the ice was more rough, and our lame companions felt their sores very galling. At noon we passed a deep bay on the south side, which is said to receive a river. Throughout the day's march the hills on each side of the lake bore a strong resemblance, in height and form, to those about Fort Enterprise. We encamped on the north main shore, among some spruce trees, having walked eight miles and a half. Three or four fish were caught with lines through holes, which the water had worn in the ice. We perceived a light westerly current at these places.

It rained heavily during the night, and this was succeeded by a dense fog on the morning of the 28th. Being short of provisions we commenced our journey, though the points of land were not discernible beyond a short distance. The surface of the ice, being honeycombed by the recent rains, presented innumerable sharp points, which tore our shoes and lacerated the feet at every step. The poor dogs, too, marked their path with their blood.

In the evening the atmosphere became clear, and, at five P.M., we reached the rapid by which Point Lake communicates with Red-Rock Lake. This rapid is only one hundred yards wide, and we were much disappointed at finding the Copper-Mine River such an inconsiderable stream. The canoes descended the rapid, but the cargoes were carried across the peninsula, and placed again on the sledges, as the next lake was still frozen. We passed an extensive arm, branching to the eastward, and encamped just below it, on the western bank, among spruce pines, having walked six miles of direct distance. The rolled stones on the beach are principally red clay slate, hence its Indian appellation, which we have retained.

We continued our journey at the usual hour next morning. At noon the variation was observed to be 47° E. Our attention was afterwards directed to some pine branches, scattered on the ice, which proved to be marks placed by our hunters, to guide us to the spot where they had deposited the carcasses of two small deer. This supply was very seasonable, and the men cheerfully dragged the additional weight. Akaitcho, judging from the appearance of the meat, thought it bad been placed here three days ago, and that the hunters were considerably in advance. We put up at six P.M., near the end of the lake, having come twelve miles and three-quarters, and found the channel open by which it is connected with the Rock-nest Lake. A river was pointed out, bearing south from our encampment, which is said to rise near Great Marten Lake. Red-Rock Lake is in general narrow, its shelving banks are well clothed with wood, and even the hills, which attain an elevation of four hundred or five hundred feet, are ornamented half way up, with stunted pines.

On June 30, the men having gummed the canoes, embarked with their burdens to descend the river; but we accompanied the Indians about five miles across a neck of land, when we also embarked. The river was about two hundred yards wide, and its course being uninterrupted, we cherished a sanguine hope of now getting on more speedily, until we perceived that the waters of Rock-nest Lake were still bound by ice, and that recourse must again be had to the sledges. The ice was much decayed, and the party were exposed to great risk of breaking through in making the traverse. In one part we had to cross an open channel in the canoes, and in another were compelled to quit the Lake, and make a portage along the land. When the party had got upon the ice again, our guide evinced much uncertainty as to the route. He first directed us towards the west end of the lake; but when we had nearly gained that point, he discovered a remarkable rock to the north-east, named by the Indians the Rock-nest, and then recollected that the river ran at its base. Our course was immediately changed to that direction, but the traverse we had then to make was more dangerous than the former one. The ice cracked under us at every step, and the party were obliged to separate widely to prevent accidents. We landed at the first point we could approach, but having found an open channel close to the shore, were obliged to ferry the goods across on pieces of ice. The fresh meat being expended we had to make another inroad on our pounded meat. The evening was very warm, and the musquitoes numerous. A large fire was made to apprise the hunters of our advance. The scenery of Rock-nest Lake is picturesque, its shores are rather low, except at the Rock's-nest, and two or three eminences on the eastern side. The only wood is the pine, which is twenty or thirty feet high, and about one foot in diameter. Our distance today was six miles.

July 1

Our guide directed us to proceed towards a deep bay on the north side of the lake, where he supposed we should find the river. In consequence of the bad state of the ice, we employed all the different modes of travelling we had previously followed in attaining this place; and, in crossing a point of land, had the misfortune to lose one of the dogs, which set off in pursuit of some reindeer. Arriving at the bay, we only found a stream that fell into it from the north-east, and looked in vain for the Copper-Mine River. This circumstance confused the guide, and lie confessed that he was now doubtful of the proper route; we, therefore, halted, and despatched him, with two men, to look for the river from the top of the high hills near the Rock-nest. During this delay a slight injury was repaired, which one of the canoes had received. We were here amused by the sight of a wolf chasing two reindeer on the ice. The pursuer being alarmed at the sight of our men, gave up the chase when near to the hindmost, much to our regret, for we were calculating upon the chance of sharing in his capture.

At four P.M. our men returned, with the agreeable information that they had seen the river flowing at the base of the Rock-nest. The canoes and stores were immediately placed on the ice, and dragged thither; we then embarked, but soon had to cut through a barrier of drift ice that blocked up the way. We afterwards descended two strong rapids, and encamped near the discharge of a small stream which flows from an adjoining lake. The Copper-Mine River, at this point, is about two hundred yards wide, and ten feet deep, and flows very rapidly over a rocky bottom. The scenery of its banks is picturesque, the hills shelve to the water-side, and are well covered with wood, and the surface of the rocks is richly ornamented with lichens. The Indians say that the same kind of country prevails as far as Mackenzie's River in this parallel; but that the land to the eastward is perfectly barren. Akaitcho and one of the Indians killed two deer, which were immediately sent for. Two of the hunters arrived in the night, and we learned that their companions, instead of being in advance, as we supposed, were staying at the place where we first found the river open. They had only seen our fires last evening, and had sent to examine who we were. The circumstance of having passed them was very vexatious, as they had three deer *en cache,* at their encampment. However, an Indian was sent to desire those who remained to join us, and bring the meat.

We embarked at nine A.M. on July 2nd, and descended a succession of strong rapids for three miles. We were carried along with extraordinary rapidity, shooting over large stones, upon which a single stroke would have been destructive to the canoes; and we were also in danger of breaking them, from the want of the long poles which lie along their bottoms and equalise their cargoes, as they plunged very much, and on one occasion the first canoe was almost filled with the waves. But there was no receding after we had once launched into the stream, and our safety depended on the skill and dexterity of the bowmen and steersmen. The banks of the river here are rocky, and the scenery beautiful; consisting of gentle elevations and dales wooded to the edge of the stream, and flanked on both sides at the distance of three or four miles by a range of round-backed barren hills, upwards of six hundred feet high. At the foot of the rapids the high lands recede to a greater distance, and the river flows with a more gentle current, in a wider channel, through a level and open country consisting of alluvial sand. In one place the passage was blocked up by drift ice, still deeply covered with snow. A channel for the canoes was made for some distance with the hatchets and poles; but on reaching the more compact part, we were under the necessity of transporting the canoes and cargoes across it; an operation of much hazard, as the snow concealed the numerous holes which the water had made in the ice. This expansion of the river being mistaken by the guide for a lake, which he spoke of as the last on our route to the sea, we sup-posed that we should have no more ice to cross, and therefore encamped after passing through it, to fit the canoes properly for the voyage, and to provide poles, which are not only necessary to strengthen them when placed in the bottom, but essentially requisite for the safe management of them in dangerous rapids. The guide began afterwards to doubt whether the lake he meant was not farther on, and he was sent with two men to examine into the fact, who returned in the evening with the information of its being below us, but that there was an open channel through it. This day was very sultry, and several plants appeared in flower.

The men were employed in repairing their canoes to a late hour, and commenced very early next morning, as we were desirous of availing ourselves of every part of this favourable weather. The hunters arrived in the course of the night. It appeared that the dog which escaped from us two days ago came into the vicinity of their encampment, howling piteously; seeing him without his harness, they came to the hasty conclusion that our whole party had perished in a rapid; and throwing away part of their baggage, and leaving the meat behind them, they set off with the utmost haste to join Long-legs. Our messenger met them in their flight, but too far advanced to admit of their returning for the meat. Akaitcho scolded them heartily for their thoughtlessness in leaving the meat, which we so much wanted. They expressed their regret, and being ashamed of their panic, proposed to remedy the evil as much as possible by going forward, without stopping, until they came to a favourable spot for hunting, which they expected to do about thirty or forty miles below our present encampment. Akaitcho accompanied them, but previous to setting off he renewed his charge that we should be on our guard against the bears, which was occasioned by the hunters having fired at one this morning as they were descending a rapid in their canoe. As their small canoes would only carry five persons, two of the hunters had to walk in turns along the banks.

In our rambles round the encampment, we witnessed with pleasure the progress which vegetation had made within the few last warm days; most of the trees had put forth their leaves, and several flowers ornamented the moss-covered ground; many of the smaller summer birds were observed in the woods, and a variety of ducks, gulls, and plovers, sported on the banks of the river. It is about three hundred yards wide at this part, is deep and flows over a bed of alluvial sand. We caught some trout of considerable size with our lines, and a few white-fish in the nets, which maintained us, with a little assistance from the pemmican. The repair of our canoes was completed this evening. Before embarking I issued an order that no rapid should in future be descended until the bowman had examined it, and decided upon its being safe to run. Wherever the least danger was to be apprehended, or the crew had to disembark for the purpose of lightening the canoe, the ammunition, guns and instruments, were always to be put out and carried along the bank, that we might be provided with the means of subsisting ourselves, in case of any accident befalling the canoes.

The situation of our encampment was ascertained to be 65° 43′ 28″ N., longitude 114° 26′ 45″ W., and the variation 42° 17′ 22″ E.

At four in the morning of July 4th we embarked and descended a succession of very agitated rapids, but took the precaution of landing the articles mentioned yesterday, wherever there appeared any hazard; notwithstanding all our precautions the leading canoe struck with great force against a stone, and the bark was split, but this injury was easily repaired, and we regretted only the loss of time. At eleven we came to an expansion of the river where the current ran with less force, and an accumulation of drift ice had, in consequence, barred the channel; over this the canoes and cargoes were carried. The ice in many places adhered to the banks, and projected in wide ledges several feet thick over the stream, which had hollowed them out beneath. On one occasion as the people were embarking from one of these ledges, it suddenly gave way, and three men were precipitated into the water, but were rescued without further damage than a sound ducking, and the canoe fortunately (and narrowly) escaped being crushed. Perceiving one of the Indians sitting on the east bank of the river, we landed, and having learned from him that Akaitcho and the hunters had gone in pursuit of a herd of musk oxen, we encamped, having come twenty-four miles and a half.

In the afternoon they brought us the agreeable intelligence of having killed eight cows, of which four were full grown. All the party were immediately despatched to bring in this seasonable supply. A young cow, irritated by the firing of the hunters, ran down to the river, and passed close to me when walking at a short distance from the tents. I tired and wounded it, when the animal instantly turned, and ran at me, but I avoided its fury by jumping aside and getting upon an elevated piece of ground. In the meantime some people came from the tents, and it took to flight.

The musk oxen, like the buffalo, herd together in bands, and generally frequent the barren grounds during the summer months, keeping near the rivers, but retire to the woods in winter. They seem to be less watchful than most other wild animals, and when grazing are not difficult to approach, provided the hunters go against the wind; when two or three men get so near a herd as to fire at them from different points, these animals, instead of separating or running away, huddle closer together, and several are generally killed; but if the wound is not mortal they become enraged and dart in the most furious manner at the hunters, who must be very dextrous to evade them. They can defend themselves by their powerful horns against the wolves and bears, which, as the Indians say, they not unfrequently kill.

The musk oxen feed on the same substances with the reindeer, and the prints of the feet of these two animals are so much alike, that it requires the eye of an experienced hunter to distinguish them. The largest killed by us did not exceed in weight three hundred pounds. The flesh has a musky disagreeable flavour, particularly when the animal is lean, which unfortunately for us was the case with all that we now killed.

During this day's march the river varied in breadth from one hundred to two hundred feet, and except in two open spaces, a very strong current marked a deep descent the whole way. It flows over a bed of gravel, of which also its immediate banks are composed. Near to our encampment it is bounded by cliffs of fine sand from one hundred to two hundred feet high. Sandy plains extend on a level with the summit of these cliffs, and at the distance of six or seven miles are terminated by ranges of hills eight hundred or one thousand feet high. The grass on these plains affords excellent pasturage for the musk oxen, and they generally abound here. The hunters added two more to our stock in the course of the night. As we had now more meat than the party could consume fresh, we delayed our voyage next day to dry it. The hunters were supplied with more ammunition, and sent forward; but Akaitcho, his brother, and another Indian, remained with us.

It may here be proper to mention, that the officers had treated Akaitcho more distantly since our departure from Point Lake, to mark their opinion of his misconduct. The diligence in hunting, however, which he had evinced at this place, induced us to receive him more familiarly when he came to the tent this evening. During our conversation he endeavoured to excite suspicions in our minds against the Hook, by saying, "I am aware that you consider me the worst man of my nation; but I know the Hook to be a great rogue, and I think he will disappoint you."

On the morning of the 6th we embarked, and descended a series of rapids, having twice unloaded the canoes where the water was shallow. After passing the mouth of the Fairy[1] Lake River the rapids ceased. The main stream was then about

1 This is an Indian name. The Northern Indian fairies are six inches high, lead a life similar to the Indians, and are excellent hunters. Those who have had the good fortune to fall in with their tiny encampments have been kindly treated, and regaled on vension. We did not learn with certainty whether the existence of these delightful creatures is known from Indian tradition, or whether the Indians own their knowledge of them to their intercourse with the traders, but think the former is probable.

three hundred yards wide, and generally deep, though, in one part, the channel was interrupted by several sandy banks, and low alluvial islands covered with willows. It flows between banks of sand thinly wooded, and as we advanced the barren hills approached the water's edge.

At ten we rejoined our hunters, who had killed a deer, and halted to breakfast. We sent them forward; one of them, who was walking along the shore afterwards, fired upon two brown bears, and wounded one of them, which instantly turned and pursued him. His companions in the canoes put ashore to his assistance, but did not succeed in killing the bears, which fled upon the reinforcement coming up. During the delay thus occasioned we overtook them, and they continued with us the rest of the day.

We encamped at the foot of a lofty range of mountains, which appear to be from twelve to fifteen hundred feet high; they are in general round backed, but the outline is not even, being interrupted by craggy conical eminences. This is the first ridge of hills we have seen in this country, that deserves the appellation of a mountain range; it is probably a continuation of the Stony Mountains crossed by Hearne. Many plants appeared in full flower near the tents, and Dr. Richardson gathered some high up on the hills. The distance we made today was fifty miles.

There was a hoar frost in the night, and the temperature, at four next morning, was 40°: embarking at that hour, we glided quickly down the stream, and by seven arrived at the Hook's encampment, which was placed on the summit of a lofty sand cliff, whose base was washed by the river. This chief had with him only three hunters, and a few old men and their families, the rest of the band having remained at their snares in Bear Lake. His brother, Long-legs, and our guide, Kaskarrah, who had joined him three days before, had communicated to him our want of provision, and we were happy to find that, departing from the general practice of Indian chiefs, he entered at once upon the business, without making a long speech. As an introductory mark of our regard, I decorated him with a medal similar to those which had been given to the other leaders. The Hook began by stating, "that he was aware of our being destitute of provision, and of the great need we had of an ample stock, to enable us to execute our undertaking; and his regret, that the unusual scarcity of animals this season, together with the circumstance of his having only just received a supply of ammunition from Fort Providence, had prevented him from collecting the quantity of meat he had wished to do for our use. The amount, indeed," he said, "is very small, but I will cheerfully give you what I have: we are too much indebted to the white people, to allow them to want food on our lands, whilst we have any to give them. Our families can live on fish until we can procure more meat, but the season is too short to allow of your delaying, to gain subsistence in that manner." He immediately desired, aloud, that the women should bring all the meat they had to us; and we soon collected sufficient to make three bags and a half of pemmican, besides some dried meat and tongues. We were truly delighted by this prompt and cheerful behaviour, and would gladly have rewarded the kindness of himself and his companions by some substantial present, but we were limited by the scantiness of our store to a small donation of fifteen charges of ammunition to each of the chiefs. In return for the provision they accepted notes on the North-West Company, to be paid at Fort Providence; and to these was subjoined an order for a few articles of clothing, as an additional present. I then endeavoured to prevail upon the Hook to remain in this vicinity with his hunters until the autumn, and to make deposits of provision in different parts of the course to the sea, as a resource for our party, in the event of our being compelled to return by this route. He required time, however, to consider this matter, and promised to give me an answer next day. I was rejoiced to find him then prepared to meet my wish, and the following plan was agreed upon: – As the animals abound, at all times, on the borders of Bear Lake, he promised to remain on the east side of it until the month of November, at that spot which is nearest to the Copper-Mine River, from whence there is a communication by a chain of lakes and portages. There the principal deposit of provision was to be made; but during the summer the hunters were to be employed in putting up supplies of dried meat at convenient distances, not only along the communication from this river, but also upon its banks, as far down as the Copper Mountain. They were also to place particular marks to guide our course to their lodges. We contracted to pay them liberally, whether we returned by this way or not; if we did, they were to accompany us to Fort Providence to receive the reward; and, at any rate, I promised to send the necessary documents by Mr. Wentzel, from the sea-coast, to ensure them an ample remuneration. With this arrangement they were perfectly satisfied, and we could not be less so, knowing they had every motive for fulfilling their promises, as the place they had chosen to remain at is their usual hunting ground. The uncommon anxiety these chiefs expressed for our safety, appeared to us likely to prompt them to every care and attention, and I record their expressions with gratitude. After representing the numerous hardships we should have to encounter in the strongest manner, though in language similar to what we had often heard from our friend Akaitcho, they earnestly entreated we would be constantly on our guard against the treachery of the Esquimaux; and no less forcibly desired we would not proceed far along the coast, as they dreaded the consequences of our being exposed to a tempestuous sea in canoes, and having to endure the cold of the autumn on a shore destitute of fuel. The Hook, having been an invalid for several years, rejoiced at the opportunity of consulting Dr. Richardson, who immediately gave him advice, and supplied him with medicine.

The pounded meat and fat were converted into pemmican, preparatory to our voyage.

The result of our observations at the Hook's encampment was, latitude 66° 45′ 11″ N., longitude 115° 42′ 23″ W., variation of the compass 46° 7′ 30″ E.

We embarked at eleven to proceed on our journey. Akaitcho and his brother, the guide, being in the first canoe, and old Keskarrah in the other. We wished to dispense with the further attendance of two guides, and made a proposition that either of them might remain here, but neither would relinquish the honour of escorting the Expedition to the sea. One of our hunters, however, was less eager for this distinction, and preferred remaining with Green-stockings, Keskarrah's fascinating daughter. The other four, with the Little Singer, accompanied us, two of them conducting their small canoes in turns, and the rest walking along the beach.

The river flows over a bed of sand, and winds in an uninterrupted channel of from three-quarters to a mile broad, between two ranges of hills, which are pretty even in their outline, and round backed, but having rather steep acclivities. The immediate borders of the stream consist either of high banks of sand, or steep gravel cliffs; and sometimes, where the hills recede to a little distance, the intervening space is occupied by high sandy ridges.

At three P.N., after passing along the foot of a high range of hills, we arrived at the portage leading to the Bear Lake, to which we have previously alluded. Its position is very remarkable, being at the most westerly part of the Copper-Mine River, and at the point where it resumes a northern course, and forces a passage through the lofty ridge of mountains, to which it has run parallel for the last thirty miles. As the Indians travel from hence, with their families, in three days to the point where they have proposed staying for us, the distance, I think, cannot exceed forty miles; and admitting the course to be due west, which is the direction the guide pointed, it would place the eastern part of Bear Lake in 118¼° W. longitude.

Beyond this spot the river is diminished in breadth and a succession of rapids are formed; but as the water was deep, we passed through them without discharging any part of the cargoes. It still runs between high ranges of mountains, though its actual boundaries are banks of mud mixed with clay, which are clothed with stunted pines. We picked up a deer which the hunters had shot, and killed another from the canoe; and also received an addition to our stock of provision of seven young geese, which the hunters had beaten down with their sticks. About six P.M.. we perceived a mark on the shore, which on examination was found to have been recently put up by some Indians: and, on proceeding farther, we discerned stronger proofs of their vicinity; we, therefore, encamped, and made a large fire as a signal, which they answered in a similar way. Mr. Wentzel was immediately sent, in expectation of getting provision from them. On his return, we learned that the party consisted of three old Copper Indians, with their families, who had supported themselves with the bow and arrow since last autumn, not having visited Fort Providence for more than a year; and so successful had they been, that they were enabled to supply us with upwards of seventy pounds of dried meat, and six moose skins fit for making shoes, which were the more valuable as we were apprehensive of being barefooted before the journey could be completed. The evening was sultry, and the musquitoes appeared in great numbers. The distance made today was twenty-five miles.

On the following morning we went down to these Indians, and delivered to them notes on the North-West Company, for the meat and skins they had furnished; and we had then the mortification of learning, that not having people to carry a considerable quantity of pounded meat, which they had intended for us, they had left it upon the Bear Lake Portage. They promised, however, to get it conveyed to the banks of this river before we could return, and we rewarded them with a present of knives and files.

After re-embarking we continued to descend the river, which was now contracted between lofty banks to about one hundred and twenty yards wide; the current was very strong. At eleven we came to a rapid which had been the theme of discourse with the Indians for many days, and which they had described to us as impassable in canoes. The river here descends for three-quarters of a mile, in a deep, but narrow and crooked, channel, which it has cut through the foot of a hill of five hundred or six hundred feet high. It is confined between perpendicular cliffs resembling stone walls, varying in height from eighty to one hundred and fifty feet, on which lies a mass of fine sand. The body of the river pent within this narrow chasm, dashed furiously round the projecting rocky columns, and discharged itself at the northern extremity in a sheet of foam. The canoes, after being lightened of part of their cargoes, ran through this defile without sustaining any injury. Accurate sketches of this interesting scene were taken by Messrs. Back and Hood. Soon after passing this rapid, we perceived the hunters running up the east side of the river, to prevent us from disturbing a herd of musk oxen, which they had observed grazing on the opposite bank; we put them across and they succeeded in killing six, upon which we encamped for the purpose of drying the meat. The country below the Rocky Defile Rapid consists of sandy plains; broken by small conical eminences also of sand; and bounded to the westward by a continuation of the mountain chain, which we had crossed at the Bear Lake Portage; and to the eastward and northward, at the distance of twelve miles, by the Copper Mountains, which Mr. Hearne visited. The plains are crowned by several clumps of moderately large spruces, about thirty feet high.

This evening the Indians made a large fire, as a signal to the Hook's party that we had passed the *terrific* rapid in safety.

The position of our encampment was ascertained to be, latitude 67° 1′ 10″ N., longitude 116° 27′ 28″ W., variation of the compass 44° 11′ 43″ E., dip of the needle 87° 31′ 18″. Some thunder showers retarded the drying of the meat, and our embarkation was delayed till next day. The hunters were sent forward to hunt at the Copper Mountains, under the superintendence of Adam, the interpreter, who received strict injunctions not to permit them to make any large fires, lest they should alarm straggling parties of the Esquimaux.

The musquitoes were now very numerous and annoying, but we consoled ourselves with the hope that their season would be short.

On the 11th we started at three A. M., and as the guide had represented the river below our encampment to be full of shoals, some of the men were directed to walk along the shore, but they were assailed so violently by the musquitoes, as to be compelled to embark very soon; and we afterwards passed over the shallow parts by the aid of the poles, without experiencing much interruption. The current ran very rapidly, having been augmented by the waters of the Mouse River and several small streams. We rejoined our hunters at the foot of the Copper Mountains, and found they had killed three musk oxen. This circumstance determined us on encamping to dry the meat, as there was wood at the spot. We availed ourselves of this delay to visit the Copper Mountains in search of specimens of the ore, agreeably to my Instructions; and a party of twenty-one persons, consisting of the officers, some of the voyagers, and all the Indians, set off on that excursion. We travelled for nine hours over a considerable space of ground, but found only a few small pieces of native copper. The range we ascended was on the west side of the river, extending W.N.W. and E.S.E. The mountains varied in height from twelve to fifteen hundred feet. The uniformity of the mountains is interrupted by narrow valleys traversed by small streams. The best specimens of metal we procured were among the stones in these valleys, and it was in such situations, that our guides desired us to search most carefully. It would appear, that when the Indians see any sparry substance projecting above the surface, they dig there; but they have no other rule to direct them, and have never found the metal in its original repository. Our guides reported that they had found copper in large pieces in every part of this range, for two days' walk to the north-west, and that the Esquimaux come hither to search for it. The annual visits which the Copper Indians were accustomed to make to these mountains, when most of their weapons and utensils were made of copper, have been discontinued since they have been enabled to obtain a supply of ice chisels and other instruments of iron by the establishment of trading posts near their hunting grounds. That none of those who accompanied us had visited them for many years was evident, from their ignorance of the spots most abundant in metal.

The impracticability of navigating the river upwards from the sea, and the want of wood for forming an establishment, would prove insuperable objections to rendering the collection of copper at this part worthy of mercantile speculation.

We had the opportunity of surveying the country from several elevated positions. Two or three small lakes only were visible, still partly frozen; and much snow remained on the mountains. The trees were reduced to a scanty fringe on the borders of the river, and every side was beset by naked mountains.

The day was unusually warm, and, therefore, favourable for drying the meat. Our whole stock of provision, calculated for preservation, was sufficient for fourteen days, without any diminution of the ordinary allowance of three pounds to each man per day. The situation of our tents was 67° 10′ 30″ N., longitude 116° 25′ 45″ W.

June 12

The Indians, knowing the course of the river below this point to be only a succession of rapids, declined taking their canoes any farther; but as I conceived one of them would be required, should we be compelled to walk along the coast, two of our men were appointed to conduct it.

As we were now entering the confines of the Esquimaux country, our guides recommended us to be cautious in lighting fires, lest we should discover ourselves, adding that the same reason would lead them to travel as much as possible in the valleys, and to avoid crossing the tops of the hills. We embarked at six A.M., taking with us only old Keskarrah. The other Indians walked along the banks of the river. Throughout this day's voyage the current was very strong, running four or five miles an hour; but the navigation was tolerable, and we had to lighten the canoes only once, in a contracted part of the river where the waves were very high. The river is in many places confined between perpendicular walls of rock to one hundred and fifty yards in width, and there the rapids were most agitated. Large masses of ice twelve or fourteen feet thick, were still adhering to many parts of the bank, indicating the tardy departure of winter from this inhospitable land, but the earth around them was rich with vegetation. In the evening two musk oxen being seen on the beach, were pursued and killed by our men. Whilst we were waiting to embark the meat the Indians rejoined us, and reported they had been attacked by a bear, which sprung upon them whilst they were conversing together. His attack was so sudden that they had not time to level their guns properly, and they all missed except Akaitcho, who, less confused than the rest, took deliberate aim, and shot the animal dead. They do not eat the flesh of the bear, but knowing that we had no such prejudice, they brought us some of the choice pieces, which upon trial we found to be very excellent meat.

The Indians having informed us that we were now within twelve miles of the rapid where the Esquimaux have invariably been found, we pitched our tents on the beach, under the shelter of a high hill whose precipitous side is washed by the river, intending to send forward some persons to determine the situation of their present abode. Some vestiges of an old Esquimaux encampment were observed near the tents, and the stumps of the trees bore marks of the stone hatchets they use. A strict watch was appointed, consisting of an officer, four Canadians, and an Indian, and directions were given for the rest of the party to sleep with their arms by their side. That as little delay as possible might be experienced in opening a communication with the Esquimaux, we immediately commenced arrangements for sending forward persons to discover whether there were any in our vicinity. Akaitcho and the guides proposed that two of the hunters should be despatched on this service, who had extremely quick sight, and were accustomed to act as scouts, an office which requires equal caution and circumspection. A strong objection, however, lay against this plan, in the probability of their being discovered by a straggling hunter, which would be destructive to every hope of accommodation. It was therefore determined to send Augustus and Junius, who were very desirous to undertake the service. These adventurous men proposed to go armed only with pistols concealed in their dress, and furnished with beads, looking-glasses, and other articles, that they might conciliate their countrymen by presents. We could not divest our minds of the apprehension, that it might be a service of much hazard, if the Esquimaux were as hostile to strangers as the Copper Indians have invariably represented them to be; and we felt great reluctance in exposing our two little interpreters, who had rendered themselves dear to the whole party, to the most distant chance of receiving injury; but this course of proceeding appeared in their opinion and our own to offer the only chance of gaining an interview. Though not insensible to the danger, they cheerfully prepared for their mission, and clothed themselves in Esquimaux dresses, which had been made for the purpose at Fort Enterprise. Augustus was desired to make his presents, and to tell the Esquimaux that the white   men had come to make peace between them and all their enemies, and also to discover a passage by which every article of which they stood in need might be brought in large ships. He was not to mention that we were accompanied by the Indians, but to endeavour to prevail on some of the Esquimaux to return with him. He was directed to come back immediately if there were no lodges at the rapid.

The Indians were not suffered to move out of our sight, but in the evening we permitted two of them to cross the river in pursuit of a musk ox, which they killed on the beach, and returned immediately. The officers, prompted an anxious solicitude for Augustus and Junius, crawled up frequently to the summit of the mountain to watch their return. The view, however, was not extensive, being bounded at the distance of eight miles by a range of hills similar to the Copper Mountains, but not so lofty. The night came without bringing any intelligence of our messengers, and our fears for their safety increased with the length of their absence.

As every one had been interested in the welfare of these men through their vivacity and good-nature, and the assistance they had cheerfully rendered in bearing their portion of whatever labour might be going on, their detention formed the subject of all our conversation, and numerous conjectures were hazarded as to the cause.

Dr. Richardson, having the first watch, had gone to the summit of the hill and remained seated, contemplating the river that washed the precipice under his feet, long after dusk had hid distant objects from his view. His thoughts were, perhaps, far distant from the surrounding scenery, when he was roused by an indistinct noise behind him, and on looking round, perceived that nine white wolves had ranged themselves in form of a crescent, and were advancing, apparently with the intention of driving him into the river. On his rising up they halted, and when he advanced they made way for his passage down to the tents. He had his gun in his hand, but forbore to fire, lest there should be Esquimaux in the neighbourhood. During Mr. Wentzel's middle watch, the wolves appeared repeatedly on the summit of the hill, and at one time they succeeded in driving a deer over the precipice. The animal was stunned by the fall, but recovering itself, swam across the stream, and escaped up the river. I may remark here, that at midnight it was tolerably dark in the valley of the river at this time, but that an object on the eminence above could be distinctly seen against the sky.

The following observations were taken at this encampment, latitude 67° 23′ 14″ N., longitude 116° 6′ 51″ W., variation 49° 46′ 24″ E. Thermometer 75° at three P.M. Sultry weather.

Augustus and Junius not having returned next morning, we were more alarmed respecting them, and determined on proceeding to find out the cause of their detention, but it was eleven A.M. before we could prevail upon the Indians to remain behind, which we wished them to do lest the Esquimaux might be suspicious of our intentions, if they were seen in our suite. We promised to send for them when we had paved the way for their reception; but Akaitcho, ever ready to augur misfortune, expressed his belief that our messengers had been killed, and that the Esquimaux, warned of our approach, were lying in wait for us, and "although," said he, "your party may be sufficiently strong to repulse any hostile attack, my band is too weak to offer effectual resistance when separated from you; and therefore, we are determined to go on with you, or to return to our lands." After much argument, however, he yielded and agreed to stay behind, provided Mr. Wentzel would remain with him. This gentleman was accordingly left with a Canadian attendant, and they promised not to pass a range of hills then in view to the northward, unless we sent notice to them.

The river during the whole of this day's voyage flowed between alternate cliffs of looses and intermixed with gravel and red sand-stone rocks, and was everywhere shallow and rapid. As its course was very crooked, much time was spent in examining the different rapids previous to running them, but the canoes descended, except at a single place, without any difficulty. Most of the officers and half the men marched along the land to lighten the canoes, and reconnoitre the country, each person being armed with a gun and a dagger. Arriving at a range of mountains which had terminated our view yesterday, we ascended it with much eagerness, expecting to see the rapid that Mr. Hearne visited near its base, and to gain a view of the sea; but our disappointment was proportionably great, when we beheld beyond, a plain similar to that we had just left, terminated by another range of trap hills, between whose tops the summits of some distant blue mountains appeared. Our reliance on the information of the guides, which had been for some time shaken was now quite at an end, and we feared that the sea was still far distant. The flat country here is covered with grass, and is devoid of the large stones, so frequent in the barren grounds, but the ranges of trap hills which seem to intersect it at regular distances are quite barren. A few decayed stunted pines were standing on the borders of the river. In the evening we had the gratification of meeting Junius, who was hastening back to inform us that they had found four Esquimaux tents at the Fall which we recognised to be the one described by Mr. Hearne. The inmates were asleep at the time of their arrival, but rose soon afterwards and then Augustus presented himself, and had some conversation across the river. He told them the white people had come, who would make them very useful presents. The information of our arrival seemed to alarm them very much, but as the noise of the rapid prevented them from hearing distinctly, one of them approached him in his canoe, and received the rest of the message. He would not, however, land on his side of the river, but returned to the tents without receiving the present. His language differed in some respects from Augustus's, but they understood each other tolerably well. Augustus trusting for a supply of provision to the Esquimaux, had neglected to carry any with him, and this was the main cause of Junius's return. We now encamped, having come fourteen miles. After a few hours' rest, Junius set off again to rejoin his companion, being accompanied by Hepburn, who was directed to remain about two miles above the fall, to arrest the canoes on their passage, lest we should too suddenly surprise the Esquimaux. About ten P.M. we were mortified by the appearance of the Indians with Mr. Wentzel, who had in vain endeavoured to restrain them from following us. The only reason assigned by Akaitcho for this conduct was, that he wished for a reassurance of my promise to establish peace between his nation and the Esquimaux. I took this occasion of again enforcing the necessity of their remaining behind, until we had obtained the confidence and good-will of their enemies. After supper Dr. Richardson ascended a lofty hill about three miles from the encampment, and obtained the first view of the sea; it appeared to be covered with ice. A large promontory, which I named Cape Hearne, bore N.E., and its lofty mountains proved to be the blue land we had seen in the forenoon, and which had led us to believe the sea was still far distant. He saw the sun set a few minutes before midnight from the same elevated situation. It did not rise during the half hour he remained there, but before be reached the encampment its rays gilded the tops of the bills.

The night was warm, and we were much annoyed by the musquitoes.

June 15

We this morning experienced as much difficulty as before in prevailing upon the Indians to remain behind, and they did not consent until I had declared that they should lose the reward which had been promised, if they proceeded any farther, before we had prepared the Esquimaux to receive them. We left a Canadian with them, and proceeded, not without apprehension that they would follow us, and derange our whole plan by their obstinacy. Two of the officers and a party of the men walked on the shore, to lighten the canoes. The river, in this part, flows between high and stony cliffs, reddish slate clay rocks and shelving banks of white clay, and is full of shoals and dangerous rapids. One of these was termed Escape Rapid, both the canoes having narrowly escaped foundering in its high waves. We had entered the rapid before we were aware, and the steepness of the cliffs preventing us from landing, we were indebted to the swiftness of our descent for preservation. Two waves made a complete breach over the canoes; a third would in all probability have filled and overset them, which must have proved fatal to every one in them. The powder fortunately escaped the water, which was soon discharged when we reached the bottom of the rapid. At noon we perceived Hepburn lying on the left bank of the river, and landed immediately to receive his information. As he represented the water to be shoal the whole way to the rapid (below which the Esquimaux were), the shore party were directed to continue their march to a sandy bay at the head of the fall, and there await the arrival of the canoes. The land in the neighbourhood of the rapid, is of the most singular form: large irregular sand hills bounding both banks, apparently so unconnected that they resemble icebergs; the country around them consisting of high round green hills. The river becomes wide in this part, and full of shoals, but we had no difficulty in finding a channel through them. On regaining the shore party, we regretted to find that some of the men had incautiously appeared on the tops of the hills, just at the time Augustus was conversing with one of the Esquimaux, who had again approached in his canoe, and was almost persuaded to land. The unfortunate appearance of so many people at this instant revived his fears, and he crossed over to the eastern bank of the river, and fled with the whole of his party. We learned from Augustus that his party, consisting of four men and as many women, had manifested a friendly disposition. Two of the former were very tall. The man who first came to speak to him, inquired the number of canoes that we had with us, expressed himself to be not displeased at our arrival, and desired him to caution us not to attempt running the rapid, but to make the portage on the west side of the river. Notwithstanding this appearance of confidence and satisfaction, it seems they did not consider their situation free from danger, as they retreated the first night to an island somewhat farther down the river, and in the morning they returned and threw down their lodges, as if to give notice to any of their nation that might arrive, that there was an enemy in the neighbourhood. From seeing all their property strewed about, and ten of their dogs left, we entertained the hope that these poor people would return after their first alarm had subsided; and therefore I determined on remaining until the next day, in the expectation of seeing them, as I considered the opening of an early communication a matter of the greatest importance in our state of absolute ignorance respecting the sea-coast. The canoes and cargoes were carried across the portage, and we encamped on the north side of it. We sent Augustus and Junius across the river to look for the runaways, but their search was fruitless. They put a few pieces of iron and trinkets in their canoes, which were lying on the beach. We also sent some men to put up the stages of fish, and secure them as much as possible from the attacks of the dogs. Under the covering of their tents were observed some stone kettles and hatchets, a few fish spears made of copper two small bits of iron, a quantity of skins, and some dried salmon, which was covered with maggots, and half putrid. The entrails of the fish were spread out to dry. A great many skins of small birds were hung up to a stage, and even two mice were preserved in the same way. Thus it would appear that the necessities of these poor people induce them to preserve every article that can be possibly used as food. Several human skulls which bore the marks of violence, and many bones were stewed about the ground near the encampment, and as the spot exactly answers the description given by Mr. Hearne, of the place where the Chipewyans who accompanied him perpetrated the dreadful massacre on the Esquimaux, we had no doubt of this being the place, notwithstanding the difference in its position as to latitude and longitude given by him, and ascertained by our observation. We have, therefore, preserved the appellation of Bloody Fall, which he bestowed upon it. Its situation by our observations is, in latitude 67° 42′ 35″ N., longitude 115° 49′ 33″ W., variation 50° 20′ 14″ E. This rapid is a sort of shelving cascade, about three hundred yards in length, having a descent of from ten to fifteen feet. It is bounded on each side by high walls of red sand-stone, upon which rests a series of lofty green hills. On its north side, close to the east bank, is the low rocky island which the Esquimaux had deserted. The surrounding scenery was accurately delineated in a sketch taken by Mr. Hood. We caught forty excellent salmon and whitefish in a single net below the rapid. We had not seen any trees during this day's journey; our fuel consisted of small willows and pieces of dried wood that were picked up near the encampment. The ground is well clothed with grass, and nourishes most of the shrubs and berry-bearing plants that we have seen north of Fort Enterprise; and the country altogether has a richer appearance than the barren lands of the Copper Indians. We had a distinct view of the sea from the summit of a hill behind the tents; it appeared choked with ice and full of islands.

On the morning of the 16th three men were sent up the river to search for dried wood to make floats for the nets. Adam, the interpreter, was also despatched with a Canadian, to inform Akaitcho of the flight of the Esquimaux. We were preparing to go down to the Sea in one of the canoes, leaving Mr. Back to await the return of the men who were absent; but just as the crew were putting the canoe in the water, Adam returned in the utmost consternation, and informed us that a party of Esquimaux were pursuing the men whom we had sent to collect floats. The orders for embarking were instantly countermanded, and we went with a part of our men to their rescue. We soon met our people returning at a slow pace, and learned that they had come unawares upon the Esquimaux party, which consisted of six men, with their women and children, who were travelling towards the rapid with a considerable number of dogs carrying their baggage. The women hid themselves on the first alarm, but the men advanced, and stopping at some distance from our men, began to dance in a circle, tossing up their hands in the air, and accompanying their motions with much shouting, to signify, I conceive, their desire of peace. Our men saluted them by pulling off their hats, and making bows, but neither party was willing to approach the other; and, at length, the Esquimaux retired to the hill, from whence they had descended when first seen. We proceeded in the hope of gaining an interview with them, but lest our appearance in a body should alarm them, we advanced in a long line, at the head of which was Augustus. We were led to their baggage, which they had deserted, by the howling of the dogs; and on the summit of a hill we found, lying behind a stone, an old man who was too infirm to effect his escape with the rest. He was much terrified when Augustus advanced, and probably expected immediate death; but that the fatal blow might not be unrevenged, he seized his spear, and made a thrust with it at his supposed enemy. Augustus, however, easily repressed the feeble effort, and soon calmed his fears by presenting him with some pieces of iron, and assuring him of his friendly intentions. Dr. Richardson and I then joined them, and, after receiving our presents, the old man was quite composed, and became communicative. His dialect differed from that used by Augustus, but they understood each other tolerably well.

It appeared that his party consisted of eight men and their families, who were returning from a hunting excursion with dried meat. After being told who we were, he said that he had heard of white people from different parties of his nation which resided on the sea-coast to the eastward; and to our inquiries respecting the provision and fuel we might expect to get on our voyage, he informed us that the reindeer frequent the coast during the summer, the fish are plentiful at the mouths of the rivers, the seals are abundant, but there are no sea-horses nor whales, although he remembered one of the latter, which had been killed by some distant tribe, having been driven on shore on his part of the coast by a gale of wind. That musk oxen were to be found a little distance up the rivers, and that we should get drift wood along the shore. He had no knowledge of the coast to tile eastward beyond the next river, which he called Nappa-arktok-towock, or Tree River. The old man, contrary to the Indian practice, asked each of our names; and in reply to a similar question on our part said his name was Terregannœuck, or the White Fox; and that his tribe denominated themselves Nagge-ook-tormœoot, or Deer-Horn Esquimaux. They usually frequent the Bloody Fall during this and the following moons, for the purpose of salting salmon, and then retire to a river which flows into the sea, a short way to the westward, (since denominated Richardson's River,) and pass the winter in snow-houses.

After this conversation Terregannœuck proposed going down to his baggage, and we then perceived he was too infirm to walk without the assistance of sticks. Augustus, therefore, offered him his arm, which he readily accepted, and, on reaching his store, he distributed pieces of dried meat to each person, which, though highly tainted, were immediately eaten; this being a universal token among the Indians of peaceable intention.

We then informed him of our desire to procure as much meat as we possibly could, and he told us that he had a large quantity concealed in the neighbourhood, which he would cause to be carried to us when his people returned.

I now communicated to him that we were accompanied by some Copper Indians, who were very desirous to make peace with his nation, and that they had requested me to prevail upon the Esquimaux to receive them in a friendly manner;

to which he replied, he should rejoice to see an end put to the hostility that existed between the nations, and therefore would most gladly welcome our companions. Having despatched Adam to inform Akaitcho of this circumstance, we left Terregannœuck, in the hope that his party would rejoin him; but as we had doubts whether the young men would venture upon coming to our tents, on the old man's bare representation, we sent Augustus and Junius back in the evening, to remain with him until they came, that they might fully detail our intentions.

The countenance of Terregannœuck was oval, with a sufficiently prominent nose, and had nothing very different from a European face, except in the smallness of his eyes, and, perhaps, in the narrowness of his forehead. His complexion was very fresh and red, and he had a longer heard than I had seen on any of the aboriginal inhabitants of America. It was between two and three inches long, and perfectly white. His face was not tattooed. His dress consisted of a shirt, or jacket with a hood, wide breeches, reaching only to the knee, and tight leggins sewed to the shoes, all of deer skins. The soles of the shoes were made of seal-skin, and stuffed with feathers instead of socks. He was bent with age, but appeared to be about five feet ten inches high. His hands and feet were small in proportion to his height. Whenever Terregannœuck received a present, he placed each article first on his right shoulder, then on his left; and when he wished to express still higher satisfaction, he rubbed it over his head. He held hatchets, and other iron instruments, in the highest esteem. On seeing his countenance in a glass for the first time, he exclaimed, "I shall never kill deer more," and immediately put the mirror down. The tribe to which he belongs repair to the sea in spring, and kill seals; as the season advances they hunt deer and musk oxen at some distance from the coast. Their weapon is the bow and arrow, and they get sufficiently nigh the deer, either by crawling, or by leading these animals by ranges of turf towards a spot where the archer can conceal himself. Their bows are formed of three pieces of fir, the centre piece alone bent, the other two lying in the same straight line with the bowstring; the pieces are neatly tied together with sinew. Their canoes are similar to those we saw in Hudson's Straits, but smaller. They get fish constantly in the rivers, and in the sea as soon as the ice breaks up. This tribe do not make use of nets, but are tolerably successful with the hook and line. Their cooking utensils are made of pot-stone, and they form very neat dishes of fir, the sides being made of thin deal, bent into an oval form, secured at the ends by sewing and fitted so nicely to the bottom as to be perfectly water-tight. They have also large spoons made of the horns of the musk oxen.

Akaitcho and the Indians arrived at our tents in the evening, and we learned that they had seen the Esquimaux the day before, and endeavoured, without success, to open a communication with them. They exhibited no hostile intention, but were afraid to advance. Akaitcho, keeping out of their sight, followed at a distance, expecting that ultimately finding themselves enclosed between our party and his, they would be compelled to come to a parley with one of us. Akaitcho had seen Terregannœuck soon after our departure; he was much terrified, and thrust his spear at him as he had done at Augustus; but was soon reconciled after the demonstrations of kindness the Indians made, in cutting off the buttons from their dress to present to him.

July 17

We waited all this forenoon in momentary expectation of the return of Augustus and Junius, but as they did not appear at two P.M., I sent Mr. Hood with a party of men, to inquire into the cause of their detention, and to bring the meat which Terregannœuck had promised us. He returned at midnight with the information that none of the Esquimaux had yet ventured to come near Terregannœuck except his aged wife, who had concealed herself amongst the rocks at our first interview; and she told him the rest of the party had gone to a river, a short distance to the westward, where there was another party of Esquimaux fishing. Augustus and Junius had erected the tent, and done everything in their power to make the old man comfortable in their absence. Terregannœuck being unable to walk to the place where the meat was concealed, readily pointed the spot out to Mr. Hood, who went thither; but after experiencing much difficulty in getting at the column of rock on which it was deposited, he found it too putrid for our use. The features of Terregannœuck's wife were remarkable for roundness and flatness; her face was much tattooed, and her dress differed little from the old man's.

In the afternoon a party of nine Esquimaux appeared on the east bank of the river, about a mile below our backs; but they turned and fled as soon as they perceived our tents. The appearance of so many different bands of Esquimaux terrified the Indians so much, that they deter-mined on leaving us the next day, lest they should be surrounded and their retreat cut off. I endeavoured, by the offer of any remuneration they would choose, to prevail upon one or two of the hunters to proceed, but in vain; and I had much difficulty even in obtaining their promise to wait at the Copper Mountains for Mr. Wentzel and the four men, whom I intended to discharge at the sea.

The fears which our interpreters, St. Germain and Adam, entertained respecting the voyage, were now greatly increased, and both of them came this evening to request their discharge, urging that their services could be no longer requisite, as the Indians were going from us. St. Germain even said that he had understood he was only engaged to accompany us as long as the Indians did, and persisted in this falsehood until his agreement to go with us throughout the voyage had been twice read to him. As these were the only two of the party on whose skill in hunting we could rely, I was unable to listen for a moment to their desire of quitting us, and lest they should leave us by stealth, their motions were strictly watched. This was not an unnecessary precaution, as I was informed that they had actually laid a plan for eloping; but the rest of the men knowing that their own safety would have been compromised had they succeeded, kept a watchful eye over them. We knew that the dread of the Esquimaux would prevent these men from leaving us as soon as the Indians were at a distance, and we trusted to their becoming reconciled to the Journey when once the novelty of a sea voyage had worn off.

July 18

As the Indians persevered in their determination of setting out this morning, I reminded them, through Mr. Wentzel and St. Germain, of the necessity of our having the deposit of provision made at Fort Enterprise, and received a renewed assurance of their attending to that point. They were also desired to put as much meat as they could *en cache* on the banks of the Copper-Mine River on their return. We then furnished them with what ammunition we could spare, and they took their departure, promising to wait three days for Mr. Wentzel at the Copper Mountains. We afterwards learned that their fears did not permit them to do so, and that Mr. Wentzel did not rejoin them until they were a day's march to the southward of the mountains.

We embarked at five A.M. and proceeded towards the sea, which is about nine miles beyond the Bloody Fall. After passing a few rapids, the river became wider, and more navigable for canoes, flowing between banks of alluvial sand. We encamped at ten on the western bank at its junction with the sea. The river is here about a mile wide, but very shallow, being barred nearly across by sand banks, which run out from the main land on each side to a low alluvial island that lies in the centre, and forms two channels; of these the westernmost only is navigable even for canoes, the other being obstructed by a stony bar. The islands to seaward are high and numerous, and fill the horizon in many points of the compass; the only open space, seen from an eminence near the encampulent, being from N.bE. to N.E.bN. Towards the east the land was like a chain of islands, the ice apparently surrounding them in a compact body, leaving a channel between its edge and the main of about three miles. The water in this channel was of a clear green colour, and decidedly salt. Mr. Hearne could have tasted it only at the mouth of the river, when he pronounced it merely brackish. A rise and fall of four inches in the water was observed. The shore is strewed with a considerable quantity of drift timber, principally of the *populus balsamifera*, but none of it of great size. We also picked up some decayed wood far out of the reach of the water. A few stunted willows were growing near the encampment. Some ducks, gulls, and partridges were seen this day. As I had to make up despatches for England to be sent by Mr. Wentzel, the nets were set in the interim, and we were rejoiced to find that they produced sufficient fish for the party. Those caught were, the Copper-Mine River salmon, white-fish, and two species of pleuronectes. We felt a considerable change of temperature on reaching the seacoast, produced by the winds changing from the southward to the N.W. Our Canadian voyagers complained much of the cold, but they were amused with their first view of the sea, and particularly with the sight of the seals that were swimming about near the entrance of the river, but these sensations gave place to despondency before the evening had elapsed. They were terrified at the idea of a voyage through an icy sea in bark canoes. They speculated on the length of the journey, the roughness of the waves, the uncertainty of provisions, the exposure to cold where we could expect no fuel, and the prospect of having to traverse the barren grounds to get to some establishment The two interpreters expressed their apprehensions with the least disguise, and again urgently applied to be discharged; but only one of the Canadians made a similar request. Judging that the constant occupation of their time as soon as we were enabled to commence the voyage would prevent them from conjuring up so many causes of fear, and that familiarity with the scenes on the coast would in a short time enable them to give scope to their natural cheerfulness, the officers endeavoured to ridicule their fears, and happily succeeded for the present. The manner in which our faithful Hepburn viewed the element to which he had been so long accustomed, contributed not a little to make them ashamed of their fears.

On the morning of the 19th, Dr. Richardson, accompanied by Augustus, paid another visit to Terregannœuck, to see if he could obtain any additional information respecting the country to the eastward; but he was disappointed at finding that his affrighted family had not yet rejoined him, and the old man could add nothing to his former communication. The Doctor remarked that Terragannœuck had a great dislike to mentioning the name of the Copper-Mine River, and evaded the question with much dexterity as often as it was put to him; but that he willingly told the name of a river to the eastward, and also of his tribe. He attempted to persuade Augustus to remain with him, and offered him one of his daughters for a wife. These Esquimaux strike fire with two stones, catching the sparks in the down of the catkins of a willow.

The despatches being finished were delivered this evening to Mr. Wentzel, who parted from us at eight P.M. with Parent, Gagnier, Dumas, and Forcier, Canadians, whom I discharged for the purpose of reducing our expenditure of provision as much as possible. The remainder of the party, including officers, amounted to twenty persons. I made Mr. Wentzel acquainted with the probable course of our future proceedings, and mentioned to him that if we were far distant from this river, when the season or other circumstances rendered it necessary to put a stop to our advance, we should, in all probability, be unable to return to it, and should have to travel across the barren grounds towards some established post: in which case I told him that we should certainly go first to Fort Enterprise, expecting that he would cause the Indians to place a supply of dried provision there, as soon as possible after their arrival in its vicinity. My instructions to him were, that he should proceed to Point Lake, transport the canoe that was left there to Fort Enterprise, where he was to embark the instruments and books, and carry them to Slave Lake, and to forward the box containing the journals, etc., with the present despatches, by the next winter packet to England. But before he quitted Fort Enterprise, he was to be assured of the intention of the Indians to lay up the provision we required, and if they should be in want of ammunition for that purpose to procure it if possible from Fort Providence, or the other forts in Slave Lake, and send it immediately to them by the hunters who accompanied him thither. I also requested him to ascertain from Akaitcho and the other leading Indians, where their different parties would be hunting in the months of September and October, and to leave this information in a letter at Fort Enterprise, for our guidance in finding them, as we should require their assistance. Mr. Wentzel was furnished with a list of the stores that had been promised to Akaitcho and his party as a remuneration for their services, as well as with an official request to the North-West Company that these goods might be paid to them on their next visit to Fort Providence, which they expected to make in the latter part of November. I desired him to mention this circumstance to the Indians as an encouragement to exertion in our behalf, and to promise them an additional reward for the supply of provision they should collect at Fort Enterprise

If Mr. Wentzel met the Hook, or any of his party, he was instructed to assure them that he was provided with the necessary documents to get them payment for any-meat they should put *en cache* for our use; and to acquaint them, that we fully relied on their fulfilling every part of the agreement they had made with us. Whenever the Indians, whom he was to join at the Copper Mountains, killed any animals on their way to Fort Enterprise, he was requested to put *en cache* whatever meat could be spared, placing conspicuous marks to guide us to them; and particularly begged he would employ them in hunting in our service, immediately after his arrival at the house.

When Mr. Wentzel's party had been supplied with ammunition, our remaining stock consisted of one thousand balls, and rather more than the requisite proportion of powder. A bag of small shot was missing, and we afterwards discovered that the Canadians had secreted and distributed it among themselves, in order that when provision should become scarce, they might privately procure ducks and geese and avoid the necessity of sharing them with the officers.

The situation of our encampment was ascertained to be, latitude 67° 47′ 50″ N., longitude 115° 36′ 49″ W., the variation of the compass 46° 25′ 52″ E., and dip of the needle 88° 5′ 07″.

It will be perceived, that the position of the mouth of the river, given by our observations, differs widely from that assigned by Mr. Hearne; but the accuracy of his description, conjoined with Indian information, assured us that we were at the very part he visited. I therefore named the most conspicuous cape we then saw "Cape Hearne," as a just tribute to the memory of that persevering traveller. I distinguished another cape by the name of Mackenzie, in honour of Sir Alexander Mackenzie, the only other European[1] who had before reached the Northern Ocean. I called the river which falls into the sea, to the westward of the Copper-Mine, Richardson, as a testimony of sincere regard for my friend and companion Dr. Richardson; and named the islands which were in view from our encampment, "Couper's Isles," in honour of a friend of his. The sun set this night at thirty minutes after eleven, apparent time.

The travelling distance from Fort Enterprise to the north of the Copper-Mine River, is about three hundred and thirty-four miles. The canoes and baggage were dragged over snow and ice for one hundred and seventeen miles of this distance.

1 Captain Parry's success was at this time unknown to us.

CHAPTER XI

*Navigation of the Polar Sea, in two Canoes, as far as Cape
Turnagain, to the Eastward, a distance exceeding Five Hundred
and Fifty Miles – Observations on the probability of a North-West
Passage.*

July 20, 1821

We intended to have embarked early this morning, and to have launched upon an element more congenial with our habits than the fresh-water navigations, with their numerous difficulties and impediments which we had hitherto encountered, but which was altogether new to our Canadian voyagers. We were detained, however by a strong north-east gale, which continued the whole day, with constant thunder showers; the more provoking as our nets procured but few fish, and we had to drawn upon our store of dried meat; which, with other provisions for the journey, amounted only to fifteen days' consumption. Indeed, we should have preferred going dinnerless to bed rather than encroach on our small stock, had we not been desirous of satisfying the appetites, and cheering the spirits of our Canadian companions at the commencement of our voyage. These thoughtless people would at any time incur the hazard of absolute starvation, at a future period, for the present gratification of their appetites; to indulge which they do not hesitate, as we more than once experienced, at helping themselves secretly; it being in their opinion no disgrace to be detected in pilfering food.

Our only luxury now was a little salt, which had long been our substitute both for bread and vegetables. Since our departure from Point Lake we had boiled the Indian tea plant, *ledum palustre*, which produced a beverage in smell much resembling rhubarb; notwithstanding which we found it refreshing, and were gratified to see this plant flourishing abundantly on the sea-shore, though of dwarfish growth.

July 21

The wind, which had blown strong through the night, became moderate in the morning, but a dense fog prevented us from embarking until noon, when we commenced our voyage on the Hyperborean Sea. Soon afterwards we landed on an island where the Esquimaux had erected a stage of drift timber, and stored up many of their fishing implements and winter sledges, together with a great many dressed seal, musk ox, and deer skins. Their spears, headed with bone, and many small articles of the same material, were worked with extreme neatness, as well as their wooden dishes, and cooking utensils of stone; and several articles, very elegantly formed of bone, were evidently intended for some game, but Augustus was unacquainted with their use. We took from this deposit four seal-skins to repair our shoes, and left in exchange a copper-kettle, some awls and beads.

We paddled all day along the coast to the eastward, on the inside of a crowded range of islands, and saw very little ice; the "blink" of it, however, was visible to the northward, and one small iceberg was seen at a distance. A tide was distinguishable among the islands by the foam floating on the water, but we could not ascertain its direction. In the afternoon St. Germain killed on an island a fat deer, which was a great acquisition to us; it was the first we had seen for some months in good condition.

Having encamped on the main shore, after a run of thirty-seven miles, we set up a pole to ascertain the rise and fall of the water, which was repeated at every halting place, and Hepburn was ordered to attend to the result. We found the coast well covered with vegetation, of moderate height, even in its outline, and easy of approach. The islands are rocky and barren, presenting high cliffs of a columnar structure. I have named the westernmost group of those we passed "Berens' Isles," in honour of the Governor of the Hudson's Bay Company; and the easternmost, "Sir Graham Moore's Islands." at the spot where we landed some mussel-shells and a single piece of seaweed lay on the beach; this was the only spot on the coast where we saw shells. We were rejoiced to find the beach strewed with abundance of small drift wood, none of it recent.

It may be remarked that the Copper-Mine River does not bring down any drift wood; nor does any other known stream except Mackenzie's River; hence, from its appearance on this part of the coast an easterly current may be inferred. This evening we were all in high glee at the progress we had made; the disappearance of the ice, and the continuance of the land in an eastern direction, and our future prospects, formed an enlivening subject of conversation. The thermometer varied during the day between 43° and 45°. The fishing-nets were set, but produced nothing.

On the 22nd we embarked at four A.M., and having the benefit of a light breeze continued our voyage along the coast under sail, until eleven, when we halted to breakfast, and to obtain the latitude. The coast up to this point presented the same general appearance as yesterday, namely, a gravelly or sandy beach, skirted by green plains; but as we proceeded, the shore became exceedingly rocky and sterile; and, at last, projecting considerably to the northward, it formed a high and steep promontory. Some ice had drifted down upon this cape, which, we feared, might check our progress; but, as the evening was fine, we ventured upon pushing the canoes through the small channels formed along it. After pursuing this kind of navigation, with some danger and more anxiety, we landed and encamped on a smooth rocky point; whence we perceived, with much satisfaction, that the ice consisted only of detached pieces, which would be removed by the first breeze. We sounded in seventeen fathoms, close to the shore, this day. The least depth ascertained by the lead, since our departure from the river, was six fathoms; and any ship might pass safely between the islands and the main. The water is of a light colour, but not very clear; and much less salt than that of the Atlantic, judging from our recollection of its taste. In the course of the day we saw geese and ducks with their young, and two deer; and experienced very great variations of temperature, from the light breezes blowing alternately from the ice and the land. The name of "Lawford's Islands" was bestowed on a group we passed in the course of the day, as a mark of my respect for Vice-Admiral Lawford, under whose auspices I first entered the naval service.

A fresh breeze blowing through the night had driven the ice from the land, and opened a channel of a mile in width; we, therefore, embarked at nine A.M. to pursue our journey along the coast, but at the distances of nine miles were obliged to seek shelter in Port Epworth, the wind having become adverse, and too strong to admit of our proceeding. The Tree River of the Esquimaux, which discharges its waters into this bay, appears to be narrow, and must interrupted by rapids. The fishing-nets were set, but obtained only one white-fish and a few bull-heads. This part of the coast is the most sterile and inhospitable that can be imagined. One trap-cliff succeeds another with tiresome uniformity, and their *Débris* cover the narrow valleys that intervene, to the exclusion of every kind of herbage. From the summit of these cliffs the ice appeared in every direction.

We obtained the following observations during our stay; latitude 67° 42′ 15″ N., longitude 112° 30′ 00″ W., variation 47° 37′ 42″ E.

The wind abating, at eight P.M. we re-embarked, and soon afterwards discovered, on an island, a reindeer, which the interpreters fortunately killed. Resuming our voyage we were much impeded by the ice, and, at length, being unable to force a passage through a close stream that had collected round a cape, we put ashore at four A.M. On the 24th, several stone fox-traps and other traces of the Esquimaux were seen near the encampment. The horizontal refraction varied so much this morning, that the upper limp of the sun twice appeared at the horizon before it finally rose.

For the last two days the water rose and fell about nine inches. The tides, however, seemed to be very irregular, and we could not determine the direction of the ebb or flood. A current setting to the eastward was running about two miles an hour during our stay. The ice having removed a short distance from the shore, by eleven A.M. we embarked, and with some difficulty effected a passage; then making a traverse across Gray's Bay,[1] we paddled up under the eastern shore against a strong wind. The interpreters landed here, and went in pursuit of a deer, but had no success. This part of the coast is indented by deep bays, which are separated by peninsulas formed like wedges, sloping many miles into the sea, and joined by low land to the main: so that often mistaking them for islands, we were led by a circuitous route round the bays. Cliffs were numerous on the islands, which were all of the trap formation.

At seven, a thunderstorm coming on, we encamped at the mouth of a river about eighty yards wide and set four nets. This stream, which received the name of Wentzel, after our late companion, discharges a considerable body of water. Its banks are sandy and clothed with herbage. The Esquimaux had recently piled up some drift timber here. A few ducks, ravens, and snow-birds were seen today. The distance made was thirty-one miles.

July 25

We had constant rain with thunder during the night. The nets furnished only three salmon-trout. We attributed the want of greater success to the entrance of some seals into the mouth of the river. Embarking at six A.M. we paddled against a cold breeze, until the spreading of a thick fog caused us to land. The rocks here consisted of a beautiful mixture of red and gray granite, traversed from north to south by veins of red felspar, which were crossed in various directions by smaller veins filled with the same substance.

At noon the wind coming from a favourable quarter tempted us to proceed, although the fog was unabated. We kept as close as we could to the main shore, but having to cross some bays, it became a matter of doubt whether we had not left the main, and were running along an island. Just as we were endeavouring to double a

1 Named after Mr. Gray, principal of the Belfast Academy. An island which lies across the mouth of this bay bears the name of our English sailor Hepburn.

bold cape, the fog partially cleared away, and allowed us an imperfect view of a chain of islands on the outside, and of much heavy ice which was pressing down upon us. The coast near us was so steep and rugged that no landing of the cargoes could be effected, and we were preserved only by some men jumping on the rocks, and thrusting the ice off with poles. There was no alternative but to continue along this dreary shore, seeking a channel between the different masses of ice which had accumulated at the various points. In this operation both the canoes were in imminent danger of being crushed by the ice, which was now tossed about by the waves that the gale had excited. We effected a passage, however, and keeping close to the shore, landed at the entrance of Detention Harbour, at nine P.M., having come twenty-eight miles. An old Esquimaux encampment was traced on this spot; and an ice chisel, a copper knife, and a small iron knife were found under the turf. I named this cape after Mr. Barrow of the Admiralty, to whose exertions are mainly owing the discoveries recently made in Arctic geography. An opening on its eastern side received the appellation of Inman Harbour, after my friend the Professor at the Royal Naval College, Portsmouth; and to a group of islands to seaward of it, we gave the name of Jameson, in honour of the distinguished Professor of Mineralogy at Edinburgh.

We had much wind and rain during the night; and by the morning of the 26th a great deal of ice had drifted into the inlet. We embarked at four and attempted to force a passage, when the first canoe got enclosed, and remained for some time in a very perilous situation: the pieces of ice, crowded together by the action of the current and wind, pressing strongly against its feeble sides. A partial opening, however, occurring, we landed without having sustained any serious injury. Two men were then set round the bay, and it was ascertained that instead of having entered a narrow passage between an island and the main, we were at the mouth of a harbour, having an island at its entrance; and that it was necessary to return by the way we came, and get a point to the northward. This was, however, impracticable, the channel being blocked up by drift ice; and we had no prospect of release except by a change of wind. This detention was extremely vexatious, as we were losing a fair wind, and expending our provision. In the afternoon the weather cleared up, and several men went hunting, but were unsuccessful. During the day the ice floated backwards and forwards in the harbour, moved by currents, not regular enough to deserve the name of tide, and which appeared to be governed by the wind. We perceived a great diminution by melting in the pieces near us. That none of this ice survives the summer is evident, from the rapidity of its decay; and because no ice of last year's formation was hanging on the rocks. Whether any body of it exists at a distance from the shore, we could not determine.

The land around Cape Barrow, and to Detention Harbour, consists of steep craggy mountains of granite, rising so abruptly from the water's edge, as to admit few landing-places even for a canoe. The higher parts attain an elevation of fourteen or fifteen hundred feet; and the whole is entirely destitute of vegetation.

On the morning of the 27th, the ice remaining stationary at the entrance, we went to the bottom of the harbour, and carried the canoes and cargoes about a mile and a half across the point of land that forms the east side of it; but the ice was not more favourable there for our advancement than at the place we had left. It consisted of small pieces closely packed together by the wind, extending along the shore, but leaving a clear passage beyond the chain of islands with which the whole of this coast is girt. Indeed, when we left the harbour we had little hope of finding a passage; and the principal object in moving was, to employ the men, in order to prevent their reflecting upon and discussing the dangers of our situation, which we knew they were too apt to do when leisure permitted. Our observations place the entrance of Detention Harbour in latitude 67° 53′ 45″, longitude 110° 41′ 20″ W., variation 40° 49′ 34″ E. It is a secure anchorage, being sheltered from the wind in every direction; the bottom is sandy.

July 28

As the ice continued in the same state, several of the men were sent out to hunt; and one of them fired no less than four times at deer, but unfortunately without success. It was satisfactory, however, to ascertain that the country was not destitute of animals. We had the mortification to discover that two of the bags of pemmican, which was our principal reliance, had become mouldy by wet. Our beef too had been so badly cured, as to be scarcely eatable, through our having been compelled, from haste, to dry it by fire instead of the sun. It was not, however, the quality of our provision that gave us uneasiness, but its diminution, and the utter incapacity to obtain any addition. Seals were the only animals that met our view at this place, and these we could never approach.

Dr. Richardson discovered near the beach a small vein of galena, traversing gneiss rocks, and the people collected a quantity of it in this hope of adding to our stock of balls; but their endeavours to smelt it, were, as may be supposed, ineffectual. The drift timber on this part of the coast consists of pine and taccamahac (*populous balsamifera*), most probably from Mackenzie's, or some other river to the westward of the Copper-Mine. It all appears to have lain long in the water, the bark being completely worn off, and the ends of the pieces rubbed perfectly smooth. There had been a sharp frost in the night, which formed a pretty thick crust of ice in a kettle of water that stood in the tents; and for several nights thin films of ice had appeared on the salt water amongst the cakes of stream ice.[1] Notwithstanding this state of temperature, we were tormented by swarms of musquitoes; we had persuaded ourselves that these pests could not sustain the cold in the vicinity of the sea, but it appears they haunt every part of this country in defiance of climate. Mr. Back made an excursion to a hill at seven or eight miles' distance, and from its summit he perceived the ice close to the shore as far as his view extended.

On the morning of the 29th the party attended divine service. About noon the ice appearing less compact, we embarked to change our situation, having consumed all the fuel within our reach. The wind came off the land just as the canoes had started, and we determined on attempting to force a passage along the shore; in which we happily succeeded, after seven hours' labour and much hazard to our frail vessels. The ice lay so close that the crews disembarked on it, and effected a passage by bearing against the pieces with their poles; but in conducting the canoes through the narrow channels thus formed, the greatest care was requisite, to prevent the sharp projecting points from breaking the bark. They fortunately received no material injury, though they were split in two places.

At the distance of three miles, we came to the entrance of a deep bay, whose bottom was filled by a body of ice so compact as to preclude the idea of a passage through it; whilst at the same time, the traverse across its mouth was attended with much danger, from the approach of a large field of ice, which was driving down before the wind. The dread of further detention, however, prevented us from hesitating; as we had the satisfaction of landing in an hour and a half on the opposite shore, where we halted to repair the canoes and to dine. I have named this

1 This is termed *bay-ice* by the Greenland-men.

bay after my friend Mr. Daniel Moor of Lincoln's Inn; to whose zeal for science, the Expedition was indebted for the use of a most valuable chronometer. Its shores are picturesque; sloping hills receding from the beach, and closed with verdure, bound its bottom and western side; and lofty cliffs of slate clay, with their intervening grassy valleys, skirt its eastern border. Embarking at midnight, we pursued our voyage without interruption, passing between the Stockport and Marcet Islands and the main, until six A.M. on July 30th; when, having rounded Point Kater, we entered Arctic Sound, and were again involved in a stream of ice, but after considerable delay extricated ourselves, and proceeded towards the bottom of the inlet in search of the mouth of a river, which we supposed it to receive, from the change in the colour of the water.

About ten A.M. we landed, to breakfast on a small deer which St. Germain had killed; and sent men in pursuit of some others in sight, but with which they did not come up. Re-embarking, we passed the river without perceiving it, and entered a deep arm of the sound; which I have named Baillie's Cove, in honour of a relative of the lamented Mr hood. As it was too late to return, we encamped, and by walking across the country discovered the river, whose mouth being barred by low sandy islands and banks, was not perceived when we passed it. Course and distance from Galena Point to this encampment were S.E.¾S. – forty-one miles.

From the accounts of Black-Meat and Boileau at Fort Chipewyan, we considered this river to be the Anatessy; and Cape Barrow to be the projection which they supposed to be the N.W. termination of America. They outline of the coast, indeed, bears some resemblance to the chart they sketched; and the distance of this river from the Copper-Mine, nearly coincides with that we estimated the Anatessy to be, from their statements. In our subsequent journey, however, across the barren grounds we ascertained that this conjecture was wrong, and that the Anatessy, which is known to come from Rum Lake, must fall into the sea to the eastward of this place.

Our stock of provision being now reduced to eight days' consumption, it had become a matter of the first importance to obtain a supply; and as we had learned from Terrregannoeuck that the Esquimaux frequent the rivers at this season, I determined on seeking a communication with them here, in the hope of obtaining relief for our present wants, or even shelter for the winter, if the season should prevent us returning either to the Hook's party, or Fort Enterprise; and I was the more induced to take this step at this time, as several deer had been seen to-day, and the river appeared good for fishing; which led me to hope we might support the party during our stay, if not add to our stock by our own exertions in hunting and fishing. Augustus, Junius, and Hepburn, were therefore furnished with the necessary presents, and desired to go along the bank of the river as far as they could, on the following day, in search of the natives, to obtain provision and leather, as well as information respecting the coast.

They started at four A.M., and at the same time our hunters were sent off in search of deer: and the rest of the party proceeded in the canoes to the first cascade in the river, at the foot of which we encamped, and set four nets. This cascade, produced by a ridge of rocks crossing the stream, is about three or four feet in height, and about two hundred and fifty yards wide. Its position by our observations in latitude 67° 19′ 23″ N., longitude 109° 44′ 30″ W., variation 41° 43′ 22″, dip 88° 58′ 48″. I have named this river Hood, as a small tribute to the memory of our lamented friend and companion. It is from three to four hundred yards wide below the cascade, but in many places very shallow. The banks, bottom, and adjacent hills, are formed of a mixture of sand and clay. The ground was overspread with small willows and the dwarf birch, both too diminutive for fuel; and the stream brought down no drift wood. We were mortified to find the nets only procured one salmon and five white-fish, and that we had to make another inroad upon our dried meat.

August 1

At two this morning the hunters returned with two small deer and a brown bear. Augustus and Junius arrived at the same time, having traced the river twelve miles farther up, without discovering any vestige of inhabitants. We had now an opportunity of gratifying our curiosity respecting the bear so much dreaded by the Indians, and of whose strength and ferocity we had heard such terrible accounts. It proved to be a lean male of a yellowish brown colour, and not longer than a common black bear. It made a feeble attempt to defend itself, and was easily despatched. The flesh was brought to the tent, but our fastidious voyagers supposing from its leanness, that the animal had been sickly, declined eating it; the officers, however, being less scrupulous, boiled the paws, and found them excellent.

We embarked at ten A.M., and proceeding down the river, took on board another deer that had been killed by Crédit last evening. We then ran along the eastern shore of Arctic Sound, distinguished by the name of Banks' Peninsula, in honour of the late Right Honourable Sir Joseph Banks, President of the Royal Society; and rounding Point Wollaston at its eastern extremity, opened another extensive sheet of water; and the remainder of the afternoon was spent in endeavouring to ascertain, from the tops of the hills, whether it was another bay, or merely a passage enclosed by a chain of islands. Appearances rather favouring the latter opinion, we determined on proceeding through it to the southward. During the delay four more deer were killed, all young and lean. It appeared that the coast is pretty well frequented by reindeer at this season; but it was rather singular, that hitherto we had killed none (excepting the first) but young ones of last season, which were all too lean to have been eaten by any but persons who had no choice.

We paddled along the western shore with the intention of encamping, but were prevented by the want of drift wood on the beach. This induced us to make a traverse to an island, where we put up at midnight, having found a small bay, whose shores furnished up with a little firewood. A heavy gale came on from the westward, attended with constant rain, and one of the squalls overthrew our tents. The course and distance made this day were north-east sixteen miles and a half. I may here mention, that Arctic Sound appeared the most convenient, and perhaps the best place for ships to anchor that we had seen along the coast; at this season especially, when they might increase their stock of provision, if provided with good marksmen. Deer are numerous in its vicinity, musk oxen also may be found up Hood's River, and the fine sandy bottom of the bays promises favourably for fishing with the seine. The hills on the western side are even in their outline and slope gradually to the water's edge. The rocks give place to an alluvial sandy soil, towards the bottom of the Sound; but on Banks' Peninsula rocky eminences again prevail, which are rugged and uneven, but intersected by valleys, at this time green; along their base is a fine sandy beach. From Point Wollaston to our encampment the coast is skirted with trap cliffs, which have often a columnar form, and are very difficult of access. These cliffs lie in ranges parallel to the shore, and the deer that we killed were feeding in small marshy grassy plats that lie in the valleys between them.

Being detained by the continuance of the gale on the 2nd August some men were sent out to hunt, and the officers visited the tops of the highest hills to ascertain the best channels to be pursued. The wind abating at ten P.M., we embarked and paddled round the southern end of the island, and continued our course to the south-east. Much doubt at this time prevailed as to the land on the right being the main shore, or merely a chain of islands. The latter opinion was strengthened by the broken appearance of the land, and the extensive view we had up Brown's Channel (named after my friend Mr. Robert Brown), the mouth of which we passed, and were in some apprehension of being led away from the main shore and, perhaps, after passing through a group of islands, of coming to a traverse greater than we durst venture upon in canoes: on the other hand, the continuous appearance of the land on the north side of the channel, and its tending to the southward excited the fear that we were entering a deep inlet.

In this state of doubt we landed often, and endeavoured, from the summits of the highest hills adjoining the shore, to ascertain the true nature of the coast, but in vain, and we continued paddling through the channel all night against a fresh breeze, which, at half-past four, increased to a violent gale, and compelled us to land. The gale diminished a short time after noon on the 3rd and permitted us to re-embark and continue our voyage until four P.M., when it returned with its former violence, and finally obliged us to encamp, having come twenty-four miles on a south-east three-quarter south course.

From the want of drift wood to make a fire we had fasted all day, and were under the necessity, in the evening, of serving out pemmican, which was done with much reluctance, especially as we had some fresh deers' meat remaining. The inlet, when viewed from a high hill adjoining to our encampment, exhibited so many arms, that the course we ought to pursue was more uncertain than ever. It was absolutely necessary, however, to see the end of it before we could determine that it was not a strait. Starting at three A.M., on the 4th, we paddled the whole day through channels, from two to five or six miles wide, all tending to the southward. In the course of the day's voyage we ascertained, that the land which we had seen on our right since yesterday morning, consisted of several large islands, which have been distinguished by the names of Goulburn, Elliott, and Young; but the land on our left preserved its unbroken appearance, and when we encamped, we were still uncertain whether it was the eastern side of a deep sound or merely a large island. It differed remarkably from the main shore, being very rugged, rocky, and sterile, whereas the outline of the main on the opposite side was even, and its hills covered with a comparatively good sward of grass, exhibiting little naked rock. There was no drift timber, but the shores near the encampment were strewed with small pieces of willow, which indicated our vicinity to the mouth of a river. This fuel enabled us to make a hearty supper from a small deer killed this evening.

The shallows we passed this day were covered with shoals of *capelin*, the angmaggoeük of the Esquimaux. It was known to Augustus, who informed us that it frequents the coast of Hudson's Bay, and is delicate eating. The course and distance made was, south by east-half-east, thirty-three miles.

After paddling twelve miles in the morning of the 5th, we had the mortification to find the inlet terminated by a river; the size of which we could not ascertain, as the entrance was blocked by shoals. Its mouth lies in latitude 66° 30′ N., longitude 107° 53′ W. I have named this stream Back, as a mark of my friendship for my associate.[1] We were somewhat consoled for the loss of time in exploring this inlet,

1 From subsequent conversation with the Copper Indians, we were inclined to suppose this may be the Thlueetessy, described by Black Meat, mentioned in a former part of the narrative.

by the success of Junius in killing a musk ox, the first we had seen on the coast; and afterwards by the acquisition of the flesh of a bear, that was shot as we were returning up the eastern side in the evening. The latter proved to be a female, in very excellent condition; and our Canadian voyagers, whose appetite for fat meat is insatiable, were delighted.

We encamped on the shores a sandy bay, and set the nets; and finding a quantity of dried willows on the beach, we were enabled to cook the bear's flesh, which was superior to any meat we tasted on the coast. The water fell two feet at this place during the night. Our nets produced a great variety of fish, namely, a salmon trout, some round fish, tittameg, bleak, star-fish, several herrings, and a flat fish resembling plaice, but covered on the back with horny excrescences.

On the 6th we were detained in the encampment by stormy weather until five P.M., when we embarked and paddled along the northern shore of the inlet; the weather still continuing foggy, but the wind moderate. Observing on the beach a she-bear with three young ones, we landed a party to attack them: but being approached without due caution, they took the alarm and scaled a precipitous rocky hill, with a rapidity that baffled all pursuit. At eight o'clock, the fog changing into rain, we encamped. Many seals were seen this day, but as they kept in deep water we did not fire at them.

On August 7th the atmosphere was charged with fog and rain all the day, but as the wind was moderate we pursued our journey; our situation, however, was very unpleasant, being quite wet and without room to stretch a limb, much less to obtain warmth by exercise. We passed a cover which I have named after my friend Mr. W. H. Tinney; and proceeded along the coast until five P.M., when we put up on a rocky point nearly opposite to our encampment on the 3rd, having come twenty-three miles on a north-north-west course.

We were detained on the 8th by a northerly gale, which blew violently throughout the day, attended by fog and rain. Some of the men went out to hunt, but they saw no other animal than a white wolf, which could not be approached. The fresh meat being expended, a little pemmican was served out this evening.

The gale abated on the morning of the 9th; and the sea, which it had raised, having greatly subsided, we embarked at seven A.M., and after paddling three or four miles, opened Sir J. A. Gordon's Bay, into which we penetrated thirteen miles, and then discovered from the summit of a hill that it would be vain to proceed in this direction, in search of a passage out of the inlet.

Our breakfast diminished our provision to two bags of pemmican, and a single meal of dried meat. The men began to apprehend absolute want of food, and we had to listen to their gloomy forebodings of the deer entirely quitting the coast in a few days. As we were embarking, however, a large bear was discovered on the opposite shore, which we had the good fortune to kill; and the sight of this fat meat relieved their fears for the present. Dr. Richardson found in the stomach of this animal the remains of a seal, several marmots (*arctomys Richardsonii*), a large quantity of the liquorice root of Mackenzie (*hedysarum*) which is common on these shores, and some berries. There was also intermixed with these substances a small quantity of grass.

We got again into the main inlet, and paddled along its eastern shore until forty minutes after eight A.M. when we encamped in a small cove. We found a single log of drift wood; it was pine, and sufficiently large to enable us to cook a portion of the bear, which had a slight fishy taste, but was deemed very palatable.

August 10

We followed up the east border of the inlet about twenty-four miles, and at length emerged into the open sea; a body of islands to the westward concealing the channel by which we had entered. Here our progress was arrested by returning bad weather. We killed a bear and its young cub of this year on the beach near our encampment. We heartily congratulated ourselves at having arrived at the eastern entrance of this inlet, which had cost us nine invaluable days in exploring. It contains several secure harbours, especially near the mouth of Back's River, where there is a sandy bottom in forty fathoms.

On the 3rd and 4th of August we observed a fall of more than two feet in the water during the night. There are various irregular and partial currents in the inlet, which may be attributed to the wind. I have distinguished it by the name of Bathurst's Inlet, after the noble Secretary of State, under whose orders I had the honour to act. It runs about seventy-six miles south-east from Cape Everitt, but in coasting its shores we went about one hundred and seventy-four geographical miles. It is remarkable that none of the Indians with whom we had spoken mentioned this inlet; and we subsequently learned, that in their journeys, they strike across from the mouth of one river to the mouth of another, without tracing the intermediate line of coast.

August 11

Embarking at five A.M. we rounded Point Everitt, and then encountered a strong breeze and heavy swell, which by causing the canoes to pitch very much, greatly impeded our progress. Some deer being seen grazing in a valley near the beach, we landed and sent St. Germain and Adam in pursuit of them, who soon killed three which were very small and lean. Their appearance, however, quite revived the spirits of our men, who had suspected that the deer had retired to the woods. It would appear, from our not having seen any in passing along the shores of Bathurst's Inlet, that at this season they confine themselves to the sea-coast and the islands. The magpie-berries (*arbutus alpina*) were found quite ripe at this place, and very abundant on the acclivities of the hills. We also ascended the highest hill and gained a view of a distant chain of islands, extending as far as the eye could reach, and perceived a few patches of ice still lingering round to some of them' but in every other part the sea was quite open. Resuming our voyage after noon, we proceeded along the coast, which is fringed by islands; and at five P.M., entered another bay, where we were for some time involved in our late difficulties by the intricacy of the passages; but we cleared them in the afternoon, and encamped near the northern entrance of the bay, at a spot which had recently been visited by a small party of Esquimaux, as the remains of some eggs containing young, were lying beside some half-burnt fire-wood. There were also several piles of stones put up by them. I have named this bay after my friend, Captain David Buchan, of the Royal Navy. It appears to be a safe anchorage, well sheltered from the wind and sea, by islands; and bottom is sandy, the shores high, and composed of red sand-stone. Two deer were seen on its beach, but could not be approached. The distance we made to-day was eighteen miles and three-quarters.

Embarking at four on the morning of the 12th, we proceeded against a fresh piercing north-east wind, which raised the waves to a height that quite terrified our people, accustomed only to the navigation of rivers and lakes. We were obliged, however, to persevere in our advance, feeling as we did, that the short season for our operations was hastening away; but after rounding Cape Croker the wind became so strong that we could proceed no farther. The distance we made was only six miles on a north-east by east course. The shore on which we encamped is formed of the *débris* of red sand-stone, and is destitute of vegetation. The beach furnished no drift wood, and we dispensed with our usual meal rather than expend our pemmican. Several deer were seen, but the hunters could not approach them; they killed two swans. We observed the latitude 68° 1′ 20″, where we had halted to breakfast this morning.

August 13

Though the wind was not much diminished, we were urged, by the want of firewood, to venture upon proceeding. We paddled close to the shore for some miles, and then ran before the breeze with reefed sails, scarcely two feet in depth. Both the canoes received much water, and one of them struck twice on sunken rocks. At the end of eighteen miles we halted to breakfast in a bay, which I have named after Vice-Admiral Sir William Johnstone Hope, one of the Lords of the Admiralty.

We found here a considerable quantity of small willows, such as are brought down by the rivers we had hitherto seen; and hence we judged, that a river discharges itself into the bottom of this bay. A paddle was also found, which Augustus, on examination, declared to be made after the fashion of the White Goose Esquimaux, a tribe with whom his countrymen had had some trading communication, as has been mentioned in a former part of the narrative.

This morning we passed the embouchure of a pretty large stream, and saw the vestiges of an Esquimaux encampment, not above a month old. Having obtained the latitude 68° 6′ 40″ N., we recommenced our voyage under sail, taking the precaution to embark all the pieces of willow we could collect, as we had found the drift wood become more scarce as we advanced. Our course was directed to a distant point, which we supposed to be a cape, and the land stretching to the westward of it to be islands; but we soon found ourselves in an extensive bay, from which no outlet could be perceived but the one by which we had entered. On examination, however, from the top of a hill, we perceived a winding shallow passage running to the north-east, which we followed for a short time, and then encamped, having come twenty-three miles north by east half east.

Some articles left by the Esquimaux attracted our attention; we found a winter sledge raised upon four stones, with some snow-shovels, and a small piece of whalebone. An ice-chisel, a knife and some beads were left at this pile. The shores of this bay, which I have named after Sir George Warrender, are low and clayey, and the country for many miles is level, and much intersected with water; but we had not leisure to ascertain whether they were branches of the bay or fresh-water lakes. Some white geese were seen this evening, and some young gray ones were caught on the beach being unable to fly. We fired at two reindeer, but without success.

On August 14th we paddled the whole day along the northern shores of the sound, returned towards its mouth. The land which we were now tracing is generally so flat, that it could not be descried from the canoes at the distance of four miles, and is invisible from the opposite side of the sound, otherwise a short traverse might have saved us some days. The few eminences that are on this side were mistaken for islands when seen from the opposite shore; they are for the most part cliffs of basalt, and are not above one hundred feet high; the subjacent strata are of white sand-stone. The rocks are mostly confined to the capes and shores, the soil inland being flat, clayey, and barren. Most of the headlands showed traces of visits from the Esquimaux, but none of them recent. Many ducks were seen, belonging to a species termed by the voyagers from their cry, "caccawees." We also saw some gray geese and swans. The only seal we procured during our voyage was killed this day; it happened to be blind, and our men imagining it to be in bad health would not taste the flesh; we, however, were less nice.

We encamped at the end of twenty-four miles' march, on the north-west side of a bay, to which I have given the name of my friend Captain Parry, now employed in the interesting research for a North-West Passage. Drift wood had become very scarce, and we found none near the encampment; a fire, however, was not required, as we served out pemmican for supper, and the evening was unusually warm.

On the following morning the breeze was fresh and the waves rather high. In paddling along the west side of Parry's Bay, we saw several deer, but owing to the openness of the country, the hunters could not approach them. They killed, however, two swans that were moulting, several cranes and many gray geese. We procured also some caccawees, which were then moulting, and assembled in immense flocks. In the evening, having rounded Point Beechy, and passed Hurd's Islands, we were exposed to much inconvenience and danger from a heavy rolling sea; the canoes receiving many severe blows, and shipping a good deal of water, which induced us to encamp at five P.M. opposite to Cape Croker, which we had passed on the morning of the 12th; the channel which lay between our situation and it, being about seven miles wide. We had now reached the northern point of entrance into this sound, which I have named in honour of Lord Viscount Melville, the first Lord of the Admiralty. It is thirty miles wide from east to west, and twenty from north to south; and in coasting it we had sailed eighty-seven and a quarter geographical miles. Shortly after the tents were pitched, Mr. Back reported from the steersmen that both canoes had sustained material injury during this day's voyage. I found on examination that fifteen timbers of the first canoe were broken, some of them in two places, and that the second canoe was so loose in the frame that its timbers could not be bound in the usual secure manner, and consequently there was danger of its bark separating from the gunwhales if exposed to a heavy sea. Distressing as were these circumstances, they have me less pain than the discovery that our people, who had hitherto displayed in following us through dangers and difficulties no less novel than appalling to them, a courage beyond our expectation, now felt serious apprehensions for their safety, which so possessed their minds that they were not restrained even by the presence of their officers from expressing them. Their fears, we imagined, had been principally excited by the interpreters, St. Germain and Adam, who from the outset had foreboded every calamity; and we now strongly suspected that their recent want of success in hunting had proceeded from an intentional relaxation in their efforts to kill deer in order that the want of provision might compel us to put a period to our voyage.

I must now mention that many concurrent circumstances had caused me, during the few last days, to meditate on the approach of this painful necessity. The strong breezes we had encountered for some days, led me to fear that the season was breaking up, and severe weather would soon ensue, which we could not sustain in a country destitute of fuel. Our stock of provision was now reduced to a quantity of pemmican only sufficient for three days' consumption, and the prospect of increasing it was not encouraging, for though reindeer were seen, they could not be easily approached on the level shores we were now coasting, besides it was to be apprehended they would soon migrate to the south. It was evident that the time spent in exploring the Arctic and Melville Sounds, and Bathurst's Inlet, had precluded the hope of reaching Repulse Bay, which at the outset of the voyage we had fondly cherished; and it was equally obvious that as our distance from any of the trading establishments would increase as we proceeded, the hazardous traverse across the barren grounds, which we should have to make, if compelled to abandon the canoes upon any part of the coast, would become greater.

I this evening communicated to the officers of my sentiments on these points, as well as respecting our return, and was happy to find that their opinions coincided with my own. We were all convinced of the necessity of putting a speedy termination to our advance, as our hope of meeting the Esquimaux and procuring provision from them, could now scarcely be retained; but yet we were desirous of proceeding, until the land should be seen trending again to the eastward; that we might be satisfied of its separation from what we had conceived, in passing from Cape Barrow to Bathurst's Inlet, to be a great chain of islands. As it was needful, however, at all events, to set a limit to our voyage, I announced my determination of returning after four days' examination, unless, indeed, we should previously meet the Esquimaux, and be enabled to make some arrangement for passing the winter with them. This communication was joyfully received by the men, and we hoped that the industry of our hunters being once more excited, we should be able to add to our stock of provision.

It may here be remarked that we observed the first regular return of the tides in Warrender's and Parry's Bays; but their set could not be ascertained. The rise of water did not amount to more than two feet. Course to-day south one quarter east – nine miles and a quarter.

August 16

Some rain fell in the night, but the morning was unusually fine. We set forward at five A.M., and the men paddled cheerfully along the coast for ten miles, when a dense fog caused us to land on Slate-clay Point. Here we found more traces of the Esquimaux, and the skull of a man placed between two rocks. The fog dispersed at noon, and we discerned a group of islands to the northward, which I have named after Vice-Admiral Sir George Cockburn, one of the Lords of the Admiralty. Re-embarking, we rounded the point and entered Walker's Bay (so called after my friend Admiral Walker), where, as in other instances, the low beach which lay between several high trap cliffs, could not be distinguished until we had coasted down the east side nearly to the bottom of the bay. When the continuity of the land was perceived, we crossed to the western shore, and on landing, discovered a channel leading through a group of islands. Having passed through this channel, we ran under sail by the Porden Islands, across Riley's Bay, and rounding a cape which now bears the name of my lamented friend Captain Flinders, had one pleasure to find the coast trending north-north-east, with the sea in the offing unusually clear of islands; a circumstance which afforded matter of wonder to our Canadians, who had not previously had an uninterrupted view of the ocean.

Out course was continued along the coast until eight P.M., when a change in the wind and a threatening thunder squall induced us to encamp; but the water was so shallow, that we found some difficulty in approaching the shore. Large pieces of drift wood gave us assurance that we had finally escaped from the bays. Our tents were scarcely pitched before we were assailed by a heavy squall and rain, which was succeeded by a violent gale from west-north-west, which thrice overset the tents during the night. The wind blew with equal violence on the following day, and the sea rolled furiously upon the beach. The Canadians had now an opportunity of witnessing the effect of a storm upon the sea; and the sight increased their desire of quitting it.

Our hunters were sent out, and saw many deer, but the flatness of the country defeated their attempts to approach them; they brought, however, a few unfledged geese. As there was no appearance of increasing our stock of provision, the allowance was limited to a handful of pemmican, and a small portion of portable soup to each man per day. The thermometer this afternoon stood to 41°. The following observations were obtained: latitude 68° 18′ 50″ N., longitude 110° 5′ 15″ W., but 109° 25′ 00″ W. was used in the construction of the chart, as the chronometers were found, on our returned to Hood's River, to have altered their rates; variation 44° 15′ 46″ E., and dip of the needles 89° 31′ 12″.

On August eighteenth the stormy weather and sea continuing, there was no prospect of our being able to embark. Dr. Richardson, Mr. Back, and I, therefore, set out on foot to discover whether the land within a day's march, inclined more to the east. We went from ten to twelve miles along the coast, which continued flat, and kept the same direction as the encampment. The most distant land we saw had the same bearing north-north-east, and appeared like two islands, which we estimated to be six or seven miles off; the shore on their side seemingly tended more to the east, so that is it probable Point Turnagain, for so this spot was named, forms the pitch of a low flat cape.

Augustus killed a deer in the afternoon, but the men were not able to find it. The hunters found the burrows of a number of white foxes, and Hepburn killed one of these animals, which proved excellent eating, equal to the young geese, with which it was boiled, and far superior to the lean deer we had upon the coast. Large flocks of geese passed over the tents, flying to the southward. The lowest temperature to-day was 38°.

Though it will appear from the chart that the position of Point Turnagain is only six degrees and a half to the east of the mouth of the Copper-Mine River; we sailed, in tracing the deeply-indented coast, five hundred and fifty-five geographical miles, which is little less than the direct distance between the Copper-Mine River and Repulse Bay; supposing the latter to be in the longitude assigned to it by Middleton.

When the many perplexing incidents which occurred during the survey of the coast are considered, in connexion with the shortness of the period during which operations of the kind can be carried on, and the distance we had to travel before we could gain a place of shelter for the winter, I trust it will be judged that we prosecuted the enterprise as far as was prudent, and abandoned it only under a well-founded conviction that a farther advance would endanger the lives of the whole party, and prevent the knowledge of what had been done from reaching England. The active assistance I received from the officers, in contending with the fears of the men, demands my warmest gratitude.

Our researches, as far as they have gone, favour the opinion of these who contend for the practicability of a North-West Passage. The general line of coast probably runs east and west, nearly in the latitude assigned to Mackenzie's River, the Sound into which Kotzebue entered, and Repulse Bay; and I think there is little doubt of a continued sea, in or about that line of direction. The existence of whales too, on this part of the coast, evidenced by a whalebone we found in Esquimaux

Cove, may be considered as an argument for an open sea; and a connexion with Hudson's Bay is rendered more probable from the same kind of fish abounding on the coasts we visited, and on those to the north of Churchill River. I allude more particularly to the Capelin of Salmo Arcticus, which we found in large shoals in Bathurst's Inlet, and which not only abounds, as Augustus told us, in bays in his country, but swarms in the Greenland firths.[1] The portion of the sea over which we passed is navigable for vessels of any size; the ice we met, particularly after quitting Detention Harbour, would not have arrested a strong boat. The chain of islands affords shelter from all heavy seas, and there are good harbours at convenient distances. I entertain, indeed, sanguine hopes that the skill and exertions of my friend Captain Parry will soon render this question no longer problematical. His task is doubtless an arduous one, and, if ultimately successful, may occupy two and perhaps three seasons; but confiding as I do, from personal knowledge, in his perseverance and talent for surmounting difficulties, the strength of his ships, and the abundance of provisions with which they are stored, I have very little apprehension of his safety. As I understand his object was to keep the coast of America close on board, he will find in the spring of the year, before the breaking up of the ice can permit him to pursue his voyage, herds of deer flocking in abundance to all parts of the coast, which may be procured without difficulty; and, even later in the season, additions to his stock of provision may be obtained on many parts of the coast, should circumstances give him leisure to send out hunting parties. With the trawl or seine nets also, he may almost everywhere get abundance of fish even without retarding his progress. Under these circumstances I do not conceive that he runs any hazard of wanting provisions, should his voyage be prolonged even beyond the latest period of time which is calculated upon. Drift timber may be gathered at many places in considerable quantities, and there is a fair prospect of his opening a communication with the Esquimaux, who come down to the coast to kill seals in the spring, previous to the ice breaking up; and from whom, if he succeeds in conciliating their good-will, he may obtain provision, and much useful assistance.

If he makes for Copper-Mine River, as he probably will do, he will not find it in the longitude as laid down on the charts; but he will probably find, what would be more interesting to him, a post, which we erected on the 26th August at the mouth of Hood's River, which is nearly, as will appear hereafter, in that longitude, with a flag upon it, and a letter at the foot of it, which may convey to him some useful information. It is possible, however, that he may keep outside of the range of islands which skirt this part of the coast.

CHAPTER XII

Journey across the barren grounds – Difficulty and delay in
crossing Copper-Mine River – Melancholy and Fatal Results
thereof – Extreme Misery of the whole Party – Murder of Mr.
Hood – Death of several of the Canadians – Desolate State of
Fort Enterprise – Distress suffered at that Place – Dr.
Richardson's Narrative – Mr. Back's Narrative – Conclusion.

August 17, 1821

My original intention, whenever the season should compel us to relinquish the survey, had been to return by the Copper-Mine River, and in pursuance of my arrangement with the Hook to travel to Slave Lake through the line of woods extending thither by the Great Bear and Marten Lakes, but our scanty stock of provision and the length of the voyage rendered it necessary to make for a nearer place. We had already found that the country, between Cape Barrow and the Copper-Mine River, would not supply our wants, and this is seemed probable would now be still the case; besides, at this advanced season, we expected the frequent recurrence of gales, which would cause great detention, if not danger in proceeding along that very rocky part of the coast.

I determined, therefore, to make at once for Arctic Sound, where we had found the animals more numerous than at any other place; and entering Hood's River, to advance up that stream as far as it was navigable, and then to construct small canoes out of the materials of the larger ones, which could be carried in crossing the barren grounds to Fort Enterprise.

August 19

We were almost beaten out of our comfortless abodes by rain during the night, and this moment the gale continued without diminution. The thermometer fell to 33°. Two men were sent with Junius to search for deer which Augustus had killed. Junius returned in the evening, bringing part of the meat, but owing to the thickness of the weather, his companions parted from him and did not make their appearance. Divine service was read. On the 20th we were presented with the most chilling prospect, the small pools of water being frozen over, the ground covered with snow, and the thermometer at the freezing-point at mid-day. Flights of geese were passing to the southward. The wind, however, was more moderate, having changed to the eastward. Considerable anxiety prevailing respecting Belanger and Michel, the two men who strayed from Junius yesterday, the rest were sent out to look for them. The search was unsuccessful, and they all returned in the evening. The stragglers were much fatigued, and had suffered severely from the cold, one of them having his thighs frozen, and what under our present circumstances was most grievous, they had thrown away all the meat. The wind during the night returned to the north-west quarter, blew more violently than ever, and raised a very turbulent sea. The next day did not improve our condition, the snow remained on the ground, and the small pools were frozen. Our hunters were sent out, but they returned after a fatiguing day's march without having seen any animals. We made a scanty meal of a handful of pemmican, after which only half a bag remained.

The wind abated after midnight, and the surf diminished rapidly, which caused us to be on the alert at a very early hour on the 22nd, but we had to wait until six A.M. for the return of Augustus, who had continued out all night on an unsuccessful pursuit of deer. It appears that he had walked a few miles farther along the coast than the party had done on the 18th, and from a sketch he drew on the sand, we were confirmed in our former opinion that the shore inclined more to the eastward beyond Point Turnagain. He also drew a river of considerable size, that discharges its waters into Walker's Bay; on the banks of which stream he saw a piece of wood, such as the Esquimaux use in producing fire, and other marks so fresh he supposed they had recently visited the spot. We therefore left several iron materials for them; and embarking without delay, prepared to retrace our steps.[1] Our men, cheered by the prospect of returning, showed the utmost alacrity; and, paddling with unusual vigour, carried us across Riley's and Walker's Bays, a distance of twenty miles, before noon, when we landed on Slate-clay Point as the wind had freshened too much to permit us to continue the voyage. The whole party went to hunt, but returned without success in the evening, drenched with the heavy rain which commenced soon after they had set out. Several deer were seen, but could not be approached in this naked country; and as our stock of pemmican did not admit of serving out two meals, we went dinnerless to bed.

Soon after our departure this day, a sealed tin-case, sufficiently buoyant to float, was thrown overboard, containing a short account of our proceedings, and the position of the most conspicuous points. The wind blew off the land, the water was smooth, and as the sea is in this part more free from islands than in any other, there was every probability of its being driven off the shore into the current; which as I have before mentioned, we suppose, from the circumstance of Mackenzie's River being the only known stream that brings down the wood we have found along the shores, to set to the eastward.

August 23

A severe frost caused us to pass and comfortless night. At two P.M. we set sail, and the men voluntarily launched out to make a traverse of fifteen miles across Melville Sound, before a strong wind and heavy sea. The privation of food, under which our voyagers were then labouring, absorbed every other terror; otherwise the most powerful persuasion could not have induced them to attempt such a traverse. It was with the utmost difficulty that the canoes were kept from turning their broadsides to the waves, though we sometimes steered with all the paddles. One of them narrowly escaped being overset by this accident, which occurred in a mid-channel, where the waves were so high that the masthead of our canoe was often hid from the other, though it was sailing within hail.

The traverse, however, was made; we were then near a high rocky lee shore, on which a heavy surf was beating. The wind being on the beam, the canoes drifted fast to leeward; and, on rounding a point, the recoil of the sea from the rocks was so great that they were with difficulty kept from foundering. We looked in vain for

1 It is a curious coincidence that our Expedition left Point Turnagain on August 22nd, – on the same day that Captain Parry sailed out of Repulse Bay. The parties were then distant from each other 539 miles.

a sheltered bay to land in; but, at length, being unable to weather another point, we were obliged to put ashore on the open beach, which fortunately was sandy at this spot. The debarkation was effected fortunately, without further injury than splitting the head of the second canoe, which was easily repaired. Our encampment being near the spot where we killed the deer on the 11th, almost the whole party went out to hunt, but returned in the evening without having seen any game. The berries, however, were ripe and plentiful, and, with the additions of some country tea, furnished a supper. There were some showers in the afternoon, and the weather was cold, the thermometer being 42°, but the evening and night were calm and fine. It may be remarked that the musquitoes disappeared when the late gales commenced.

August 24

Embarking at three A.M., we stretched across the eastern entrance of Bathurst's Inlet, and arrived at an island, which I have named after the Right Hon, Colonel Barry, of Newton Barry. Some deer being seen on the beach, the hunters went in pursuit of them, and succeeded in killing three females, which enabled us to save our last remaining meal of pemmican. They saw also some fresh tracks of musk oxen on the banks of a small stream which flowed into a lake in the centre of the island. These animals must have cross a channel, at least three miles wide, to reach the nearest of these islands. Some specimens of variegated pebbles and jasper were found here imbedded in the amygdaloidal rock.

Re-embarking at two P.M., and continuing through what was supposed to be a channel between two islands, we found our passage barred by a gravelly isthmus of only yen yards in width; the canoes and cargoes were carried across it, and we passed into Bathurst's Inlet through another similar channel, bounded on both sides by steep rocky hills. The wind then changing from S.E. top N.W. brought heavy rain, and we encamped at seven P.M., having advanced eighteen miles.

August 25

Starting this morning with a fresh breeze in our favour, we soon reached the part of Barry's Island where the canoes were detained on the 2nd and 3rd of this month, and contrary to what we then experienced, the deer were now plentiful. The hunters killed two, and relieved us from all apprehension of immediate want of food. From their assembling at this time in such numbers on the islands nearest to the coast, we conjectured that they were about to retire to the main shore. Those we saw were generally females with their young, and all of them very lean.

The wind continued in the same direction until we had rounded Point Wollaston, and then changed to a quarter, which enabled us to steer for Hood's River, which we ascended as high as the first rapid and encamped. Here terminated our voyage on the arctic Sea, during which we had gone over six hundred and fifty geographical miles. Our Canadian voyagers could not restrain their joy at having turned their backs on the sea, and passed the evening in talking over their past adventures with much humour and no little exaggeration. The consideration that the most painful, and certainly the most hazardous part of the journey was yet to come, did not depress their spirits at all. It is due to their character to mention that they displayed much courage in encountering the dangers of the sea, magnified to them by their novelty.

The shores between Cape Barrow and Cape Flinders, including the extensive branches of Arctic and Melville Sounds, and Bathurst's Inlet, may be comprehended in one great gulf, which I have distinguished by the appellation of George IV.'s Coronation Gulf, in honour of His Most Gracious Majesty, the latter name being added to mark the time of its discovery. The archipelago of islands which fringe the coast from Copper-Mine River to Point Turnagain, I have named in honour of His Royal Highness the Duke of York.

It may be deserving of notice that the extremes in temperature of the sea water during our voyage were 53° and 35°, but its general temperature was between 43° and 48°. Throughout our return from Point Turnagain we observed that the sea had risen several feet above marks left at our former encampments. This may, perhaps, be attributed to the north-west gales.

August 26

Previous to our departure this morning an assortment of iron materials, beads, looking-glasses, and other articles were put up in a conspicuous situation for the Esquimaux, and the English Union was planted on the loftiest sand-hill, where it might be seen by any ships passing in the offing. Here also, was deposited in a tin box, a letter containing an outline of our proceedings, the latitude and longitude of the principal places, and the course we intended to pursue towards Slave River.

Embarking at eight A.M. we proceeded up the river, which is full of sandy shoals, but sufficiently deep for canoes in the channels. It is from one hundred to two hundred yards wide, and is bounded by high and steep banks of clay. We encamped at a cascade of eighteen or twenty feet high, which is produced by a ridge of rock crossing the river, and the nets were set. A mile below this cascade Hood's River is joined by a stream half its own size, which I have called James' Branch. Bear and deer tracks had been numerous on the banks of the river when we were here before, but not a single recent one was to be seen at this time. Crédit, however, killed a small deer at some distance inland, which, with the addition of berries, furnished a delightful repast this evening. The weather was remarkably fine, and the temperature so mild, that the musquitoes again made their appearance, but not in any great numbers. Our distance made to-day was not more than six miles.

The next morning the net furnished with ten white-fish and trout. Having made a further deposit of iron work for the Esquimaux we pursued our voyage up the river, but the shoals and rapids in this part were so frequent, that we walked along the banks the whole day, and the crews laboured hard in carrying the canoes thus lightened over the shoals or dragging them up the rapids, yet our journey in a direct line was only about seven miles. In the evening we encamped at the lower end of a narrow chasm through which the river flows for upwards of a mile. The walls of this chasm are upwards of two hundred feet high, quite perpendicular, and in some places only a few yards apart. The river precipitates itself into it over a rock, forming two magnificent and picturesque falls close to each other. The upper fall is about sixty feet high, and the lower one at least one hundred; but perhaps considerable more, for the narrowness of the chasm into which it fell prevented us from seeing its bottom, and we could merely discern the top of the spray far beneath our feet. The lower fall is divided into two by an insulated column of rock which rises about forty feet above it. The whole descent of the river at this place probably exceeds two hundred and fifty feet. The rock is very fine felspathose sand-stone. It has a smooth surface and a light red colour. I have named these magnificent cascades "Wilberforce Falls," as a tribute to my respect for that distinguished philanthropist and Christian. Messrs. Back and Hood took beautiful sketches of this majestic scene.

The river being surveyed from the summit of a hill, above these falls, appeared so rapid and shallow, that it seemed useless to attempt proceeding any farther in the large canoes. I therefore determined on constructing out of their materials two smaller ones of sufficient size to contain three persons, for the purpose of crossing any river that might obstruct our progress. This operation was accordingly commenced, and by the 31st both the canoes being finished, we prepared for our departure on the following day.

The leather which had been preserved for making shoes was equally divided among the men, two pairs of flannel socks were given to each person, and such articles of warm clothing as remained, were issued to those who most required them. They were also furnished with one of the officers' tents. This being done, I communicated to the men my intention of proceeding in as direct a course as possible to the part of Point Lake, opposite our spring encampment, which was only distant one hundred and forty-nine miles in a straight line. They received the communication cheerfully, considered the journey to be short, and left me in high spirits, to arrange their own packages. The stores, books, etc., which were not absolutely necessary to be carried, were then put up in boxes to be left *en caches* here, in order that the men's burdens might be a light as possible.

The next morning was warm, and very fine. Every one was on the alert at an early hour, being anxious to commence the journey. Our luggage consisted of ammunition, nets, hatchets, ice chisels, astronomical instruments, clothing, blankets, three kettles, and the two canoes, which were each carried by one man. The officers carried such a portion of their own things as their strength would permit; the weight carried by each man was about ninety pounds, and with this we advanced at the rate of about a mile an hour, including rests. In the evening the hunters killed a lean cow, out of a large drove of musk oxen; but the men were too much laden to carry more than a small portion of its flesh. The alluvial soil, which towards the mouth of the river spreads into plains, covered with grass and willows, was now giving place to a more barren and hilly country; so that we could but just collect sufficient brushwood to cook our suppers. The part of the river we skirted this day was shallow, and flowed over a bed of sand; its width about one hundred and twenty yards. About midnight our tent was blown down by a squall, and we were completely drenched with rain before it could be re-pitched.

On the morning of the 1st of September a fall of snow took place; the canoes became a cause of delay, from the difficulty of carrying them in a high wind, and they sustained much damage through the falls of those who had charge of them. The face of the country was broken by hills of moderate elevation, but the ground was plentifully strewed with small stones, which, to men bearing heavy burdens, and whose feet were protected only by soft moose-skin shoes, occasioned great pain. At the end of eleven miles we encamped, and sent for a musk ox and a deer, which St. Germain and Augustus had killed. The day was extremely cold, the thermometer varying between 34° and 36°. In the afternoon a heavy fall of snow took place, on the wind changing from north-west to south-east. We found no wood at the encampment, but made a fire of moss to cook the supper, and crept under our blankets for warmth. At sunrise the thermometer was at 31°, and the wind fresh from north-west; but the weather became mild in the course of the forenoon, and the snow disappeared from the gravel. The afternoon was remarkably fine, and the thermometer rose to 50°. One of the hunters killed a musk ox. The hills in this part are lower, and more round-backed than those we passed yesterday, exhibiting but little naked rock; they were covered with lichens.

Having ascertained from the summit of the highest hill near the tents that the river continued to preserve a west course; and fearing that by pursuing it farther we might lose much time, and unnecessarily walk over a great deal of ground, I determined on quitting its banks the next day, and making as directly as we could for Point Lake. We accordingly followed the river on the 3rd, only to the place where the musk ox had been killed last evening, and after the meat was procured, crossed the river in our two canoes lashed together. We now emerged from the valley of the river, and entered a level, but very barren, country, varied only by small lakes and marshes, the ground being covered with small stones. Many old tracks of reindeer were seen in the clayey soil, and some more recent traces of the musk ox. We encamped on the borders of Wright's River, which flows to the eastward; the direct distance walked to-day being ten miles and three-quarters. The next morning was very fine, and, as the day advanced, the weather became quite warm. We set out at six A.M., and, having forded the river, walked over a perfectly level country, interspersed with small lakes, which communicated with each other, by streams running in various directions. No berry-bearing plants were found in this part, the surface of the earth being thinly covered in the moister places with a few grasses, and on the drier spots with lichens.

Having walked twelve miles and a half, we encamped at seven P.M., and distributed our last piece of pemmican, and a little arrowroot for supper, which afforded but a scanty meal. This evening was warm, but dark clouds overspread the sky. Our men now began to find their burdens very oppressive, and were much fatigued by this day's march, but did not complain. One of them was lame from an inflammation in the knee. Heavy rain commenced at mid-night, and continued without intermission until five in the morning, when it was succeeded by snow on the wind changing to north-west, which soon increased to a violent gale. As we had nothing to eat, and were destitute of the means of making a fire, we remained in our beds all the day; but the covering of our blankets was insufficient to prevent us from feeling the severity of the frost, and suffering inconvenience from the drifting of the snow into our tents. There was no abatement of the storm next day; our tents were completely frozen, and the snow had drifted around them to a depth of three feet, and even in the inside there was a covering of several inches on our blankets. Our suffering from cold, in a comfortless canvas tent in such weather, with the temperature at 20°, and without fire, will easily be imagined; it was, however, less than that which we felt from hunger.

The morning of the 7th cleared up a little but the wind was still strong, and the weather extremely cold. From the unusual continuance of the storm, we feared the winter had set in with all its vigour, and that by longer delay we should only be exposed to an accumulation of difficulties; we therefore prepared for our journey, although we were in a very unfit condition for starting, being weak from fasting, and our garments stiffened by the frost. We had no means of making a fire to thaw them, the moss, at all times difficult to kindle, being now covered with ice and snow. A considerable time was consumed in packing up the frozen tents and bed clothes, the wind blowing so strong that no one could keep his lands long out of his mittens.

Just as we were about to commence our march, I was seized with a fainting fit, in consequence of exhaustion and sudden exposure to the wind; but after eating a morsel of portable soup, I recovered so far as to be able to move on. I was unwilling at first to take this morsel of soup, which was diminishing the small and only remaining meal for the party; but several of the men urged me to it, with much kindness. The ground was covered a foot deep with snow, the margins of the lakes

JOURNEY
TO THE
POLAR SEA

244

were encrusted with ice, and the swamps over which we had to pass were entirely frozen; but the ice not being sufficiently strong to bear us, we frequently plunged knee-deep in water. Those who carried the canoes were repeated blown down by the violence of the wind, and they often fell, from making an insecure step on a slippery stone; on one of these occasions, the largest canoe was so much broken as to be rendered utterly unserviceable. This we felt was a serious disaster, as the remaining canoe having through mistake been made too small, it was doubtful whether it would be sufficient to carry us across a river. Indeed we had found it necessary in crossing Hood's River, to lash the two canoes together. As there was some suspicion that Benoit, who carried the canoe, had broken it intentionally, he having on a former occasion been overheard by some of the men to say that he would do so when he got it in charge, we closely examined him on the point; he roundly denied having used the expressions attributed to him, and insisted that it was broken by his falling accidentally; and as he brought men to attest the latter fact, who saw him tumble, we did not press the matter further. I may here remark that our people had murmured a good deal at having the carry two canoes, though they were informed of the necessity of taking both, in case it should be deemed advisable to divide the party; which it had been thought probable we should be obliged to do if animals proved scarce, in order to give the whole the better chance of procuring subsistence, and also for the purpose of sending forward some of the best walkers to search for Indians, and to get them to meet us with supplies of provision. The power of doing this was now at an end. As the accident could not be remedied, we turned it to the best account, but making a fire of the bark and timbers of the broken vessel, and cooked the remaineder for our portable soup and arrowroot. This was a scanty meal after three days' fasting, but it served to allay the pangs of hunger, and enabled us to proceed at a quicker pace than before. The depth of the snow caused us to march in Indian file, that is in each other's steps; the voyagers taking it in turn to lead the party. A distant object was pointed out to this man in the direction we wished to take, and Mr. Hood followed immediately behind him, to renew the bearings, and keep him from deviating more than could be helped from the mark. It may be here observed, that we proceeded in this manner throughout our route across the barren grounds.

In the afternoon we got into a more hilly country, where the ground was strewed with large stones. The surface of these was covered with lichens of the genus *gyrophora* which the Canadians term *tripe de roche*. A considerable quantity was gathered, and with half a partridge each, (which we shot in the course of the day). Furnished a slender supper, which we cooked with a few willows, dug up from beneath the snow. We passed a comfortless night in our damp clothes, but took the prevention of sleeping upon our socks and shoes to prevent them from freezing. This plan was afterwards adopted throughout the journey.

At half-past five in the morning we proceeded; and after walking about two miles, came to Cracroft's River, flowing to the westward with a very rapid current over a rocky channel. We had much difficulty in crossing this, the canoe being useless, not only from the bottom of the channel being obstructed by large stones, but also from its requiring gumming, an operation which, owing to the want of wood and the frost, we were unable to perform. However, after following the course of the river some distance we effected a passage by means of a range of large rocks that crossed a rapid. As the current was strong, and many of the rocks were covered with water to the depth of two or three feet, the men were exposed to much danger in carrying their heavy burdens across, and several of them actually slipped into the stream, but were immediately rescued by the others.

Junius went farther up the river in search of a better crossing-place and did not rejoin us this day. As several of the party were drenched from head to foot, and we were all wet to the middle, our clothes became stiff with the frost, and we walked with much pain for the remainder of the day. The march was continued to a late hour from our anxiety to rejoin the hunters who had gone before, but we were obliged to encamp at the end of ten miles and a quarter, without seeing them. Our only meal to-day consisted of a partridge each (which the hunters shot), mixed with *tripe de roche*. This repast, although scanty for men with appetites such as our daily fatigue created, proved a cheerful one, and was received with thankfulness. Most of the men had to sleep in the open air, in consequence of the absence of Crédit, who carried their tent; but we fortunately found an unusual quantity of roots to make a fire, which prevented their suffering much from the cold, though the thermometer was at 17°.

We started at six on the 9th, and at the end of two miles regained our hunters, who were halting on the borders of a lake amidst a clump of stunted willows. This lake stretched to the westward as far as we could see, and its waters were discharged by a rapid stream one hundred and fifty yards wide. Being entirely ignorant where we might be led by pursuing the course of the lake, and dreading the idea of going a mile unnecessarily out of the way, we determined on crossing the river if possible; and the canoe was gummed for the purpose, the willows furnishing us with fire. But we had to await the return of Junius before we could make the traverse. In the meantime we gathered a little *tripe de roche*, and breakfasted upon it and a few partridges that were killed in the morning. St. Germain and Adam were sent upon some recent tracks of deer. Junius arrived in the afternoon and informed us that he had seen a large herd of musk oxen on the banks of Cracroft's River, and had wounded one of them, but it escaped. He brought about four pounds of meat, the remains of a deer that had been devoured by the wolves. The poor fellow was much fatigued, having walked throughout the night, but as the weather was particularly favourable for our crossing the river, we could not allow him to rest. After he had taken some refreshment we proceeded to the river. The canoe being put into the water was found extremely ticklish, but it was managed with much dexterity by St. Germain, Adam, and Peltier, who ferried over one passenger at a time, causing him to lie flat in its bottom, by no means an pleasant position, owing to its leakiness, but there was no alternative. The transport of the whole party was effected by five o'clock and we walked about two miles farther and encamped having come five miles and three-quarters on a south-west course. Two young alpine hares were shot by St. Germain, which, with the small piece of meat brought in by Junius, furnished the supper of the whole party. There was no *tripe de roche* here. The country had now become decidedly hilly, and was covered with snow. The lake preserved its western direction, as far as I could see from the summit of the highest mountain near the encampment. We subsequently learned from the Copper Indians, that the part at which we had crossed the river was the *Congecatha-wha-chaga* of Hearne, of which I had little idea at the time, not only from the difference of latitude, but also from its being so much farther east of the mouth of the Copper-Mine River than his track is laid down; he only making one degree and three-quarters' difference of longitude, and we, upwards of four. Had I been aware of the fact, several days' harassing march, and a disastrous accident would have been prevented by keeping on the western side of the lake, instead of crossing the river. We were informed also, that this river is the Anatessy or River of Strangers, and is supposed to fall into Bathurst's Inlet; but although the Indians have visited its mouth, their description was not sufficient to identify it with any of the rivers whose mouths we had seen. It probably discharges itself in that part of the coast which was hid from our view by Goulbourn's or Elliott's Islands.

September 10

We had a cold north wind, and the atmosphere was foggy. The thermometer 18° at five A.M. In the course of our march this morning, we passed many small lakes; and the ground becoming higher and more hilly as we receded from the river, was covered to a much greater depth with snow. This rendered walking not only extremely laborious, but also hazardous in the highest degree; for the sides of the hills, as is usual throughout the barren grounds, abounding in accumulations of large angular stones, it often happened that the men fell into the interstices with their loads on their backs, being deceived by the smooth appearance of the drifted snow. If any one had broken a limb here, his fate would have been melancholy indeed; we could neither have remained with him, nor carried him on. We halted at ten to gather *tripe de roche*, but it was so frozen, that we were quite benumbed with cold before a sufficiency could be collected even for a scanty meal. On proceeding our men were somewhat cheered by observing on the sandy summit of a hill, from whence the snow had been blown, the summer track of a man; and afterwards by seeing several deer tracks on the snow. About noon the weather cleared up a little, and to our great joy, we saw a heard of musk oxen grazing in a valley below us. The party instantly halted, and the best hunters were sent out; they approached the animals with the utmost caution, no less than two hours being consumed before they got within gunshot. In the meantime we beheld their proceedings with extreme anxiety, and many secret prayers were, doubtless, offered up for their success. At length they opened their fire, and we had the satisfaction of seeing one of the largest cows fall; another was wounded, but escaped. This success infused spirit into our starving party. To skin and cut up the animal was the work of a few minutes. The contents of its stomach were devoured upon the spot, and the raw intestines, which were next attacked, were pronounced by the most delicate amongst us to be excellent. A few willows, whose tops were seen peeping through the snow in the bottom of the valley, were quickly grubbed, the tents pitched, and supper cooked, and devoured with avidity. This was the sixth day since we had had a good meal; the *tripe de roche*, even where we got enough, only serving to allay the pangs of hunger for a short time. After supper, two of the hunters went in pursuit of the herd, but could not get near them. I do not think that we witnessed through the course of our journey a more striking proof of the wise dispensation of the Almighty, and of the weakness of our own judgment than on this day. We had considered the dense fog which prevailed throughout the morning, as almost the greatest inconvenience that could have befallen us, since it rendered the air extremely cold, and prevented us from distinguishing any distance object towards which our course could be directed. Yet this very darkness enabled the party to get to the top of the hill which bounded the valley wherein the musk oxen were grazing with being perceived. Had the herd discovered us and taken alarm, our hunters in their present state of debility would in all probability have failed in approaching them.

We were detained all the next day by a strong southerly wind, and were much incommoded in the tents by the drift snow. The temperature was about 20°. The average for the last ten days about 24°. We restricted ourselves to one meal this day, as we were at rest, and there was only meat remaining sufficient for the morrow.

The gale had not diminished on the 12th, and, as we were fearful of its continuance for some time, we determined on going forward; our only doubt regarded the preservation of the canoe, but the men promised to pay particular attention to it, and the most careful persons were appointed to take it in charge. The snow was two feet deep and the ground much broken, which rendered the march extremely painful. The whole party complained more of faintness and weakness than they had ever done before; their strength seemed to have been impaired by the recent supply of animal food. In the afternoon the wind abated, and the snow ceased; cheered with the change, we proceeded forward at a quicker pace and encamped at six P.M., having come eleven miles. Our supper consumed the last of our meat.

We set out on the 13th, in thick hazy weather, and, after an hour's march, had the extreme mortification to find ourselves on the borders of a large lake; neither of its extremities could be seen, and as the portion which lay to the east seemed the widest, we coasted along to the westward portion in search of a crossing-place. This lake being bounded by steep and lofty hills, our march was very fatiguing. Those sides which were exposed to the sun, were free from snow, and we found upon them some excellent berries. We encamped at six P.M., having come only six miles and a half. Crédit was then missing, and he did not return during the night. We supped off a single partridge and some *tripe de roche*; this unpalatable weed was now quite nauseous to the whole party, and in several it produced bowel complaints. Mr. Hood was the greatest sufferer from this cause. This evening we were extremely distressed, at discovering that our improvident companions, since we left Hood's River had thrown away three of the fishing-nets, and burnt the floats; they knew we had brought them to procure subsistence for the party, when the animals should fail, and we could scarcely believe the fact of their having wilfully deprived themselves of this resource, especially when we considered that most of them had passed the greater part of their servitude in situations where the nets alone had supplied them with food. Being thus deprived of our principal resource, that of fishing, and the men evidently getting weaker every day, it became necessary to lighten their burdens of everything except ammunition, clothing, and the instructions that were required to find our way. I, therefore, issued directions to deposit at this encampment the dipping needle, azimuth compass, magnet, a large thermometer, and a few books we had carried, having torn out of these, such parts as we should require to work the observations for latitude and longitude. I also promised, as an excitement to the efforts in hunting, my gun to St. Germain, and an ample compensation to Adam or any of the other men who should kill any animals. Mr. Hood, on this occasion, lent his gun to Michel, the Iroquois, who was very eager in the chase, and often successful.

September 14

This morning the officers being assembled round a small fire, Perrault presented each of us with a small piece of meat which he had saved from his allowance. It was received with great thankfulness, and such an act of self-denial and kindness being totally unexpected in a Canadian voyager filled our eyes with tears. In directing our course to a river issuing from the lake, we met Crédit, who communicated the joyful intelligence of his having killed two deer in the morning. We instantly halted, and having shared the seer that was nearest to us, prepared breakfast. After which, the other deer was sent for, and we went down to the river, which was about three hundred yards wide, and flowed with great velocity through a broken rocket channel. Having searched for a part where the current was most smooth, the canoe was placed in the water at the head of a rapid, and St. Germain, Solomon Belanger, and I, embarked in order to cross it. We went from the shore very well, but in mid-channel the canoe became difficult to manage under our burden as the breeze was fresh. The current drove us to the edge of the rapid, when Belanger unluckily applied his paddle to avert the apparent danger of being forced down it, and lost his balance. The canoe was overset in consequence in the middle of the rapid. We fortunately kept hold of it, until we touched a rock where the water did not reach higher than our waists; here we kept our footing, notwithstanding the strength of the current, until the water was emptied out of the canoe. Belanger then held the canoe steady whilst St. Germain placed me in it, and afterwards embarked himself in a very dexterous manner. It was impossible, however, to embark Belanger, as the canoe would have hurried down the rapid the moment he should have raised his foot from the rock on which he stood. We were, therefore, compelled to leave him in his perilous situation. We had not gone twenty yards before the canoe, striking on a sunken rock, went down. The place being shallow, we were again enabled to empty it, and the third attempt brought us to the shore. In the mean time Belanger was suffering extremely, immersed to his middle in the centre of a rapid, the temperature of which was very little above the freezing-point, and the upper part of his body covered with wet clothes, exposed in a temperature not much above zero, to a strong breeze. He called piteously for relief, and St. Germain on his return endeavoured to embark him, but in vain. The canoe was hurried down the rapid, and when he landed he was rendered by the cold incapable of further exertion, and Adam attempted to embark Belanger, but found it impossible. An attempt was next made to carry out to him a line, made of the sling's of the men's loads. This also failed, the current acting so strongly upon it, as to prevent the canoe from steering, and it was finally broken and carried down the stream. At length, when Belanger's strength seemed almost exhausted, the canoe reached him with a small cord belonging to one of the nets, and he was dragged perfectly senseless through the rapid. By the direction of Dr. Richardson, he was instantly stripped, and being rolled up in blankets, two men undressed themselves and went to bed with him: but it was some hours before he recovered his warmth and sensations. As soon as Belanger was placed in his bed, the officers sent over my blankets, and a person to make a fire. Augustus brought the canoe over, and in returning he was obliged to descend both the rapids, before he could get across the stream; which hazardous service he performed with the greatest coolness and judgment. It is impossible to describe my sensations as I witnessed the various unsuccessful attempts to relieve Belanger. The distance prevented my seeing distinctly what was going on, and I continued pacing up and down upon the rock on which I landed, regardless of the coldness of my drenched and stiffening garments. The canoe, in every attempt to reach him, was hurried down the rapid, and was lost view amongst the rocky islets, with a rapidity that seemed to threaten certain destruction; once, indeed, I fancied that I saw it overwhelmed in the waves. Such an event would have been fatal to the whole party. Separated as I was from my companions, without gun, ammunition, hatchet, or the means of making a fire, and in wet clothes, my doom would have been speedily sealed. My companions, too, driven to the necessity of coasting the lake, must have sunk under the fatigue of rounding it innumerable arms and bays, which, as we have learned from the Indians, are very extensive. But the goodness of Providence, however, we were spared at that time, and some of us have been permitted to offer up our thanksgivings, in a civilised land, for the signal deliverances we then and afterwards experienced.

By this incident I had the misfortune to lose my port-folio, containing my journal from Fort Enterprise, together with all the astronomical and meteorological observations made during the descent of the Copper-Mine River, and along the sea-coast (except those for the dip and variation). I was in the habit of carrying it strapped across my shoulders, but had taken it off on entering the canoe, to reduce the upper weight. The results of most of the observations for latitude and longitude had been registered in the sketch-books, so that we preserved the requisites for the construction of the charts. The meteorological observations, not having been copied, were lost. My companions, Dr. Richardson, Mr. Back, and Mr. Hood, had been so careful in noting every occurrence in their journals, that the loss of mine could fortunately be well supplied. These friends immediately offered me their documents, and every assistance in drawing up another narrative, of which kindness I availed myself at the earliest opportunity afterwards.

September 15

The rest of the party were brought across this morning, and we were delighted to find Belanger so much recovered as to be able to proceed, but we could not set out until noon, as the men had to prepare substitutes fro the slings which were lost yesterday. Soon after leaving the encampment we discerned a herd of deer, and after a long chase a fine male was killed by Perrault, several others were wounded but they escaped. After this we passed round the north end of the a branch of the lake, and ascended the Willingham Mountains, keeping near the border of the lake. These hills were steep, craggy, and covered with snow. We encamped at seven and enjoyed a substantial meal. The party were in good spirits this evening at the recollection of having crossed the rapid, and being in possession of provision for the next day. Besides, we had taken the precaution of bringing away the skin of the deer to eat when the meat should fail. The temperature at six P.M. was 30°.

We started at seven next morning and marched until ten, when the appearance of a few willows peeping through the snow induced us to halt and breakfast. Recommencing the journey at noon, we passed over a more rugged country, where the hills were separated by deep ravines, whose steep sides were equally difficult to descend and to ascend, and the toil and suffering we experienced were greatly increased.

The party was quite fatigued when we encamped, having come ten miles and three-quarters. We observed many summer deer roads, and some recent tracks. Some marks that had been put up by the Indians were also noticed. We have since learned that this is a regular deer pass, and on that account, annually frequented by the Copper Indians. The lake is called by them Contwoy-to, or Rum Lake; in consequence of Mr. Hearne having here given the Indians who accompanied him some of that liquor. Fish is not found here.

We walked next day over a more level country, but it was strewed with large stones. These galled our feet a good deal; we contrived, however, to wade through the snow at a tolerably quick pace until five P.M., having proceeded twelve miles and a half. We had made to-day our proper course, south by east, which we could not venture upon doing before, for fear of falling again upon some branch of the Contwoy-to. Some deer were seen in the morning, but the hunters failed of killing any, and in the afternoon we fell into the tracks of a large herd, which had passed the day before, but did not overtake them. In consequence of this want of success we had no breakfast, and but a scanty supper; but we allayed the pangs of hunger, by eating pieces of singed hide. A little *tripe de roche*[1] was also obtained. These would have satisfied us in ordinary times, but we were now almost exhausted by slender fare and travel, and our appetites had become ravenous. We looked, however, with humble confidence to the Great Author and Giver of all good, for a

1 The different kinds of *gyrophora*, are termed indiscriminately by the voyagers, *tripe de roche*.

continuance of the support which had hitherto been always supplied to us at our greatest need. The thermometer varied to-day between 25° and 28°. The wind blew fresh from the south.

On the eighteenth the atmosphere was hazy, but the day was more pleasant for walking than usual. The country was level and gravelly, and the snow very deep. We went for a short time along a deeply-beaten road made by the reindeer, which turned suddenly off to the south-west, a direction so wide of our course that we could not venture upon following it. All the small lakes were frozen, and we marched across those which lay in our track. We supped off the *tripe de roche* which had been gathered during our halts in the course of the march. Thermometer at six P.M. 32°.

Showers of snow fell without intermission through the night, but they ceased in the morning, and we set out at the usual hour. The men were very faint from hunger, and marched with difficulty, having to oppose a fresh breeze, and to wade through snow two feet deep. We gained, however, ten miles by four o'clock, and then encamped. The canoe was unfortunately broken by the fall of the person who had it in charge. No *tripe de roche* was seen to-day, but in clearing the snow to pitch the tents we found a quantity of Iceland moss, which was boiled for supper. This weed, not having been soaked, proved so bitter, that few of the party could eat more than a few spoonfuls.

Our blankets did not suffice this evening to keep us in tolerable warmth; the slightest breeze seeming to pierce through our debilitated frames. The reader will, probably, be desirous to know how we passed our time in such a comfortless situation: the first operation after encampment was to thaw our frozen shoes, if a sufficient fire could be made, and dry ones were put on; each person then wrote his notes of the daily occurrences, and evening prayers were read; as soon as supper was prepared it was eaten, generally in the dark, and we went to bed, and kept up a cheerful conversation until our blankets were thawed by the heat of our bodies, and we had gathered sufficient warmth to enable us to fall asleep. On many nights we had not even the luxury of going to bed in dry clothes, and when the fire was insufficient to dry our shoes, we durst not venture to pull them off, lest they should freeze so hard as to be unfit to put on in the morning, and, therefore, inconvenient to carry.

On the 20th we got into a hilly country, and the marching became much more laborious, even the stoutest experienced great difficulty in climbing the craggy eminences. Mr. Hood was particularly weak, and was obliged to relinquish his station of second in the line, which Dr. Richardson now took, to direct the leading man in keeping the appointed course. I was also unable to keep pace with the men, who put forth their upmost speed, encouraged by the hope, which our reckoning had led us to form, of seeing Point Lake in the evening, but we were obliged to encamp without gaining a view of it. We had not seen either deer or their tracks through the day, and this circumstance, joined to the disappointment of not discovering the lake, rendered our voyagers very desponding, and the meagre supper of *tripe de roche* was little calculated to elevate their spirits. They now threatened to throw away their bundles, and quit us, which rash act they would probably have committed, if they had known what track to pursue.

September 21

We set out at seven this morning in dark foggy weather, and changed our course two points to the westward. The party were very feeble, and the men much dispirited; we made slow progress, having to march over a hilly and very rugged country.

Just before noon the sun beamed through the haze for the first time for six days, and we obtained an observation in latitude 65° 7′ 06″ N., which was six miles to the southward of that part of Point Lake to which our course was directed. By this observation we discovered that we had kept to the eastward of the proper course, which may be attributed partly to the difficulty in preserving a straight line through an unknown country, unassisted by celestial observations, and in such thick weather, that our view was often limited to a few hundred yards; but chiefly to our total ignorance of the amount of the variation of the compass.

We altered the course immediately to west-south-west, and fired guns to apprise the hunters who were out of our view, and ignorant of our having done so. After walking about two miles we waited to collect the stragglers. Two partridges were killed, and these with some *tripe de roche*, furnished our supper. Notwithstanding a full explanation was given to the men of the reasons for altering the course, and they were assured that the observation had enabled us to discover our exact distance from Fort Enterprise, they could not divest themselves of the idea of our having lost our way, and a gloom was spread over every countenance. At this encampment Dr. Richardson was obliged to deposit his specimens of plants and minerals, collected on the sea-coast, being unable to carry them any further. The way made to-day was five miles and a quarter.

September 22

After walking about two miles this morning, we came upon the borders of an extensive lake, whose extremities could not be discerned in consequence of the density of the atmosphere; but as its shores seemed to approach nearer to each other to the southward than to the northward, we determined on tracing it in that direction. We were grieved at finding the lake expand very much beyond the contracted part we had first seen, and incline to the eastward of south. As, however, it was considered more than probable, from the direction and size of the body of water we were now tracing, that it was a branch of Point Lake; and as, in any case, we knew that by passing round its south end, we must shortly come to the Copper-Mine River, our course was continued in that direction. The appearance of some dwarf pines and willows, larger than usual, induced us to suppose the river was near. We encamped early, having come eight miles. Our supper consisted of *tripe de roche* and half a partridge each.

Our progress next day was extremely slow, from the difficulty in managing the canoe in passing over the hills, as the breeze was fresh. Peltier who had it in charge, having received several severe falls, became impatient, and insisted on leaving his burden, as it had already been much injured by the accidents of this day; and no arguments we could use were sufficient to prevail on him to continue carrying it. Vaillant was, therefore, directed to take it, and we proceeded forward. Having found that he got on very well, and was walking even faster than Mr. Hood could follow, in his present debilitated state, I pushed forward to stop the rest of the party, who had got out of sight during the delay which the discussion respecting the canoe had occasioned. I accidentally passed the body of men, and followed the tracks of two persons who had separated from the rest, until two P.M., when not seeing any person, I retraced my steps, and on my way met Dr. Richardson, who had also missed the party whilst he was employed gathering *tripe de roche*, and we went back together in search of them. We found they had halted among some willows, where they had picked up some pieces of skin and a few bones of deer that had been devoured by the wolves last spring. They had rendered the bones friable by burning, and eaten them as well as the skin; and several of them had added their old shoes to the repast. Peltier and Vaillant were with them, having left the canoe, which, they said, was so completely broken by another fall, as to be rendered incapable of repair, and entirely useless. The anguish this intelligence occasioned may be conceived, but it is beyond my power to describe it. Impressed, however, with the necessity of taking it forward, even in the state these men represented it to be, we urgently desired them to fetch it; but they declined going, and the strength of the officers was inadequate to the task. To their infatuated obstinacy on this occasion, a great portion of the melancholy circumstances which attended our subsequent progress may, perhaps, be attributed. The men now seemed to have lost all hope of being preserved; and all the arguments we could use failed in stimulating them to the least exertion. After consuming the remains of the bones and horns of the deer we resumed our march, and in the evening, reached a contracted part of the lake, which perceiving it to be shallow, we forded, and encamped on the opposite side. Heavy rain began soon afterwards, and continued all night. On the following morning the rain had so wasted the snow, that the tracks of Mr. Back and his companions, who had gone before with the hunters, were traced with difficulty; and the frequent showers during the day almost obliterated them. The men became furious at the apprehension of being deserted by the hunters, and some of the strongest throwing down their bundles, prepared to set out after them, intending to leave the more weak to follow as they could. The entreaties and threats of the officers, however, prevented their executing this mad scheme; but not before Solomon Belanger was despatched with orders for Mr. Back to halt until we should join him. Soon afterwards a thick fog came on, but we continued our march and overtook Mr. Back, who had been detained in consequence of his companions having followed some recent tracks of deer. After halting an hour, during which we refreshed ourselves with eating our old shoes, and a few scraps of leather, we set forward in the hope of ascertaining whether an adjoining piece of water was the Copper-Mine River or not, but were soon compelled to return and encamp, for fear of separation of the party, as we could not see each other at ten yards' distance. The fog diminishing towards evening, Augustus was sent out to examine the water, but having lost his way he did not reach the tents before midnight, when he brought the information of its being a lake. We supper upon *tripe de roche*, and enjoyed a comfortable fire, having found some pines, seven or eight feet high, in a valley near the encampment.

The bounty of Providence was most seasonably manifested to us next morning, in our killing five small deer out of a herd, which came in sight as we were on the point of starting. This unexpected supply re-animated the drooping spirits of our men, and filled every heart with gratitude.

The voyagers instantly petitioned for a day's rest which we were most reluctant to grant, being aware of the importance of every moment at this critical period of our journey. But they so earnestly and strongly pleaded their recent sufferings, and their conviction that the quiet enjoyment of two substantial meals, after eight days' famine, would enable them to proceed next day more vigorously, that we could not resist their entreaties. The flesh, the skins, and even the contents of the stomachs of the deer were equally distributed among the party by Mr. Hood, who had volunteered, on the departure of Mr. Wentzel, to perform the duty of issuing the provision. This invidious task he had all along performed with great impartiality, but seldom without producing some grumbling amongst the Canadians; and, on the present occasion, the hunters were displeased that the heads and some other parts, had not been added to their portion. It is proper to remark, that Mr. Hood always took the smallest portion for his own mess, but this weighed little with these men, as long as their own appetites remained unsatisfied. We all suffered much inconvenience from eating animal food after our long abstinence, but particularly those men who indulged themselves beyond moderation. The Canadians, with their usual thoughtlessness, had consumed above a third of their portions of meat that evening.

We set out early on the 26th, and after walking about three miles along the lake, came to the river which we at once recognised, from its size, to be the Copper-Mine. It flowed to the northward, and after winding about five miles, terminated in Point Lake. Its current was swift, and there were two rapids in this part of its course, which in a canoe we could have crossed with ease and safety. These rapids, we well as every other part of the river, were carefully examined in search of a ford; but finding none, the expedients occurred, of attempting to cross on a raft made of the willows which were growing there, or in a vessel framed with willows, and covered with the canvas of the tents; but both these schemes were abandoned, through the obstinacy of the interpreters and the most experienced voyagers, who declared that they would prove inadequate to the conveyance of the party, and that much time would be lost in the attempt. The men, in fact, did not believe that this was the Copper-Mine River, and so little confidence had they in our reckoning, and so much had they bewildered themselves on the march that some of them asserted it was Hood's River, and others that it was the Bethe-tessy. (A river which rises from a lake to the northward of Rum Lake, and holds a course to the sea parallel with than of the Copper-Mine.) In short, their despondency had returned, and they all despaired of seeing Fort Enterprise again. However, the steady assurances of the officers that we were actually on the banks of the Copper-Mine River, and that the distance to Fort Enterprise did not exceed forty miles, made some impression upon them, which was increased upon our finding some bear-berry plants (*arbutus uva ursi*), which are reported by the Indians not to grow to the eastward of that river. They then adopted their folly and impatience in breaking the canoe, being all of opinion, that had it not been so completely demolished on the 23rd, it might have been repaired sufficiently to take the party over. We again closely interrogated Peltier and Vaillant as to its state, with the intention of sending for it; but they persisted in the declaration that it was in a totally unserviceable condition. St. Germain being again called upon to endeavour to construct a canoe frame with willows, stated that he was unable to make one sufficiently large. It became necessary, therefore, to search for pines of sufficient size to form a raft; and being aware that such trees grow on the borders of Lake Point, we considered it best to trace its shores in search of them; we, therefore, resumed our march, carefully looking, but in vain, for a fordable part, and encamped at the east end of Point Lake.

As there was little danger of our losing the path of our hunters whilst we coasted the shores of this lake, I determined on again sending Mr. Back forward, with the interpreters to hunt. I had in view, in this arrangement, the further object of enabling Mr. Back to get across the lake with two of these men, to convey the earliest possible account of our situation to the Indians. Accordingly I instructed him to halt at the first pines he should come to, and then prepare a raft; and if his hunters had killed animals, so that they party could be supported whilst we were making our raft, he was to cross immediately with St. Germain and Beauparlant, and send the Indians to us as quickly as possible with supplies of meat.

We had this evening the pain of discovering that two of our men had stolen part of the officers' provision, which had been allotted to us with strict impartiality.

This conduct was the more reprehensible, as it was plain that we were suffering, even in a greater degree than themselves, from the effects of famine, owing to our being of a less robust habit, and less accustomed to privations. We had no means of punishing this crime, but by the threat that they should forfeit their wages, which had now ceased to operate.

Mr. Back and his companions set out at six in the morning, and we started at seven. As the snow had entirely disappeared, and there were no means of distinguishing the footsteps of stragglers, I gave strict orders, previously to setting out, for all the party to keep together: and especially I desired the two Esquimaux not to leave us, they having often strayed in search of the remains of animals. Our people, however, through despondency, had become careless and disobedient, and had ceased to dread punishment, or hope of reward. Much time was lost in halting and firing guns to collect them, but the labour of walking was so much lightened by the disappearance of the snow, that we advanced seven or eight miles along the lake before noon, exclusive of the loss of distance in rounding its numerous bays. At length we came to an arm, running away to the north-east, and apparently connected with the lake which we had coasted on the 22nd, 23rd, and 24th, of the month.

The idea of again rounding such an extensive piece of water and of travelling over so barren a country was dreadful, and we feared that other arms, equally large, might obstruct our path, and that the strength of the party would entirely fail, long before we could reach the only part where we were certain of finding wood, distant in a direct line twenty-five miles. While we halted to considered of this subject, and to collect the party, the carcass of a deer was discovered in the cleft of a rock into which it had fallen in the spring. It was putrid, but little less acceptable to us on that account, in our present circumstances; and a fire being kindled, a large portion was devoured on the spot, affording us an unexpected breakfast, for in order to husband our small remaining portion of meat, we had agreed to make only one scanty meal a day. The men, cheered by this unlooked-for supply, became sanguine in the hope of being able to cross the stream on a raft of willows, although they had declared such a project impracticable, and they unanimously entreated us to return back to the rapid, a request which accorded with our own opinion, and was therefore acceded to. Crédit and Junius, however, were missing, and it was also necessary to send notice of our intention to Mr. Back and his party. Augustus being promised a reward, undertook the task, and we agreed to wait for him at the rapid. It was supposed he could not fail meeting with the two stragglers on his way to or from Mr. Back, as it was likely they would keep on the borders of the lake. He accordingly set out after Mr. Back, whilst we returned about a mile towards the rapid, and encamped in a deep valley amongst some large willows. We supped on the remains of the putrid deer, and the men having gone to the spot where it was found, scraped together the contents of its intestines which were scattered on the rocks, and added them to their meal. We also enjoyed the luxury of to-day eating a large quantity of excellent blue-berries and cran-berries (*vaccinium uliginosum* and *v. Vitis idaea*) which were laid bare by the melting of the snow, but nothing could allay our inordinate appetites.

In the night we heard the report of Crédit's gun in answer to our signal muskets, and he rejoined us in the morning, but we got no intelligence of Junius. We set out about an hour after daybreak, and encamped at two P.M. between the rapids, where the river was about one hundred and thirty yards wide, being its narrowest part.

Eight deer were seen by Michel and Crédit, who loitered behind the rest of the party, but they could not approach them. A great many shots were fired by those in the rear at partridges, but they missed, or at least did not choose to add what they killed to the common stock. We subsequently learned that the hunters often secreted the partridges they shot, and ate them unknown to the officers. Some *tripe de roche* was collected, which we boiled for supper, with the moiety of the remainder of our deer's meat. The men commenced cutting the willows for the construction of the raft. As an incitement to exertion, I promised a reward of three hundred livres to the first person who should convey a line across the river, by which the raft could be managed in transporting the party.

September 29

Strong south-east winds with fog in the morning, more moderate in the evening. Temperature of the rapid 38°. The men began at an early hour to bind the willows in fagots for the construction of the raft, and it was finished by seven; but as the willows were green, it proved to be very little buoyant, and was unable to support more than one man at a time. Even on this, however, we hoped the whole party might be transported, by hauling it from one side to the other, provided a line could be carried to the other bank. Several attempts were made by Belanger and Benoit, the strongest men of the party, to convey the raft across the stream, but they failed for want of oars. A pole was constructed by tying the tent poles together, was too short to reach the bottom at a short distance from the shore; and a paddle which had been carried from the sea-coast by Dr. Richardson, did not possess sufficient power to move the raft in opposition to a strong breeze, which blew from the other side. All the men suffered extremely from the coldness of the water, in which they were necessarily immersed up to the waists, in their endeavours to aid Belanger and Benoit; and having witnessed repeated failures, they began to consider the scheme as hopeless. At this time Dr. Richardson, prompted by a desire of relieving his suffering companions, proposed to swim across the stream with a line, and to haul the raft over. He launched into the stream with the line round his middle, but when he got a short distance from the bank, his arms became benumbed with cold, and he lost the power of moving them; still he persevered, and, turning on his back, had nearly gained the opposite bank, when his legs also became powerless, and to our infinite alarm we beheld him sink. We instantly hauled upon the line and he came again on the surface, and was gradually drawn ashore in an almost lifeless state. Being rolled up in blankets, he was placed before a good fire of willows, and fortunately was just able to speak sufficiently to give some slight directions respecting the manner of treating him. He recovered strength gradually, and through the blessing of God was enabled in the course of a few hours to converse, and by the evening was sufficiently recovered to remove into the tent. We then regretted to learn that the skin on his whole left side was deprived of feeling, in consequence of exposure to too great heat. He did not perfectly recover the sensation of that side until the following summer. I cannot describe what every one felt at beholding the skeleton which the Doctor's debilitated frame exhibited. When he stripped, the Canadians simultaneously exclaimed, "Ah! Que nous sommes maigres!" I shall best explain his state and that of the party, by the following extract from his journal: "It may be worthy of remark that I should have had little hesitation in any former period of my life, at plunging into water even below 38° Fahrenheit; but at this time I was reduced almost to skin and bone, and, like the rest of the party, suffered from degrees of cold that would have been disregarded in health and vigour. During the whole of our march we experienced that no quantity of clothing could keep us warm whilst we fasted, but on those occasions on which we were enabled to go to bed with full stomachs, we passed the night in a warm and comfortable manner."

In following the detail of our friend's narrow escape, I have omitted to mention, that when he was about to step into the water, he put his foot on a dagger, which cut him to the bone; but this misfortune could not stop him from attempting the execution of his generous undertaking.

In the evening Augustus came in. He had walked a day and a half beyond the place from whence we turned back, but had neither seen Junius nor Mr. Back. Of the former he had seen no traces, but he had followed the tracks of Mr. Back's party for a considerable distance, until the hardness of the ground rendered them imperceptible. Junius was well equipped with ammunition, blankets, knives, a kettle, and other necessaries; and it was the opinion of Augustus that when he found he could not rejoin the party, he would endeavour to gain the woods on the west end of the Point Lake, and follow the river until he fell in with the Esquimaux, who frequent its mouth. The Indians too with whom we have since conversed upon this subject, are confident that he would be able to subsist himself during the winter. Crédit, on his hunting excursion to-day, found a cap, which our people recognised to belong to one of the hunters who had left us in the spring. This circumstance produced the conviction of our being on the banks of the Copper-Mine River, which all the assertions of the officers had hitherto failed in effecting with some of the party; and it had the happy consequence of reviving their spirits considerably. We consumed the last of our deer's meat this evening at supper.

Next morning the men went out in search of dry willows, and collected eight large fagots, with which they formed a more buoyant raft than the former, but the wind being still adverse and strong, they delayed attempting to cross until a more favourable opportunity. Pleased, however, with the appearance of this raft, they collected some *tripe de roche*, and made a cheerful supper. Dr. Richardson was gaining strength, but his leg was much swelled and very painful. An observation for latitude placed the encampment in 65° 00′ 00″ N., the longitude being 112° 20′ 00″ W., deduced from the last observation.

On the morning of the 1st of October, the wind was strong, and the weather as unfavourable as before for crossing on the raft. We were rejoiced to see Mr. Back and his party in the afternoon. They had traced the lake about fifteen miles farther than we did, and found it undoubtedly connected, as we had supposed, with the lake we fell in with on the 22nd September; and dreading, as we had done, the idea of coasting its barren shores, they returned to make an attempt at crossing here. St. Germain now proposed to make a canoe of the fragments of painted canvas in which we wrapped our bedding. This scheme appearing practicable, a party was sent to our encampment of the 24th and 25th last, to collect pitch amongst the small pines that grew there, to pay over the seams of the canoe.

In the afternoon we had a heavy fall of snow, which continued all night. A small quantity of *tripe de roche* was gathered; and Crédit, who had been hunting, brought in the antlers and back bone of a deer which had been killed in the summer. The wolves and birds of prey had picked them cleaned, but there still remained a quantity of the spinal marrow which they had not been able to extract. This, although putrid, was esteemed a valuable prize, and the spine being divided into portions, was distributed equally. After eating the marrow, which was so acrid as to excoriate the lips, we rendered the bones friable by burning, and ate them also.

On the following morning the ground was covered with snow to the depth of a foot and a half, and the weather was very stormy. These circumstances rendered the men again extremely despondent; a settled gloom hung over their countenances, and they refused to pick *tripe de roche*, choosing rather to entirely without eating, than to make any exertion. They party which went for gum returned early in the morning without having found any; but St. Germain said he could still make the canoe with the willows, covered with canvas, and removed with Adam to a clump of willows for that purpose. Mr. Back accompanied them to stimulate his exertion, as we feared the lowness of his spirits would cause him to be slow in his operations. Augustus went to fish at the rapid, but a large trout having carried away his bait, we had nothing to replace it.

The snow-storm continued all the night, and during the forenoon of the 3rd. Having persuaded the people to gather some *tripe de roche*, I partook of a meal with them; and afterwards set out with the intention of going to St. Germain to hasten his operations, but those he was only three-quarters of a mile distant, I spent three hours in a vain attempt to reach him, my strength being unequal to the labour of wading through the deep snow; and I returned quite exhausted, and much shaken by the numerous falls I had got. My associates were all in the same debilitated state, and poor Hood was reduced to a perfect shadow, from the severe bowel complaints which the *tripe de roche* never failed to give him. Back was so feeble as to require the support of a stick in walking; and Dr. Richardson had lameness superadded to weakness. The voyagers were somewhat stronger than ourselves, but more indisposed to exertion, on account of the despondency. The sensation of hunger was no longer felt by any of us, yet we were scarcely able to converse upon any other subject than the pleasures of eating. We were much indebted to Hepburn at this crisis. The officers were unable from weakness to gather *tripe de roche* themselves, and Samandré, who had acted as our cook on the journey from the coast, sharing in the despair of the rest of the Canadians, refused to make the slightest exertion. Hepburn, on the contrary, animated by a firm reliance on beneficence of the Supreme Being, tempered with resignation to His will, was indefatigable in his exertions to serve us, and daily collected all the *tripe de roche* that was used in the officers' mess. Mr. Hood could not partake of this miserable fare, and a partridge which had been reserved for him was, I lament to say, this day stolen by one of the men.

October 4

The canoe being finished, it was brought to the encampment, and the whole party being assembled in anxious expectation on the beach, St. Germain embarked, and amidst our prayers for his success, succeeded in reaching the opposite shore. The canoe was then drawn back again, and another person transported, and in this manner by drawing it backwards and forwards, we were all conveyed over without any serious accident. By these frequent traverses the canoe was materially injured; and latterly it filled each time with water before reaching the shore, so that all our garments and bedding were wet, and there was not a sufficiency of willows upon the side on which we now were, to make a fire to dry them.

That no time might be lost in procuring relief, I immediately despatched Mr. Back with St. Germain, Solomon Belanger, and Beauparlant, to search for the Indians, directing him to go to Fort Enterprise, where we expected they would be, or where, at least, a note from Mr. Wentzel would be found to direct us in our search for them. If St. Germain should kill any animals on his way, a portion of the meat was to be put up securely for us, and conspicuous marks placed over it.

It is impossible to imagine a more gratifying change than was produced in our voyagers after we were all safely landed on the southern banks of the river. Their spirits immediately revived, each of them shook the officers cordially by the hand, and declared they now considered the worst of their difficulties over, as they did not doubt of reaching Fort Enterprise in a few days, even in their feeble condition. We had, indeed, every reason to be grateful, and our joy would have been complete had it not been mingled with sincere regret at the separation of our poor Esquimaux, the faithful Junius.

The want of *tripe de roche* caused us to go supperless to bed. Showers of snow fell frequently during the night. The breeze was light next morning, the weather cold and clear. We were all on foot by daybreak, but from the frozen state of our tents and bed-clothes, it was long before the bundles could be made, and as usual, the men lingered over a small fire they had kindled, so that it was eight o'clock before we started. Our advance, from the depths of the snow, was slow, and about noon, coming to a spot where there was some *tripe de roche*, we stopped to collect it and breakfasted. Mr. Hood, who was now very feeble, and Dr. Richardson, who attached himself to him, walked together at a gentle pace in the rear of the party. I kept with the foremost men, to cause them to halt occasionally, until the stragglers came up. Resuming our march after breakfast, we followed the track of Mr. Back's party, and encamped early, as all of us were much fatigued, particularly Crédit, who having to-day carried the men's tent, it being his turn so to do, was so exhausted, that when he reached the encampment he was unable to stand. The *tripe de roche* disagreed with this man and with Vaillant, in consequence of which, they were the first whose strength totally failed. We had a small quantity of this weed in the evening, and the rest of our supper was made up of scraps of roasted leather. The distance walked to-day was six miles. As Crédit was very weak in the morning, his load was reduced to little more than his personal luggage, consisting of his blanket, shoes, and gun. Previous to setting out, the whole party ate the remains of their old shoes, and whatever scraps of leather they had, to strengthen their stomachs for the fatigue of the day's journey. We left the encampment at nine, and pursued our route over a range of black hills. The wind having increased to a strong gale in the course of the morning, became piercingly cold, and the drift rendered it difficult for those in the rear to follow the track over the heights; whilst in the valleys, where it was sufficiently marked, from the depth of the snow, the labour of walking was pro-portionably great. Those in advance made, as usual, frequent halts, yet being unable from the severity of the weather to remain long still they were obliged to move on before the rear could come up, and the party, of course, straggled very much.

About noon Samandré coming up, informed us that Crédit and Vaillant could advance no farther. Some willows being discovered in a valley near us, I proposed to half the party there, whilst Dr. Richardson went back to visit them. I hoped too, that when the sufferers received the information of a fire being kindled at so short a distance they would be cheered, and use their utmost efforts to reach it, but this proved a vain hope. The Doctor found Vaillant about a mile and a half in the rear, much exhausted with cold and fatigue. Having encouraged him to advance to the fire, after repeated solicitations he made the attempt, but fell down amongst the deep snow at every step. Leaving him in this situation, the Doctor went about half a mile farther back to the spot where Crédit was said to have halted, and the track being nearly obliterated by the snow drift, it became unsafe for him to go farther. Returning he passed Vaillant, who having moved only a few yards in his absence, had fallen down, was unable to rise, and could scarcely answer his questions. Being unable to afford him any effectual assistance, he hastened on to inform us of his situation. When J. B. Belanger had heard the melancholy account, he went immediately to aid Vaillant, and bring up his burden. Respecting Crédit, we were informed by Samandré, that he had stopped a short distance behind Vaillant, but that his intention was to return to the encampment of the preceding evening.

When Belanger came back with Vaillant's load, he informed us that he had found him lying on his back, benumbed with cold, and incapable of being roused. The stoutest men of the party were now earnestly entreated to bring him to the fire, but they declared themselves unequal to the task; and, on the contrary, urged me to allow them to throw down their loads, and proceed to Fort Enterprise with utmost speed. A compliance with their desire would have caused the loss of the whole party, for the men were totally ignorant of the course to be pursued, and none of the officers, who could have directed the march, were sufficiently strong to keep up at the pace they would then walk; besides, even supposing them to have found their way, the strongest men would certainly have deserted the weak. Something, however, was absolutely necessary to be done to relieve them as much as possible from their burdens, and the officers consulted on the subject. Mr. Hood and Dr. Richardson proposed to remain behind, with a single attendant, at the first place where sufficient wood and *tripe de roche* should be found for ten days' consumption; and that I should proceed as expeditiously as possible with the men to the house, and thence send them immediate relief. They strongly urged that this arrangement would contribute to the safety of the rest of the party, by relieving them from the burden of a tent, and several other articles; and that they might afford aid to Crédit, if he should unexpectedly come up. I was distressed beyond description at the thought of leaving them in such a dangerous situation, and for a long time combated their proposal; but they strenuously urged, that this step afforded the only chance of safety for the party, and I reluctantly acceded to it. The ammunition, of which we had a small barrel, was also to be left with them, and it was hoped that this deposit would be a strong inducement for the Indians to venture across the barren grounds to their aid. We communicated this resolution to the men, who were cheered at the slightest prospect of alleviation to their present miseries, and promised with great appearance of earnestness to return to those officers, upon the first supply of food.

The party then moved on; Vaillant's blanket and other necessaries were left in the track, at the request of the Canadians, without any hope, however, of his being able to reach them. After marching till dusk without seeing a favourable place for encamping, night compelled us to take shelter under the less of a hill, amongst some willows, with which, after many attempts, we at length made a fire. It was not sufficient, however, to warm the whole party, much less to thaw our shoes; and the weather not permitting the gathering of *tripe de roche*, we had nothing to cook. The painful retrospection of the melancholy events of the day banished sleep, and we shuddered as we contemplated the dreadful effects of this bitterly cold night on our two companions, if still living. Some faint hopes were entertained of Crédit's surviving the storm, as he was provided with a good blanket, and had leather to eat.

The weather was mild next morning. We left the encampment at nine, and a little before noon came to a pretty extensive thicket of small willows, near which there appeared a supply of *tripe de roche* on the face of the rocks. At this place Dr. Richardson and Mr. Hood determined to remain, with John Hepburn, who volunteered to stop with them. The tent was securely pitched, a few willows collected, and the ammunition and all other articles were deposited, except each man's clothing, one tent, a sufficiency of ammunition for the journey, and the officers' journals. I had only one blanket, which was carried for me, and two pairs of shoes. The offer was now made for any of the men, who felt themselves too weak to proceed, to remain with the officers, but none of them accepted it. Michel alone felt some inclination to do so. After we had united in thanksgiving and prayers to Almighty God, I separated from my companions, deeply afflicted that a train of melancholy circumstances should have demanded of me the severe trial of parting, in such a condition, from friends who had become endeared to me by their constant kindness and co-operation, and a participation of numerous sufferings. This trial I could not have been induced to undergo, but for the reasons they had so strongly urged the day before, to which my own judgment assented, and for the sanguine hope I felt of either finding a supply of provision at Fort Enterprise, or meeting the Indians in the immediate vicinity of that place, according to my arrangements with Mr. Wentzel and Akaitcho. Previously to our starting, Peltier and Benoit repeated their promises, to return to them with provision, if any should be found at the house, or to guide the Indians to them, if any were met.

Greatly as Mr. Hood was exhausted, and indeed, incapable as he must have proved, of encountering the fatigue of our very next day's journey, so that I felt his resolution to be prudent, I was sensible that his determination to remain, was chiefly prompted by the disinterest and generous wish to remove impediments to the progress of the rest. Dr. Richardson and Hepburn, who were both in a state of strength to keep pace with the men, besides this motive which they shared with him, were influenced in their resolution to remain, the former by the desire which had distinguished his character, throughout the Expedition, of devoting himself to the succour of the weak, and the latter by the zealous attachment he had ever shown towards his officers.

We set out without waiting to take any of the *tripe de roche*, and walking at a tolerable pace, in an hour arrived at a fine group of pines, about a mile and a quarter from the tent. We sincerely regretted not having seen these before we separated from our companions, as they would have been better supplied with fuel here, and there appeared to be more *tripe de roche* than where we had left them.

Descending afterwards into a more level country, we found the snow very deep, and the labour of wading through it so fatigued the whole party, that we were compelled to encamp, after a march of four miles and a half. Belanger and Michel were left far behind, and when they arrived at the encampment appeared quite exhausted. The former, bursting into tears, declared his inability to proceed, and begged me to let him go back next morning to the tent, and shortly afterwards Michel made the same request. I was in hopes they might recover a little strength by the night's rest, and therefore deferred giving any permission *until* morning. The sudden failure in the strength of these men cast a gloom over the rest, which I tried in vain to remove, by repeated assurances that the distance to Fort Enterprise was short, and that we should, in all probability, reach it in four days. Not being able to find any *tripe de roche*, we drank an infusion of the Labrador tea plant (*ledum palustre*), and ate a few morsels of burnt leather for supper. We were unable to raise the tent, and found its weight too great to carry it on; we, therefore, cut it up, and took a part of the canvas for a cover. The night was bitterly cold, and though we lay as close to each other as possible, having no shelter, we could not keep ourselves sufficiently warm to sleep. A strong gale came on after midnight, which increased the severity of the weather. In the morning Belanger and Michel renewed their request to be permitted to go back to the tent, assuring me they were still weaker than on the preceding evening, and less capable of going forward; and they urged, that the stopping at a place where there was a supply of *tripe de roche* was their only chance of preserving life; under these circumstances, I could not do otherwise than yield to their desire. I wrote a note to Dr. Richardson and Mr. Hood, informing them of the pines we had passed, and recommending their removing thither. Having found that Michel was carrying a considerable quantity of ammunition, I desired him to divide it among my party, leaving him only ten balls and a little shot, to kill any animals he might meet on his way to the tent. This man was very particularly in his inquiries respecting the direction of the house, and the course we meant to pursue; he also said, that if he should be able, he would go and search for Vaillant and Crédit; and he requested my permission to take Vaillant's blanket, if he should find it, to which I agreed, and mentioned it in my notes to the officers.

Scarcely were these arrangements finished, before Perrault and Fontano were seized with a fit of dizziness, and betrayed other symptoms of extreme debility. Some tea was quickly prepared for them, and after drinking it, and eating a few morsels of burnt leather, they recovered, and expressed their desire to go forward; but the other men, alarmed at what they had just witnessed, became doubtful of their own strength, and, giving want to absolute dejection, declared their inability to move. I now earnestly pressed upon them the necessity of continuing our journey, as the only means of saving their own lives, as well as those of our friends at the tent; and, after much entreaty, got them to set out at ten A.M.: Belanger and Michel were left at the encampment, and proposed to start shortly afterwards. By the time we had gone about two hundred yards, Perrault became again dizzy, and desired us to halt, which we did, until he, recovering, offered to march on. Ten minutes more had hardly elapsed before he again desired us to stop, and bursting into tears, declared he was totally exhausted, and unable to accompany us farther. As the encampment was not more than a quarter of a mile distance, we recommended that he should return to it, and rejoin Belanger and Michel, whom we knew to be still there, from perceiving the smoke of a fresh fire; and because they had not made any preparation for starting when we quitted them. He readily acquiesced in the proposition, and having taken a friendly leave of each of us, and enjoined us to make all the haste we could in sending relief, he turned back, keeping his gun and ammunition. We watched him until he was nearly at the fire, and then proceeded. During these detentions, Augustus becoming impatient of the delay had walked on, and we lost sight of him. The labour we experienced in wading through the deep snow induced us to cross a moderate size lake, which lay in our track, but we found this operation far more harassing. As the surface of the ice was perfectly smooth, we slipped at almost every step, and were frequently blown down by the wind with such a force as to shake our whole frames.

Poor Fontano was completely exhausted by the labour of this traverse, and we made a halt until his strength was recruited, by which time the party was benumbed with cold. Proceeding again, he got on tolerably well for a little time; but being again seized with faintness and dizziness, he fell often, and at length exclaimed that he could go no farther. We immediately stopped, and endeavoured to encourage him to persevere, until we should find some willows to camp; he insisted, however, that he could not march any longer through this deep snow; and said, that if he should even reach our encampment this evening, he must be left there, provided *tripe de roche* could not be procured to recruit his strength. The poor man was overwhelmed with grief, and seemed desirous to remain at that spot. We were about two miles from the place where the other men had been left, and as the track to it was beaten, we proposed to him to return thither, as we thought it probable he would find the men still there; at any rate, he would be able to get fuel to keep him warm during the night; and, on the next day, he could follow their track to the officers' tent; and, should the path be covered by the snow, the pines we had passed yesterday would guide him, as they were yet in view.

I cannot describe my anguish on the occasion of separating from another companion under circumstances so distressing. There was, however, no alternative.

The extreme debility of the rest of the party put the carrying him quite out of the question, as he himself admitted; and it was evident that the frequent delays he must occasion if he accompanied us, and did not gain strength, would endanger the lives of the whole. By returning he had the prospect of getting to the tent where *tripe de roche* could be obtained, which agreed with him better than with any other of the party, and which he was always very assiduous in gathering. After some hesitation he determined on going back, and set out, having bid each of us farewell in the tenderest manner. We watched him with inexpressible anxiety for some time, and were rejoiced to find, though he got on slowly, that he kept on his legs better than before. Antonio Fontano was an Italian, and had served many years in De Meuron's regiment. He had spoken to me that very morning, and after his first attack of dizziness, about his father; and had begged, that should he survive, I would take him with me to England, and put him in the way of reaching home.

The party was now reduced to five persons, Adam, Peltier, Benoit, Samandré, and myself. Continuing the journey we came, after an hour's walk, to some willows, and encamped under the shelter of a rock, having walked in the whole four miles and a half. We made an attempt to gather some *tripe de roche*, but could not, owing to the severity of the weather. Our supper, therefore, consisted of tea and a few morsels of leather.

Augustus did not make his appearance, but we felt no alarm at his absence, supposing he would go to the tent if he missed our track. Having fire, we procured a little sleep. Next morning the breeze was light and the weather mild, which enabled us to collect some *tripe de roche*, and to enjoy the only meal we had had for four days. We derived great benefit from it, and walked with considerably more ease than yesterday. Without the strength it supplied, we should certainly have been unable to oppose the strong breeze we met in the afternoon. After walking about five miles, we came upon the borders of Marten Lake, and were rejoiced to find it frozen, so that we could continue our course straight for Fort Enterprise. We encamped at the first rapid in Winter River amidst willows and alders; but these were so frozen, and the snow fell so thick, that the men had great difficulty in making a fire. This proving insufficient to warm us, or even thaw our shoes, and having no food to prepare, we crept under our blankets. The arrival of a well-known part raised the spirits of the men to a high pitch, and we kept up a cheerful conversation until sleep overpowered us. The night was very stormy, and the morning scarcely less so; but, being desirous to reach the house this day, we commenced our journey very early. We were gratified by the sight of a large herd of reindeer on the side of the hill near the track, but our only hunter, Adam, was too feeble to pursue them. Our shoes and garments were stiffened by the frost, and we walked in great pain until we arrived at some stunted pines, at which we halted, made a good fire, and procured the refreshment of tea. The weather becoming fine in the afternoon, we continued our journey, passed the Dog-Rib Rock, and encamped among a clump of pines of considerable growth, about a mile father on. Here we enjoyed the comfort of a large fire for the first time since our departure from the sea-coast; but this gratification was purchased at the expense of many severe falls in crossing a stony valley to get to these trees. There was no *tripe de roche*, and we drank tea and ate some of our shoes for supper. Next morning after taking the usual repast of tea, we proceeded to the house. Musing on what we were likely to find there, our minds were agitated between hope and fear, and, contrary to the custom we had kept up, of supporting our spirits by conversation, we went silently forward.

At length we reached Fort Enterprise, and to our infinite disappointment and grief found it a perfectly desolate habitation. There was no deposit of provision, no trace of the Indians, no letter from Mr. Wentzel to point out where the Indians might be found. It would be impossible to describe our sensations after entering this miserable abode, and discovering how we had been neglected: the whole party shed tears, not so much for our own fate, as for that of our friends in the rear, whose lives depended entirely on our sending immediate relief from this place.

I found a note, however, from Mr. Back, stating that he had reached the house two days before and was going in search of the Indians, at a part where St. Germain deemed it probable they might be found. If he was unsuccessful, he purposed walking to Fort Providence, and sending succour from thence: but he doubted whether either he or his party could perform the journey to that place in their present debilitated state. It was evident that any supply that could be sent from Fort Providence would be long in reaching us, neither could it be sufficient to enable us to afford any assistance to our companions behind, and that the only relief for them must be procured from the Indians. I resolved, therefore, on going also in search of them; but my companions were absolutely incapable of proceeding, and I thought by halting two or three days they might gather a little strength, whilst the delay would afford us the chance of learning whether Mr. Back had seen the Indians.

We now looked round for the means of subsistence, and were gratified to find several deer-skins, which had been thrown away during our former residence. The bones were gathered from the heap of ashes; these with the skins, and the addition of *tripe de roche*, we considered would support us tolerably well for a time. As to the house, the parchment being torn from the windows, the apartment we selected for our abode was exposed to all the rigour of the season. We endeavoured to exclude the wind as much as possible, by placing loose boards against the apertures. The temperature was now between 15° and 20° below zero. We procured fuel by pulling up the flooring of the other rooms, and water for cooking, by melting the snow. Whilst we were seated round the fire, singeing the deer-skin for supper, we were rejoiced by the unexpected entrance of Augustus. He had followed quite a different course from ours, and the circumstance of his having found his way through a part of the country he had never been in before, must be considered a remarkable proof of sagacity. The unusual earliness of the winter became manifest to us from the state of things at this spot. Last year at the same season, and still later there had been very little snow on the ground, and we were surrounded by vast herds of reindeer; now there were but few recent tracks of these animals, and the snow was upwards of two feet deep. Winter River was then open, now it was frozen two feet thick.

When I arose the following morning, my body and limbs were so swollen that I was unable to walk more than a few yards. Adam was in a still worse condition, being absolutely incapable of rising without assistance. My other companions happily experienced this inconvenience in a less degree, and went to collect bones, and some *tripe de roche* which supplied us with two meals. The bones were quite acrid, and the soup extracted from them excoriated the mouth if taken alone, but it was somewhat milder when boiled with *tripe de roche*, and we even thought the mixture quite palatable, with the addition of salt, of which a cask had been fortunately left here in the spring. Augustus to-day set two fishing-lines below the rapid. On his way thither he saw two deer, but had not strength to follow them.

On the 13th the wind blew violently from south-east, and the snow drifted so much that the party were confined to the house. In the afternoon of the following day Belanger arrived with a note from Mr. Back, stating that he had seen no trace of the Indians, and desiring further instructions as to the course he should pursue. Belanger's situation, however, required our first care, as he came in almost speechless, and covered with ice, having fallen into a rapid, and, for the third time since we left the coast, narrowly escaped drowning. He did not recover sufficiently to answer our questions, until we had rubbed him for some time, changed his dress, and given him some warm soup. My companions nursed him with the greatest kindness, and the desire of restoring him to health, seemed to absorb all regard for their own situation. I witnessed with peculiar pleasure this conduct, so different from that which they had recently pursued, when every tender feeling was suspended by the desire of self-preservation. They now no longer betrayed impatience or despondency, but were composed and cheerful, and had entirely given up the practice of swearing, to which the Canadian voyagers are so lamentably addicted. Our conversation naturally turned upon the prospect of getting relief, and upon the means which were bed adapted for obtaining. The absence of all traces of Indians on Winter River, convinced me that they were at this time on the way to Fort Providence, and that by proceeding towards that post we should overtake them, as they move slowly when they have their families with them. This route also offered us the prospect of killing deer, in the vicinity of Reindeer Lake, in which neighbourhood, our men in their journey to and fro last winter, had always found them abundant. Upon these grounds I determined on taking the route to Fort Providence as soon as possible, and wrote to Mr. Back, desiring him to join me at Reindeer Lake, and detailing the occurrences since we parted, that our friends might receive relief, in case of any accident happening to me.

Belanger did not recover sufficient strength to leave us before the 18th. His answers as to the exact part of Round-Rock Lake in which he had left Mr. Back, were very unsatisfactory; and we could only collect that it was at a considerable distance, and that he was still going on with the intention of halting at the place where Akaitcho was encamped last summer, about thirty miles off. This distance appeared so great, that I told Belanger it was very unsafe for him to attempt it alone, and that he would be several days in accomplishing it. He stated, however, that as the track was beaten, he should experience little fatigue, and seemed so confident, that I suffered him to depart with a supply of singed hide. Next day I received information which explained why he was so unwilling to acquaint us with the situation of Mr. Back's party. He dreaded that I should resolve upon joining it, when our numbers would be so great as to consume at once everything St. Germain might kill, if by accident he should be successful in hunting. He even endeavoured to entice away our other hunter, Adam, and proposed to him to carry off the only kettle we had, and without which we could not have subsisted two days. Adam's inability to move, however, precluded him from agreeing to the proposal, but he could assign no reason for not acquainting me with it previous to Belanger's departure. I was at first inclined to consider the whole matter as a fiction of Adam's, but he persisted in his story without wavering; and Belanger, when we met again, confessed that every part of it was true. It is painful to have to record a fact so derogatory to human nature, but I have deemed it proper to mention it, to show the difficulties we had to contend with, and the effect which distress had in warping the feelings and understanding of the most diligent and obedient of our party; for such Belanger had been always esteemed up to this time.

In making arrangements for our departure, Adam disclosed to me, for the first time, that he was affected with oedematous swellings in some parts of the body, to such a degree as to preclude the slightest attempt at marching; and upon my expressing my surprise at his having hitherto concealed from me the extent of his malady, among other explanations the details of the preceding story came out. It now became necessary to abandon my original intention of proceeding with the whole party towards Fort Providence, and Peltier and Samandré having volunteered to remain with Adam, I determined on setting out with Benoit and Augustus, intending the send them relief by the first party of Indians we should meet. My clothes were so much torn, as to be quite inadequate to screen me from the wind, and Peltier and Samandrè fearing that I might suffer on the journey in consequence, kindly exchanged with me parts of their dress, desiring me to send them skins in return by the Indians. Having patched up three pairs of snow-shoes, and singed a quantity of skin for the journey, we started on the morning of the 20th. Previous to my departure, I packed up the journals of the officers, the charts, and some other documents, together with a letter addressed to the Under-Secretary of State, detailed the occurrences of the Expedition up to this period, which package was given in charge to Peltier and Samandré with directions that it should be brought away by the Indians who might come to them. I also instructed them to send succour immediately on its arrival to our companions in the rear, which they solemnly promised to do, and I left a letter for my friends, Richardson and Hood, to be sent at the same time. I thought it necessary to admonish Peltier, Samandré, and Adam, to eat two meals every day, in order to keep up their strength, which they promised me they would do. No language that I can use could adequately describe the parting scene. I shall only say there was far more calmness and resignation to the Divine will evinced by every one than could have been expected. We were all cheered by the hope that the Indians would be found by the one party, and relief sent to the other. Those who remained entreated us to make all the haste we could, and expressed their hope of seeing the Indians in ten or twelve days.

At first starting we were so feeble as scarcely to be able to move forwards, and the descent of the bank of the river through the deep snow was a sever labour. When we came upon the ice, where the snow was less deep, we got on better, but after walking six hours we had only gained four miles, and were then compelled by fatigue to encamp on the borders of Round-Rock Lake. Augustus tried for fish here, but without success, so that our fare was skin and tea. Composing ourselves to rest, we lay close to each other for warmth. We found the night bitterly cold, and the wind pierced through our famished frames.

The next morning was mild and pleasant for travelling, and we set out after breakfast. We had not, however, gone many yards before I had the misfortune to break my snow-shoes by falling between two rocks. This accident prevented me from keeping pace with Benoit and Augustus, and in the attempt I became quite exhausted. Feeling convinced that their being delayed on my account might prove of fatal consequence to the rest, I resolved on returning to the house, and letting them proceed alone in search of the Indians. I therefore halted them only whilst I wrote a note to Mr. Back, stating the reason for my return, and desiring he would send meat from Reindeer Lake by these men, if St. Germain should kill any animal there. If Benoit should miss Mr. Back, I directed him to proceed to Fort Providence, and furnished him with a letter to the gentleman in charge of it, requesting that immediate supplies might be sent to us.

On my return to the house, I found Samandré very dispirited, and too weak, as he said, to render any assistance to Peltier; upon whom the whole labour of getting wood and collecting the means of subsistence would have devolved. Conscious, too, that his strength would have been unequal to these tasks, they had determined upon taking only one meal each day; so that I felt my going back particularly fortunate, as I hoped to stimulate Samandré to exertion, and at any rate could contribute some help to Peltier. I undertook the office of cooking, and insisted they should eat twice a day whenever food could be procured; but as I was too weak to pound the bones, Peltier agreed to do that in addition to his more fatiguing task of getting wood. We had a violent snow-storm all the next day, and this gloomy weather increased the depression of spirits under which Adam and Samandré were labouring. Neither of them would quit their beds, and they scarcely ceased from shedding tears all day; in van did Peltier and myself endeavour to cheer them. We had even to use much entreaty before they would take the meals we had prepared for them. Our situation was indeed distressing, but in comparison with that of our friends in the rear, we thought it happy. Their condition gave us unceasing solicitude, and as the principal subject of our conversation.

Though the weather was stormy on the 26th, Samandré assisted me to gather *tripe de roche*. Adam, who was very ill, and could now be prevailed upon to eat this weed, subsisted principally on bones, though he also partook of the soup. The *tripe de roche* had hitherto afforded us out chief support, and we naturally felt great uneasiness at the prospect of being deprived of it, by its being so frozen as to render it impossible for us to gather it.

We perceived our strength decline every day, and every exertion began to be irksome; when we were once seated the greatest effort was necessary in order to rise, and we had frequently to lift each other from our seats; but even in this pitiable condition we conversed cheerfully, being sanguine as to the speedy arrival of the Indians. We calculated indeed that if they should be near the situation where they had remained last winter, our men would have reached them by this day. Having expended all the wood which we could procure from our present dwelling, without danger or its fall, Peltier began this day to pull down the partitions of the adjoining houses. These there were only distant about twenty yards, yet the increase of labour in carrying the wood fatigued him so much, that by the evening he was exhausted. On the next day his weakness was such, especially in the arms, of which he chiefly complained, that he with difficulty lifted the hatchet; still he persevered, whilst Samandré and I assisted him in bringing in the wood, but our united strength could only collect sufficient to replenish the fire four times in the course of the day. As the insides of our mouths had become sore from eating the bone-soup, we relinquished the use of it, and now boiled the skin, which mode of dressing we found more palatable than frying it, as he had hitherto done.

On the 29th Peltier felt his pains more severe, and could only cut a few pieces of wood. Samandré, who was still almost as weak, relieved him a little time, and I aided them in carrying in the wood. We endeavoured to pick some *tripe de roche*, but in vain, as it was entirely frozen. In turning up the snow, in searching for bones, I found several pieces of bark, which proved a valuable acquisition, as we were almost destitute of dry wood proper for kindling the fire. We saw a herd of reindeer sporting on the river, about half a mile from the house; they remained there a long time, but none of the party felt themselves strong enough to go after them, nor was there one of us who could have fired a gun without resting it.

Whilst we were seating round the fire this evening, discoursing about the anticipated relief, the conversation was suddenly interrupted by Peltier's exclaiming with joy, "*Ah! le monde!*" imagining that he heard the Indians in the other room; immediately afterwards, to his bitter disappointment, Dr. Richardson and Hepburn entered, each carrying his bundle. Peltier, however, soon recovered himself enough to express his delight at their safe arrival, and his regret that their companions were not with them. When I saw them alone my own mind was instantly filled with apprehensions respecting my friend Hood, and our other companions, which were immediately confirmed by the Doctor's melancholy communication, the Mr. Hood and Michel were dead. Perrault and Fontano had neither reached the tent, nor been heard of by them. This intelligence produced a melancholy despondency in the minds of my party, and on that account the particulars were deferred until another opportunity. We were all shocked at beholding the emaciated countenances of the Doctor and Hepburn, as they strongly evidenced their extremely debilitated state. The alteration in our appearance was equally distressing to them, for since the swellings had subsided we were little more than skin and bone. The Doctor particularly remarked at sepulchral tone of our voices, which he requested us to make more cheerful if possible, unconscious that his own partook of the same key.

Hepburn having shot a partridge, which was brought to the house, the Doctor tore out the feathers, and having held it to the fire a few minutes divided it into six portions. I and my three companions ravenously devoured our shares, as it was the first morsel of flesh any of us had tasted for thirty-one days, unless, indeed, the small grisly particles which we found occasionally adhering to the pounded bones may be termed flesh. Our spirits were revived by this small supply, and the Doctor endeavoured to raise them still higher by the prospect of Hepburn's being able to kill a deer next day, as they had seen, and even fired at several near the house. He endeavoured, too, to rouse us into some attention to the comfort of our apartment, and particularly to roll up, in the day, our blankets, which (expressly for the convenience of Adam and Samandré), we had been in the habit of leaving by the fire where we lay on them. The Doctor having brought his prayer-book and testament, some prayers and psalms, and portions of scripture, appropriate to our situation, were read, and we retired to bed.

Next morning the Doctor and Hepburn went out early in search of deer; but though they saw several herbs and fired some shots, they were not so fortunate as to kill any, being too weak to hold their guns steadily. The cold compelled the former to return soon, but Hepburn persisted until late in the evening.

My occupation was to search for skins under the snow, it being now out object immediately to get all that we would, but I had not strength to drag in more than two of those which were within twenty yards of the house until the Doctor came and assisted me. We made up our stock to twenty-six, but several of them were putrid, and scarcely eatable, even by men suffering the extremity of famine. Peltier and Samandré continued very weak and dispirited, and they were unable to cut firewood. Hepburn had in consequence that laborious task to perform after he came back. The Doctor having scarified the swelled parts of Adam's body, a large quantity of water flowed out, and he obtained some ease, but still kept his bed.

After our usual supper of singed skin and bone-soup, Dr, Richardson acquainted me with the afflicting circumstances attending the death of Mr. Hood and Michel, and detailed the occurrences subsequent to my departure from them, which I shall give from his Journal, in his own words; but I must here be permitted to express the heartfelt sorrow with which I was overwhelmed at the loss of so many companions; especially of my fried Mr. Hood, to whose zealous and able co-operation I had been indebted for so much invaluable assistance during the Expedition, whilst the excellent qualities of his heart engaged my warmest regard. His scientific observations, together with his maps and drawings (a small part of which only appear in this work), evince a variety of talent, which, had his life been spared, must have rendered him a distinguished ornament to his profession, and which will cause his death to be felt as a loss to the service.

DR. RICHARDSON'S NARRATIVE

After Captain Franklin had bidden us farewell we remained seated by the fireside as long as the willows the men had cut for us before they departed, lasted. We had no *tripe de roche* that day, but drank an infusion of the country tea-plant, which was grateful from its warmth, although it afforded no sustenance. We then retired to bed, where we remained all the next day, as the weather was stormy, and the snow-drift so heavy, as to destroy every prospect of success in our endeavours to light a fire with the green and frozen willows, which were our only fuel. Through the extreme kindness and forethought of a lady, the party, previous to leaving London, had been furnished with a small collection of religious books, of which we still retained two or three of the most portable, and they proved of incalculable benefit to us. We read portions of them to each other as we lay in bed, in addition to the morning and evening service, and found that they inspired us on each perusal with so strong a sense of the omnipresence of a beneficent God, that our situation, even in these wilds, appeared no longer destitute; and we conversed, not only with calmness, but with cheerfulness, detailed with unrestrained confidence the past events of our lives, and dwelling with hope on our future prospects. Had my poor friend been spared to revisit his native land, I should look back to this period with unalloyed delight.

On the morning of the 9th, the weather, although still cold, was clear, and I went out in quest of *tripe de roche*, leaving Hepburn to cut willows for a fire, and Mr. Hood in bed. I had no success, as yesterday's snow-drift was so frozen on the surface of the rocks that I could not collect any of the weed; but on my return to the tent, I found that Michel, the Iroquois, had come with a note from Mr. Franklin, which stated, that this man and Jean Baptiste Belanger being unable to proceed, were about to return to us, and that a mile beyond our present encampment there was a clump of pine-trees, to which he recommended us to remove the tent. Michel informed us that he quitted Mr. Franklin's party yesterday morning, but, that having missed his way, he had passed the night on the snow a mile or two to the northward of us. Belanger, he said, being impatient, left the fire about two hours earlier, and, as he had not arrived, he supposed must have gone astray. It will be seen in the sequel, that we had more than sufficient reason to doubt the truth of this story.

Michel now produced a hare and a partridge which he had killed in the morning. This unexpected supply of provision was received by us with a deep sense of gratitude to the Almighty for His goodness, and we looked upon Michel as the instrument He had chosen to preserve all our lives. He complained of cold, and Mr. Hood offered to share his buffalo robe with him at night: I gave him one of two shirts which I wore, whilst Hepburn in the warmth of his heart, exclaimed, "How I shall love this man if I find that he does not tell lies like the others." Our meals being finished, we arranged that the greatest part of the things should be carried to the pines the next day; and, after reading the evening service retired to bed full of hope.

Early in the morning Hepburn, Michel, and myself, carried the ammunition, and most of the other heavy articles to the pines. Michel was our guide, and it did not occur to us at the time that his conducting us perfectly straight was incompatible with his story of having mistaken his road in coming to us. He now informed us that he had, on his way to the tent, left on the hill above the pines and gun and forty-eight balls, which Perrault had given to him when with the rest of Franklin's party, he took leave of him. It will be seen, on a reference to Mr. Franklin's journal, that Perrault carried his gun and ammunition with him when they parted from Michel and Belanger. After we had made a fire, and drank a little of the country tea, Hepburn and I returned to the tent, where we arrived in the evening, much exhausted with our journey. Michel preferred sleeping where he was, and requested us to leave him the hatchet, which we did, after he had promised to come early in the morning to assist us in carrying the tent and bedding. Mr. Hood remained in bed all day. Seeing nothing of Belanger to-day, we gave him up for lost.

On the 11th, after waiting until late in the morning for Michel, who did not come, Hepburn and I loaded ourselves with the bedding, and, accompanied by Mr. Hood, set out for the pines. Mr. Hood was much affected with dimness of sight, giddiness, and other symptoms of extreme debility, which caused us to move very slowly, and to make frequent halts.

On arriving at the pines, we were much alarmed to find that Michel was absent. We feared that he had lost his way in coming to us in the morning, although it was not easy to conjecture how that could have happened, as our footsteps of yesterday were very distinct. Hepburn went back for the tent, and returned with it after dusk, completely worn out with the fatigue of the day. Michel, too, arrived at the same time, and relieved our anxiety on his account. He reported that he had been in chase of some deer which passed near his sleeping-place in the morning, and although he did not come up with them, yet that he found a wolf which had been killed by the stroke of a deer's horn, and had brought a part of it. We implicitly believed this story then, but afterwards became convinced from circumstances, the detail of which may be spared, that it must have been a portion of the body of Belanger or Perrault. A question of moment here presents itself; namely, whether he actually murdered these men, or either of them, or whether he found the bodies in the snow. Captain Franklin, who is the best able to judge of this matter, from knowing their situation when he parted from them, suggested the former idea, and that both Belanger and Perrault had been sacrificed. When Perrault turned back, Captain Franklin watched him until he reached a small group of willows, which was immediately adjoining to the fire, and concealed it from view, and at this time the smoke of fresh fuel was distinctly visible. Captain Franklin conjectures, that Michel having already destroyed Belanger, completed his crime by Perrault's death, in order to screen himself from detection. Although this opinion is founded only on circumstances, and is unsupported by direct evidence, it has been judged proper to mention it, especially as the subsequent conduct of the man showed that he was capable of committing such a deed. The circumstances are very strong. It is not easy to assign any other adequate motive for his concealing from us that Perrault had turned back; while his request over-night that we should leave him the hatchet, and his cumbering himself with it when he went out in the morning, unlike a hunter who makes use only of his knife when he kills a deer, seem to indicate that he took it for the purpose of cutting up something that he knew to be frozen. These opinions, however, are the result of subsequent consideration. We passed this night in the open air.

On the following morning the tent was pitched; Michel went out early, refused my offer to accompany him, and remained out the whole day. He would not sleep in the tent at night, but chose to lie at the fireside.

On the 13th there was a heavy gale of wind, and we passed the day by the fire. Next day, about two P.M., the gale abating, Michel set out as he said to hunt, but returned unexpectedly in a very short time. This conduct surprised us, and his contradictory and evasory answers to our questions excited some suspicions, but they did not turn towards the truth.

October 15th

In the course of this day Michel expressed much regret that he had stayed behind Mr. Franklin's party, and declared that he would set out for the house at once if he knew the way. We endeavoured to soothe him, and to raise his hopes of the Indians speedily coming to our relief, but without success. He refused to assist us in cutting wood, but about noon, after much solicitation, he set out to hunt. Hepburn gathered a kettleful of *tripe de roche*, but froze his fingers. Both Hepburn and I fatigued ourselves much to-day in pursuing a flock of partridges from one part to another of the group of willows, in which the hut was situated, but we were too weak to be able to approach them with sufficient caution. In the evening Michel returned, having met with no success.

Next day he refused either to hunt or cut wood, spoke in a very surly manner, and threatened to leave us. Under these circumstances, Mr. Hood and I deemed it better to promise if he would hunt diligently for four days, that then we would give Hepburn a letter for Mr. Franklin, a compass, inform him what course to pursue, and let them proceed together to the fort. The non-arrival of the Indians to our relief, now led us to fear that some accident had happened to Mr. Franklin, and we placed no confidence in the exertions of the Canadians that accompanied him, but we had the fullest confidence in Hepburn's returning the moment he could obtain assistance.

On the 17th I went to conduct Michel to where Vaillant's blanket was left, and after walking about three miles, pointed out the hills to him at a distance, and returned to the hut, having gathered a bagful of *tripe de roche* on the way. It was easier to gather this weed on a march than at the tent, for the exercise of walking produced a glow of heat, which enabled us to withstand for a time the cold to which we were exposed in scraping the frozen surface of the rocks. On the contrary, when we left the fire, to collect it in the neighbourhood of the hut, we became chilled at once, and were obliged to return very quickly.

Michel proposed to remain out all night, and to hunt next day on his way back. He returned in the afternoon of the 18th, having found the blanket, together with a bag containing two pistols, and some other things which had been left beside it. We had some *tripe de roche* in the evening, but Mr. Hood from the constant griping it produced, was unable to eat more than one or two spoonfuls. He was now so weak as to be scarcely able to sit up at the fireside, and complained that the least breeze of wind seemed to blow through his frame. He also suffered much from cold during the night. We lay close to each other, but the heat of the body was no longer sufficient to thaw the frozen rime formed by our breaths on the blankets that covered him.

At this period we avoided as much as possible conversing upon the hopelessness of our situation, and generally endeavoured to lead the conversation towards our future prospects in life. The fact is, that with the decay of our strength, our minds decayed, and we were no longer able to bear the contemplation of the horrors that surrounded us. Each of us, if I may be allowed to judge from my own case, excused himself from so doing by a desire of not shocking the feelings of others, for we were sensible of one another's weakness of intellect though blind to our own. Yet we were calm and resigned to our fate, not a murmur escaped us, and we were punctual and fervent in our addresses to the Supreme Being.

On the 19th Michel refused to hunt, or even to assist in carrying a log of wood to the fire, which was too heavy for Hepburn's strength and mine. Mr. Hood endeavoured to point out to him the necessity and duty of exertion, and the cruelty of his quitting us without leaving something for our support; but the discourse, far from producing any beneficial effect, seemed only to excite his anger, and amongst other expressions, he made use of the following remarkable one: "It is no use hunting, there are no animals, you had better kill and eat me." At length, however, he went out, but returned very soon, with a report that he had seen three deer, which he was unable to follow from having wet his foot in a small stream of water thinly covered with ice, and being consequently obliged to come to the fire. The day was rather mild, and Hepburn and I gathered a large kettleful of *tripe de roche*; Michel slept in the tent this night.

Sunday, October 20

In the morning we again urged Michel to go hunting that he might if possible leave us some provision, to-morrow being the day appointed for his quitting us; but he showed great unwillingness to go out, and lingered about the fire, under the pretence of cleaning his gun. After we had read the morning service I went about noon to gather some *tripe de roche*, leaving Mr. Hood sitting before the tent at the fireside arguing with Michel; Hepburn was employed cutting down a tree at a short distance from the tent, being desirous of accumulating a quantity of firewood before he left us. A short time after I went out, I heard the report of a gun, and about ten minutes afterwards Hepburn called to me in a voice of great alarm, to come directly. When I arrived I found poor Hood lying lifeless at the fireside, a ball having apparently entered his forehead. I was at first horror-struck with the idea, that in a fit of despondency he had hurried himself into the presence of his Almighty Judge, by an act of his own hand; but the conduct of Michel soon gave rise to other thoughts, and excited suspicions which were confirmed, when upon examining the body, I discovered that the shot had entered the back part of the head, and passed out at the forehead, and that the muzzle of the gun had been applied so close as to set fire to the night-cap behind. The gun, which was of the longest kind supplied to the Indians, could not have been placed in a position to inflict such a wound, except by a second person. Upon inquiring of Michel how it happened, he replied that Mr. Hood had sent him into the tent for the short gun, and that during his absence the long gun had gone off, he did not know whether by accident or not. He held the short gun in his hand at the time he was speaking to me. Hepburn afterwards informed me that previous to the report of the gun Mr. Hood and Michel were speaking to each other in an elevated angry tone; that Mr. Hood being seated at the fireside, was hid from him by intervening willows, but that on hearing the report he looked up and saw Michel rising up from before the tent-door, or just behind where Mr. Hood was seated, and then going into the tent. Thinking that the gun had been discharged for the purpose of cleaning it, he did not go to the fire at first; and when Michel called to him that Mr. Hood was dead, a considerable time had elapsed. Although I dared not openly to evince any suspicion that I thought Michel guilty of the deed, yet he repeatedly protested that he was incapable of committing such an act, kept constantly on his guard, and carefully avoided leaving Hepburn and me together. He was evidently afraid of permitting us to converse in private, and whenever Hepburn spoke, he inquired if he accused him of the murder. It is to be remarked, that he understood English very imperfectly, yet sufficiently to render it unsafe for us to speak on the subject in his presence. We removed the body into a clump of willows behind the tent, and, returning to the fire, read the funeral service in addition to the evening prayers. The loss of a young officer, of such distinguished and varied talents and applications, may be felt and duly appreciated by the eminent characters under whose command he had served; but the calmness with which he contemplated the probable termination of a life of uncommon promise, and the patience and fortitude with which he sustained, I may venture to say, unparalleled boldily sufferings, can only be known to the companions of his distress. Owing to the effect that the *tripe de roche* invariably had, when he ventured to taste it, he undoubtedly suffered more than any of the survivors of the party. *Bickersteth's Scripture Help* was lying open beside the body, as if it had fallen from his hand, and it is probable, that he was reading it at the instant of his death. We passed the night in the tent together without rest, every one being on his guard. Next day, having determined on going to the fort, we began to patch and prepare our clothes for the journey. We singed the hair off a part of the buffalo robe that belonged to Mr. Hood, and boiled and ate it. Michel tried to persuade me to go to the woods on the Copper-Mine River, and hunt for deer instead of going to the fort. In the afternoon a flock of partridges coming near the tent, he killed several which he shared with us.

Thick snowy weather and a head wind prevented us from starting the following day, but on the morning of the 23rd we set out, carrying with us the remainder of the singed robe. Hepburn and Michel each had a gun, and I carried a small pistol which Hepburn had loaded for me. In the course of the march Michel alarmed us much by his gestures and conduct, was constantly muttering to himself, expressed an unwillingness to go to the fort, and tried to persuade me to go to the southward to the woods, where he said he could maintain himself all the winter by killing deer. In consequence of this behaviour, and the expression of his countenance, I requested him to leave us, and to go to the southward by himself. This proposal increased his ill-nature, he threw out some obscure hints of freeing himself from all restraint on the morrow; and I overheard his muttering threats against Hepburn, whom he openly accused of having told stories against him. He also, for the first time, assumed such a tone of superiority in addressing me, as evinced that he considered us to be completely in his power, and he gave vent to several expressions of hatred towards the white people, or as he termed us in the idiom of the voyagers, the French, some of whom, he said, had killed and eaten his uncle and two of his relations. In short, taking every circumstance of his conduct into consideration, I came to the conclusion that he would attempt to destroy us on the first opportunity that offered, and that he had hitherto abstained from doing so from his ignorance of his way to the fort, but that he would never suffer us to go thither in company with him. In the course of the day he had several times remarked that we were pursuing the same course that Mr. Franklin was doing when he left him, and by keeping towards the setting sun he could find his way himself. Hepburn and I were not in a condition to resist even an open attack, nor could we by any device escape from him. Our united strength was far inferior to his, and, beside his gun, he was armed with two pistols, an Indian bayonet and a knife. In the afternoon, coming to a rock on which there was some *tripe de roche*, he halted, and said he would gather it whilst we went on, and that he would soon overtake us. Hepburn and I were now left together for the first time since Mr. Hood's death, and he acquainted me with several material circumstances which he had observed of Michel's behaviour, and which confirmed me in the opinion that there was no safety for us except in his death, and he offered to be the instrument of it. I determined, however, as I was thoroughly convinced of the necessity of such a dreadful act, to take the whole responsibility upon myself; and immediately upon Michel's coming up, I put an end to his life by shooting him through the head with a pistol. Had my own life alone been threatened, I would not have purchased it by such a measure; but I considered myself as entrusted also with the protection of Hepburn's, a man who, by in humane attentions and devotedness, had so endeared himself to me, that I felt more anxiety for his safety than for my own. Michel had gathered no *tripe de roche*, and it was evident to us that he had halted for the purpose of putting his gun in order, with the intention of attacking us, perhaps, whilst we were in the act of encamping.

I have dwelt in the preceding part of the narrative upon many circumstance's of Michel's conduct, not for the purpose of aggravating his crime, but to put the reader in possession of the reasons that influenced me in depriving a fellow-creature of life. Up to the period of his return to the tent, his conduct had been good and respectful to the officers, and in a conversation between Captain Franklin, Mr. Hood, and myself, at Obstruction Rapid, it had been proposed to give him a reward upon our arrival at a post. His principles, however, unsupported by a belief in the divine truths of Christianity, were unable to withstand the pressures of severe distress. His countrymen, the Iroquois, are generally Christians, but he was totally uninstructed and ignorant of the duties inculcated by Christianity; and from his long residence in the Indian country, seems to have imbibed, or retained, the rules of conduct which the southern Indians prescribe to themselves.

On the two following days we had mild but thick snowy weather, and as the view was too limited to enable us to preserve a straight course, we remained encamped amongst a few willows and dwarf pines, and five miles from the tent. We found a species of *cornicularia*, a kind of lichen, that was good to eat when moistened and toasted over the fire; and we had a good many pieces of singed buffalo hide remaining.

On the 26th, the weather being clear and extremely cold, we resumed our march which was very painful from the depth of the snow, particularly on the margins of the small lakes that lay in our route. We frequently sunk under the load of our blankets, and were obliged to assist each other in getting up. After walked about three miles and a half, however, we were cheered by the sight of a large herd of reindeer, and Hepburn went in pursuit of them; but his hand being unsteady through weakness he missed. He was so exhausted by this fruitless attempt that we were obliged to encamp upon the spot, although it was a very unfavourable one.

Next day, we had fine and clear, but cold, weather. We set out early, and, in crossing a hill, found a considerable quantity of *tripe de roche*. About noon we fell upon Little Marten Lake, having walked about two miles. The sight of a place that we knew inspired us with fresh vigour, and there being comparatively little snow on the ice, we advanced at a pace to which we had lately been unaccustomed. In the afternoon we crossed a recent track of a wolverine, which, from a parallel mark in the snow, appeared to have been dragging something. Hepburn traced it, and upon the borders of the lake found the spine of a deer, that it had dropped. It was clean picked, and at least one season old; but we extracted the spinal marrow from it; which, even in its frozen state, was so acrid as to excoriate the lips. We encamped within sight of the Dog-Rib Rock, and from the coldness of the night and the want of fuel, rested very ill.

On the 28th we rose at daybreak, but from the want of the small fire, that we usually made in the mornings to warm our fingers, a very long time was spent in making up our bundles. This task fell to Hepburn's share, as I suffered so much from the cold as to be unable to take my hands out of my mittens. We kept a straight course for the Dog-Rib Rock, but, owing to the depth of the snow in the valleys we had to cross, did not reach it until late in the afternoon. We would have encamped, but did not like to pass a second night without fire; and though scarcely able to drag our limbs after us, we pushed on to a clump of pines, about a mile to the southward of the rock, and arrived at them in the dusk of the evening. During the last few hundred yards of our march, our track lay over some large stones, amongst which I fell down upwards of twenty times, and became at length so exhausted that I was unable to stand. If Hepburn had not exerted himself far beyond his strength, and speedily made the encampment and kindled a fire, I must have perished on the spot. This night we had plenty of dry wood.

On the 29th we had clear and fine weather. We set out at sunrise, and hurried on in our anxiety to reach the house, but our progress was much impeded by the great depth of the snow in the valleys. Although every spot of ground over which we travelled to-day had been repeatedly trodden by us, yet we got bewildered in a small lake. We took it for Marten Lake, which was three times its size, and fancied that we saw the rapids and the grounds about the fort, although they were still far distant. Our disappointment when this illusion was dispelled, by our reaching the end of the lake, so operated on our feeble minds as to exhaust our strength, and we decided upon encamping; but upon ascending a small eminence to look for a clump of wood, we caught a glimpse of the Big Stone, a well-known rock upon the summit of a hill opposite to the fort, and determined upon proceeding. In the evening we saw several large herds of reindeer, but Hepburn, who used to be considered a good marksman, was now unable to hold the gun straight, and although he got near them all his efforts proved fruitless. In passing through a small clump of pines we saw a flock of partridges, and he succeeded in killing one after firing several shots. We came in sight of the fort at dusk, and it is impossible to describe our sensations, when on attaining the eminence that overlooks it, we beheld the smoke issuing from one of the chimneys. From not having met with any footsteps in the snow, as we drew nigh our once cheerful residence, we had been agitated by many melancholy forebodings. Upon entering the now desolate building, we had the satisfaction of embracing Captain Franklin, but no words can convey the idea of the filth and wretchedness that met our eyes on looking around. Our own misery had stolen upon us by degrees, and we were accustomed to the contemplation of each others emaciated figures, but the ghastly countenances, dilated eye-balls, and sepulchral voices of Captain Franklin and those with him were more than we could at first bear.

Conclusion of Dr. Richardson's Narrative.

The morning of the 31st was very cold, the wind being strong from the north. Hepburn went again in quest of deer, and the Doctor endeavoured to kill some partridges: both were unsuccessful. A large herd of deer passed close to the house, the Doctor fired once at them, but was unable to pursue them. Adam was easier this day, and left his bed. Peltier and Samandré were much weaker, and could not assist in the labours of the day. Both complained of soreness in the throat, and Samandré suffered much from cramps in his fingers. The Doctor and Hepburn began this day to cut the wood, and also brought it to the house. Being too weak to aid in these laborious tasks, I was employed in searching for bones, and cooking, and attending to our more weakly companions. In the evening Peltier, complaining much of cold, requested of me a portion of blanket to repair his shirt and drawers. The mending of these articles occupied him and Samandré until past one A.M., and their spirits were so much revived by the employment, that they conversed even cheerfully the whole time. Adam sat up with them. The Doctor, Hepburn, and myself, went to bed. We were afterwards agreeably surprised to see Peltier and Samandré carry three or four logs of wood across the room to replenish the fire, which induced us to hope they still possessed more strength than we had supposed.

November, 1

This day was fine and mild. Hepburn went hunting, but was as usual unsuccessful. As his strength was rapidly declining, we advised him to desist from the pursuit of deer; and only to go out for a short time, and endeavour to kill a few partridges for Peltier and Samandré. The Doctor obtained a little *tripe de roche*, but Peltier could not eat any of it, and Samandré only a few spoonfuls, owing to the soreness of their throats. In the afternoon Peltier was so much exhausted, that he sat up with difficulty, and looked piteously; at length he slided from his stool upon his bed, as we supposed to sleep, and in this composed state he remained upwards of two hours, without our apprehending any danger. We were then alarmed by hearing a rattling in his throat, and on the Doctor's examining him, he was found to be speechless. He died in the course of the night. Samandré sat up the greater part of the day, and even assisted in pounding some bones; but on witnessing the melancholy state of Peltier, he became very low, and began to complain of cold and stiffness of the joints. Being unable to keep up a sufficient fire to warm him, we laid him down and covered him with several blankets. He did not, however, appear to get better, and I deeply lament to add he also died before daylight. We removed the bodies of the deceased into the opposite part of the house, but our united strength was inadequate to the task of interring them, or even carrying them down to the river.

It may be worthy of remark that poor Peltier, from the time of Benoit's departure, had fixed on the first of November as the time when he should cease to expect any relief from the Indians, and had repeatedly said that if they did not arrive by that day, he should not survive.

Peltier had endeared himself to each of us by his cheerfulness, his unceasing activity, and affectionate care and attentions, ever since our arrival at this place. He had nursed Adam with the tenderest solicitude the whole time. Poor Samandré was willing to have taken his share in the labours of the party, had he not been wholly incapacitated by his weakness and low spirits. The severe shock occasioned by the sudden dissolution of our two companions rendered us very melancholy. Adam became low and despondent, a change which we lamented the more, as we had perceived he had been gaining strength and spirits for the two preceding days. I was particularly distressed by the thought that the labour of collecting wood must now devolve upon Dr. Richardson and Hepburn, and that my debility would disable me from affording them any material assistance; indeed both of them most kindly urged me not to make the attempt. They were occupied the whole of the next day in tearing down the logs of which the store-house was built, but the mud plastered between them was so hard frozen that the labour of separation exceeded their strength, and they were completely exhausted by bringing in wood sufficient for less than twelve hours' consumption.

I found it necessary in their absence, to remain constantly near Adam, and to converse with him, in order to prevent his reflecting on our condition, and to keep up his spirits as far as possible. I also lay by his side at night.

On the 3rd the weather was very cold, though the atmosphere was cloudy. This morning Hepburn was affected with swelling in his limbs, his strength as well as that of the Doctor, was rapidly declining; they continued, however, to be full of hope. Their utmost exertions could only supply wood, to renew the fire thrice, and on making it up the last time we went to bed. Adam was in rather better spirits, but he could not bear to be left alone. Our stock of bones was exhausted by a small quantity of soup we made this evening. The toil of separating the hair from the skins, which in fact were our chief support, had now become so wearisome as to prevent us from eating as much as we should otherwise have done.

November 4. – Calm and comparatively mild weather. The Doctor and Hepburn, exclusive of their usual occupation, gathered some *tripe de roche*. I went a few hundred yards from the house in search of bones, and returned quite fatigued, having found but three. The Doctor again made incisions in Adam's leg, which discharged a considerable quantity of water, and gave him great relief. We read prayers and a portion of the New Testament in the morning and evening, as had been our practice since Dr. Richardson's arrival; and I may remark that the performance of these duties always afforded us the greatest consolation, serving to re-animate our hope in the mercy of the Omnipotent, who alone could save and deliver us.

On the 5th the breezes were light, with dark cloudy weather, and some snow. The Doctor and Hepburn were getting much weaker, and the limbs of the latter were now greatly swelled. They came into the house frequently in the course of the day to rest themselves, and when once seated, were unable to rise without the help of one another, or of a stick. Adam was for the most part in the same low spirit as yesterday, but sometimes he surprised us by getting up and walking with an appearance of increased strength. His looks were now wild and ghastly, and his conversation was often incoherent.

The next day was fine, but very cold. The swellings in Adam's limps having subsided, he was free from pain, and arose this morning in much better spirits, and spoke of cleaning his gun ready for shooting partridges, or any animals that might appear near the house, but his tone entirely changed before the day was half over; he became again dejected, and could scarcely be prevailed upon to eat. The Doctor and Hepburn were almost exhausted. The cutting of one log of wood occupied the latter half and hour; and the other took as much time to drag it into the house, though the distance did not exceed thirty yards. I endeavoured to help the Doctor, but my assistance was very trifling. Yet it was evident that, in a day or two, if their strength should continue to decline at the same rate, I should be the strongest of the party.

I may here remark that owing to our loss of flesh, the hardness of the floor, from which we were only protected by a blanket, produced soreness over the body, and especially those parts on which the weight rested in lying, yet to turn ourselves for relief was a matter of toil and difficulty. However, during this period, and indeed all along after the acute pains of hunger, which lasted but three or four days, had subsided, we generally enjoyed the comfort of a few hours' sleep. The dreams which for the most part, but not always accompanied it, were usually (though not invariably) of a pleasant character, being very often about the enjoyments of feasting. In the daytime we fell into the practice of conversing on common and light subjects, although we sometimes discussed with seriousness and earnestness topics connected with religion. We generally avoided speaking directly of our present sufferings, or even of the prospect of relief. I observed, that in proportion as our strength decayed, our minds exhibited symptoms of weakness, evinced by a kind of unreasonable pettishness with each other. Each of us thought the other weaker in intellect than himself, and more in need of advice and assistance. So trifling a circumstance as a change of place, recommended by one as being warmer and more comfortable, and refused by the other from a dread of motion, frequently called forth fretful expressions which were no soon uttered than atoned for, to be repeated perhaps in the course of a few minutes. The same thing often occurred when we endeavoured to assist each other in carrying wood to the fire; none of us were willing to receive assistance, although the task was disproportioned to our strength. On one of these occasions, Hepburn was so convinced of this waywardness that he exclaimed, "Dear me, if we are spared to return to England, I wonder if we shall recover our understandings."

November 7

Adam had passed a restless night, being disquieted by gloomy apprehensions of approaching death, which we tried in vain to dispel. He was so low in the morning as to be scarcely able to speak. I remained in bed by his side to cheer him as much as possible. The Doctor and Hepburn went to cut wood. They had hardly begun their labour, when they were amazed at hearing the report of a musket. They could scarcely believe that there was really any one near, until they heard a shout, and immediately espied three Indians close to the house. Adam and I heard the latter noise, and I was fearful that a part of the house had fallen upon one of my companions, a disaster which had in fact been thought not unlikely. My alarm was only momentary, Dr. Richardson came in to communicate the joyful intelligence that relief had arrived. He and myself immediately addressed thanksgivings to the throne of mercy for this deliverance, but poor Adam was in so low a state that he could scarcely comprehend the information. When the Indians entered, he attempted to rise but sank down again. But for this seasonable interposition of Providence, his existence must have terminated in a few hours, and that of the rest probably in not many days.

The Indians had left Akaitcho's encampment on the 5th November, having been sent by Mr. Back with all possible expedition, after he had arrived at their tents. They brought but a small supply of provision that they might travel quickly. It consisted of dried deer's meat, some fat, and a few tongues. Dr. Richardson, Hepburn, and I eagerly devoured the food, which they imprudently presented to us, in too great abundance, and in consequence we suffered dreadfully from indigestion, and had no rest the whole night. Adam being unable to feed himself, was more judiciously treated by them, and suffered less; his spirits revived hourly. The circumstance of our eating more food than was proper in our present condition, was another striking proof of the debility of our minds. We were perfectly aware of the danger, and Dr. Richardson repeatedly cautioned us to be moderate; but he was himself unable to practise the caution he so judiciously recommended.

Boudell-kell, the youngest of the Indians, after resting about an hour, returned to Akaitcho with the intelligence of our situation, and he conveyed a note from me to Mr. Back, requesting another supply of meat as soon as possible. The two others, "Crooked-Foot and the Rat," remained to take care of us, until we should be able to move forward.

The note received by the Indians from Mr. Back, communicated a tale of distress, with regard to himself and his party, as painful as that which we had suffered; as will be seen hereafter, by his own narrative.

November 8

The Indians this morning requested us to remove to an encampment on the banks of the river, as they were unwilling to remain in the house where the bodies of our deceased companions were lying exposed to view. We agreed, but the day proved too stormy, and Dr. Richardson and Hepburn having dragged the bodies to a short distance, and covered them with snow, the objections of the Indians to remain in the house were dissipated, and they began to clear our room of the accumulation of dirt, and fragments of pounded bones. The improved state of our apartment, and the large and cheerful fires they kept up, produced in us a sensation of comfort to which we had long been strangers. In the evening they brought in a pile of dried wood, which was lying on the river-side, and towards which we had often cast a wishful eye, being unable to drag it up the bank. The Indians set about everything with an activity that amazed us. Indeed, contrasted with our emaciated figures and extreme debility, their frames appeared to us gigantic, and their strength supernatural. These kind creatures next turned their attention to our personal appearance, and prevailed upon us to shave and wash ourselves. The beards of the Doctor and Hepburn had been untouched since they had left the sea-coast, had were become of a hideous length, and peculiarly offensive to the Indians. The Doctor and I suffered extremely from distension, and there ate sparingly.[1] Hepburn was getting better, and Adam recovered his strength with amazing rapidity.

November 9

This morning was pleasantly fine. Crooked-Foot caught four large trout in Winter Lake, which were very much prized, especially by the Doctor and myself, who had taken a dislike to meat, in consequence of our sufferings from repletion, which rendered us almost incapable of moving. Adam and Hepburn in a good measure escaped this pain. Though the night was stormy, and our apartment freely admitted the wind, we felt no inconvenience, the Indians were so very careful in covering us up, and in keeping a good fire; and our plentiful cheer gave such power of resisting the cold, that we could scarcely believe otherwise than that the season had become milder.

On the 13th, the weather was stormy, with constant snow. The Indians became desponding at the non-arrival of the supply, and would neither go to hunt nor fish. They frequently expressed their fears of some misfortune having befallen Boudel-kell; and, in the evening, went off suddenly, without apprising us of their intention, having first given to each of us a handful of pounded meat, which they had reserved. Their departure, at first, gave rise to a suspicion of their having deserted us, not meaning to return, especially as the explanations of Adam, who appeared to be in their secret, were very unsatisfactory. At length, by interrogations, we got from him the information that they designed to march night and day, until they should reach Akaitcho's encampment, whence they would send us aid. As we had combated their fears about Boudell-kell, they, perhaps, apprehended that we should oppose their determination, and therefore concealed it. We were now left a second time without food, and with appetites recovered, and strongly excited by recent indulgence.

On the following day the Doctor and Hepburn resumed their former occupation of collecting wood, and I was able to assist a little in bringing it into the house. Adam, whose expectation of the arrival of the Indians had been raised by the fineness of the weather, became, towards night, very desponding, and refused to eat the singed skin. The night was stormy, and there was a heavy fall of snow. The next day he became still more dejected. About eleven, Hepburn, who had gone out for the wood, came in with the intelligence that a party appeared upon the river.

1 The first alvine discharges after we received food, were, as Hearne remarks on a similar occasion, attended with excessive pain. Previous to the arrival of the Indians the urinary secretion was extremely abundant, and we were obliged to rise from bed in consequence upwards of ten times in a night. This was an extreme annoyance in our reduced state. It may, perhaps, be attributed to the quantity of the country tea that we drank.

The room was instantly swept, and in compliance with prejudices of the Indians, every scrap of skin was carefully removed out of sight: for these simple people imagine, that burning deer-skin renders them unsuccessful in hunting. The party proved to be Crooked-Foot, Thooee-yorre, and the Fop, with the wives of the two latter dragging provisions. They were accompanied by Benoit, one of our own men.

We were rejoiced to learn, by a note from Mr. Back, dated November 11, that he and his companions had so recruited their strength that they were preparing to proceed to Fort Providence. Adam recovered his spirits on the arrival of the Indians and even walked about the room with an appearance of strength and activity that surprised us all. As it was of consequence to get amongst the reindeer before our present supply should fail we made preparations for quitting Fort Enterprise the next day; and, accordingly, at an early hour, on the 16th, having united in thanksgiving and prayer, the whole party left the house after breakfast. Our feelings on quitting the fort where we had formerly enjoyed much comfort, if not happiness, and, latterly, experienced a degree of misery scarcely to be paralleled, may be more easily conceived than described. The Indians treated us with the utmost tenderness, gave us their snow-shoes, and walked without themselves, keeping by our sides, that they might lift us when we fell. We descended Winter River, and, about noon, crossed the head of Round-Rock Lake, distant about three miles from the house, where we were obliged to halt, as Dr. Richardson was unable to proceed. The swellings in his limbs rendered him by much the weakest of the party. The Indians prepared our encampment, cooked for us, and fed us as if we had been children; evincing humanity that would have done honour to the most civilised people. The night was mild, and fatigue made us sleep soundly.

From this period to the 26th November, we gradually improved, through their kindness and attention; and on that day arrived in safety at the abode of our chief and companion Akaitcho. We were received by the party assembled in the leader's tent, with looks of compassion, and profound silence, which lasted about a quarter of an hour, and by which they meant to express their condolence for our sufferings. The conversation did not begin until we had tasted food. The chief, Akaitcho, showed us the most friendly hospitality, and all sorts of personal attention, even to cooking for us with his own hands, an office which he never performs for himself. Annoethai-yazzeh and Humpy, the chief's two brothers, and several of our hunters, with their families, were encamped here, together with a number of old men and women. In the course of the day we were visited by every person of the band, not merely from curiosity, but a desire to evince their tender sympathy in our late distress. We learned that Mr. Back, with St. Germain and Belanger, had gone to Fort Providence; and that, previous to his departure he had left us a letter in a *cache* of pounded meat, which we had missed two days ago. As we supposed that this letter might acquaint us with his intentions more fully than we could gather from the Indians, through our imperfect knowledge of their language, Augustus, the Esquimaux, whom we found here in perfect health, and an Indian lad, were despatched to bring it.

We found several of the Indian families in great affliction for the loss of three of their relatives who had been drowned in the August preceding, by the upsetting of a canoe near Fort Enterprise. They bewailed the melancholy accident every morning and evening, by repeating the names of the persons in a loud singing tone, which was frequently interrupted by bursts of tears. One woman was so affected by the loss of her only son, that she seemed deprived of reason, and wandered about the tents the whole day, crying and singing out his name.

On the 1st of December we removed with the Indians to the southward.

On the 4th we again set off after the Indians about noon, and soon overtook them, as they had halted, to drag from the water and cut up and share a moose-deer, that had been drowned in a rapid part of the river, partially covered with ice. These operations detained us a long time, which was the more disagreeable, as the weather was extremely unpleasant from cold low fogs. We were all much fatigued at the hour of encampment, which was after dark, though the day's journey did not exceed four miles. At every halt the elderly men of the tribe made holes in the ice and put in their lines. One of them shares the produce of his fishery with us this evening.

In the afternoon of the 6th, Belanger, and another Canadian, arrived from Fort Providence, sent by Mr. Weeks with two trains of dogs, some spirits and tobacco for the Indians, a change of dress for ourselves, and a little tea and sugar. They also brought letters for us from England, and from Mr. Back and Mr. Wentzel. By the former we received the gratifying intelligence of the successful termination of Captain Perry's voyage; and were informed of the promotion of myself and Mr. Back, and of poor Hood, our grief for whose loss was renewed by this intelligence.

The letter from Mr. Back stated that the rival Companies in the fur trade had united; but that, owing to some cause which had not been explained to him, the goods intended as rewards to Akaitcho and his band, which we had demanded in the spring from the North-West Company, were not sent. There were, however, some stores lying for us at Moose-Deer Island, which had been ordered for the equipment of our voyagers; and Mr. Back had gone across to that establishment, to make a selection of the articles we could spare for a temporary present to the Indians. The disappointment at the non-arrival of the goods was seriously felt by us, as we had looked forward with pleasure to the time when we should be enabled to recompense our kind Indian friends for their tender sympathy in our distresses, and the assistance they had so cheerfully and promptly rendered. I now regretted to find, that Mr. Wentzel and his party, in their return from the sea, had suffered severely on their march along the Copper-Mine River, having on one occasion, as he mentioned, had no food but *tripe de roche* for eleven days.

All the Indians flocked to our encampment to learn the news, and to receive the articles brought for them. Having got some spirits and tobacco, they withdrew to the tent to the chief, and passed the greater part of the night in singing. We had now the indescribable gratification of changing our linen, which had been worn ever since our departure from the sea-coast.

December 8

After a long conference with Akaitcho, we took leave of him and his kind companions, and set out with two sledges heavily laden with provision and bedding, drawn by the dogs, and conducted by Belanger and the Canadian sent by Mr. Weeks. Hepburn and Augustus jointly dragged a smaller sledge, laden principally with their own bedding. Adam and Benoit were left to follow with the Indians. We encamped on the Grassy-Lake Portage, having walked about nine miles, principally on the Yellow Knife River. It was open at the rapids, and in these places we had to ascend its banks, and walk through the woods for some distance, which was very fatiguing, especially to Dr. Richardson, whose feet were severely galled in consequence of some defect in his snow-shoes.

On the 11th, however, we arrived at the fort, which was still under the charge of Mr. Weeks. He welcomed us in the most kind manner, immediately gave us changes of dress, and did everything in his power to make us comfortable.

Our sensations on being once more in a comfortable dwelling, after the series of hardships and miseries we had experienced, may be imagined. Our first act was again to return our grateful praises to the Almighty for the manifold instances of His mercy towards us. Having found here some articles which Mr. Back had sent across from Moose-Deer Island, I determined on awaiting the arrival of Akaitcho and his party, in order the present these to them, and to assure them of the promised reward, as soon as it could possibility be procured.

In the afternoon of the 14th, Akaitcho, with his whole band came to the fort. He smoked his customary pipe, and made an address to Mr. Weeks in the hall previous to his coming into the room in which Dr. Richardson and I were. We discovered at the commencement of his speech to us, that he had been informed that our expected supplies had not come. He spoke of this circumstance as a disappointment, indeed, sufficiently severe to himself, to whom his band looked up for the protection of their interests, but without attaching any blame to us. "The world goes badly," he said, "all are poor; you are poor, the traders appear to be poor, I and my party are poor likewise; and since the goods have not come in, we cannot have them. I do not regret having supplied you with provisions, for a Copper Indian can never permit white men to suffer from want of food on his lands, without flying to their aid. I trust, however, that we shall, as you say, receive what is due next autumn; and at all events," he added, in a tone of good-humour, "it is the first time that the white people have been indebted to the Copper Indians." We assured him the supplies should certainly be sent to him by the autumn, if not before. He then cheerfully received the small present we made to himself; and although we could give a few things only to those who had been most active in our service, the others, who, perhaps, thought themselves equally deserving, did not murmur at being left out in the distribution. Akaitcho afterwards expressed a strong desire that we should represent the character of his nation in a favourable light to our countrymen. "I know," he said, "you write down every occurrence in your books; but probably you have only noticed the bad things we have said and done, and have omitted the good." In the course of the desultory conversation which ensued, he said, that he had been always told by us to consider the traders in the same light as ourselves; and that, for his part, he looked upon both as equally respectable. This assurance, made in the presence of Mr. Weeks, was particularly gratifying to us, as it completely disproved the defence that had been set up, respecting the injurious reports circulated against us amongst the Indians in the spring; namely, that they were in retaliation for our endeavours to lower the traders in the eyes of the Indians. I take this opportunity of stating my opinion, that Mr. Weeks, in spreading these reports, was actuated by a mistaken idea that he was serving the interest of his employers. On the present occasion, we felt indebted to him for the sympathy he displayed for our distresses, and the kindness with which he administered to our personal wants. After this conference, such Indians as were indebted to the Company were paid for the provision they had given us, by deducting a corresponding sum from their debts; in the same way we gave a reward of sixteen skins of beaver to each of the persons who had come to our relief at Fort Enterprise. As the debts of Akaitcho and his hunters had been effaced at the time of his engagement with us, we placed a sum equal to the amount of provision they had recently supplied, to their credit on the Company's books. These things being, through the moderation of the Indians, adjusted with an unexpected facility, we gave them a keg of mixed liquors, (five parts water), and distributed among them several fathoms of tobacco, and they retired to their tents to spend the night in merriment.

Adam, our interpreter, being desirous of uniting himself with the Copper Indians, applied to me for his discharge, which I granted, and gave him a bill on the Hudson's Bay Company for the amount of his wages. These arrangements being completed, we prepared to cross the lake.

Mr. Weeks provided Dr. Richardson and I with a cariole each, and we set out at eleven A.M., on the 15th, for Moose-Deer Island. Our party consisted of Belanger, who had charge of a sledge laden with the bedding, and drawn by two dogs, our two cariole men, Benoit and Augustus. Previous to our departure, we had another conference with Akaitcho, who, as well as the rest of his party, bade us farewell, with a warmth of manner rare among Indians.

The badness of Belanger's dogs, and the roughness of the ice, impeded our progress very much, and obliged us to encamp early. We had a good fire made of drift wood, which lines the shores of this lake in great quantities. The next day was very cold. We began the journey at nine A.M., and encamped at the Big Cape, having made another short march, in consequence of the roughness of the ice.

On the 17th, we encamped on the most southerly of the Reindeer Islands. This night was very stormy, but the wind abating in the morning, we proceeded, and by sunset reached the fishing-huts of the Company at Stony Point. Here we found Mr. Andrews, a clerk of the Hudson's Bay Company, who regaled us with a supper of excellent white-fish, for which this part of Slave Lake is particularly celebrated. Two men with sledges arrived soon afterwards, sent by Mr. M'Vicar, who expected us about this time. We set off in the morning before daybreak, with several companions, and arrived at Moose-Deer Island about one P.M. Here we were received with the utmost hospitality by Mr. M'Vicar, the chief trader of the Hudson's Bay Company in this district, as well as by his assistant Mr. M'Auley. We had also the happiness of joining our friend, Mr. Back; our feelings on this occasion can be well imagined, and we were deeply impressed with gratitude to him for his exertions in sending the supply of food to Fort Enterprise, to which, under Divine Providence, we felt the preservation of our lives to be owing. He gave us an affecting detail of the proceedings of his party since our separation; the substance of which I shall convey to the reader, by the following extracts from his Journal.

MR. BACK'S NARRATIVE

October 4, 1821

Captain Franklin having directed me to proceed with St. Germain, Belanger, and Beauparlant, to Fort Enterprise, in the hope of obtaining relief for the party, I took leave of my companions, and set out on my journey, through a very swampy country, which with the cloudy state of the weather and a keen north-east wind, accompanied by frequent snow showers, retarded us so much, that we had scarcely got more than four miles before we halted for the night, and made a meal of *tripe de roche* and some old leather.

On the 5th we set out early, amidst extremely deep snow, sinking frequently in it up to the thighs, a labour in our enfeebled and almost worn out state that nothing but the cheering hopes of reaching the house and affording relief to our friends could have enabled us to support. As we advanced we found to our mortification, the *tripe de roche*, hitherto our sole dependence, began to be scarce, so that we could only collect sufficient to make half a kettleful, which, with the addition of a partridge each, that St. Germain had killed, yielded a tolerable meal; during this day I felt very weak and sore in the joints, particularly between the shoulders. At eight we encamped among a small clump of willows.

On the 6th we set out an early hour, pursuing our route over a range of hills at the foot of one of which we saw several large pines, and a great quantity of willows; a sight that encouraged us to quicken our pace, as we were now certain we could not be too far from the woods. In deed we were making considerable progress, when Belanger unfortunately broke through the ice, and sank up to the hips. The weather being cold, he was in danger of freezing, but some brushwood on the borders of the lake enabled us to make a fire to dry him. At the same time we took the opportunity of refreshing ourselves with a kettle of swamp tea.

My increasing debility had for some time obliged me to use a stick for the purpose of extending my arms; the pain in my shoulders being so acute, that I could not bear them to remain in the usual position for two minutes together. We halted at five among some small brushwood, and made a sorry meal of an old pair of leather trowsers, and some swamp tea.

The night was cold with a hard frost, and though two persons slept together, yet we could not by any means keep ourselves warm, but remained trembling the whole time. The following morning we crossed several lakes, occasionally seeing the recent track's of deer, and at noon we fell upon Marten Lake; it happened to be at the exact spot where we had been the last year with the canoes, yet though I immediately recognised the place, the men would not believe it to be the same; at length, by pointing out several marks, and relating circumstances connected with them, they recovered their memory, and a simultaneous expression of "Mon Dieu, nous sommes sauvès," broke from the whole. Contrary to our expectations the lake was frozen sufficiently to bear us, so that we were excused from making the tours of the different bays. This circumstance seemed to import fresh vigour to us, and we walked as fast as the extreme smoothness of the ice would permit, intending to reach the Slave Rock that night; but an unforeseen and almost fatal accident prevented the prosecution of our plan: Belanger (who seemed the victim of misfortune) again broke through the ice, in a deep part near the head of the rapid, but was timely saved by our fastening our worsted belts together, and pulling him out. By urging him forwards as quick as his icy garments would admit, to prevent his freezing, we reached a few pines, and kindled a fire; but it was late before he even felt warm, though he was so near the flame as to burn is hair twice; and to add to our distress, (since we could not pursue them,) three wolves crossed the lake close to us.

The night of the 7th was extremely stormy, and about ten the following morning, on attempting to go on, we found it totally impossible, being too feeble to oppose the wind and drift which frequently blew us over, and on attempting to cross a small lake that lay in our way, drove us faster backwards, than with every effort, we could get forwards; we therefore encamped under the shelter of a small clump of pines, secure from the south-west storm that was raging around us. In the evening, there being no *tripe de roche*, we were compelled to satisfy, or rather allay the cravings of hunger, by eating a gun cover and a pair of old shoes; at this time I had scarcely strength to get on my legs.

The wind did not in the least abate during the night, but in the morning of the 9th it changed to north-east and became moderate. We took advantage of this circumstance, and rising with great difficulty, set out; though had it not been for the hope of reaching the house, I am certain, from the excessive faintness which almost over-powered me, that I must have remained where I was. We passed the Slave Rock, and making frequent halts, arrived within a short distance of Fort Enterprise; but as we perceived neither any marks of Indians, nor even of animals, the men began absolutely to despair: on a nearer approach, however, the tracks of large herds of deer, which had only passed a few hours, tended a little to revive their spirits, and shortly after we crossed the ruinous threshold of the long-sought spot; but what was our surprise, what our sensations, at beholding everything in the most desolate and neglected state; the doors and windows of that room in which we expected to find provision, had been thrown down and the wild animals of the woods had resorted there as to a place of shelter and retreat. Mr. Wentzel had taken away the trunks and papers, but had left no note to guide us to the Indians. This was to us the most grievous disappointment: without assistance of the Indians, bereft of every resource, we felt ourselves reduced to the most miserable state, which was rendered still worse, from the recollection that our friends in the rear were as miserable as ourselves. For the moment, however, hunger prevailed, and each began to gnaw the scraps of putrid and frozen meat that were lying about, without waiting to prepare them. A fire, however, was made, and the neck and bones of a deer, found in the house, were boiled and devoured.

I determined to remain a day here to repose; then to go in search of the Indians, and in the event of missing them, to proceed to the first trading establishment, which was distant about one hundred and thirty miles, and from thence to send succour to my companions. This indeed I should have done immediately, as the most certain manner of executing my purpose, had there been any probability of the river and lakes being frozen to the southward, or had we possessed sufficient strength to have clambered over the rocks and mountains which impeded the direct way; but as we were aware of our inability to do so, I listened to St. Germain's proposal, which was, to follow the deer into the woods, (so long as they did not lead us out of our route to the Indians,) and if possible to collect sufficient food to carry us to Fort Providence. We now set about making mittens and snow-shoes, whilst Belanger searched under the snow, and collected a mass of old bones, which when burned and used with a little salt we found palatable enough, and made a tolerable meal. At night St. Germain returned, having seen plenty of tracks, but no animals; the day was cloudy, with fresh breezes, and the river was frozen at the borders.

On the 11th we prepared for our journey, having first collected a few old skins of deer, to serve us as food; and written a note to be left for our commander, to apprise him of our intentions. We pursued the course of the river to the lower lake, when St. Germain fell in, which obliged us to encamp directly to prevent his being frozen; indeed we were all grad to rest, for in our meagre and reduced state it was impossible to resist the weather, which at any other time would have been thought fine; my toes were frozen, and although wrapped up in a blanket I could not keep my hands warm.

The 12th was excessively cold with fresh breezes. Our meal at night consisted of scraps of old deer-skins and swamp tea, and the men complained greatly of their increasing debility. The following morning I sent St. Germain to hunt, intending to go some distance down the lake, but the weather becoming exceedingly thick with snow-storms, we were prevented from moving. He returned without success, not having seen any animals. We had nothing to eat.

In the morning of the 14th the part of the lake before us was quite frozen. There was so much uncertainty in St. Germain's answer as to the chance of any Indians being in the direction we were then going (although he had previously said that the leader had told him he should be there), and he gave so much dissatisfaction in his hunting excursions, that I was induced to send a note to the Commander, whom I supposed to be by this time at Fort Enterprise, to inform him of our situation; not that I imagined for a moment he could amend it, but that by all returning to the fort we might, perhaps, have better success in hunting; with this view I despatched Belanger, much against his inclination, and told him to return as quickly as possible to a place about four miles farther on, where we intended to fish, and to await his arrival. The men were so weak this day, that I could get neither of them to move from the encampment; and it was only necessity that compelled them to cut wood for fuel, in performing which operation Beauparlant's face became so dreadfully swelled that he could scarcely see; I myself lost my temper on the most trivial circumstances, and was become very peevish; the day was fine but cold, with a freezing north-east wind. We had nothing to eat.

October 15

The night was calm and clear, but it was not before two in the afternoon that we set out; and the one was so weak, and the other so full of complaints, that we did not get more than three-quarters of a mile from our last encampment before we were obliged to put up; but in this distance we were fortunate enough to kill a partridge, the bones of which were eaten, and the remainder reserved for baits to fish with. We, however, collected sufficient *tripe de roche* to make a meal: and I anxiously awaited Belanger's return, to know what course to take. I was now so much reduced, that my shoulders were as if they would fall from my body, my legs seemed unable to support me, and in the disposition in which I then found myself, had it not been for the remembrance of my friends behind, who relied on me for relief, as well as the persons of whom I had charge, I certainly should have preferred remaining where I was, to the miserable pain of attempting to move.

October 16

We waited until two in the afternoon for Belanger; but not seeing anything of him on the lake, we set out, purposing to encamp at the Narrows, the place which was said to be so good for fishing, and where, according to St. Germain's account, the Indians never failed to catch plenty; its distance at most could not be more than two miles. We had not proceeded far before Beauparlant began to complain of increasing weakness; but this was so usual with us that no particular notice was taken of it; for in fact there was little difference, all being alike feeble: among other things, he said whilst we were resting, that he should never get beyond the next encampment, for his strength had quite failed him. I endeavoured to encourage him by explaining the mercy of the Supreme Being, who ever beholds with an eye of pity those that seek His aid. This passed as common discourse, when he inquired where we were to put up; St. Germain pointed to a small clump of pines near us, the only place indeed that offered for fuel. "Well," replied the poor man, "take your axe, Mr. Back, and I will follow at my leisure, I shall join you by the time the encampment is made." This is a usual practice of the country, and St. Germain and myself went on towards the spot; it was five o'clock and not very cold, but rather milder than we had experienced it for some time, when on leaving the ice, we saw a number of crows perched on top of some high pines near us. St. Germain immediately said there must be some dead animal thereabouts, and proceeded to search, when he saw several heads of deer half buried in the snow and ice, without eyes or tongues: the previous severity of the weather having obliged the wolves and other animals to abandon them. An expression of "Oh merciful God! we are saved," broke from us both; and with feelings more easily imagined than described, we shook hands, not knowing what to say for joy. It was twilight, and a fog was rapidly darkening the surface of the lake, when St. Germain commenced making the encampment; the task was too laborious for me to render him any assistance, and had we not thus providentially found provision, I feel convinced that the next twenty-four hours would have terminated my existence. But this good fortune in some measure renovated me for the moment, and putting out my whole strength I contrived to collect a few heads, and with incredible difficulty carried them singly about thirty paces to the fire.

Darkness stole on us apace, and I became extremely anxious about Beauparlant; several guns were fired, to each of which he answered. We then called out, and again heard his responses though faintly, when I told St. Germain to go and look for him, as I had not the strength myself, being quite exhausted. He said that he had already placed a pine branch on the ice, and he could then scarcely find his way back, but if he went now he should certainly be lost. In this situation I could only hope that as Beauparlant had my blanket, and everything requisite to light a fire, he might have encamped at a little distance from us.

October 17

The night was cold and clear, but we could not sleep at all, from the pains of having eaten. We suffered the most excruciating torments, though I in particular did not eat a quarter of what would have satisfied me; it might have been from using a quantity of raw or frozen sinews of the legs of the deer, which neither of us could avoid doing, so great was our hunger. In the morning, being much agitated for the safety of Beauparlant, I desired St. Germain to go in search of him, and to return with him as quick as possible, when I would have something prepared for them to eat.

It was, however, late when he arrived, with a small bundle which Beauparlant was accustomed to carry, and with tears in his eyes, told me he had found our poor companion dead. Dead! I could not believe him. "It is so, sir," said St. Germain, "after hallooing and calling his name to no purpose, I went towards our last encampment, about three-quarters of a mile, and found him stretched upon his back on a sand bank frozen to death, his limbs all extended and swelled enormously, and as hard as the ice that was near him; his bundle was behind him, as if it had rolled away when he fell, and the blanket which he wore around his neck and shoulders thrown on one side. Seeing that there was no longer life in him. I threw your covering over him, and place his snow-shoes on the top of it."

I had not even thought of so serious an occurrence in our little party, and for a short time was obliged to give vent to my grief. Left with one person and both of us weak, no appearance of Belanger, a likelihood that great calamity had taken place amongst our other companions still upwards of seventeen days' march from the nearest establishment, and myself unable to carry a burden; all these things pressed heavy on me; and how to get to the Indians or to the fort I did not know; but that I might not depress St. Germain's spirits, I suppressed the feelings to which these thoughts gave rise, and made some arrangements for the journey to Fort Providence.

October 18

While we were this day occupied in scraping together the remains of some deer's meat, we observed Belanger coming round a point apparently scarcely moving. I went to meet him, and made immediate enquiries about my friends. Five, with the Captain, he said, were at the house, the rest were left near the river, unable to proceed; but he was too weak to relate the whole. He was conducted to the encampment, and paid every attention to, and by degrees we heard the remainder of his tragic tale, at which the interpreter could not avoid crying. He then gave me a letter from my friend the Commander, which indeed was truly afflicting. The simple story of Belanger I could hear, but when I read it in another language, mingled with the pious resignation of a good man, I could not sustain it any longer. The poor man was much affected by the death of our lamented companion, but his appetite prevailed over every other feeling; and, had I permitted it, he would have done himself an injury; for after two hours' eating, principally skin and sinews, he complained of hunger. The day was cloudy, with snow and fresh breezes from the north-east by east.

The last evening, as well as this morning, the 19th, I mentioned my wishes to the men, that we should proceed towards Reindeer Lake, but this proposal met with a direct refusal. Belanger stated his inability to move, and St. Germain used similar language; adding, for the first time, that he did not know the route, and that it was of no use to go in the direction I mentioned, which was the one agreed upon between the Commander and myself. I then insisted that we should go by the known route, and join the Commander, but they would not hear of it; they would remain where they were until they had regained their strength; they said, I wanted to expose them again to death (*faire perir*). In vain did I use every argument to the contrary, for they were equally heedless to all. Thus situated I was compelled to remain; and from this time to the 25th we employed ourselves in looking about for the remnants of the deer and pieces of skin, which even the wolves had left; and by pounding the bones, we were enabled to make a sort of soup, which strengthened us greatly, though each still complained of weakness. It was not without the greatest difficulty that I could restrain the men from eating every scrap they found, though they were well aware of the necessity there was of being economical in our present situation, and to save whatever they could for our journey; yet they could not resist the temptation, and whenever my back was turned they seldom failed to snatch at the nearest piece to them, whether cooked or raw.

We had set fishing-lines, but without any success; and we often saw large herds of deer crossing the lake at full speed, and wolves pursuing them.

The night of the 25th was cold with hard frost. Early the next morning I sent the men to cover the body of our departed companion Beauparlant with the trunks and branches of trees, which they did; and shortly after their return I opened his bundle, and found it contained two papers of vermilion, several strings of beads, some firesteels, flints, awls, fish-hooks, rings, linen, and the glass of an artificial horizon. My two men began to recover a little as well as myself, though I was by far the weakest of the three; the soles of my feet were cracked all over, and the other parts were as hard as horn, from constant walking. I again urged the necessity of advancing to join the Commander's party, but they said they were not sufficiently strong.

On the 27th we discovered the remains of a deer, on which we feasted. The night was unusually cold, and coruscations of the Aurora were beautifully brilliant; they served to show us eight wolves, which we had some trouble to frighten away from our collection of deer's bones; and, between their howling and the constant cracking of the ice, we did not get much rest.

Having collected with great care, and by self-denial, two small packets of dried meat or sinews, sufficient (for men who knew what it was to fast) to last for eight days, at the rate of one indifferent meal per day, we prepared to set out on the 30th. I calculated that we should be about fourteen days in reaching Fort Providence; and allowing that we neither killed deer nor found Indians, we could but be unprovided with food six days, and this we heeded not whilst the prospect of obtaining full relief was before us. Accordingly we set out against a keen north-east wind, in order to gain the known route to Fort Providence. We saw a number of wolves and some crows on the middle of the lake, and supposing such an assemblage was not met idly, we made for them and came for a share of a deer which they had killed a short time before, and thus added a couple of meals to our stock. By four P.M. we gained the head of the lake, or the direct road to Fort Providence, and some dry wood being at hand, we encamped; by accident it was the same place where the Commander's party had slept on the 19th, the day on which I supposed they had left Fort Enterprise; but the encampment was so small, that we feared great mortality had taken place amongst them; and I am sorry to say the stubborn resolution of my men, not to go to the house, prevented me from determining this most anxious point, so that I now almost dreaded passing their encampment, lest I should see some of our unfortunate friends dead at each spot. Our fire was hardly kindled when a fine herd of deer passed close to us. St. Germain pursued them a short distance, but with his usual want of success, so that we made a meal off the muscles and sinews we had dried, though they were so tough that we could scarcely cut them. My hands were benumbed throughout the march, and we were all stiff and fatigued. The marching of two days weakened us all very much, and the more so on account of our exertion to follow the tracks of our Commander's party; but we lost them, and concluded that they were not before us. Though the weather was not cold, I was frozen in the face and was so reduced and affected by these constant calamities, as well in mind as in body, that I found much difficulty in proceeding even with the advantages I had enjoyed.

November 3

We set out before day, though, in fact, we were all much fitter to remain, from the excessive pain which we suffered in our joints, and proceeded till one P.M., without halting, when Belanger, who was before, stopped, and cried out, "Footsteps of Indians." It is needless to mention the joy that brightened the countenances of each at this unlooked-for sight; we knew relief must be at hand, and considered our sufferings at an end. St. Germain inspected the tracks, and said that three persons had passed the day before; and that he knew the remainder must be advancing to the southward, as was customary with these Indians, when they sent to the trading establishment on the first ice. On this information we encamped, and being too weak to walk myself, I sent St. Germain to follow the tracks, with instructions to the chief of the Indians to provide immediate assistance for such of our friends as might be at Fort Enterprise, as well as for ourselves, and to lose no time in returning to me. I was now so exhausted, that had we not seen the tracks this day, I must have remained at the next encampment, until the men could have sent aid from Fort Providence. We had finished our small portion of sinews, and were preparing for rest, when an Indian boy made his appearance with meat. St. Germain had arrived before sunset at the tents of Akaitcho, whom he found at the spot where he had wintered last year: but imagine my surprise, when he gave me a note from the Commander, and said that Benoit and Augustus, two of the men, had just joined them. The note was so confused, by the pencil marks being partly rubbed out, that I could not decipher it clearly; but it informed me, that he had attempted to come with the two men, but finding his strength inadequate to the task, he relinquished his design, and returned to Fort Enterprise, to await relief with the others. There was another note for the gentleman in charge of Fort Providence, desiring him to send meat, blankets, shoes, and tobacco. Akaitcho wished me to join him on the ensuing day, at a place which the boy knew, where they were going to fish; and I was the more anxious to do so, on account of my companions: but particularly that I might hear a full relation of what had happened, and of the Commander's true situation, which I suspected to be much worse than he had described.

In the afternoon I joined the Indians, and repeated to Akaitcho what St. Germain had told him; he seemed much affected, and said, he would have sent relief directly, though I had not been there; indeed, his conduct was generous and humane. The next morning, at an early hour, three Indians, with loaded sledges of meat, skins, shoes, and a blanket, set out for Fort Enterprise; one of them was to return directly with an answer from Captain Franklin, to whom I wrote; but in the event of his death, he was to bring away all the papers he could find; and he promised to travel with such haste, as to be able to return to us on the fourth day. I was now somewhat more at ease, having done all in my power to succour my unfortunate companions; but was very anxious for the return of the messenger. The Indians brought me meat in small quantities, though sufficient for our daily consumption; and, as we had a little ammunition, many were paid on the spot for what they gave.

On the 9th I had the satisfaction of seeing the Indian arrive from Fort Enterprise. At first he said they were all dead, but shortly after he gave me a note, which was from the Commander, and then I learned all the fatal particulars which had befallen them. I now proposed that the chief should immediately send three sledges, loaded with meat, to Fort Enterprise, should make a *cache* of provision at our present encampment, and also, that he should there await the arrival of the Commander. By noon two large trains, laden with meat, were sent off for Fort Enterprise. The next day we proceeded on our journey, and arrived at Fort Providence on the 21st of November.

Conclusion of Mr. Back's Narrative.

I have little now to add to the melancholy detail into which I felt it proper to enter; but I cannot omit to state, that the unremitting care and attentions of our kind friends, Mr. M'Vicar and Mr. M'Auley, united with our improved diet, to promote to the restoration of our health; so that, by the end of February, the swellings of our limbs, which had returned upon us, entirely subsided, and we were able to walk to any part of the island. Our appetites gradually moderated, and we nearly regained our ordinary state of body before the spring. Hepburn alone suffered from a severe attack of rheumatism, which confined him to his bed for some weeks. The usual symptoms of spring having appeared, on the 25th of May we prepared to embark for Fort Chipewyan. Fortunately, on the following morning, a canoe arrived from that place with the whole of the stores which we required for the payment of Akaitcho and the hunters. It was extremely gratifying to us to be thus enabled, previous to our departure, to make arrangements respecting the requital of our late Indian companions; and the more so, as we had recently discovered that Akaitcho, and the whole of his tribe, in consequence of the death of the leader's mother, and the wife of our old guide Keskarrah, had broken and destroyed every useful article belonging to them, and were in the greatest distress. It was an additional pleasure to find our stock of ammunition more than sufficient to pay them what was due, and that we could make a considerable present of this most essential article to every individual that had been attached to the Expedition.

We quitted Moose-Deer Island at five P.M. on the 26th, accompanied by Mr. M'Vicar and Mr. M'Auley, and nearly all the voyagers at the establishment, having resided there about five months, not a day of which had passed without our having cause of gratitude for the kind and unvaried attentions of Mr. M'Vicar and Mr. M'Auley. These gentlemen accompanied us as far as Fort Chipewyan, where we arrived on the 2nd June; here we met Mr. Wentzel, and the four men, who had been sent with him from the mouth of the Copper-Mine River; and I think it due to that gentleman, to give his own explanation of the unfortunate circumstances which prevented him from fulfilling my instructions respecting the provisions to have been left for us at Fort Enterprise.[1]

In a subsequent conversation he stated to me, that the two Indians, who were actually with him at Fort Enterprise, whilst he remained there altering his canoe, were prevented from hunting; one by an accidental lameness, the other by the fear of meeting alone some of the Dog-Rib Indians.

We were here furnished with a canoe by Mr. Smith, and a bowman, to act as our guide; and having left Fort Chipewyan on the 5th, we arrived, on the 4th of July, at Norway House. Finding at this place that canoes were about to go down to Montreal, I gave all our Canadian voyagers their discharges, and sent them by those vessels, furnishing them with orders on the Agent of the Hudson's Bay Company for the amount of their wages. We carried Augustus down to York Factory, where we arrived on the 14th of July, and were received with every mark of attention and kindness by Mr. Simpson, the Governor, Mr. M'Tavish, and, indeed, by all the officers of the United Companies. And thus terminated our long, fatiguing, and disastrous travels in North America, having journeyed by water and by land (including our navigation of the Polar Sea) five thousand five hundred and fifty miles.

1. See page 291 for extended footnote.

1 "After you sent me back from the mouth of the Copper-Mine River, and I had overtaken the Leader, Guides, and Hunters, on the fifth day, leaving the sea-coast, as well as our journey up the River, they always expressed the same desire of fulfilling their promises, although somewhat dissatisfied at being exposed to privation while on our return, from a scarcity of animals; for, as I have already stated in my first communication from Moose-Deer Island, we had been eleven days with no other food but *tripe de roche*. In the course of this time an Indian, with his wife and child, who were travelling in company with us, were left in the rear, and are since supposed to have perished through want, as no intelligence had been received of them at Fort Providence in December last. On the seventh day after I had joined the Leader, etc. etc., and journeying on together, all the Indians, excepting Petit Pied and Bald-Head, left me to seek their families, and crossed Point Lake at the Crow's Nest, where Humpy had promised to meet his brother Ekehcho[a] with the families, but did not fulfil, nor did any of my party of Indians know where to find them; for we had frequently made fires to apprise them of our approach, yet none appeared in return as answers. This disappointment, as might be expected, served to increase the ill-humour of the Leader and party, the brooding of which (agreeably to Indian custom) was liberally discharged on me, in bitter reproach for having led them from their families, and exposed them to dangers and hardships, which but for my influence, they said, they might have spared themselves. Nevertheless, they still continued to profess the sincerest desire of meeting your wishes in making *caches* of provisions, and remaining until a late season on the road that leads from Fort Enterprise to Fort Providence, through which the Expedition-men had travelled so often the year before – remarking, however, at the same time, that they had not the least hopes of ever seeing one person return from the Expedition. These alarming fears I never could persuade them to dismiss from their minds; they always sneered at what they called 'my credulity.' – 'If,' said the Gros Pied,[b] 'the Great Chief (meaning Captain Franklin), or any of his party, should pass at my tents, he or they shall be welcome to all my provisions, or anything else that I may have.' And I am sincerely happy to understand, by your communication, that in this he had kept his word – in sending you with such promptitude and liberality the assistance your truly dreadful situation required. But the party of Indians on whom I had placed the utmost confidence and dependence, was Humpy and the White Capot Guide, with their sons, and several of the discharged hunters from the Expedition. This party was well-disposed, and readily promised to collect provisions for the possible return of the Expedition, provided they could get a supply of ammunition from Fort Providence; for when I came up with them they were actually starving, and converting old axes into ball, having no other substitute – this was unlucky. Yet they were well inclined, and I expected to find means at Fort Providence to send them with a supply, in which I was, however, disappointed, for I found that establishment quite destitute of necessaries; and then, shortly after I had left them, they had the misfortune of losing three of their hunters, who were drowned in Marten Lake: this accident was, of all others, the most fatal that could have happened – a truth which no one, who has the least knowledge of the Indian character, will deny; and as they were nearly connected by relationship to the Leader, Humpy, and White Capot Guide, the three leading men of this part of the Copper Indian Tribe, it had the effect of unhinging (if I may use the expression) the minds of all these families, and finally destroying all the fond hopes I had so sanguinely conceived of their assisting the Expedition, should it come back by the Annadessé River, of which they were not certain.

"As to my not leaving a letter at Fort Enterprise, it was because, by some mischance, you had forgotten to give me paper when we parted.[c]

"I, however, wrote this news on a plank, in pencil, and placed it in the top of your former bedstead, where I left it. Since it has not been found there, some Indians must have gone to the house after my departure, and destroyed it. These details, Sir, I have been induced to enter into (rather unexpectedly) in justification of myself, and hope it will be satisfactory."

a Akaitcho the Leader.

b Also Akaitcho.

c I certainly offered Mr. Wentzel some paper when he quitted us, but he declined it, having then a note-book; and Mr. Back gave him a pencil.